Wilhelm Meister's Apprenticeship and Travels, Volume 1

Thomas Carlyle, Johann Wolfgang Von Goethe

Nabu Public Domain Reprints:

You are holding a reproduction of an original work published before 1923 that is in the public domain in the United States of America, and possibly other countries. You may freely copy and distribute this work as no entity (individual or corporate) has a copyright on the body of the work. This book may contain prior copyright references, and library stamps (as most of these works were scanned from library copies). These have been scanned and retained as part of the historical artifact.

This book may have occasional imperfections such as missing or blurred pages, poor pictures, errant marks, etc. that were either part of the original artifact, or were introduced by the scanning process. We believe this work is culturally important, and despite the imperfections, have elected to bring it back into print as part of our continuing commitment to the preservation of printed works worldwide. We appreciate your understanding of the imperfections in the preservation process, and hope you enjoy this valuable book.

WILHELM MEISTER'S

APPRENTICESHIP AND TRAVELS.

LONDON:
PRINTED BY LEVEY, ROBSON, AND FRANKLYN,
Great New Street and Fetter Lane.

TRANSLATIONS FROM THE GERMAN

BY

THOMAS CARLYLE.

WILHELM MEISTER'S

APPRENTICESHIP AND TRAVELS.

VOL. I.

LONDON:
CHAPMAN AND HALL, 193 PICCADILLY.
M.DCCC.LVIII.

47587.26

TO THE READER.

These two Translations, *Meister's Apprenticeship* and *Meister's Travels*, have long been out of print, but never altogether out of demand; nay, it would seem, the originally somewhat moderate demand has gone on increasing, and continues to increase. They are therefore here republished; and the one being in some sort a sequel to the other, though in rather unexpected sort, they are now printed together. The English version of *Meister's Travels* has been extracted, or extricated, from a Compilation of very various quality named *German Romance*; and placed by the side of the *Apprenticeship*, its forerunner, which, in the translated as in the original state, appeared hitherto as a separate work.

In the *Apprenticeship*, the first of these Translations, which was executed some fifteen years ago, under questionable auspices, I have made many little changes; but could not, unfortunately, change it into a right translation: it hung, in many places, stiff and laboured, too like some unfortunate buckram cloak round the light harmonious movement of the original; and, alas, still hangs so, here and there; and may now hang. In the second Translation, *Meister's Travels*, two years later in date, I have changed little or nothing: I might have added much; for the original, since that time, was as it were taken to pieces by the Author himself in his last years, and constructed anew; and in the Final Edition of his Works appears with multifarious intercalations, giving a great expansion both of size and of scope. Not Pedagogy only, and Husbandry and Art and Religion and Human Conduct in the Nineteenth Century, but Geology, Astronomy, Cotton-spinning, Metallurgy, Anatomical Lecturing, and much else, are typically shadowed forth in this second form of the *Travels*; which, however, continues a Fragment like the first, significantly pointing on all hands towards infinitude; not more complete than the first was, or indeed perhaps less so. It will well reward the trustful student of Goethe to read this new form of the *Travels*; and see how in that great mind, beaming in mildest mellow splendour, beaming if also trembling, like a great sun on the verge of the horizon, near now to its long farewell, all these things were illuminated and illustrated: but for the mere English reader there are probably in our prior edition of the *Travels* already novelties enough; for us, at all events, it seemed unadvisable to meddle with it farther at present.

Goethe's position towards the English Public is greatly altered since these Translations first made their appearance. Criticisms, near the mark, or farther from the mark, or even altogether far and away from any mark; of these there has been enough. These pass on their road; the man and his works remain what they are and were; more and more recognisable for what they are. Few English readers can require now to be apprised that these two Books, named Novels, come not under the Minerva-Press category, nor the Ballantyne-Press category, nor any such category; that the Author is one whose secret, by no means worn upon his sleeve, will never, by any ingenuity, be got at in that way.

For a Translator, in the present case, it is enough to reflect that he who imports into his own country any true delineation, a rationally spoken word on any subject, has done well. Ours is a wide world, peaceably admitting many different modes of speech. In our wide world, there is but one altogether fatal personage—the dunce; he that speaks *irrationally*, that sees not, and yet thinks he sees. A genuine seer and speaker, under what conditions soever, shall be welcome to us: has he not *seen* somewhat, of great Nature our common Mother's bringing forth; seen it, loved it, laid his heart open to it and to the Mother of it, so that he can now rationally speak it for us? He is our brother, and a good not a bad man; his words are like gold, precious, whether stamped in our mint, or in what mint soever stamped.

T. CARLYLE.

London, Nov. 1839.

TRANSLATOR'S PREFACE

TO THE

FIRST EDITION OF MEISTER'S APPRENTICESHIP.

[*Edinburgh*, 1824.]

WHETHER it be that the quantity of genius among ourselves and the French, and the number of works more lasting than brass produced by it, have of late been so considerable as to make us independent of additional supplies; or that, in our ancient aristocracy of intellect, we disdain to be assisted by the Germans, whom, by a species of second sight, we have discovered, before knowing any thing about them, to be a tumid, dreaming, extravagant, insane race of mortals; certain it is, that hitherto our literary intercourse with that nation has been very slight and precarious. After a brief period of not too judicious cordiality, the acquaintance on our part was altogether dropped: nor, in the few years since we partially resumed it, have our feelings of affection or esteem been materially increased. Our translators are unfortunate in their selection or execution, or the public is tasteless and absurd in its demands; for, with scarcely more than one or two exceptions, the best works of Germany have lain neglected, or worse than neglected, and the Germans are yet utterly unknown to us. Kotzebue still lives in our minds as the representative of a nation that despises him; Schiller is chiefly known to us by the monstrous production of his boyhood; and Klopstock by a hacked and mangled image of his *Messias*, in which a beautiful poem is distorted into a theosophic rhapsody, and the brother of Virgil and Racine ranks little higher than the author of Meditations among the Tombs.

But of all these people there is none that has been more unjustly dealt with than Johann Wolfgang von Goethe. For half a century the admiration, we might almost say the idol of his countrymen, to us he is still a stranger. His name, long echoed and re-echoed through reviews and magazines, has become familiar to our ears: but it is a sound and nothing more; it excites no definite idea in almost any mind. To such as know him by the faint and garbled version of his *Werter*, Goethe figures as a sort of poetic Heraclitus; some woe-begone hypochondriac, whose eyes are overflowing with perpetual tears, whose long life has been spent in melting into ecstasy at the sight of waterfalls, and clouds, and the moral sublime, or dissolving into hysterical wailings over hapless love-stories and the miseries of human life. They are not aware that Goethe smiles at this performance of his youth; or that the German Werter, with all his faults, is a very different person from his English namesake; that his Sorrows are in the original recorded in a tone of strength and sarcastic emphasis, of which the other offers no vestige, and intermingled with touches of powerful thought, glimpses of a philosophy deep as it is bitter, which our sagacious translator has seen proper wholly to omit. Others again, who have fallen in with Retzsch's *Outlines* and the extracts from *Faust*, consider Goethe as a wild mystic, a dealer in demonology and osteology, who draws attention by the aid of skeletons and evil spirits, whose excellence it is to be extravagant, whose chief aim it is to do what no one but himself has tried. The tyro in German may tell us that the charm of *Faust* is altogether unconnected with its preternatural import; that the work delineates the fate of human enthusiasm struggling against doubts and errors from within, against scepticism, contempt and selfishness from without; and that the witchcraft and magic, intended merely as a shadowy frame for so complex and mysterious a picture of the moral world and the human soul, are introduced for the purpose not so much of being trembled at as laughed at. The voice of the tyro is not listened to; our indolence takes part with our ignorance; *Faust* continues to be called a monster; and Goethe is regarded as a man of "some genius," which he has perverted to produce all manner of misfashioned prodigies; things false, abortive, formless, Gorgons and Hydras and Chimæras dire.

Now, it must no doubt be granted, that so long as our invaluable constitution is preserved in its pristine purity, the British nation may exist in a state of comparative prosperity with very inadequate ideas of Goethe: but, at the same time, the present arrangement is an evil in its kind; slight, it is true, and easy to be borne, yet still more easy to be remedied, and which therefore ought to have been remedied ere now. Minds like Goethe's are the common property of all nations; and, for many reasons, all should have correct impressions of them.

It is partly with the view of doing something to supply this want, that *Wilhelm Meisters Lehrjahre* is now presented to the English public. Written in its Author's forty-fifth year, embracing hints or disquisitions on almost every leading point in life and literature, it affords us a more distinct view of his matured genius, his manner of thought and favourite subjects, than any of his other works. Nor is it Goethe alone whom it portrays; the prevailing taste of Germany is likewise indicated by it. Since the year 1795, when it first appeared at Berlin, numerous editions of *Meister* have been printed: critics of all ranks, and some of them dissenting widely from its doctrines, have loaded it with encomiums; its songs and poems are familiar to every German ear; the people read it, and speak of it, with an admiration approaching in many cases to enthusiasm.

That it will be equally successful in England, I am far indeed from anticipating. Apart from the above considerations, from the curiosity, intelligent or idle, which it may awaken, the number of admiring, or even approving judges it will find can scarcely fail of being very limited. To the great mass of readers, who read to drive away the tedium of mental vacancy, employing the crude phantasmagoria of a modern novel, as their grandfathers employed tobacco and diluted brandy, *Wilhelm Meister* will appear beyond endurance weary, flat, stale and unprofitable. Those in particular, who take delight in "King Cambyses' vein," and open *Meister* with the thought of *Werter* in their minds, will soon pause in utter dismay, and their paroxysm of dismay will pass by degrees into unspeakable contempt. Of romance interest there is next to none in *Meister*; the characters are samples to judge of, rather than persons to love or hate; the incidents are contrived for other objects than moving or affrighting us; the hero is a milksop, whom, with all his gifts, it takes an effort to avoid despising. The author himself, far from "doing it in a passion," wears a face of the most still indifference throughout the whole affair; often it is even wrinkled by a slight sardonic grin. For the friends of the sublime, then, for those who cannot do without heroical sentiments, and "moving accidents by flood and field," there is nothing here that can be of any service.

Nor among readers of a far higher character can it be expected that many will take the praiseworthy pains of Germans, reverential of their favourite author, and anxious to hunt out his most elusive charms. Few among us will disturb themselves about the allegories and typical allusions of the work; will stop to inquire whether it includes a remote emblem of human culture, or includes no such matter; whether this is a light airy sketch of the development of man in all his endowments and faculties, gradually proceeding from the first rude exhibitions of puppets and mountebanks, through the perfection of poetic and dramatic art, up to the unfolding of the principle of religion, and the greatest of all arts, the art of life,—or is nothing more than a bungled piece of patch-work, presenting in the shape of a novel much that should have been suppressed entirely, or at least given out by way of lecture. Whether the characters do or do not represent distinct classes of men, including various stages of human nature, from the gay material vivacity of Philina to the severe moral grandeur of the Uncle and the splendid accomplishment of Lothario, will to most of us be of small importance: and the everlasting disquisitions about plays and players, and politeness and activity, and art and nature, will weary many a mind that knows not and heeds not whether they are true or false. Yet every man's judgment is, in this free country, a lamp to himself: whoever is displeased will censure; and many, it is to be feared, will insist on judging *Meister* by the common rule, and what is worse, condemning it, let Schlegel bawl as loudly as he pleases. "To judge," says he, "of this book,—new and peculiar as it is, and only to be understood and learned from itself, by our common notion of the novel, a notion pieced together and produced out of custom and belief, out of accidental and arbitrary requisitions,—is as if a child should grasp at the moon and stars, and insist on packing them into its toy-box."[1] Unhappily, the most of us have boxes; and some of them are very small!

Yet, independently of these its more recondite and dubious qualities, there are beauties in *Meister*, which cannot but secure it some degree of favour at the hands of many. The philosophical discussions it contains; its keen glances

---

[1] *Charakteristik des Meister.*

into life and art; the minute and skilful delineation of men; the lively genuine exhibition of the scenes they move in; the occasional touches of eloquence, and tenderness, and even of poetry, the very essence of poetry; the quantity of thought and knowledge embodied in a style so rich in general felicities, of which, at least, the new and sometimes exquisitely happy metaphors have been preserved,—cannot wholly escape an observing reader, even on the most cursory perusal. To those who have formed for themselves a picture of the world, who have drawn out, from the thousand variable circumstances of their being, a philosophy of life, it will be interesting and instructive to see how man and his concerns are represented in the first of European minds: to those who have penetrated to the limits of their own conceptions, and wrestled with thoughts and feelings too high for them, it will be pleasing and profitable to see the horizon of their certainties widened, or at least separated with a firmer line from the impalpable obscure which surrounds it on every side. Such persons I can fearlessly invite to study *Meister*. Across the disfigurement of a translation, they will not fail to discern indubitable traces of the greatest genius in our times. And the longer they study, they are likely to discern them the more distinctly. New charms will successively arise to view; and of the many apparent blemishes, while a few superficial ones may be confirmed, the greater and more important part will vanish, or even change from dark to bright. For, if I mistake not, it is with *Meister* as with every work of real and abiding excellence, the first glance is the least favourable. A picture of Raphael, a Greek statue, a play of Sophocles or Shakspeare, appears insignificant to the unpractised eye; and not till after long and patient and intense examination, do we begin to descry the earnest features of that beauty, which has its foundation in the deepest nature of man, and will continue to be pleasing through all ages.

If this appear excessive praise, as applied in any sense to *Meister*, the curious sceptic is desired to read and weigh the whole performance, with all its references, relations, purposes; and to pronounce his verdict after he has clearly seized and appreciated them all. Or if a more faint conviction will suffice, let him turn to the picture of Wilhelm's states of mind in the end of the first Book, and the beginning of the second; the eulogies of commerce and poesy, which follow; the description of Hamlet; the character of histrionic life in Serlo and Aurelia; that of sedate and lofty manhood in the Uncle and Lothario. But above all, let him turn to the history of Mignon. This mysterious child, at first neglected by the reader, gradually forced on his attention, at length overpowers him with an emotion more deep and thrilling than any poet since the days of Shakspeare has succeeded in producing. The daughter of enthusiasm, rapture, passion and despair, she is of the earth, but not earthly. When she glides before us through the light mazes of her fairy dance, or twangs her cithern to the notes of her homesick verses, or whirls her tambourine and hurries round us like an antique Mænad, we could almost fancy her a spirit; so pure is she, so full of fervour, so disengaged from the clay of this world. And when all the fearful particulars of her story are at length laid together, and we behold in connected order the image of her hapless existence, there is, in those dim recollections, those feelings so simple, so impassioned and unspeakable, consuming the closely-shrouded, woe-struck, yet ethereal spirit of the poor creature, something which searches into the inmost recesses of the soul. It is not tears which her fate calls forth; but a feeling far too deep for tears. The very fire of heaven seems miserably quenched among the obstructions of this earth. Her little heart, so noble and so helpless, perishes before the smallest of its many beauties is unfolded; and all its loves and thoughts and longings do but add another pang to death, and sink to silence utter and eternal. It is as if the gloomy porch of Dis, and his pale kingdoms, were realised and set before us, and we heard the ineffectual wail of infants reverberating from within their prison-walls forever.

Continuò auditæ voces, vagitus et ingens,
Infantumque animæ flentes in limine primo:
Quos dulcis vitæ exsortes, et ab ubere raptos,
Abstulit atra dies, et funere mersit acerbo.

The history of Mignon runs like a thread of gold through the tissue of the narrative, connecting with the heart much that were else addressed only to the head. Philosophy and eloquence might have done the rest; but this is poetry in the highest meaning of the word. It must be for the power of producing such creations and emotions, that Goethe is by many of his countrymen ranked at the side of Homer and Shakspeare, as one of the only three men of genius that have ever lived.

But my business here is not to judge of *Meister* or its Author, it is only to prepare others for judging it; and for this purpose the most that I had room to say is said. All I ask in the name of this illustrious foreigner is, that the court which tries him be pure, and the jury instructed in the cause; that the work be not condemned for wanting what it was not meant to have, and by persons nowise called to pass sentence on it.

Respecting my own humble share in the adventure, it is scarcely necessary to say anything. Fidelity is all the merit I have aimed at: to convey the Author's sentiments, as he himself expressed them; to follow the original, in all the variations of its style, has been my constant endeavour. In many points, both literary and moral, I could have wished devoutly that he had not written as he has done; but to alter anything was not in my commission. The literary and moral persuasions of a man like Goethe are objects of a rational curiosity; and the duty of a translator is simple and distinct. Accordingly, except a few phrases and sentences, not in all amounting to a page, which I have dropped as evidently unfit for the English taste, I have studied to present the work exactly as it stands in German. That my success has been indifferent, I already know too well. In rendering the ideas of Goethe, often so subtle, so capriciously expressive, the meaning was not always easy to seize, or to convey with adequate effect. There were thin tints of style, shades of ridicule or tenderness, or solemnity, resting over large spaces, and so slight as almost to be evanescent: some of these I may have failed to see; to many of them I could do no justice. Nor, even in plainer matters, can I pride myself in having always imitated his colloquial familiarity without falling into sentences bald and rugged, into idioms harsh or foreign; or in having copied the flowing oratory of other passages, without at times exaggerating or defacing the swelling cadences and phrases of my original. But what work, from the translating of a German novel to the writing of an epic, was ever as the workman wished and meant it? This version of *Meister*, with whatever faults it may have, I honestly present to my countrymen: if, while it makes any portion of them more familiar with the richest, most gifted of living minds, it increase their knowledge, or even afford them a transient amusement, they will excuse its errors, and I shall be far more than paid for all my labour.

WILHELM MEISTER'S APPRENTICESHIP.

BOOK I.

CHAPTER I.

THE play was late in breaking up: old Barbara went more than once to the window, and listened for the sound of carriages. She was waiting for Mariana, her pretty mistress, who had that night, in the afterpiece, been acting the part of a young officer, to the no small delight of the public. Barbara's impatience was greater than it used to be, when she had nothing but a frugal supper to present: on this occasion, Mariana was to be surprised with a packet, which Norberg, a young and wealthy merchant, had sent by the post, to show that, in absence, he still thought of his love.

As an old servant, as confidante, counsellor, manager and housekeeper, Barbara assumed the privilege of opening seals; and this evening she the less had been able to restrain her curiosity, as the favour of the open-handed gallant was more a matter of anxiety with herself than with her mistress. On breaking up the packet, she had found, with unfeigned satisfaction, that it held a piece of fine muslin and some ribbons of the newest fashion, for Mariana; with a quantity of calico, two or three neckerchiefs, and a moderate rouleau of money, for herself. Her esteem for the absent Norberg was of course unbounded: she meditated only how she might best present him to the mind of Mariana, best bring to her recollection what she owed him, and what he had a right to expect from her fidelity and thankfulness.

The muslin, with the ribbons half unrolled, to set it off by their colours, lay like a Christmas-present on the small table; the position of the lights increased the glitter of the gift; all was in order, when the old woman heard Mariana's step on the stairs, and hastened to meet her. But what was her disappointment, when the little female officer, without deigning to regard her caresses, rushed past her with unusual speed and agitation; threw her hat and sword upon the table, and walked hastily up and down, bestowing not a look on the lights, or any portion of the apparatus!

"What ails thee, my darling?" exclaimed the astonished Barbara; "for Heaven's sake, what is the matter? Look here, my pretty child! See what a present! And who could have sent it but thy kindest of friends? Norberg has given thee the muslin to make a night-gown of: he will soon be here himself; he seems to be fonder and more generous than ever."

Barbara went to the table, that she might exhibit the memorials with which Norberg had likewise honoured *her*, when Mariana, turning away from the presents, exclaimed with vehemence, "Off! off! Not a word of all this tonight! I have yielded to thee; thou hast willed it; be it so! When Norberg comes, I am his, am thine, am any one's; make of me what thou pleasest: but till then I will be my own; and, if thou hadst a thousand tongues, thou shouldst never talk me from my purpose. All, all that *is* my own will I give up to him who loves me; whom I love. No sour faces! I will abandon myself to this affection, as if it were to last forever."

The old damsel had abundance of objections and serious considerations to allege; in the progress of the dialogue, she was growing bitter and keen, when Mariana sprang at her, and seized her by the breast. The old damsel laughed aloud. "I must have a care," she cried, "that you don't get into pantaloons again, if I mean to be sure of my life! Come, doff you! The girl will beg my pardon for the foolish things the boy is doing to me. Off with the frock! Off with them all! The dress beseems you not; it is dangerous for you, I observe; the epaulets make you too bold."

Thus speaking, she had laid hands upon her mistress: Mariana pushed her off, exclaiming, "Not so fast! I expect a visit tonight."

"Visit!" rejoined Barbara; "you surely do not look for Meister, the young, soft-hearted, callow merchant's son?"

"Just for him," replied Mariana.

"Generosity appears to be growing your ruling passion," said the old woman with a grin; "you connect yourself with minors and moneyless people, as if they were the chosen of the earth. Doubtless it is charming to be worshiped as a benefactress."

"Jeer as thou pleasest. I love him! I love him! With what

rapture do I now, for the first time, speak the word! *This* is the passion which I have mimicked so often, when I knew not what it meant. Yes! I will throw myself about his neck; I will clasp him as if I could hold him forever. I will show him all my love; will enjoy all his in its whole extent."

"Moderate yourself," said the old dame coolly; "moderate yourself! A single word will interrupt your rapture: Norberg is coming! Coming in a fortnight! Here is the letter that arrived with the packet."

"And, though the morrow were to rob me of my friend, I would conceal it from myself and him. A fortnight! An age! Within a fortnight, what may not happen, what may not alter?"

Here Wilhelm entered. We need not say how fast she flew to meet him; with what rapture he clasped the red uniform, and pressed the beautiful wearer of it to his bosom. It is not for us to describe the blessedness of two lovers. Old Barbara went grumbling away: we shall retire with her, and leave the happy two alone.

CHAPTER II.

When Wilhelm saluted his mother, next morning, she informed him that his father was very greatly discontented with him, and meant to forbid him these daily visits to the playhouse. "Though I myself often go with pleasure to the theatre," she continued, "I could almost detest it entirely, when I think that our fireside-peace is broken by your excessive passion for that amusement. Your father is ever repeating: What is the use of it? How can any one waste his time so?"

"He has already told me this," said Wilhelm; "and perhaps I answered him too hastily: but, for Heaven's sake, mother, is nothing then of use but what immediately puts money in our purse; but what procures us some property that we can lay our hands on? Had we not, for instance, room enough in the old house; and was it indispensable to build a new one? Does not my father every year expend a large part of his profit in ornamenting his chambers? Are these silk carpets, this English furniture, likewise of no use? Might we not content ourselves with worse? For my own part, I confess, these striped walls, these hundred times repeated flowers, and knots, and baskets, and figures, produce a really disagreeable effect upon me. At best, they but remind me of the front curtain of our theatre. But what a different thing it is to sit and look at that! There, if you must wait for a while, you are always sure that it will rise at last, and disclose to you a thousand curious objects, to entertain, to instruct and to exalt you."

"But you go to excess with it," said the mother; "your father wishes to be entertained in the evenings as well as you; besides, he thinks it dissipates your attention; and when he grows ill-humoured on the subject, it is I that must bear the blame. How often have I been upbraided with that miserable puppet-show, which I was unlucky enough to provide for you at Christmas, twelve years ago! It was the first thing that put these plays into your head."

"O, do not blame the poor puppets; do not repent of your love and motherly care! It was the only happy hour I had enjoyed in the new empty house. I never can forget that hour; I see it still before me; I recollect how surprised I was, when, after we had got our customary presents, you made us seat ourselves before the door that leads to the other room. The door opened; but not as formerly, to let us pass and repass; the entrance was occupied by an unexpected show. Within it rose a porch, concealed by a mysterious curtain. All of us were standing at a distance; our eagerness to see what glittering or jingling article lay hid behind the half-transparent veil was mounting higher and higher, when you bade us each sit down upon his stool and wait with patience.

"At length all of us were seated and silent: a whistle gave the signal; the curtain rolled aloft, and showed us the interior of the Temple, painted in deep red colours. The high-priest Samuel appeared with Jonathan, and their strange alternating voices seemed to me the most striking thing on earth. Shortly after entered Saul, overwhelmed with confusion at the impertinence of that heavy-limbed warrior, who had defied him and all his people. But how glad was I when the little dapper son of Jesse, with his crook and shepherd's pouch and sling, came hopping forth and said: 'Dread king and sovereign lord! let no one's heart sink down because of this; if your Majesty will grant me leave, I will go out to battle with this blustering giant.' Here ended the first act; leaving the spectators more curious than ever to see what further would happen, each praying that the music might soon be done. At last the curtain rose again. David devoted the flesh of the monster to the fowls of the air and the beasts of the field; the Philistine scorned and bullied him, stamped mightily with both his feet, and at length fell like a mass of clay, affording a splendid termination to the piece. And then the virgins sang: 'Saul hath slain his thousands, but David his ten thousands!' The giant's head was borne before his little victor, who received the King's beautiful daughter to wife. Yet withal, I remember, I was vexed at the dwarfish stature of this lucky prince; for the great Goliath and the small David had both been formed, according to the common notion, with a due regard to their figures and proportions. I pray you, mother, tell me what has now become of those puppets? I promised to show them to a friend, whom I was lately entertaining with a history of all this child's work."

"I can easily conceive," said the mother, "how these things should stick so firmly in your mind: I well remember what an interest you took in them; how you stole the little book from me, and learned the whole piece by heart. I first noticed it one evening when you had made a Goliath and a David of wax; you set them both to declaim against each other, and at length gave a deadly stab to the giant, fixing his shapeless head, stuck upon a large pin with a wax handle, in little David's hand. I then felt such a motherly contentment at your fine recitation and good memory, that I resolved to give you up the whole wooden troop to your own disposal. I did not then foresee that it would cause me so many heavy hours."

"Do not repent of it," said Wilhelm; "this little sport has often made us happy." So saying, he got the keys; made haste to find the puppets; and, for a moment, was transported back into those times when they almost seemed to him alive, when he felt as if he himself could give them life by the cunning of his voice and the movements of his hands. He took them to his room, and locked them up with care.

CHAPTER III.

IF the first love is indeed, as I hear it everywhere maintained to be, the most delicious feeling which the heart of man, before it or after, can experience,—then our hero must be reckoned doubly happy, as permitted to enjoy the pleasure of this chosen period in all its fulness. Few men are so peculiarly favoured; by far the greater part are led by the feelings of their youth into nothing but a school of hardship, where, after a stinted and checkered season of enjoyment, they are at length constrained to renounce their dearest wishes, and to learn forever to dispense with what once hovered before them as the highest happiness of existence.

Wilhelm's passion for that charming girl now soared aloft on the wings of imagination: after a short acquaintance, he had gained her affections; he found himself in possession of a being whom with all his heart he not only loved, but honoured: for she had first appeared before him in the flattering light of theatric pomp, and his passion for the stage combined itself with his earliest love for woman. His youth allowed him to enjoy rich pleasures, which the activity of his fancy exalted and maintained. The situation of his mistress, too, gave a turn to her conduct, which greatly enlivened his emotions. The fear, lest her lover might, before the time, detect the real state in which she stood, diffused over all her conduct an interesting tinge of anxiety and bashfulness; her attachment to the youth was deep; her inquietude itself appeared but to augment her tenderness; she was the loveliest of creatures while beside him.

When the first tumult of joy had passed, and our friend began to look back upon his life and its concerns, everything appeared new to him; his duties seemed holier, his inclinations keener, his knowledge clearer, his talents stronger, his purposes more decided. Accordingly, he soon fell upon a plan to avoid the reproaches of his father, to still the cares of his mother, and at the same time to enjoy Mariana's love without disturbance. Through the day he punctually transacted his business, commonly forbore attending the theatre, strove to be entertaining at table in the evening; and when all were asleep, he glided softly out into the garden, and hastened, wrapt up in his mantle, with all the feelings of Leander in his bosom, to meet his mistress without delay.

"What is this you bring?" inquired Mariana, as he entered one evening, with a bundle, which Barbara, in hopes it might turn out to be some valuable present, fixed her eyes upon with great attention. "You will never guess," said Wilhelm.

Great was the surprise of Mariana, great the scorn of Barbara, when the napkin being loosened gave to view a perplexed multitude of span-long puppets. Mariana laughed aloud, as Wilhelm set himself to disentangle the confusion of the wires, and show her each figure by itself. Barbara glided sulkily out of the room.

A very little thing will entertain two lovers; and accordingly our friends, this evening, were as happy as they wished to be. The little troop was mustered; each figure was minutely examined, and laughed at, in its turn. King Saul, with his golden crown and his black velvet robe, Mariana did not like; he looked, she said, too stiff and pedantic. She was far better pleased with Jonathan, his sleek chin, his turban, his cloak of red and yellow. She soon got the art of turning him deftly on his wire; she made him bow, and repeat declarations of love. On the other hand, she refused to give the least attention to the prophet Samuel, though Wilhelm commended the pontifical breastplate, and told her that the taffeta of the cassock had been taken from a gown of his own grandmother's. David she thought too small, Goliath was too large; she held by Jonathan. She grew to manage him so featly, and at last to extend her caresses from the puppet to its owner, that, on this occasion, as on others, a silly sport became the introduction to happy hours.

Their soft, sweet dreams were broken in upon by a noise which arose on the street. Mariana called for the old dame, who, as usual, was occupied in furbishing the changeful materials of the playhouse wardrobe for the service of the piece next to be acted. Barbara said, the disturbance arose from a set of jolly companions, who were just then sallying out of the Italian Tavern, hard by, where they had been busy discussing fresh oysters, a cargo of which had just arrived, and by no means sparing their champaign.

"Pity," Mariana said, "that we did not think of it in time; we might have had some entertainment to ourselves."

"It is not yet too late," said Wilhelm, giving Barbara a louis-d'or: "get us what we want; then come and take a share with us."

The old dame made speedy work; ere long a trimly-covered table, with a neat collation, stood before the lovers. They made Barbara sit with them; they ate and drank, and enjoyed themselves.

On such occasions, there is never want of enough to say. Mariana soon took up little Jonathan again, and the old dame turned the conversation upon Wilhelm's favourite topic. "You were once telling us," she said, "about the first exhibition of a puppet-show on Christmas-eve: I remember you were interrupted, just as the ballet was going to begin. We have now the pleasure of a personal acquaintance with the honourable company by whom those wonderful effects were brought about."

"O yes!" cried Mariana, "do tell us how it all went on, and how you felt then."

"It is a fine emotion, Mariana," said the youth, "when we bethink ourselves of old times, and old harmless errors; especially if this is at a period when we have happily gained some elevation, from which we can look around us, and survey the path we have left behind. It is so pleasant to think, with composure and satisfaction, of many obstacles, which often with painful feelings we may have regarded as invincible; pleasant to compare what we now are, with what we then were struggling to become. But I am happy above others in this matter, that I speak to you about the past, at a moment when I can also look forth into the blooming country, which we are yet to wander through together, hand in hand."

VOL. I.   C

"But how was it with the ballet?" said Barbara. "I fear it did not quite go off as it should have done."

"I assure you," said Wilhelm, "it went off quite well. And certainly the strange caperings of these Moors and Mooresses, these shepherds and shepherdesses, these dwarfs and dwarfesses, will never altogether leave my recollection, while I live. When the curtain dropped, and the door closed, our little party skipped away, frolicking as if they had been tipsy, to their beds; for myself, however, I remember that I could not go to sleep: still wanting to have something told me on the subject, I continued putting questions to every one, and would hardly let the maid away who had brought me up to bed.

"Next morning, alas! the magic apparatus had altogether vanished; the mysterious veil was carried off, the door permitted us again to go and come through it without obstruction; the manifold adventures of the evening had passed away, and left no trace behind. My brothers and sisters were running up and down with their playthings; I alone kept gliding to and fro; it seemed to me impossible that two bare door-posts could be all that now remained, where the night before so much enchantment had displayed itself. Alas! the man that seeks a lost love can hardly be unhappier than I then thought myself."

A rapturous look, which he cast on Mariana, convinced her that he was not much afraid of ever having a misfortune such as this to strive with.

CHAPTER IV.

"My sole wish now," continued Wilhelm, "was to witness a second exhibition of the piece. For this purpose I had recourse, by constant entreaties, to my mother; and she attempted in a favourable hour to persuade my father. Her labour, however, was in vain. My father's principle was, that none but enjoyments of rare occurrence were adequately prized; that neither young nor old could set a proper value on pleasures which they tasted every day.

"We might have waited long, perhaps till Christmas returned, had not the contriver and secret director of the spectacle himself felt a pleasure in repeating the display of it; partly incited, I suppose, by the wish to produce a brand-new Harlequin expressly prepared for the afterpiece.

"A young officer of the artillery, a person of great gifts in all sorts of mechanical contrivance, had served my father in many essential particulars during the building of the house; for which, having been handsomely rewarded, he felt desirous of expressing his thankfulness to the family of his patron, and so made us young ones a present of this complete theatre, which, in hours of leisure, he had already carved and painted and strung together. It was this young man, who, with the help of a servant, had himself managed the puppets, disguising his voice to pronounce their various speeches. He had no great difficulty in persuading my father, who granted, out of complaisance to a friend, what he had denied from conviction to his children. In short, our theatre was again set up, some little ones of the neighbourhood were invited, and the piece was again represented.

"If I had formerly experienced the delights of surprise and astonishment, I enjoyed on this second occasion the pleasure of examining and scrutinising. *How* all this happened was my present concern. That the puppets themselves did not speak, I had already decided; that of themselves they did not move, I also conjectured: but then how came it all to be so pretty, and to look just as if they both spoke and moved of themselves; and where were the lights, and the people that managed the deception? These enigmas perplexed me the more, as I wished at once to be among the enchanters and the enchanted, at once to have a secret hand in the play, and to enjoy, as a looker-on, the pleasure of illusion.

"The piece being finished, preparations were making for the farce; the spectators had risen, and were all busy talking together. I squeezed myself closer to the door, and heard, by the rattling within, that the people were packing up some articles. I lifted the lowest screen, and poked in my head between the posts. As our mother noticed it, she drew me back; but I had seen well enough, that here friends and foes, Saul and Goliath, and whatever else their names might be, were lying quietly down together in a drawer; and thus my half-contented curiosity received a fresh excitement. To my great surprise, moreover, I had noticed the lieutenant very diligently occupied in the interior of the shrine. Henceforth, Jack-pudding, however he might clatter with his heels, could not any longer entertain me. I sank into deep meditation; my discovery at once made me more satisfied, and less so than before. After a little, it first struck me that I yet comprehended nothing; and here I was right; for the connexion of the parts with each other was entirely unknown to me, and everything depends on that.

CHAPTER V.

"In well adjusted and regulated houses," continued Wilhelm, "children have a feeling not unlike what I conceive rats and mice to have; they keep a sharp eye on all crevices and holes, where they may come at any forbidden dainty; they enjoy it also with a fearful, stolen satisfaction, which forms no small part of the happiness of childhood.

"More than any other of the young ones, I was in the habit of looking out attentively to see if I could notice any cupboard left open, or key standing in its lock. The more reverence I bore in my heart for those closed doors, on the outside of which I had to pass by for weeks and months, catching only a furtive glance when our mother now and then opened the consecrated place to take something from it,—the quicker was I to make use of any opportunities which the forgetfulness of our housekeepers at times afforded me.

"Among all the doors, that of the store-room was, of course, the one I watched most narrowly. Few of the joyful anticipations in life can equal the feeling which I used to have, when my mother happened to call me, that I might help her to carry out anything, after which I might pick up a few dried plums, either with her kind permission, or by help of my own dexterity. The accumulated treasures of this chamber took hold of my imagination by their magnitude; the very fragrance exhaled by so multifarious a collection of sweet-smelling spices produced such a craving effect on me, that I never failed, when passing near, to linger for a little, and regale myself at least on the unbolted atmosphere. At length, one Sunday morning, my mother, being hurried by the ringing of the church-bells, forgot to take this precious key with her on shutting the door, and went away, leaving all the house in a deep Sabbath stillness. No sooner had I marked this oversight, than gliding softly once or twice to and from the place, I at last approached very gingerly, opened the door, and felt myself, after a single step, in immediate contact with these manifold and long-wished-for means of happiness. I glanced over glasses, chests and bags, and drawers and boxes, with a quick and doubtful eye, considering what I ought to choose and take; turned finally to my dear withered plums, provided myself also with a few dried apples, and completed the forage with an orange chip. I was quietly retreating with my plunder, when some little chests, lying piled over one another, caught my attention; the more so, as I noticed a wire, with hooks at the end of it, sticking through the joint of the lid in one of them. Full of eager hopes, I opened this singular package; and judge of my emotions, when I found my glad world of heroes all sleeping safe within! I meant to pick out the topmost, and, having examined them, to pull up those below; but in this attempt, the wires got very soon entangled, and I fell into a fright and flutter, more particularly as the cook just then began making some stir in the kitchen, which lay close by; so that I had nothing for it but to squeeze the whole together the best way I could, and to shut the chest, having stolen from it nothing but a little written book, which happened to be lying above, and contained the whole drama of Goliath and David. With this booty I made good my retreat into the garret.

"Henceforth all my stolen hours of solitude were devoted to perusing the play, to learning it by heart, and picturing in thought how glorious it would be, could I but get the figures, to make them move along with it. In idea, I myself became David and Goliath by turns. In every corner of the court-yard, of the stables, of the garden, under all kinds of circumstances, I laboured to stamp the whole piece upon my mind; laid hold of all the characters, and learned their speeches by heart, most commonly, however, taking up the parts of the chief personages, and allowing all the rest to move along with them, but as satellites, across my memory. Thus day and night the heroic words of David, wherewith he challenged the braggart giant, Goliath of Gath, kept their place in my thoughts. I often muttered them to myself, while no one gave heed to me, except my father, who, frequently observing some such detached exclamation, would in secret praise the excellent memory of his boy, that had retained so much from only two recitations.

"By this means, growing always bolder, I one evening repeated almost the entire piece before my mother, whilst I was busied in fashioning some bits of wax into players. She observed it, questioned me hard, and I confessed.

"By good fortune, this detection happened at a time when the lieutenant had himself been expressing a wish to initiate me in the mysteries of the art. My mother forthwith gave him notice of these unexpected talents; and he now contrived to make my parents offer him a couple of chambers in the top story, which commonly stood empty, that he might accommodate the spectators in the one, while the other held his actors, the proscenium again filling up the opening of the door. My father had allowed his friend to arrange all this; himself, in the mean time, seeming only to look at the transaction, as it were, through his fingers; for his maxim was, that children should not be allowed to see the kindness which is felt towards them, lest their pretensions come to extend too far. He was of opinion, that, in the enjoyments of the young, one should assume a serious air; often interrupting the course of their festivities, to prevent their satisfaction from degenerating into excess and presumption.

CHAPTER VI.

"The lieutenant now set up his theatre, and managed all the rest. During the week I readily observed, that he often came into the house at unusual hours, and I soon guessed the cause. My eagerness increased immensely; for I well understood, that till Sunday evening I could have no share in what was going on. At last the wished-for day arrived. At five in the evening, my conductor came and took me up with him. Quivering with joy, I entered, and descried, on both sides of the frame-work, the puppets all hanging in order as they were to advance to view. I considered them narrowly, and mounted on the steps, which raised them above the scene, and allowed me to hover aloft over all that little world. Not without reverence did I look down between the pieces of board, and recollect what a glorious effect the whole would produce, and feel into what mighty secrets I was now admitted. We made a trial, which succeeded well.

"Next day, a party of children were invited: we performed rarely; except that once, in the fire of action, I let poor Jonathan fall, and was obliged to reach down with my hand and pick him up again; an accident which sadly marred the illusion, produced a peal of laughter, and vexed me unspeakably. My father, however, seemed to relish this misfortune not a little. Prudently shrouding up the contentment he felt at the expertness of his little boy, after the piece was finished, he dwelt on the mistakes we had committed, saying it would all have been very pretty, had not this or that gone wrong with us.

"I was vexed to the heart at these things, and sad for all the evening. By next morning, however, I had quite slept off my sorrow; and was blessed in the persuasion that, but for this one fault, I had played delightfully. The spectators also flattered me with their unanimous approval; they all maintained, that though the lieutenant, in regard to the coarse and the fine voices, had done great things, yet his declamation was in general too stiff and affected; whereas the new aspirant spoke his Jonathan and David with exquisite grace. My mother in particular commended the gallant tone in which I had challenged Goliath, and acted the modest victor before the king.

"From this time, to my extreme delight, the theatre continued open; and as the spring advanced, so that fires could be dispensed with, I passed all my hours of recreation lying in the garret, and making the puppets caper and play together. Often I invited up my comrades, or my brothers and sisters; but when they would not come, I stayed by myself not the less. My imagination brooded over that tiny world, which soon afterwards acquired another form.

"Scarcely had I once or twice exhibited the first piece, for which my scenery and actors had been formed and decorated, till it ceased to give me any pleasure. On the other hand, among some books of my grandfather's, I had happened to fall in with the *German Theatre*, and a few translations of Italian operas; in which works I soon got very deeply immersed, on each occasion first reckoning up the characters, and then, without farther ceremony, proceeding to exhibit the piece. King Saul, with his black velvet cloak, was therefore now obliged to personate Darius or Cato, or some other pagan hero; in which cases, it may be observed, the plays were never wholly represented; for most part, only the fifth acts, where the cutting and stabbing lay.

"It was natural that the operas, with their manifold adventures and vicissitudes, should attract me more than anything beside. In these compositions I found stormy seas, gods descending in chariots of cloud, and, what most of all delighted me, abundance of thunder and lightning. I did my best with pasteboard, paint and paper: I could make night very prettily; my lightning was fearful to behold; only my thunder did not always prosper, which, however, was of less importance. In operas, moreover, I found frequent opportunities of introducing my David and Goliath, persons whom the regular drama would hardly admit. Daily I felt more attachment for the hampered spot where I enjoyed so many pleasures; and, I must confess, the fragrance which the puppets had acquired from the store-room added not a little to my satisfaction.

"The decorations of my theatre were now in a tolerable state of completeness. I had always had the knack of drawing with compasses, and clipping pasteboard, and colouring figures; and here it served me in good stead. But the more sorry was I, on the other hand, when, as frequently happened, my stock of actors would not suffice for representing great affairs.

"My sisters dressing and undressing their dolls, awoke in me the project of furnishing my heroes by and by with garments, which might also be put off and on. Accordingly, I slit the scraps of cloth from off their bodies; tacked the fragments together as well as possible; saved a particle of money to buy new ribbons and lace; begged many a rag of taffeta; and so formed, by degrees, a full theatrical wardrobe, in which hoop-petticoats for the ladies were especially remembered.

"My troop was now fairly provided with dresses for the most important piece, and you might have expected that henceforth one exhibition would follow close upon the heels of another: but it happened with me, as it often happens with children; they embrace wide plans, make mighty preparations, then a few trials, and the whole undertaking is abandoned. I was guilty of this fault. My greatest pleasure lay in the inventive part, and the employment of my fancy. This or that piece inspired me with interest for a few scenes of it, and immediately I set about providing new apparel suitable for the occasion. In such fluctuating operations, many parts of the primary dresses of my heroes had fallen into disorder, or totally gone out of sight; so that now the first great piece could no longer be exhibited. I surrendered myself to my imagination; I rehearsed and prepared forever; built a thousand castles in the air, and saw not that I was at the same time undermining the foundations of these little edifices."

During this recital, Mariana had called up and put in action all her courtesy for Wilhelm, that she might conceal her sleepiness. Diverting as the matter seemed on one side, it was too simple for her taste, and her lover's view of it too serious. She softly pressed her foot on his, however, and gave him all visible signs of attention and approval. She drank out of his glass: Wilhelm was convinced that no word of his history had fallen to the ground. After a short pause, he said: "It is now your turn, Mariana, to tell me what were your first childish joys. Till now, we have always been too busy with the present to trouble ourselves, on either side, about our previous way of life. Let me hear, Mariana, under what circumstances you were reared; what are the first lively impressions which you still remember?"

These questions would have very much embarrassed Mariana, had not Barbara made haste to help her. "Think you," said the cunning old woman, "we have been so mindful of what happened to us long ago, that we have merry things like these to talk about; and though we had, that we could give them such an air in talking of them?"

"As if they needed it!" cried Wilhelm. "I love this soft, good, amiable creature so much, that I regret every instant of my life which has not been spent beside her. Allow me, at least in fancy, to have a share in thy bygone life: tell me everything; I will tell everything to thee! If possible, we will deceive ourselves, and win back those days that have been lost to love."

"If you require it so eagerly," replied the old dame, "we can easily content you. Only, in the first place, let us hear how your taste for the theatre gradually reached a head; how you practised, how you improved so happily, that now you can pass for a superior actor. No doubt, you must have met with droll adventures in your progress. It is not worth while to go to bed now: I have still one flask in reserve; and who knows whether we shall soon all sit together so quiet and cheery again?"

Mariana cast a mournful look upon her, which Wilhelm not observing, proceeded with his narrative.

CHAPTER VII.

"THE recreations of youth, as my companions began to increase in number, interfered with this solitary, still enjoyment. I was by turns a hunter, a soldier, a knight, as our games required me; and constantly I had this small advantage above the rest, that I was qualified to furnish them suitably with the necessary equipments. The swords, for example, were generally of my manufacture; I gilded and decorated the scabbards; and a secret instinct allowed me not to stop, till our militia was accoutred according to the antique model. Helmets, with plumes of paper, were got ready; shields, even coats of mail, were provided; undertakings in which such of the servants as had aught of the tailor in them, and the sempstresses of the house, broke many a needle.

"A part of my comrades I had now got well equipped; by degrees, the rest were likewise furbished up, though on a thriftier plan; and so a very seemly corps at length was mustered. We marched about the court-yards and gardens; smote fearfully upon each other's shields and heads: many flaws of discord rose among us, but none that lasted.

"This diversion greatly entertained my fellows; but scarcely had it been twice or thrice repeated, till it ceased to content me. The aspect of so many harnessed figures naturally stimulated in my mind those ideas of chivalry, which, for some time, since I had commenced the reading of old romances, were filling my imagination.

"Koppen's translation of *Jerusalem Delivered* at length fell into my hands, and gave these wandering thoughts a settled direction. The whole poem, it is true, I could not read; but there were pieces of it which I learned by heart, and the images expressed in these hovered round me. Particularly was I captivated with Clorinda, and all her deeds and bearing. The masculine womanhood, the peaceful completeness of her being, had a greater influence upon my mind, just beginning to unfold itself, than the factitious charms of Armida, though the garden of that enchantress was by no means an object of my contempt.

"But a hundred and a hundred times, while walking in the evenings on the balcony which stretches along the front of the house, and looking over the neighbourhood, as the quivering splendour streamed up at the horizon from the departed sun, and the stars came forth, and night pressed forward from every cleft and hollow, and the small shrill tone of the cricket tinkled through the solemn stillness,—a hundred and a hundred times have I repeated to myself the history of the mournful duel between Tancred and Clorinda.

"However strongly I inclined by nature to the party of the Christians, I could not help declaring for the Paynim heroine with all my heart, when she engaged to set on fire the great tower of the besiegers. And when Tancred in the darkness met the supposed knight, and the strife began between them under that veil of gloom, and the two battled fiercely, I could never pronounce the words,

> But now the sure and fated hour is nigh,
> Clorinda's course is ended, she must die!

without tears rushing into my eyes, which flowed plentifully, when the hapless lover, plunging his sword into her breast, opened the departing warrior's helmet, recognised the lady of his heart, and, shuddering, brought water to baptise her.

"How did my heart run over, when Tancred struck with his sword that tree in the enchanted wood; when blood flowed from the gash, and a voice sounded in his ears, that now again he was wounding Clorinda; that destiny had marked him out ever unwittingly to injure what he loved beyond all else!

"The recital took such hold of my imagination, that the passages I had read of the poem began dimly, in my mind, to conglomerate into a whole; wherewith I was so taken that I could not but propose to have it some way represented. I meant to have Tancred and Rinaldo acted; and for this purpose, two coats of mail, which I had before manufactured, seemed expressly suitable. The one, formed of dark-gray paper with scales, was to serve for the solemn Tancred; the other, of silver and gilt paper, for the magnificent Rinaldo. In the vivacity of my anticipations, I told the whole project to my comrades, who felt quite charmed with it, only could not well comprehend how so glorious a thing could be exhibited, and, above all, exhibited by them.

" Such scruples I easily set aside. Without hesitation, I took upon me in idea the management of two rooms in the house of a neighbouring playmate; not calculating that his venerable aunt would never give them up, or considering how a theatre could be made of them, whereof I had no settled notion, except that it was to be fixed on beams, to have side-scenes made of parted folding-screens, and on the floor a large piece of cloth. From what quarter these materials and furnishings were to come, I had not determined.

" So far as concerned the forest, we fell upon a good expedient. We betook ourselves to an old servant of one of our families, who had now become a woodman, with many entreaties that he would get us a few young firs and birches; which actually arrived more speedily than we had reason to expect. But, in the next place, great was our embarrassment as to how the piece should be got up before the trees were withered. Now was the time for prudent counsel! We had no house, no scenery, no curtains; the folding-screens were all we had.

" In this forlorn condition we again applied to the lieutenant, giving him a copious description of all the glorious things we meant to do. Little as he understood us, he was very helpful: he piled all the tables he could get in the house or neighbourhood, one above the other, in a little room; to these he fixed our folding-screens; and made a back-view with green curtains, sticking up our trees along with it.

" At length the appointed evening came; the candles were lit, the maids and children were sitting in their places, the piece was to go forward, the whole corps of heroes was equipped and dressed, —when each for the first time discovered that he knew not what he was to say. In the heat of invention, being quite immersed in present difficulties, I had forgotten the necessity of each understanding what and where he was to speak; nor, in the midst of our bustling preparations, had it once occurred to the rest; each believing he could easily enact a hero, easily so speak and bear himself, as became the personage into whose world I had transplanted him. They all stood wonderstruck, asking: What was to come first? I alone, having previously got ready Tancred's part, entered *solus* on the scene, and began reciting some verses of the epic. But as the passage soon changed into narrative, and I, while speaking, was at once transformed into a third party, and the bold

Godfredo when his turn came would not venture forth, I was at last obliged to take leave of my spectators under peals of laughter; a disaster which cut me to the heart. Thus had our undertaking proved abortive; but the company still kept their places, still wishing to see something. All of us were dressed; I screwed my courage up, and determined, foul or fair, to give them David and Goliath. Some of my companions had before this helped me to exhibit the puppet-play; all of them had often seen it: we shared the characters among us; each promised to do his best; and one small grinning urchin painted a black beard upon his chin, and undertook, if any lacuna should occur, to fill it up with drollery as Harlequin; an arrangement to which, as contradicting the solemnity of the piece, I did not consent without extreme reluctance; and I vowed within myself, that, if once delivered out of this perplexity, I would think long and well before risking the exhibition of another piece."

CHAPTER VIII.

MARIANA, overpowered with sleep, leaned upon her lover, who clasped her close to him, and proceeded in his narrative, while the old damsel prudently sipped up the remainder of the wine.

"The embarrassment," he said, "into which, along with my companions, I had fallen, by attempting to act a play that did not anywhere exist, was soon forgotten. My passion for representing each romance I read, each story that was told me, would not yield before the most unmanageable materials. I felt convinced that whatever gave delight in narrative must produce a far deeper impression when exhibited: I wanted to have everything before my eyes, everything brought forth upon the stage. At school, when the elements of general history were related to us, I carefully marked the passages where any person had been slain or poisoned in a singular way; and my imagination, glancing rapidly along the exposition and intrigue, hastened to the interesting fifth act. Indeed I actually began to write some pieces from the end backwards; without, however, in any of them reaching the beginning.

"At the same time, partly by inclination, partly by the counsel of my good friends, who had caught the fancy of acting plays, I read a whole wilderness of theatrical productions, as chance put them into my hands. I was still in those happy years when all things please us, when number and variety yield us abundant satisfaction. Unfortunately, too, my taste was corrupted by another circumstance. Any piece delighted me especially, in which I could hope to give delight; there were few which I did not peruse in this agreeable delusion; and my lively conceptive power enabling me to transfer myself into all the characters, seduced me to believe that I might likewise represent them all. Hence, in the distribution of the parts, I commonly selected such as did not fit me; and always more than one part, if I could by any means accomplish more.

"In their games, children can make all things out of any: a staff becomes a musket, a splinter of wood a sword, any bunch of cloth a puppet, any crevice a chamber. Upon this principle was our private theatre got up. Totally unacquainted with the measure of our strength, we undertook all; we stuck at no *qui pro quo*, and felt convinced that every one would take us for what we gave ourselves out to be. Now, however, our affairs went on so soberly and smoothly, that I have not even a curious insipidity to tell you of. We first played all the few pieces in which only males are requisite; next, we travestied some of ourselves; and at last took our sisters into the concern along with us. In one or two houses, our amusement was looked upon as profitable, and company invited to see it. Nor did our lieutenant of artillery now turn his back upon us. He showed us how we ought to make our exits and our entrances; how we should declaim, and with what attitudes and gestures. Yet generally he earned small thanks for his toil: we conceived ourselves to be much deeper in the secrets of theatrical art than he himself was.

"We very soon began to grow tired of tragedy: for all of us believed, as we had often heard, that it was easier to write or represent a tragedy than to attain proficiency in comedy. In our first attempts, accordingly, we had felt as if exactly in our element: dignity of rank, elevation of character, we studied to approach by stiffness and affectation, and imagined that we succeeded rarely: but our happiness was not complete, except we might rave outright, might stamp with our feet, and cast ourselves upon the ground, full of fury and despair.

"Boys and girls had not long carried on these amusements in concert, till nature began to take her course, and our society branched itself off into sundry little love-associations, as generally more than one sort of comedy is acted in the playhouse. Behind the scenes, each happy pair pressed hands in the most tender style; they floated in blessedness, appearing to one another quite ideal persons, when so transformed and decorated, whilst, on the other hand, unlucky rivals consumed themselves with envy, and out of malice and spite worked every species of mischief.

"Our amusements, though undertaken without judgment, and carried on without instruction, were not without their use to us. We trained our memories and persons; we acquired more dexterity in speech and gesture than is usually met with at so early an age. But for me in particular this time was in truth an epoch; my mind turned all its faculties exclusively to the theatre, and my highest happiness was in reading, in writing, or in acting plays.

"Meanwhile the labours of my regular teachers continued; I had been set apart for the mercantile life, and placed under the guidance of our neighbour in the counting-house; yet my spirit at this very time recoiled more forcibly than ever from all that was to bind me to a low profession. It was to the stage that I aimed at consecrating all my powers; on the stage that I meant to seek all my happiness and satisfaction.

"I recollect a poem, which must be among my papers, where the Muse of tragic art and another female form, by which I personified Commerce, were made to strive very bravely for my most important self. The idea is common, and I recollect not that the verses were of any worth; but you shall see it, for the sake of the fear, the abhorrence, the love and passion, which reign in it. How repulsively did I paint the old housewife, with the distaff in her girdle, the bunch of keys by her side, the spectacles on her nose; ever toiling, ever restless, quarrelsome and penurious, pitiful and dissatisfied! How feelingly did I describe the condition of that poor man who has to cringe beneath her rod, and earn his slavish day's-wages by the sweat of his brow!

"And how differently advanced the other! What an apparition for the overclouded mind! Formed as a queen, in her thoughts and looks she announced herself the child of freedom. The feeling of her own worth gave her dignity without pride: her apparel became her, it veiled her form without constraining it; and the rich folds repeated, like a thousand-voiced echo, the graceful movements of the goddess. What a contrast! How easy for me to decide! Nor had I forgotten the more peculiar characteristics of my muse. Crowns and daggers, chains and masks, as my predecessors had delivered them, were here produced once more. The contention was keen; the speeches of both were palpably enough contrasted, for at fourteen years of age one usually paints the black lines and the white pretty near each other. The old lady spoke as beseemed a person that would pick up a pin from her path; the other, like one that could give away kingdoms. The warning threats of the housewife were disregarded: I turned my back upon her promised riches; disinherited and naked, I gave myself up to the muse; she threw her golden veil over me, and called me hers.

"Could I have thought, my dearest," he exclaimed, pressing Mariana close to him, "that another and a more lovely goddess would come to encourage me in my purpose, to travel with me on my journey, the poem might have had a finer turn, a far more interesting end. Yet it is no poetry; it is truth and life that I feel in thy arms; let us prize the sweet happiness, and consciously enjoy it."

The pressure of his arms, the emotion of his elevated voice, awoke Mariana, who hastened by caresses to conceal her embarrassment; for no word of the last part of his story had reached her. It is to be wished, that in future, our hero, when recounting his favourite histories, may find more attentive hearers.

CHAPTER IX.

THUS Wilhelm passed his nights in the enjoyment of confiding love; his days in the expectation of new happy hours. When desire and hope had first attracted him to Mariana, he already felt as if inspired with new life; felt as if he were beginning to be another man: he was now united to her; the contentment of his wishes had become a delicious habitude. His heart strove to ennoble the object of his passion; his spirit to exalt with it the young creature whom he loved. In the shortest absence, thoughts of her arose within him. If she had once been necessary to him, she was now grown indispensable, now that he was bound to her by all the ties of nature. His pure soul felt that she was the half, more than the half of himself. He was grateful and devoted without limit.

Mariana, too, succeeded in deceiving herself for a season; she shared with him the feeling of his liveliest blessedness. Alas! if the cold hand of self-reproach had not often come across her heart! She was not secure from it even in Wilhelm's bosom, even under the wings of his love. And when she was again left alone, again left to sink from the clouds, to which passion had exalted her, into the consciousness of her real condition, then she was indeed to be pitied. So long as she had lived among degrading perplexities, disguising from herself her real situation, or rather never thinking of it, frivolity had helped her through; the incidents she was exposed to had come upon her each by itself; satisfaction and vexation had cancelled one another; humiliation had been compensated by vanity; want by frequent, though momentary superfluity; she could plead necessity and custom as a law or an excuse; and hitherto all painful emotions from hour to hour, and from day to day, had by these means been shaken off. But now, for some instants, the poor girl had felt herself transported to a better world; aloft as it were, in the midst of light and joy, she had looked down upon the abject desert of her life, had felt what a miserable creature is the woman who, inspiring desire, does not also inspire reverence and love; she regretted and repented, but found herself outwardly or inwardly no better for regret. She had nothing that she could accomplish or resolve upon. Looking into herself and searching, all was waste and void within her soul; her heart had no place of strength or refuge. But the more sorrowful her state was, the more vehemently did her feelings cling to the man whom she loved; her passion for him even waxed stronger daily, as the danger of losing him came daily nearer.

Wilhelm, on the other hand, soared serenely happy in higher regions; to him also a new world had been disclosed, but a world rich in the most glorious prospects. Scarcely had the first excess of joy subsided, when all that had long been gliding dimly through his soul stood up in bright distinctness before it. She is thine! She has given herself away to thee! She, the loved, the wished-for, the adored, has given herself away to thee in trust and faith; she shall not find thee ungrateful for the gift. Standing or walking, he talked to himself; his heart constantly overflowed; with a copiousness of splendid words, he uttered to himself the loftiest emotions. He imagined that he understood the visible beckoning of fate reaching out its hand by Mariana to save him from the stagnant, weary, drudging life out of which he had so often wished for deliverance. To leave his father's house and people now appeared a light matter. He was young, and had not tried the world; his eagerness to range over its expanses, seeking fortune and contentment, was stimulated by his love. His vocation to the theatre was now clear to him; the high goal, which he saw raised before him, seemed nearer whilst he was advancing to it with Mariana's hand in his; and in his comfortable prudence, he beheld in himself the embryo of a great actor; the future founder of that national theatre, for which he heard so much and various sighing on every side. All that till now had slumbered, in the most secret corners of his soul, at length awoke. He painted for himself a picture of his manifold ideas, in the colours of love, upon a canvas of cloud: the figures of it, indeed, ran sadly into one another; yet the whole had an air but the more brilliant on that account.

CHAPTER X.

He was now in his chamber at home, ransacking his papers, making ready for departure. Whatever savoured of his previous employment he threw aside, meaning at his entrance upon life to be free even from recollections that could pain him. Works of taste alone, poets and critics, were, as acknowledged friends, placed among the chosen few. Heretofore he had given little heed to the critical authors: his desire for instruction now revived, when, again looking through his books, he found the theoretical part of them lying generally still uncut. In the full persuasion that such works were absolutely necessary, he had bought a number of them; but, with the best disposition in the world, he had not reached midway in any.

The more steadfastly, on the other hand, he had dwelt upon examples; and in every kind that was known to him, had made attempts himself.

Werner entered the room; and seeing his friend busied with the well-known sheets, he exclaimed: "Again among your papers? And without intending, I dare swear, to finish any one of them! You look them through and through once or twice, then throw them by, and begin something new."

"To finish is not the scholar's care; it is enough if he improves himself by practice."

"But also completes according to his best ability."

"And still the question might be asked, Is there not good hope of a youth who, on commencing some unsuitable affair, soon discovers its unsuitableness, and discontinues his exertions, not choosing to spend toil and time on what never can be of any value?"

"I know well enough it was never your concern to bring aught to a conclusion; you have always sickened on it before it came half-way. When you were the director of our puppet-show, for instance, how many times were fresh clothes got ready for the dwarfish troop, fresh decorations furbished up? Now this tragedy was to be played, now that; and at the very best you gave us some fifth act, where all was going topsy-turvy, and people cutting one another's throats."

"If you talk of those times, whose blame really was it that we ripped off from our puppets the clothes that fitted them, and were fast stitched to their bodies, and laid out money for a large and useless wardrobe? Was it not yours, my good friend, who had always some fragment of ribbon to traffic with; and skill, at the same time, to stimulate my taste, and turn it to your profit?"

Werner laughed, and continued: "I still recollect, with pleasure, how I used to extract gain from your theatrical campaigns, as army-contractors do from war. When you mustered for the 'Deliverance of Jerusalem,' I, for my part, made a pretty thing of profit, like the Venetians in the corresponding case. I know of nothing in the world more rational than to turn the folly of others to our own advantage."

"Perhaps it were a nobler satisfaction to cure men of their follies."

"From the little I know of men, this might seem a vain endeavour. But something towards it is always done, when any individual man grows wise and rich; and generally this happens at the cost of others."

"Well, here is *The Youth at the Parting of the Ways*; it has just come into my hand," said Wilhelm, drawing out a bunch of papers from the rest; "this at least is finished, whatever else it may be."

"Away with it, to the fire with it!" cried Werner. "The invention does not deserve the smallest praise: that affair has plagued me enough already, and drawn upon yourself your father's wrath. The verses may be altogether beautiful; but the meaning of them is fundamentally false. I still recollect your Commerce personified; a shrivelled, wretched-looking sibyl she was. I suppose you picked up the image of her from some miserable huckster's shop. At that time, you had no true idea at all of trade; whilst I could not think of any man whose spirit was, or needed to be, more enlarged than the spirit of a genuine merchant. What a thing is it to see the order which prevails throughout his business! By means of this he can at any time survey the general whole, without needing to perplex himself in the details. What advantages does he derive from the system of book-keeping by double entry! It is among the finest inventions of the human mind; every prudent master of a house should introduce it into his economy."

"Pardon me," said Wilhelm, smiling; "you begin by the form, as if it were the matter: you traders commonly, in your additions and balancings, forget what is the proper net-result of life."

"My good friend, you do not see how form and matter are in this case one; how neither can exist without the other. Order and arrangement increase the desire to save and get. A man embarrassed in his circumstances, and conducting them imprudently, likes best to continue in the dark; he will not gladly reckon up the debtor entries he is charged with. But on the other hand, there is nothing to a prudent manager more pleasant than daily to set before himself the sums of his growing fortune. Even a mischance, if it surprise and vex, will not affright him; for he knows at once what gains he has acquired to cast into the other scale. I am convinced, my friend, that if you once had a proper taste for our employments, you would grant that many faculties of the mind are called into full and vigorous play by them."

"Possibly this journey I am thinking of may bring me to other thoughts."

"O, certainly. Believe me, you want but to look upon some great scene of activity to make you ours forever; and when you come back, you will joyfully enroll yourself among that class of men whose art it is to draw towards themselves a portion of the money, and materials of enjoyment, which circulate in their appointed courses through the world. Cast a look on the natural and artificial productions of all the regions of the earth; consider how they have become, one here, another there, articles of necessity for men. How pleasant and how intellectual a task is it to calculate, at any moment, what is most required, and yet is wanting, or hard to find; to procure for each easily and soon what he demands; to lay in your stock prudently beforehand, and then to enjoy the profit of every pulse in that mighty circulation. This, it appears to me, is what no man that has a head can attend to without pleasure."

Wilhelm seemed to acquiesce, and Werner continued.

"Do but visit one or two great trading-towns, one or two seaports, and see if you can withstand the impression. When you observe how many men are busied, whence so many things have come, and whither they are going, you will feel as if you too could gladly mingle in the business. You will then see the smallest piece of ware in its connexion with the whole mercantile concern; and for that very reason you will reckon nothing paltry, because everything augments the circulation by which you yourself are supported."

Werner had formed his solid understanding in constant intercourse with Wilhelm; he was thus accustomed to think also of *his* profession, of *his* employments, with elevation of soul; and he firmly believed that he did so with more justice than his otherwise more gifted and valued friend, who, as it seemed to him, had placed his dearest hopes, and directed all the force of his mind, upon the most imaginary objects in the world. Many a time he thought this false enthusiasm would infallibly be got the better of, and so excellent a soul be brought back to the right path. So, hoping in the present instance, he continued: "The great ones of the world have taken this earth of ours to themselves; they live in the midst of splendour and superfluity. The smallest nook of the land is already a possession, none may touch it or meddle with it; offices and civic callings bring in little profit; where, then, will you find more honest acquisitions, juster conquests, than those of trade? If the princes of this world hold the rivers, the highways, the havens in their power, and take a heavy tribute from everything that passes through them, may not we embrace with joy the opportunity of levying tax and toll, by *our* activity, on those commodities which the real or imaginary wants of men have rendered indispensable? I can promise you, if you would rightly apply your poetic view, my goddess might be represented as an invincible, victorious queen, and boldly opposed to yours. It is true, she bears the olive rather than the sword; dagger or chain she knows not; but she, too, gives crowns to her favourites; which, without offence to yours be it said, are of true gold from the furnace and the mine, and glance with genuine pearls, which she brings up from the depths of the ocean, by the hands of her unwearied servants."

This sally somewhat nettled Wilhelm; but he concealed his sentiments, remembering that Werner used to listen with composure to *his* apostrophes. Besides, he had fairness enough to be pleased at seeing each man think the best of his own peculiar craft; provided only *his*, of which he was so passionately fond, were likewise left in peace.

"And for you," exclaimed Werner, "who take so warm an interest in human concerns, what a sight will it be to behold the fortune which accompanies bold undertakings distributed to men before your eyes. What is more spirit-stirring than the aspect of a ship arriving from a lucky voyage, or soon returning with a rich capture? Not alone the relatives, the acquaintances, and those that share with the adventurers, but every unconcerned spectator also is excited, when he sees the joy with which the long-imprisoned shipman springs on land before his keel has wholly reached it, feeling that he is free once more, and now can trust what he has rescued from the false sea to the firm and faithful earth. It is not, my friend, in figures of arithmetic alone that gain presents itself before us; fortune is the goddess of breathing men; to feel her favours truly, we must live and be men who toil with their living minds and bodies, and enjoy with them also."

CHAPTER XI.

It is now time that we should know something more of Wilhelm's father and of Werner's; two men of very different modes of thinking, but whose opinions so far coincided, that both regarded commerce as the noblest calling, and both were peculiarly attentive to every advantage which any kind of speculation might produce to them. Old Meister, when his father died, had turned into money a valuable collection of pictures, drawings, copperplates and antiquities: he had entirely rebuilt and furnished his house in the newest style, and turned his other property to profit in all possible ways. A considerable portion of it he had embarked in trade, under the direction of the elder Werner, a man noted as an active merchant, whose speculations were commonly favoured by fortune. But nothing was so much desired by Meister as to confer upon his son those qualities of which himself was destitute, and to leave his children advantages which he reckoned it of the highest importance to possess. Withal, he felt a peculiar inclination for magnificence; for whatever catches the eye, and possesses at the same time real worth and durability. In his house, he would have all things solid and massive; his stores must be copious and rich; all his plate must be heavy; the furniture of his table must be costly. On the other hand, his guests were seldom invited; for every dinner was a festival, which, both for its expense and for its inconvenience, could not often be repeated. The economy of his house went on at a settled, uniform rate; and everything that moved or had place in it was just what yielded no one any real enjoyment.

The elder Werner, in his dark and hampered house, led quite another sort of life. The business of the day, in his narrow counting-house, at his ancient desk, once done, Werner liked to eat well, and, if possible, to drink better. Nor could he fully enjoy good things in solitude; with his family he must always see at table his friends, and any stranger that had the slightest connexion with his house. His chairs were of unknown age and antic fashion; but he daily invited some to sit on them. The dainty victuals arrested the attention of his guests, and none remarked that they were served up in common ware. His cellar held no great stock of wine; but the emptied niches were usually filled by more of a superior sort.

So lived these two fathers, often meeting to take counsel about their common concerns. On the day we are speaking of, it had been determined to send Wilhelm out from home, for the despatch of some commercial affairs.

"Let him look about him in the world," said old Meister, "and at the same time carry on our business in distant parts. One cannot do a young man any greater kindness, than initiate him early in the future business of his life. Your son returned so happily from his first expedition, and transacted his affairs so cleverly, that I am very curious to see how mine will do: *his* experience, I fear, will cost him dearer."

Old Meister had a high notion of his son's faculties and capabilities; he said this in the hope that his friend would contradict him, and hold up to view the admirable gifts of the youth. Here, however, he deceived himself: old Werner, who, in practical concerns, would trust no man but such as he had proved, answered placidly: "One must try all things; we can send him on the same journey, we shall give him a paper of directions to conduct him. There are sundry debts to be gathered in, old connexions are to be renewed, new ones to be made. He may likewise help the speculation I was lately talking of; for without punctual intelligence gathered on the spot, there is little to be done in it."

"He must prepare," said Meister, "and set forth as soon as possible. Where shall we get a horse for him to suit this business?"

"We shall not seek far. The shopkeeper in H——, who owes us somewhat, but is withal a good man, has offered me a horse instead of payment. My son knows it, and tells me it is a serviceable beast."

"He may fetch it himself; let him go with the diligence: the day after tomorrow he is back again betimes; we have his saddle-bags and letters made ready in the mean time; he can set out on Monday morning."

Wilhelm was sent for, and informed of their determination. Who so glad as he, now seeing the means of executing his purpose put into his hands, the opportunity made ready for him, without coöperation of his own! So intense was his love, so full was his conviction of the perfect rectitude of his intention to escape from the pressure of his actual mode of life, and follow a new and nobler career, that his conscience did not in the least rebel; no anxiety arose within him; he even reckoned the deception he was meditating holy. He felt certain that, in the long-run, parents and relations would praise and bless him for this resolution: he acknowledged in these concurring circumstances the signal of a guiding fate.

How slowly the time passed with him till night, till the hour when he should again see his Mariana! He sat in his chamber, and revolved the plan of his journey; as a conjuror, or a cunning thief in durance often draws out his feet from the fast-locked irons, to cherish in himself the conviction that his deliverance is possible, nay nearer than short-sighted turnkeys believe.

At last the appointed hour struck; he went out, shook off all anxiety, and hastened through the silent streets. In the middle of the great square, he raised his hands to the sky, feeling as if all was behind him and below him; he had freed himself from all. One moment he figured himself as in the arms of his beloved, the next as glancing with her in the splendours of the stage; he soared aloft in a world of hopes, only now and then the call of some watchman brought to his recollection that he was still wandering on the vulgar earth.

Mariana came to the stairs to meet him; and how beautiful, how lovely! She received him in the new white *négligé;* he thought he had never seen her so charming. Thus did she handsel the gift of her absent lover in the arms of a present one; with true passion, she lavished on her darling the whole treasure of those caresses, which nature suggested, or art had taught: need we ask if he was happy, if he was blessed?

He disclosed to her what had passed, and showed her, in general terms, his plan and his wishes. He would try, he said, to find a residence, then come back for her; he hoped she would not refuse him her hand. The poor girl was silent; she concealed her tears, and pressed her friend against her bosom. Wilhelm, though interpreting her silence in the most favourable manner, could have wished for a distinct reply; and still more, when at last he inquired of her in the tenderest and most delicate terms, if he might not think himself a father. But to this she answered only with a sigh, with a kiss.

CHAPTER XII.

NEXT morning Mariana awoke only to new despondency; she felt herself very solitary, she wished not to see the light of day, but stayed in bed, and wept. Old Barbara sat down by her, and tried to persuade and console her; but it was not in her power so soon to heal the wounded heart. The moment was now at hand, to which the poor girl had been looking forward as to the last of her life. Who could be placed in a more painful situation! The man she loved was departing; a disagreeable lover was threatening to come; and the most fearful mischiefs were to be anticipated, if the two, as might easily happen, should meet together.

"Calm yourself, my dear," said the old woman; "do not spoil your pretty eyes with crying. Is it then so terrible a thing to have two lovers? And though you can bestow your love but on the one, yet be thankful to the other, who, caring for you as he does, certainly deserves to be named your friend."

"My poor Wilhelm," said the other, all in tears, "had warning that a separation was at hand. A dream discovered to him what we strove so much to hide. He was sleeping calmly at my side; on a sudden I heard him muttering some unintelligible sounds; I grew frightened, and awoke him. Ah! with what love and tenderness and warmth did he clasp me! 'O Mariana!' cried he, 'what a horrid fate have you freed me from! How shall I thank you for deliverance from such torment! I dreamed that I was far from you in an unknown country, but your figure hovered before me; I saw you on a beautiful hill, the sunshine was glancing over it all; how charming did you look! But it had not lasted long, till I observed your image sinking down, sinking, sinking; I stretched out my arms towards you; they could not reach you through the distance. Your image still kept gliding down; it approached a great sea that lay far extended at the foot of the hill, a marsh rather than a sea. All at once a man gave you his hand, and seemed meaning to conduct you upwards, but he led you sidewards, and appeared to draw you after him. I cried out; as I could not reach you, I hoped to warn you. If I tried to walk, the ground seemed to hold me fast; if I could walk, the water hindered me; and even my cries were smothered in my breast.' So said the poor youth, while recovering from his terror, and reckoning himself happy to dissipate a frightful dream by the most delicious reality."

Barbara made every effort to reduce, by her prose, the poetry of her friend to the domain of common life; employing, in the present case, the ingenious craft which so often succeeds with birdcatchers, when they imitate with a whistle the tones of those luckless creatures which they soon hope to see by dozens safely lodged in their nets. She praised Wilhelm; she expatiated on his figure, his eyes, his love. The poor girl heard her with a gratified heart; then arose, let herself be dressed, and appeared calmer. "My child, my darling," continued the old woman in a cozening tone, "I will not trouble you or injure you; I cannot think of tearing from you your dearest happiness. Could you mistake my intention? Have you forgotten, that on all occasions I have cared for you more than for myself? Tell me only what you wish; we shall soon see how it may be brought about."

"What can I wish?" said Mariana; "I am miserable, miserable for life; I love him, and he loves me; yet I see that I must part with him, and know not how I shall survive it. Norberg comes, to whom we owe our whole subsistence, whom we cannot live without. Wilhelm is straitened in his fortune, he can do nothing for me."

"Yes, unfortunately, he is of those lovers who bring nothing but their hearts; and these people too have the highest pretensions of any."

"No jesting! The unhappy youth thinks of leaving his home, of going upon the stage, of offering me his hand."

"Of empty hands we have already four."

"I have no choice," continued Mariana; "do you decide for me! Cast me away to this side or to that; mark only one thing: I think I carry in my bosom a pledge that ought to unite me with him still more closely. Consider and determine: whom shall I forsake? whom shall I follow?"

After a short silence, Barbara exclaimed: "Strange, that youth should always be for extremes! To my view, nothing would be easier than for us to combine both the profit and enjoyment. Do you love the one, let the other pay for it: all we have to mind is being sharp enough to keep the two from meeting."

"Do as you please; I can imagine nothing, but I will follow."

"We have this advantage, we can humour the Manager's caprice, and pride about the morals of his troop. Both lovers are accustomed already to go secretly and cunningly to work. For hours and opportunity I will take thought; only henceforth you must play the part that I prescribe to you. Who knows what circumstances may arise to help us? If Norberg would arrive even now, when Wilhelm is away! Who can hinder you from thinking of the one in the arms of the other? I wish you a son, and good fortune with him; he will have a rich father."

These projects lightened Mariana's despondency only for a very short time. She could not bring her situation into harmony with her feelings, with her convictions; she would fain have forgotten the painful relations in which she stood, and a thousand little circumstances forced them back every moment to her recollection.

CHAPTER XIII.

In the mean time, Wilhelm had completed the small preliminary journey. His merchant being from home, he delivered the letter of introduction to the mistress of the house. But neither did this lady give him much furtherance in his purposes; she was in a violent passion, and her whole economy was in confusion.

He had not waited long till she disclosed to him, what in truth could not be kept a secret, that her step-daughter had run off with a player; a person who had parted lately from a small strolling company, and had stayed in the place, and commenced teaching French. The father, distracted with grief and vexation, had run to the Amt to have the fugitives pursued. She blamed her daughter bitterly, and vilified the lover, till she left no tolerable quality with either: she deplored at great length the shame thus brought upon the family; embarrassing our hero not a little, who here felt his own private scheme beforehand judged and punished, in the spirit of prophecy as it were, by this frenzied sibyl. Still stronger and deeper was the interest he took in the sorrows of the father, who now returned from the Amt, and with fixed sorrow, in broken sentences, gave an account of the errand to his wife; and strove to hide the embarrassment and distraction of his mind, while, after looking at the letter, he directed that the horse it spoke of should be given to Wilhelm.

Our friend thought it best to mount his steed immediately, and quit a house, where in its present state he could not possibly be comfortable; but the honest man would not allow the son of one to whom he had so many obligations to depart without tasting of his hospitality, without remaining at least a night beneath his roof.

Wilhelm assisted at a melancholy supper; wore out a restless night; and hastened to get rid of these people, who, without knowing it, had, by their narratives and condolences, been constantly wounding him to the quick.

In a musing mood, he was riding slowly along, when all at once he observed a number of armed men coming through the fields. By their long loose coats with enormous cuffs, by their shapeless hats, clumsy muskets, by their unpretending gait and contented bearing of the body, he recognised in these people a detachment of provincial militia. They halted beneath an old oak; set down their fire-arms; and placed themselves at their ease upon the sward to smoke a pipe of tobacco. Wilhelm lingered near them, and entered into conversation with a young man who came up on horseback. The history of the two runaways, which he already knew too well, was again detailed to him; and that with comments, not particularly flattering either to the young pair themselves or to the parents. He learned also that the military were come hither to take the loving couple into custody, who had already been seized and detained in a neighbouring village. After some time, accordingly, a cart was seen advancing to the place, encircled with a city-guard more ludicrous than appalling. An amorphous Town-clerk rode forth, and made his compliments to the Actuarius (for such was the young man whom Wilhelm had been speaking to), on the border of their several districts, with great conscientiousness and wonderful grimaces; as perhaps the ghost and the conjuror do, when they meet, the one within the circle and the other out of it, in their dismal midnight operations.

But the chief attention of the lookers-on was directed to the cart: they could not behold without compassion the poor misguided creatures, who were sitting upon bundles of straw, looking tenderly at one another, and scarcely seeming to observe the bystanders. Accident had forced their conductors to bring them from the last village in that unseemly style; the old chaise, which had previously transported the lady, having there broken down. On that occurrence she had begged for permission to sit beside her friend; whom, in the conviction that his crime was of a capital sort, the rustic bailiffs had brought along so far in irons. These irons certainly contributed to give the tender group a more interesting appearance, particularly as the young man moved and bore himself with great dignity, while he kissed more than once the hands of his fair companion.

"We are unfortunate," she cried to the bystanders; "but not so guilty as we seem. It is thus that savage men reward true love; and parents, who entirely neglect the happiness of their children, tear them with fury from the arms of joy, when it has found them after many weary days."

The spectators were expressing their sympathy in various ways, when the officers of law having finished their ceremonial, the cart went on, and Wilhelm, who took a deep interest in the fate of the lovers, hastened forward by a footpath to get some acquaintance with the Amtmann before the procession should arrive. But scarcely had he reached the Amthaus, where all was in motion, and ready to receive the fugitives, when his new friend, the Actuarius, laid hold of him; and, giving him a circumstantial detail of the whole proceedings, and then launching out into a comprehensive eulogy of his own horse, which he had got last night by barter, put a stop to every other sort of conversation.

The luckless pair, in the mean time, had been set down behind at the garden, which communicated by a little door with the Amthaus, and thus brought in unobserved. The Actuarius, for this mild and handsome treatment, accepted of a just encomium from Wilhelm; though in truth his sole object had been to mortify the crowd collected in front of the Amthaus, by denying them the satisfaction of looking at a neighbour in disgrace.

The Amtmann, who had no particular taste for such extraordinary occurrences, being wont on these occasions to commit frequent errors, and with the best intentions to be often paid with sour admonitions from the higher powers, went with heavy steps into his office-room, the Actuarius with Wilhelm and a few respectable citizens following him.

The lady was first produced; she advanced without pertness, calm and self-possessed. The manner of her dress, the way in which she bore herself, showed that she was a person not without value in her own eyes. She accordingly began, without any questions being put, to speak not unskilfully about her situation.

The Actuarius bade her be silent, and held his pen over the folded sheet. The Amtmann gathered up his resolution, looked at his assistant, cleared his throat by two or three hems, and asked the poor girl what was her name, and how old she was.

"I beg your pardon, sir," said she, "but it seems very strange to me that you ask my name and age; seeing you know very well what my name is, and that I am just of the age of your oldest son. What you do want to know of me, and need to know, I will tell freely without circumlocution:—Since my father's second marriage, my situation in his house has not been of the most enviable sort. Oftener than once I have had it in my power to make a suitable marriage, had not my stepmother, dreading the expense of my portion, taken care to thwart all such proposals. At length I grew acquainted with the young Melina; I felt constrained to love him; and as both of us foresaw the obstacles that stood in the way of our regular union, we determined to go forth together, and seek in the wide world the happiness which was denied us at home. I took nothing with me that was not my own; we did not run away like thieves and robbers, and my lover does not merit to be hauled about in this way with chains and handcuffs. The Prince is just, and will not sanction such severity. If we are liable to punishment, it is not punishment of this kind."

The old Amtmann hereupon fell into double and treble confusion. Sounds of the most gracious eulogies were already humming through his brain; and the girl's voluble speech had entirely confounded the plan of his protocol. The mischief increased, when to repeated official questions she refused giving any answer, but constantly referred to what she had already said.

"I am no criminal," she said. "They have brought me hither on bundles of straw to put me to shame; but there is a higher court that will bring us back to honour."

The Actuarius, in the mean time, had kept writing down her words: he whispered the Amtmann, "just to go on; a formal protocol might be made out by and by."

The senior then again took heart; and began, with his heavy words, in dry prescribed formulas, to seek information about the sweet secrets of love.

The red mounted into Wilhelm's cheeks, and those of the pretty criminal likewise glowed with the charming tinge of modesty. She was silent, she stammered, till at last her embarrassment itself seemed to exalt her courage.

"Be assured," she cried, "that I should have strength enough to confess the truth, though it made against myself: and shall I now hesitate and stammer, when it does me honour? Yes, from the moment when I first felt certain of his love and faith, I looked upon him as my husband; I freely gave him all that love requires, that a heart once convinced cannot long refuse. Now do with me what you please. If I hesitated for a moment to confess, it was owing to fear alone lest the admission might prove hurtful to my lover."

On hearing this confession, Wilhelm formed a high opinion of the young woman's feelings; while her judges marked her as an impudent strumpet; and the townsfolk present thanked God that, in their families, no such scandal had occurred, or at least been brought to light.

Wilhelm transported his Mariana into this conjuncture, answering at the bar; he put still finer words in her mouth, making her uprightness yet more affecting, her confession still nobler. The most violent desire to help the two lovers took possession of him. Nor did he conceal this feeling; but signified in private to the wavering Amtmann, that it were better to end the business, all being clear as possible, and requiring no farther investigation.

This was so far of service that the young woman was allowed to retire; though, in her stead, the lover was brought in, his fetters having previously been taken off him at the door. This person seemed a little more concerned about his fate. His answers were more careful; and if he showed less heroic generosity, he recommended himself by the precision and distinctness of his expressions.

When this audience also was finished, and found to agree in all points with the former, except that, from regard for his mistress, Melina stubbornly denied what had already been confessed by herself,—the young woman was again brought forward; and a scene took place between the two, which made the heart of our friend entirely their own.

What usually occurs nowhere but in romances and plays, he saw here in a paltry court-room before his eyes; the contest of reciprocal magnanimity, the strength of love in misfortune.

"Is it then true," said he internally, "that timorous affection which conceals itself from the eye of the sun and of men, not daring to taste of enjoyment save in remote solitude and deep secrecy, yet, if torn rudely by some cruel chance into light, will show itself more courageous, strong and resolute, than any of our loud and ostentatious passions?"

To his comfort, the business now soon came to a conclusion. The lovers were detained in tolerable quarters: had it been possible, he would that very evening have brought back the young lady to her parents. For he firmly determined to act as intercessor in this case, and to forward a happy and lawful union between the lovers.

He begged permission of the Amtmann to speak in private with Melina; a request which was granted without difficulty.

CHAPTER XIV.

THE conversation of these new acquaintances very soon grew confidential and lively. When Wilhelm told the downcast youth of his connexion with the lady's parents, and offered to mediate in the affair, showing at the same time the strongest expectation of success, a light was shed across the dreary and anxious mind of the prisoner; he felt himself already free, already reconciled with the parents of his bride; and now began to speak about his future occupation and support.

"On this point," said our friend, "you cannot long be in difficulty; for you seem to me directed, not more by your circumstances than by nature, to make your fortune in the noble profession you have chosen. A pleasing figure, a sonorous voice, a feeling heart! Could an actor be better furnished? If I can serve you with a few introductions, it will give me the greatest pleasure."

"I thank you with all my heart," replied the other; "but I shall hardly be able to make use of them; for it is my purpose, if possible, not to return to the stage."

"Here you are certainly to blame," said Wilhelm, after a pause, during which he had partly recovered out of his astonishment; for it had never once entered his head, but that the player, the moment his young wife and he were out of durance, would repair to some theatre. It seemed to him as natural and as necessary as for the frog to seek pools of water. He had not doubted of it for a moment; and he now heard the contrary with boundless surprise.

"Yes," replied Melina, " I have it in view not to reappear upon the stage; but rather to take up some civil calling, be it what it will, so that I can but obtain one."

" This is a strange resolution, which I cannot give my approbation to. Without especial reasons, it can never be advisable to change the mode of life we have begun with; and, besides, I know of no condition that presents so much allurement, so many charming prospects, as the condition of an actor."

" It is easy to see that you have never been one," said the other.

"Alas, sir," answered Wilhelm, " how seldom is any man contented with the station where he happens to be placed! He is ever coveting that of his neighbour, from which the neighbour in his turn is longing to be free."

" Yet still there is a difference," said Melina, " between bad and worse. Experience, not impatience, makes me determine as you see. Is there in the world any creature whose morsel of bread is attended with such vexation, uncertainty and toil? It were almost as good to take the staff and wallet, and beg from door to door. What things to be endured from the envy of rivals, from the partiality of managers, from the ever-altering caprices of the public! In truth, one would need to have a hide like a bear's, that is led about in a chain along with apes and dogs of knowledge, and cudgelled into dancing at the sound of a bagpipe before the populace and children."

Wilhelm thought a thousand things, which he would not vex the worthy man by uttering. He merely, therefore, led the conversation round them at a distance. His friend explained himself the more candidly and circumstantially on that account. "Is not the manager obliged," said he, " to fall down at the feet of every little Stadtrath, that he may get permission, for a month between the fairs, to cause another groschen or two to circulate in the place? Ours, on the whole a worthy man, I have often pitied; though at other times he gave me cause enough for discontentment. A good actor drains him by extortion; of the bad he cannot rid himself; and, should he try to make his income at all equal to his outlay, the public immediately takes umbrage, the house stands empty; and, not to go to wreck entirely, he must continue acting in the midst of sorrow and vexation. No, no, sir! Since you are so good as undertake to help me, have the kindness, I entreat you, to plead with the parents of my bride; let them get me a little post of clerk or collector, and I shall think myself well dealt with."

After exchanging a few words more, Wilhelm went away with the promise to visit the parents early in the morning, and see what could be done. Scarcely was he by himself, when he gave utterance to his thoughts in these exclamations: "Unhappy Melina! not in thy condition, but in thyself lies the mean impediment over which thou canst not gain the mastery. What mortal in the world, if without inward calling he take up a trade, an art, or any mode of life, will not feel his situation miserable? But he who is born with capacities for any undertaking, finds in executing this the fairest portion of his being. Nothing upon earth without its difficulties! It is the secret impulse within; it is the love and the delight we feel, that help us to conquer obstacles, to clear out new paths, and to overleap the bounds of that narrow circle in which others poorly toil. For *thee* the stage is but a few boards; the parts assigned thee are but what a task is to a schoolboy. The spectators thou regardest as on work-days they regard each other. For thee then it may be well to wish thyself behind a desk, over ruled ledgers, collecting tolls, and picking out reversions. Thou feelest not the coöperating, co-inspiring whole, which the mind alone can invent, comprehend and complete; thou feelest not that in man there lives a spark of purer fire, which, when it is not fed, when it is not fanned, gets covered by the ashes of indifference and daily wants; yet not till late, perhaps never, can be altogether quenched. Thou feelest in thy soul no strength to fan this spark into a flame, no riches in thy heart to feed it when aroused. Hunger drives thee on, inconveniences withstand thee; and it is hidden from thee, that, in every human condition, foes lie in wait for us, invincible except by cheerfulness and equanimity. Thou dost well to wish thyself within the limits of a common station; for what station that required soul and resolution couldst thou rightly fill! Give a soldier, a statesman, a divine thy sentiments, and as justly will he fret himself about the miseries of *his* condition. Nay, have there not been men so totally forsaken by all feeling of existence, that they have held the life and nature of mortals as a nothing, a painful, short and tarnished gleam of being? Did the forms of active men rise up living in thy soul; were thy breast warmed by a sympathetic fire; did the vocation which proceeds from within diffuse itself over all thy frame; were the tones of thy voice, the words of thy mouth, delightful to hear; didst thou feel thy own being sufficient for thyself,—then wouldst thou doubtless seek place and opportunity likewise to feel it in others."

Amid such words and thoughts, our friend undressed himself, and went to bed, with feelings of the deepest satisfaction. A whole romance of what he now hoped to do, instead of the worthless occupations which should have filled the approaching day, arose within his mind; pleasant fantasies softly conducted him into the kingdom of sleep, and then gave him up to their sisters, sweet dreams, who received him with open arms, and encircled his reposing head with the images of heaven.

Early in the morning he was awake again, and thinking of the business that lay before him. He revisited the house of the forsaken family, where his presence caused no small surprise. He introduced his proposal in the most prudent manner, and soon found both more and fewer difficulties than he had anticipated. For one thing, the evil was already *done;* and though people of a singularly strict and harsh temper are wont to set themselves forcibly against the past, and thus to increase the evil that cannot now be remedied; yet, on the other hand, what is actually done exerts a resistless effect upon most minds; an event which lately appeared impossible takes its place, so soon as it has really occurred, with what occurs daily. It was accordingly soon settled, that Herr Melina was to wed the daughter; who, however, in return, because of her misconduct, was to take no marriage-portion with her, and to promise that she would leave her aunt's legacy, for a few years more, at an easy interest, in her father's hands. But the second point, touching a civil provision for Melina, was attended with greater difficulties. They liked not to have the luckless pair continually living in their sight; they would not have a present object ever calling to their minds the connexion of a mean vagabond with so respectable a family, a family which could number even a Superintendent among its relatives; nay, it was not to be looked for, that the government would trust him with a charge. Both parents were alike inflexible in this matter; and Wilhelm, who pleaded very hard, unwilling that a man whom he contemned should return to the stage, and convinced that he deserved not such a happiness, could not, with all his rhetoric, produce the slenderest impression. Had he known the secret springs of the business, he would have spared himself the labour of attempting to persuade. The father would gladly have kept his daughter near him, but he hated the young man, because his wife herself had cast an eye upon him; while the latter could not bear to have, in her stepdaughter, a happy rival constantly before her eyes. So Melina, with his young wife, who already manifested no dislike to go and see the world, and be seen of it, was obliged, against his will, to set forth in a few days, and seek some place in any acting company where he could find one.

VOL. I.   E

CHAPTER XV.

Happy season of youth! Happy times of the first wish of love! A man is then like a child that can for hours delight itself with an echo, can support alone the charges of conversation, and be well contented with its entertainment, if the unseen interlocutor will but repeat the concluding syllables of the words addressed to it.

So was it with Wilhelm in the earlier and still more in the later period of his passion for Mariana: he transferred the whole wealth of his own emotions to her, and looked upon himself as a beggar that lived upon her alms; and as a landscape is more delightful, nay is delightful only, when it is enlightened by the sun, so likewise in his eyes were all things beautified and glorified which lay round her or related to her.

Often would he stand in the theatre behind the scenes, to which he had obtained the freedom of access from the manager. In such cases, it is true, the perspective magic was away; but the far mightier sorcery of love then first began to act. For hours he could stand by the sooty light-frame, inhaling the vapour of tallow lamps, looking out at his mistress; and when she returned and cast a kindly glance upon him, he could feel himself lost in ecstasy, and though close upon laths and bare spars, he seemed transported into paradise. The stuffed bunches of wool denominated lambs, the waterfalls of tin, the paper roses and the one-sided huts of straw, awoke in him fair poetic visions of an old pastoral world. Nay, the very dancing-girls, ugly as they were when seen at hand, did not always inspire him with disgust: they trod the same floor with Mariana. So true is it, that love, which alone can give their full charm to rose-bowers, myrtle-groves and moonshine, can also communicate, even to shavings of wood and paper-clippings, the aspect of animated nature. It is so strong a spice, that tasteless, or even nauseous soups are by it rendered palatable.

So potent a spice was certainly required to render tolerable, nay at last agreeable, the state in which he usually found her chamber, not to say herself.

Brought up in a substantial burgher's house, cleanliness and order were the element in which he breathed; and inheriting as he did a portion of his father's taste for finery, it had always been his care, in boyhood, to furbish up his chamber, which he regarded as his little kingdom, in the stateliest fashion. His bed-curtains were drawn together in large massy folds, and fastened with tassels, as they are usually seen in thrones: he had got himself a carpet for the middle of his chamber, and a finer one for his table; his books and apparatus he had, almost instinctively, arranged in such a manner, that a Dutch painter might have imitated them for groups in his still-life scenes. He had a white cap, which he wore straight up like a turban; and the sleeves of his nightgown he had caused to be cut short, in the mode of the Orientals. By way of reason for this, he pretended that long wide sleeves encumbered him in writing. When, at night, the boy was quite alone, and no longer dreaded any interruption, he usually wore a silk sash tied round his body, and often, it is said, he would fix in his girdle a sword, which he had appropriated from an old armory, and thus repeat and declaim his tragic parts; nay, in the same trim he would kneel down and say his evening prayer.

In those times, how happy did he think the players, whom he saw possessed of so many splendid garments, trappings and arms; and in the constant practice of a lofty demeanour, the spirit of which seemed to hold up a mirror of whatever, in the opinions, relations and passions of men, was stateliest and most magnificent. Of a piece with this, thought Wilhelm, is also the player's domestic life; a series of dignified transactions and employments, whereof their appearance on the stage is but the outmost portion; like as a mass of silver, long simmering about in the purifying furnace, at length gleams with a bright and beautiful tinge in the eye of the refiner, and shows him, at the same time, that the metal now is cleansed of all foreign mixture.

Great, accordingly, was his surprise at first, when he found himself beside his mistress, and looked down, through the cloud that environed him, on tables, stools and floor. The wrecks of a transient, light and false decoration lay, like the glittering coat of a skinned fish, dispersed in wild disorder. The implements of personal cleanliness, combs, soap, towels, with the traces of their use, were not concealed. Music, portions of plays and pairs of shoes, washes and Italian flowers, pincushions, hair-skewers, rouge-pots and ribbons, books and straw-hats; no article despised the neighbourhood of another; all were united by a common element, powder and dust. Yet as Wilhelm scarcely noticed in her presence aught except herself; nay, as all that had belonged to her, that she had touched, was dear to him, he came at last to feel, in this chaotic housekeeping, a charm which the proud pomp of his own habitation never had communicated. When, on this hand, he lifted aside her bodice, to get at the harpsichord; on that, threw her gown upon the bed, that he might find a seat; when she herself, with careless freedom, did not seek to hide from him many a natural office, which, out of respect for the presence of a second person, is usually concealed; he felt as if by all this he was coming nearer to her every moment, as if the communion betwixt them was fastening by invisible ties.

It was not so easy to reconcile with his previous ideas the behaviour of the other players, whom, on his first visits, he often met with in her house. Ever busied in being idle, they seemed to think least of all on their employment and object; the poetic worth of a piece they were never heard to speak of, or to judge of, right or wrong; their continual question was simply: How much will it *bring?* Is it a stock-piece? How long will it run? How often think you it may be played? and other inquiries and observations of the same description. Then commonly they broke out against the manager, that he was stinted with his salaries, and especially unjust to this one or to that; then against the public, how seldom it recompensed the right man with its approval, how the German theatre was daily improving, how the player was ever growing more honoured, and never could be honoured enough. Then they would descant largely about wine-gardens and coffee-houses; how much debt one of their comrades had contracted, and must suffer a deduction from his wages on account of; about the disproportion of their weekly salaries; about the cabals of some rival company: on which occasions they would pass again to the great and merited attention which the public now bestowed upon them; not forgetting the importance of the theatre to the improvement of the nation and the world.

All this, which had already given Wilhelm many a restless hour, came again into his memory, as he walked his horse slowly homewards, and contemplated the various occurrences in which he had so lately been engaged. The commotion produced by a girl's elopement, not only in a decent family, but in a whole town, he had seen with his own eyes; the scenes upon the highway and in the Amthaus, the views entertained by Melina, and whatever else he had witnessed, again arose before him, and brought his keen forecasting mind into a sort of anxious disquietude; which no longer to endure, he struck the spurs into his horse, and hastened towards home.

By this expedient, however, he but ran to meet new vexations. Werner, his friend and future brother-in-law, was waiting for him, to begin a serious, important, unexpected conversation.

Werner was one of those tried sedate persons, with fixed principles and habits, whom we usually denominate cold characters, because on emergencies they do not burst forth quickly or very visibly. Accordingly, his intercourse with Wilhelm was a perpetual contest; which, however, only served to knit their mutual affection the more firmly; for, notwithstanding their very opposite modes of thinking, each found his account in communicating with the other. Werner was very well contented with himself, that he could now and then lay a bridle on the exalted but commonly extravagant spirit of his friend; and Wilhelm often felt a glorious triumph, when the staid and thinking Werner could be hurried on with him in warm ebullience. Thus each exercised himself upon the other; they had been accustomed to see each other daily; and you would have said, their eagerness to meet and talk together had even been augmented by the inability of each to understand the other. At bottom, however, being both goodhearted men, they were both travelling together towards one goal; and they could never understand how it was that neither of the two could bring the other over to his own persuasion.

For some time, Werner had observed that Wilhelm's visits had been rarer; that in his favourite discussions he was brief and absent-minded; that he no longer abandoned himself to the vivid depicting of singular conceptions; tokens by which, in truth, a mind getting rest and contentment in the presence of a friend, is most clearly indicated. The considerate and punctual Werner first sought for the root of the evil in his own conduct; till some rumours of the neighbourhood set him on the proper trace, and some unguarded proceedings on the part of Wilhelm brought him nearer to the certainty. He began his investigation; and ere long discovered, that for some time Wilhelm had been openly visiting an actress, had often spoken with her at the theatre, and accompanied her home. On discovering the nightly visits of his friend, Werner's anxiety increased to a painful extent; for he heard that Mariana was a most seductive girl, who probably was draining the youth of his money, while, at the same time, she herself was supported by another and a very worthless lover.

Having pushed his suspicions as near certainty as possible, he had resolved to make a sharp attack on Wilhelm: he was now in full readiness with all his preparations, when his friend returned, discontented and unsettled, from his journey.

That very evening, Werner laid the whole of what he knew before him, first calmly, then with the emphatic earnestness of a well-meaning friendship. He left no point of the subject undiscussed; and made Wilhelm taste abundance of those bitter things, which men at ease are accustomed, with virtuous spite, to dispense so liberally to men in love. Yet, as might have been expected, he accomplished little. Wilhelm answered with interior commotion, though with great confidence: "You know not the girl! Appearances, perhaps, are not to her advantage; but I am certain of her faithfulness and virtue, as of my love."

Werner maintained his accusations, and offered to bring proofs and witnesses. Wilhelm waved these offers; and parted with his friend out of humour and unhinged; like a man in whose jaw some unskilful dentist has been seizing a diseased yet fast-rooted tooth, and tugging at it harshly to no purpose.

It exceedingly dissatisfied Wilhelm to see the fair image of Mariana overclouded and almost deformed in his soul, first by the capricious fancies of his journey, and then by the unfriendliness of Werner. He adopted the surest means of restoring it to complete brilliancy and beauty, by setting out at night, and hastening to his wonted destination. She received him with extreme joy: on entering the town, he had ridden past her window; she had been expecting his company; and it is easy to conceive that all scruples were soon driven from his heart. Nay, her tenderness again opened up the whole stores of his confidence; and he told her how deeply the public, how deeply his friend, had sinned against her.

Much lively talking led them at length to speak about the earliest period of their acquaintance; the recollection of which forms always one of the most delightful topics between two lovers. The first steps that introduce us to the enchanted garden of love are so full of pleasure, the first prospects so charming, that every one is willing to recall them to his memory. Each party seeks a preference above the other; each has loved sooner, more devotedly; and each, in this contest, would rather be conquered than conquer.

Wilhelm repeated to his mistress, what he had so often told her before, how she soon abstracted his attention from the play, and fixed it on herself; how her form, her acting, her voice inspired him; how at last he went only on the nights when *she* was to appear; how, in fine, having ventured behind the scenes, he had often stood by her unheeded: and he spoke with rapture of the happy evening when he found an opportunity to do her some civility, and lead her into conversation.

Mariana, on the other hand, would not allow that she had failed so long to notice him; she declared that she had seen him in the public walk, and for proof she described the clothes which he wore on that occasion; she affirmed that even then he pleased her before all others, and made her long for his acquaintance.

How gladly did Wilhelm credit all this! How gladly did he catch at the persuasion, that when he used to approach her, she had felt herself drawn towards him by some resistless influence;

that she had gone with him between the side-scenes, on purpose to see him more closely, and get acquainted with him; and that, in fine, when his backwardness and modesty were not to be conquered, she had herself afforded him an opportunity, and as it were compelled him to hand her a glass of lemonade!

In this affectionate contest, which they pursued through all the little circumstances of their brief romance, the hours passed rapidly away; and Wilhelm left his mistress, with his heart at peace, and firmly determined on proceeding forthwith to the execution of his project.

CHAPTER XVI.

The necessary preparations for his journey his father and mother had attended to; some little matters, that were yet wanting to his equipage, delayed his departure for a few days. Wilhelm took advantage of this opportunity to write to Mariana, meaning thus to bring to a decision the proposal, about which she had hitherto avoided speaking with him. The letter was as follows:

"Under the kind veil of night, which has often overshadowed us together, I sit and think, and write to thee; all that I meditate and do is solely on thy account. O Mariana! with me, the happiest of men, it is as with a bridegroom who stands in the festive chamber, dreaming of the new universe that is to be unfolded to him, and by means of him, and, while the holy ceremonies are proceeding, transports himself in longing thought before the mysterious curtains, from which the loveliness of love whispers out to him.

"I have constrained myself not to see thee for a few days; the sacrifice was easy, when united with the hope of such a recompense, of being always with thee, of remaining ever thine! Need I repeat what I desire? I must; for it seems as if yet thou hadst never understood me.

"How often, in the low tones of true love, which, though wishing to gain all, dares speak but little, have I sought in thy heart for the desire of a perpetual union. Thou hast understood me, doubtless; for in thy own heart the same wish must have arisen; thou *didst* comprehend me, in that kiss, in the intoxicating peace of that happy evening. Thy silence testified to me thy modest honour; and how did it increase my love! Another woman would have had recourse to artifice, that she might ripen by superfluous sunshine the purpose of her lover's heart, might elicit a proposal, and secure a firm promise. Mariana, on the contrary, drew back;

she repelled the half-opened confidence of him she loved, and sought to conceal her approving feelings by apparent indifference. But I have understood thee! What a miserable creature must I be, if I did not by these tokens recognise the pure and generous love that cares not for itself, but for its object! Confide in me, and fear nothing. We belong to one another; and neither of us leaves aught or forsakes aught, if we live for one another.

"Take it, then, this hand! Solemnly I offer this unnecessary pledge! All the joys of love we have already felt; but there is a new blessedness in the firm thought of duration. Ask not how; care not. Fate takes care of love, and the more certainly as love is easy to provide for.

"My heart has long ago forsaken my paternal home; it is with thee, as my spirit hovers on the stage. O my darling! to what other man has it been given to unite all his wishes, as it is to me? No sleep falls upon my eyes; like the redness of an everlasting dawn, thy love and thy happiness still glow around me.

"Scarcely can I hold myself from springing up, from rushing forth to thee, and forcing thy consent, and, with the first light of tomorrow, pressing forward into the world for the mark I aim at. But no! I will restrain myself; I will not act like a thoughtless fool; will do nothing rashly; my plan is laid, and I will execute it calmly.

"I am acquainted with the Manager Serlo; my journey leads me directly to the place where he is. For above a year he has frequently been wishing that his people had a touch of my vivacity, and my delight in theatrical affairs; I shall doubtless be very kindly received. Into your company I cannot enter, for more than one reason. Serlo's theatre, moreover, is at such a distance from this, that I may there begin my undertaking without any apprehension of discovery. With him I shall thus at once find a tolerable maintenance; I shall look about me in the public, get acquainted with the company, and then come back for thee.

"Mariana, thou seest what I can force myself to do, that I may certainly obtain thee. For such a period not to see thee; for such a period to know thee in the wide world! I dare not view it closely. But yet if I recall to memory thy love, which assures me of all; if thou shalt not disdain my prayer, and give me, ere we part, thy hand, before the priest; I may then depart in peace. It is but a form between us, yet a form so touching; the blessing of Heaven to the blessing of the earth. Close by thy house, in the Ritterschaftliche Chapel, the ceremony will be soon and secretly performed.

"For the beginning I have gold enough; we will share it between us; it will suffice for both; and before that is finished, Heaven will send us more.

"No, my darling, I am not downcast about the issue. What is begun with so much cheerfulness must reach a happy end. I have never doubted that a man may force his way through the world, if he really is in earnest about it; and I feel strength enough within me to provide a liberal support for two, and many more. The world, we are often told, is unthankful; I have never yet discovered that it was unthankful, if one knew how, in the proper way, to do it service. My whole soul burns at the idea, that *I* shall at length step forth and speak to the hearts of men something they have long been yearning to hear. How many thousand times has a feeling of disgust passed through me, alive as I am to the nobleness of the stage, when I have seen the poorest creatures fancying they could speak a word of power to the hearts of the people! The tone of a man's voice singing treble sounds far pleasanter and purer to my ear: it is incredible how these blockheads, in their coarse inoptitude, deform things beautiful and venerable.

"The theatre has often been at variance with the pulpit; they ought not, I think, to quarrel. How much is it to be wished, that in both the celebration of nature and of God were intrusted to none but men of noble minds! These are no dreams, my darling! As I have felt in thy heart that thou couldst love, I seize the dazzling thought, and say—no, I will not say, but I will hope and trust—that we two shall yet appear to men as a pair of chosen spirits, to unlock their hearts, to touch the recesses of their nature, and prepare for them celestial joys, as surely as the joys I have tasted with thee deserved to be named celestial, since they drew us from ourselves, and exalted us above ourselves.

"I cannot end. I have already said too much; and know not whether I have yet said all, all that concerns *thy* interests; for to express the agitations of the vortex that whirls round within myself is beyond the power of words.

"Yet take this sheet, my love! I have again read it over; I observe it ought to have begun more cautiously; but it contains in it all that thou hast need to know; enough to prepare thee for the hour when I shall return with the lightness of love to thy bosom. I seem to myself like a prisoner that is secretly filing his irons asunder. I bid good-night to my soundly sleeping parents. Farewell, my beloved, farewell! For this time I conclude; my eyelids have more than once dropped together; it is now deep in the night."

CHAPTER XVII.

It seemed as if the day would never end, while Wilhelm, with the letter beautifully folded in his pocket, longed to meet with Mariana. The darkness had scarcely come on, when, contrary to custom, he glided forth to her house. His plan was to announce himself for the night; then to quit his mistress for a short time, leaving the letter with her ere he went away; and, returning at a late hour, to obtain her reply, her consent, or to force it from her by the power of his caresses. He flew into her arms, and pressed her in rapture to his bosom. The vehemence of his emotions prevented him at first from noticing that, on this occasion, she did not receive him with her wonted heartiness; yet she could not long conceal her painful situation, but imputed it to slight indisposition. She complained of a headache, and would not by any means consent to his proposal of coming back that night. Suspecting nothing wrong, he ceased to urge her; but felt that this was not the moment for delivering his letter. He retained it, therefore; and as several of her movements and observations courteously compelled him to take his leave, in the tumult of unsatiable love he snatched up one of her neckerchiefs, squeezed it into his pocket, and forced himself away from her lips and her door. He returned home, but could not rest there; he again dressed himself, and went out into the open air.

After walking up and down several streets, he was accosted by a stranger inquiring for a certain inn. Wilhelm offered to conduct him to the house. In the way, his new acquaintance asked about the names of the streets, the owners of various extensive edifices, then about some police-regulations of the town; so that by the time they reached the door of the inn, they had fallen into quite an interesting conversation. The stranger compelled his guide to enter, and drink a glass of punch with him. Ere long he had told his name and place of abode, as well as the business that had brought him hither; and he seemed to expect a like confidence from Wilhelm. Our friend, without any hesitation, mentioned his name and the place where he lived.

"Are you not a grandson of the old Meister, who possessed that beautiful collection of pictures and statues?" inquired the stranger.

"Yes, I am so. I was ten years old when my grandfather died; and it grieved me very much to see these fine things sold."

"Your father got a fine sum of money for them."

"You know of it, then?"

"O yes; I saw that treasure ere it left your house. Your grandfather was not merely a collector, he had a thorough knowledge of art. In his younger happy years he had been in Italy; and had brought back with him such treasures as could not now be got for any price. He possessed some exquisite pictures by the best masters. When you looked through his drawings, you would scarcely have believed your eyes. Among his marbles were some invaluable fragments; his series of bronzes was instructive and well chosen; he had also collected medals, in considerable quantity, relating to history and art; his few gems deserved the greatest praise. In addition to all which, the whole was tastefully arranged, although the rooms and hall of the old house had not been symmetrically built."

"You may conceive," said Wilhelm, "what we young ones lost, when all these articles were taken down and sent away. It was the first mournful period of my life. I cannot tell you how empty the chambers looked, as we saw those objects vanishing one by one, which had amused us from our earliest years, and which we considered equally unalterable with the house or the town itself."

"If I mistake not, your father put the capital produced by the sale into some neighbour's stock, with whom he commenced a sort of partnership in trade."

"Quite right; and their joint speculations have prospered in their hands. Within the last twelve years, they have greatly increased their fortunes, and are now the more vehemently bent on gaining. Old Werner also has a son, who suits that sort of occupation much better than I."

"I am sorry the place should have lost such an ornament to it as your grandfather's cabinet was. I saw it but a short time prior to the sale: and I may say, I was myself the cause of its being then disposed of. A rich nobleman, a great amateur, but one who, in such important transactions, does not trust to his own solitary judgment, had sent me hither, and requested my advice. For six days I examined the collection; on the seventh, I advised my friend to pay down the required sum without delay. You were then a lively boy, often running about me; you explained to me the subjects of the pictures; and in general, I recollect, could give a very good account of the whole cabinet."

"I remember such a person; but I should not have recognised him in you."

"It is a good while ago, and we all change more or less. You had, if I mistake not, a favourite piece among them, to which you were ever calling my attention."

"O yes; it represented the history of that king's son dying of a secret love for his father's bride."

"It was not, certainly, the best picture; badly grouped, of no superiority in colouring, and executed altogether with great mannerism."

"This I did not understand, and do not yet; it is the subject that charms me in a picture, not the art."

"Your grandfather seemed to have thought otherwise. The greater part of his collection consisted of excellent pieces; in which, represent what they might, one constantly admired the talent of the master. This picture of yours had accordingly been hung in the outermost room, a proof that he valued it slightly."

"It was in that room where we young ones used to play, and where the piece you mention made on me a deep impression; which not even your criticism, greatly as I honour it, could obliterate, if we stood before the picture at this moment. What a melancholy object is a youth that must shut up within himself the sweet impulse, the fairest inheritance which nature has given us, and conceal in his own bosom the fire which should warm and animate himself and others, so that his vitals are wasted away by unutterable pains! I feel a pity for the ill-fated man that would consecrate himself to another, when the heart of that other has already found a worthy object of true and pure affection."

"Such feelings are, however, very foreign to the principles by which a lover of art examines the works of great painters; and most probably you too, had the cabinet continued in your family, would have by and by acquired a relish for the works themselves; and have learned to see in the performances of art something more than yourself and your individual inclinations."

"In truth, the sale of that cabinet grieved me very much at the time; and often since I have thought of it with regret; but, when I consider that it was a necessary means of awakening a taste in me, of developing a talent, which will operate far more powerfully on my history than ever those lifeless pictures could have done, I easily content myself, and honour destiny, which knows how to bring about what is best for me, and what is best for every one."

"It gives me pain to hear this word destiny in the mouth of a young person, just at the age when men are commonly accustomed to ascribe their own violent inclinations to the will of higher natures."

"Do you then believe in no destiny? No power that rules over us, and directs all for our ultimate advantage?"

"The question is not now of my belief; nor is this the place to explain how I may have attempted to form for myself some not impossible conception of things which are incomprehensible to all of us: the question here is: What mode of viewing them will profit us the most? The fabric of our life is formed of necessity and chance; the reason of man takes its station between them, and may rule them both: it treats the necessary as the groundwork of its being; the accidental it can direct and guide and employ for its own purposes; and only while this principle of reason stands firm and inexpugnable, does man deserve to be named the god of this lower world. But woe to him who, from his youth, has used himself to search in necessity for something of arbitrary will; to ascribe to chance a sort of reason, which it is a matter of religion to obey! Is conduct like this aught else than to renounce one's understanding, and give unrestricted scope to one's inclinations? We think it is a kind of piety to move along without consideration; to let accidents that please us determine our conduct; and finally, to bestow on the result of such a vacillating life the name of providential guidance."

"Was it never your case that some little circumstance induced you to strike into a certain path, where some accidental occurrence ere long met you, and a series of unexpected incidents at length brought you to some point which you yourself had scarcely once contemplated? Should not lessons of this kind teach us obedience to destiny, confidence in some such guide?"

"With opinions like these, no woman could maintain her virtue, no man could keep the money in his purse; for occasions enough are occurring to get rid of both. He alone is worthy of respect, who knows what is of use to himself and others, and who labours to control his self-will. Each man has his own fortune in his hands; as the artist has a piece of rude matter, which he is to fashion to a certain shape. But the art of living rightly is like all arts: the capacity alone is born with us; it must be learned, and practised with incessant care."

These discussions our two speculators carried on between them to considerable length; at last they parted, without seeming to have wrought any special conviction in each other, but engaging to meet at an appointed place next day.

Wilhelm walked up and down the streets for a time; he heard a sound of clarionets, hunting-horns and bassoons; it swelled his bosom with delightful feelings. It was some travelling showmen that produced this pleasant music. He spoke with them: for a piece of coin they followed him to Mariana's house. The space in front of the door was adorned with lofty trees; under them he placed his artists; and himself resting on a bench at some distance, he surrendered his mind without restraint to the hovering tones which floated round him in the cool mellow night. Stretched out beneath the kind stars, he felt his existence like a golden dream. "She, too, hears these flutes," said he within his heart; "she feels whose remembrance, whose love of her it is that makes the night full of music. In distance even, we are united by these melodies; as in every separation, by the ethereal accordance of love. Ah! two hearts that love each other are as two magnetic needles; whatever moves the one must move the other with it; for it is one power that works in both, one principle that pervades them. Can I in her arms conceive the possibility of parting from her? And yet I am soon to be far from her; to seek out a sanctuary for our love, and then to have her ever with me.

"How often, when absent from her, and lost in thoughts about her, happening to touch a book, a piece of dress or aught else, have I thought I felt her hand, so entirely was I invested with her presence! And to recollect those moments which shunned the light of day and the eye of the cold spectator; which to enjoy, the gods might determine to forsake the painless condition of their pure blessedness! To recollect them? As if by memory we could renew the tumultuous thrilling of that cup of joy, which encircles our senses with celestial bonds, and lifts them beyond all earthly hindrances. And her form"—He lost himself in thoughts of her; his rest passed away into longing; he leaned against a tree, and cooled his warm cheek on its bark; and the winds of the night wafted speedily aside the breath, which proceeded in sighs from his pure and impassioned bosom. He groped for the neckerchief he had taken from her; but it was forgotten, it lay in his other clothes. His frame quivered with emotion.

The music ceased, and he felt as if fallen from the element in which his thoughts had hitherto been soaring. His restlessness increased, as his feelings were no longer nourished and assuaged by the melody. He sat down upon her threshold, and felt more peace. He kissed the brass knocker of her door; he kissed the threshold over which her feet went out and in, and warmed it by the fire of his breast. He again sat still for a moment, and figured her behind her curtains in the white nightgown, with the red ribbon round her head, in sweet repose; he almost fancied that he was himself so near her, she must needs be dreaming of him. His thoughts were beautiful, like the spirits of the twilight; rest and desire alternated within him; love ran with a quivering hand, in a thousand moods, over all the chords of his soul: it was as if the spheres stood mute above him, suspending their eternal song to watch the low melodies of his heart.

Had he then had about him the master-key with which he used to open Mariana's door, he could not have restrained himself from penetrating into the sanctuary of love. Yet he went away slowly; he slanted half-dreaming in beneath the trees, set himself for home, and constantly turned round again; at last, with an effort, he constrained himself, and actually departed. At the corner of the street, looking back yet once, he imagined that he saw Mariana's door open, and a dark figure issue from it. He was too distant for seeing clearly; and, before he could exert himself and look sharply, the appearance was already lost in the night: yet afar off he thought he saw it again gliding past a white house. He stood and strained his eyes; but, ere he could arouse himself and follow the phantom, it had vanished. Whither should he pursue it? What street had the man taken, if it were a man?

A nightly traveller, when at some turn of his path he has seen the country for an instant illuminated by a flash of lightning, will, with dazzled eyes, next moment, seek in vain for the preceding forms and the connexion of his road: so was it in the eyes and the heart of Wilhelm. And as a spirit of midnight, which awakens unutterable terror, is, in the succeeding moments of composure, regarded as a child of imagination, and the fearful vision leaves doubts without end behind it in the soul: so likewise was Wilhelm in extreme disquietude, as, leaning on the corner-stone of the street, he heeded not the clear gray of the morning, and the crowing of the cocks; till the early trades began to stir, and drove him home.

On his way, he had almost effaced the unexpected delusion from his mind by the most sufficient reasons, yet the fine harmonious feelings of the night, on which he now looked back as if they too had been a vision, were also gone. To soothe his heart, and put the last seal on his returning belief, he took the neckerchief from the pocket of the dress he had been last wearing. The rustling of a letter which fell out of it took the kerchief away from his lips; he lifted and read:

"As I love thee, little fool, what ailed thee last night? This evening I will come again. I can easily suppose that thou art sick of staying here so long: but have patience; at the fair I will return for thee. And observe, never more put me on that abominable black-green-brown jacket; thou lookest in it like the witch of Endor. Did I not send the white nightgown that I might have a snowy little lambkin in my arms? Send thy letters always by the ancient sibyl; the Devil himself has selected her as Iris."

BOOK II.

CHAPTER I.

Whoever strives in our sight with vehement force to reach an object, be it one that we praise or that we blame, may count on exciting an interest in our minds; but when once the matter is decided, we turn our eyes away from him; whatever once lies finished and done, can no longer at all fix our attention, especially if we at first prophesied an evil issue to the undertaking.

Therefore we shall not try to entertain our readers with any circumstantial account of the grief and desperation into which the ill-fated Wilhelm was cast, when he saw his hopes so unexpectedly and instantaneously ruined. On the contrary, we shall even pass over several years, and again take up our friend, where we hope to find him in some sort of activity and comfort. First, however, we must shortly set forth a few matters necessary for maintaining the connexion of our narrative.

The pestilence, or a malignant fever, rages with more fierceness and speedier effect, if the frame which it attacks was before healthy and full of vigour; and in like manner, when a luckless unlooked-for fate overtook the wretched Wilhelm, his whole being in a moment was laid waste. As when by chance, in the preparation of some artificial firework, any part of the composition kindles before its time; and the skilfully bored and loaded barrels, which, arranged, and burning after a settled plan, would have painted in the air a magnificently varying series of flaming images,—now hissing and roaring, promiscuously explode with a confused and dangerous crash; so, in our hero's case, did happiness and hope, pleasure and joys, realities and dreams, clash together with destructive tumult, all at once in his bosom. In such desolate moments, the friend that has hastened to deliverance stands fixed in astonishment; and for him who suffers, it is a benefit that sense forsakes him.

Days of pain, unmixed, ever-returning and purposely renewed, succeeded next; still even these are to be regarded as a grace from nature. In such hours Wilhelm had not yet quite lost his mistress; his pains were indefatigable struggles, still to hold fast the happiness that was gliding from his soul; again to luxuriate in thought on the possibility of it; to procure a brief after-life for his joys that had departed forever. Thus one may look upon a body as not utterly dead while the putrefaction lasts, while the forces that in vain seek to work by their old appointment still labour in dissevering the particles of that frame which they once animated; and not till all is disunited and inert, till we see the whole mouldered down into indifferent dust,—not till then does there rise in us the mournful vacant sentiment of death; death, not to be recalled save by the breath of Him that lives forever.

In a temper so new, so entire, so full of love, there was much to tear asunder, to desolate, to kill; and even the healing force of youth gave nourishment and violence to the power of sorrow. The stroke had extended to the roots of his whole existence. Werner, by necessity his confidant, attacked the hated passion itself with fire and sword, resolutely zealous to search into the monster's inmost life. The opportunity was lucky, the evidence at hand, and many were the histories and narratives with which he backed it out. With such unrelenting vehemence did he make his advances, leaving his friend not even the respite of the smallest momentary self-deception, but treading down every lurking-place, in which he might have saved himself from desperation, that nature, not inclined to let her darling perish utterly, visited him with sickness, to make an outlet for him on the other side.

A violent fever, with its train of consequences, medicines, overstraining and exhaustion, besides the unwearied attentions of his family, the love of his brothers and sisters, which first becomes truly sensible in times of distress and want, were so many fresh occupations to his mind, and thus formed a kind of painful entertainment. It was not till he grew better, in other words, till his strength was exhausted, that Wilhelm first looked down with horror into the gloomy abyss of a barren misery, as one looks down into the hollow crater of an extinguished volcano.

He now bitterly reproached himself, that after so great a loss he could yet enjoy one painless, restful, indifferent moment. He despised his own heart, and longed for the balm of tears and lamentation.

To awaken these again within him, he would recall to memory the scenes of his bygone happiness. He would paint them to his fancy in the liveliest colours, transport himself again into the days when they were real; and when standing on the highest elevation he could reach, when the sunshine of past times again seemed to animate his limbs and heave his bosom, he would look back into the fearful chasm, would feast his eye on its dismembering depth, then plunge down into its horrors, and thus force from nature the bitterest pains. With such repeated cruelty did he tear himself in pieces; for youth, which is so rich in undeveloped force, knows not what it squanders, when to the anguish which a loss occasions, it adds so many sorrows of its own production, as if it meant then first to give the right value to what is gone forever. He likewise felt so convinced that his present loss was the sole, the first, the last which he ever could experience in life, that he turned away from every consolation which aimed at showing that his sorrows might be less than endless.

CHAPTER II.

Accustomed in this way to torment himself, he now also attacked what still remained to him, what next to love, and along with it, had given him the highest joys and hopes, his talent as a poet and actor, with spiteful criticisms on every side. In his labours he could see nothing but a shallow imitation of prescribed forms, without intrinsic worth; he looked on them as stiff school-exercises, destitute of any spark of nature, truth, or inspiration. His poems now appeared nothing more than a monotonous arrangement of syllables, in which the most trite emotions and thoughts were dragged along and kept together by a miserable rhyme. And thus did he also deprive himself of every expectation, every pleasure, which, on this quarter at least, might have aided the recovery of his peace.

With his theatric talent it fared no better. He blamed himself for not having sooner detected the vanity, on which alone this pretension had been founded. His figure, his gait, his movements, his mode of declamation, were severally taxed; he decisively renounced every species of advantage or merit, that might have raised him above the common run of men, and so doing he increased his mute despair to the highest pitch. For, if it is hard to give up a woman's love, no less painful is the task to part from the fellowship of the Muses, to declare ourselves forever undeserving to be of their community; and to forego the fairest and most immediate kind of approbation, what is openly bestowed on our person, our voice and our demeanour.

Thus then our friend had long ago entirely resigned himself, and set about devoting his powers with the greatest zeal to the business of trade. To the surprise of friends, and to the great contentment of his father, no one was now more diligent than Wilhelm, on the exchange or in the counting-house, in the sale-room or the warehouses; correspondence and calculations, all that was intrusted to his charge, he attended to and managed with the greatest diligence and zeal. Not in truth with that warm diligence which to the busy man is its own reward, when he follows with constancy and order the employment he was born for; but with the silent diligence of duty, which has the best principle for its foundation, which is nourished by conviction, and rewarded by conscience; yet, which oft, even when the clearest testimony of our minds is crowning it with approbation, can scarcely repress a struggling sigh.

In this manner he had lived for a time, assiduously busied, and at last persuaded that his former hard trial had been ordained by fate for the best. He felt glad at having thus been timefully, though somewhat harshly warned about the proper path of life; while many are constrained to expiate more heavily, and at a later age, the misconceptions into which their youthful inexperience has betrayed them. For, each man commonly defends himself as long as possible from casting out the idols which he worships in his soul, from acknowledging a master error, and admitting any truth which brings him to despair.

Determined as he was to abandon his dearest projects, some time was still necessary to convince him fully of his misfortune. At last, however, he had so completely succeeded by irrefragable reasons in annihilating every hope of love, of poetical performance, or stage-representation, that he took courage to obliterate entirely all the traces of his folly, all that could in any way remind him of it. For this purpose he had lit a fire in his chamber one cool evening, and brought out a little chest of reliques, among which were multitudes of small articles, that, in memorable moments, he had begged or stolen from Mariana. Each withered flower brought to his mind the time when it bloomed fresh among her hair; each little note the happy hour to which it had invited him; each ribbon-knot the lovely resting-place of his head, her beautiful bosom. So occupied, was it not to be expected that each emotion, which he thought long since quite dead, should again begin to move? Was it not to be expected that the passion, over which, when separated from his mistress, he had gained the victory, should, in the presence of these memorials, again gather strength? We first observe how dreary and disagreeable an overclouded day is, when a single sunbeam pierces through, and offers to us the exhilarating splendour of a serene hour.

Accordingly, it was not without disturbance that he saw these reliques, long preserved as sacred, fade away from before him in smoke and flame. Sometimes he shuddered and hesitated in his task; he had still a pearl necklace and a flowered neckerchief in his hands, when he resolved to quicken the decaying fire with the poetical attempts of his youth.

Till now he had carefully laid up whatever had proceeded from his pen, since the earliest unfolding of his mind. His papers yet lay tied up in a bundle at the bottom of the chest, where he had packed them, purposing to take them with him in his elopement. How altogether different were his feelings now in opening them, and his feelings then in tying them together!

If we happen, under certain circumstances, to have written and sealed and despatched a letter to a friend, which, however, does not find him, but is brought back to us, and we open it at the distance of some considerable time, a singular emotion is produced in us, on breaking up our own seal, and conversing with our altered self as with a third person. A similar and deep feeling seized our friend, as he now opened this packet, and threw the scattered leaves into the fire; which was flaming fiercely with its offerings, when Werner entered, expressed his wonder at the blaze, and asked what was the matter.

"I am now giving proof," said Wilhelm, "that I am serious in abandoning a trade for which I was not born." And with these words, he cast the second packet likewise into the fire. Werner made a motion to prevent him, but the business was already done.

"I cannot see how thou shouldst bring thyself to such extremities," said Werner. "Why must these labours, because they are not excellent, be annihilated?"

"Because either a poem is excellent, or it should not be allowed to exist. Because each man, who has no gift for producing first-rate works, should entirely abstain from the pursuit of art, and seriously guard himself against every deception on that subject. For it must be owned, that in all men there is a certain vague desire to imitate whatever is presented to them; and such desires do not prove at all that we possess the force within us necessary for succeeding in these enterprises. Look at boys, how, whenever any rope-dancers have been visiting the town, they go scrambling up and down, and balancing on all the planks and beams within their reach, till some other charm calls them off to other sports, for which perhaps they are as little suited. Hast thou never marked it in the circle of our friends? No sooner does a dilettante introduce himself to notice, than numbers of them set themselves to learn playing on his instrument. How many wander back and forward on this bootless way! Happy they, who soon detect the chasm that lies between their wishes and their powers!"

Werner contradicted this opinion; their discussion became lively, and Wilhelm could not without emotion employ against his friend the arguments with which he had already so frequently tormented himself. Werner maintained that it was not reasonable wholly to relinquish a pursuit for which a man had some propensity and talent, merely because he never could succeed in it to full perfection. There were many vacant hours, he said, which might be filled up by it; and then by and by some result might be produced, which would yield a certain satisfaction to himself and others.

Wilhelm, who in this matter was of quite a different opinion, here interrupted him, and said with great vivacity:

"How immensely, dear friend, do you err in believing that a work, the first presentation of which is to fill the whole soul, can be produced in broken hours scraped together from other extraneous employment. No, the poet must live wholly for himself, wholly in the objects that delight him. Heaven has furnished him internally with precious gifts; he carries in his bosom a treasure that is ever of itself increasing; he must also live with this treasure, undisturbed from without, in that still blessedness which the rich seek in vain to purchase with their accumulated stores. Look at men, how they struggle after happiness and satisfaction! Their wishes, their toil, their gold, are ever hunting restlessly; and after what? After that which the poet has received from nature,—the right enjoyment of the world; the feeling of himself in others; the harmonious conjunction of many things that will seldom exist together.

"What is it that keeps men in continual discontent and agitation? It is, that they cannot make realities correspond with their conceptions, that enjoyment steals away from among their hands, that the wished-for comes too late, and nothing reached and acquired produces on the heart the effect which their longing for it at a distance led them to anticipate. Now fate has exalted the poet above all this, as if he were a god. He views the conflicting tumult of the passions; sees families and kingdoms raging in aimless commotion; sees those inexplicable enigmas of misunderstanding, which frequently a single monosyllable would suffice to explain, occasioning convulsions unutterably baleful. He has a fellow-feeling of the mournful and the joyful in the fate of all human beings. When the man of the world is devoting his days to wasting melancholy, for some deep disappointment; or, in the ebullience of joy, is going out to meet his happy destiny, the lightly-moved and all-conceiving spirit of the poet steps forth, like the sun from night to day, and with soft transitions tunes his harp to joy or woe. From his heart, its native soil, springs up the lovely flower of wisdom; and if others, while waking, dream, and are pained with fantastic delusions from their every sense, he passes the dream of life like one awake, and the strangest of incidents is to him a part both of the past and of the future. And thus the poet is at once a teacher, a prophet, a friend of gods and men. How! thou wouldst have him descend from his height to some paltry occupation? He who is fashioned like the bird to hover round the world, to nestle on the lofty summits, to feed on buds and fruits, exchanging gaily one bough for another, *he* ought also to work at the plough like an ox; like a dog to train himself to the harness and draught; or perhaps, tied up in a chain, to guard a farm-yard by his barking!"

Werner, it may well be supposed, had listened with the greatest surprise. "All true," he rejoined, "if men were but made like birds, and though they neither spun nor weaved, could yet spend peaceful days in perpetual enjoyment; if, at the approach of winter, they could as easily betake themselves to distant regions, could retire before scarcity, and fortify themselves against frost."

"Poets have lived so," exclaimed Wilhelm, "in times when true nobleness was better reverenced; and so should they ever live. Sufficiently provided for within, they had need of little from without; the gift of communicating lofty emotions and glorious images to men, in melodies and words that charmed the ear, and fixed themselves inseparably on whatever objects they referred to, of old enraptured the world, and served the gifted as a rich inheritance. At the courts of kings, at the tables of the great, beneath the windows of the fair, the sound of them was heard, while the ear and the soul were shut for all beside; and men felt, as we do when delight comes over us, and we stop with rapture if among the dingles we are crossing the voice of the nightingale starts out touching and strong. They found a home in every habitation of the world, and the lowliness of their condition but exalted them the more. The hero listened to their songs; and the conqueror of the earth did reverence to a poet, for he felt that without poets, his own wild and vast existence would pass away like a whirlwind, and be forgotten forever. The lover wished that he could feel his longings and his joys so variedly and so harmoniously as the poet's inspired lips had skill to show them forth; and even the rich man could not of himself discern such costliness in his idol grandeurs, as when they were presented to him shining in the splendour of the poet's spirit, sensible to all worth, and exalting all. Nay, if thou wilt have it, who but the poet was it that first formed gods for us; that exalted us to them, and brought them down to us?"

"My friend," said Werner, after some reflection, "it has often grieved me, that thou shouldst strive by force to banish from thy soul what thou feelest so vividly. I am greatly mistaken, if it were not better for thee in some degree to yield to these propensities, than to waste thyself by the contradictions of so hard a piece of self-denial, and with the enjoyment of this one guiltless pleasure to renounce the enjoyment of all others."

"Shall I confess it," said the other, "and wilt thou not laugh at me if I acknowledge, that these ideas pursue me constantly; that let me fly them as I will, when I explore my heart, I find all my early wishes yet rooted there, firmly, nay more firmly than ever? Yet what now remains for me, wretched that I am? Ah! whoever should have told me that the arms of my spirit, with which I was grasping at infinity, and hoping with certainty to clasp something great and glorious, would so soon be crushed and smote in pieces; whoever should have told me this, would have brought me to despair. And yet now, when judgment has been passed against me; now when *she*, that was to be as my divinity to guide me to my wishes, is gone forever, what remains but that I yield up my soul to the bitterest woes? O my brother! I will not deceive you: in my secret purposes, she was as the hook on which the ladder of my hopes was fixed: See! With daring aim the mounting adventurer hovers in the air; the iron breaks, and he lies broken and dismembered on the earth. No, there is no hope, no comfort for me more! I will not," he cried out, springing to his feet, "leave a single fragment of these wretched papers from the flames." He then seized one or two packets of them, tore them up, and threw them into the fire. Werner endeavoured to restrain him, but in vain. "Let me alone!" cried Wilhelm; "what should these miserable leaves do here? To me they give neither pleasant recollections, nor pleasant hopes. Shall they remain behind to vex me to the end of my life? Shall they perhaps one day serve the world for a jest, instead of awakening sympathy and horror? Woe to me! my doom is woe! Now I comprehend the wailings of the poets, of the wretched whom necessity has rendered wise. How long did I look upon myself as invulnerable and invincible; and alas! I am now made to see that a deep and early sorrow can never heal, can never pass away; I feel that I shall take it with me to my grave. No! not a day of my life shall escape this anguish, which at last must crush me down; and *her* image too shall stay with me, shall live and die with me, the image of the worthless—O my friend! if I must speak the feeling of my heart—the perhaps not altogether worthless! Her situation, the crookedness of her destiny, have a thousand times excused her in my mind. I have been too cruel; you steeled me in your own cold unrelenting harshness; you held my wavering senses captive, and hindered me from doing for myself and her what I owed to both. Who knows to what a state I may have brought her; my conscience by degrees presents to me, in all its heaviness, in what helplessness, in what despair I may have left her. Was it not possible that she might clear herself? Was it not possible? How many misconceptions throw the world into perplexity; how many circumstances may extort forgiveness for the greatest fault? Often do I figure her as sitting by herself in silence, leaning on her elbows. 'This,' she says, 'is the faith, the love he swore to me! With this hard stroke to end the delicious life which made us one!'" He broke out into a stream of tears, while he threw himself down with his face upon the table, and wetted the remaining papers with his weeping.

Werner stood beside him in the deepest perplexity. He had not anticipated this fierce ebullition of feeling. More than once he had tried to interrupt his friend, more than once to lead the conversation elsewhere, but in vain; the current was too strong for him. It remained that long-suffering friendship should again take up her office. Werner allowed the first shock of sorrow to pass over, while by his silent presence he testified a pure and honest sympathy. And thus they both remained that evening: Wilhelm sunk in the dull feeling of old sorrows; and the other terrified at this new outbreaking of a passion, which he thought his prudent counsels and keen persuasion had long since mastered and destroyed.

CHAPTER III.

AFTER such relapses, Wilhelm usually applied himself to business and activity with augmented ardour; and he found it the best means to escape the labyrinth into which he had again been tempted to enter. His attractive way of treating strangers, the ease with which he carried on a correspondence in any living language, more and more increased the hopes of his father and his trading friends; and comforted them in their sorrow for his sickness, the origin of which had not been known, and for the pause which had thus interrupted their plan. They determined a second time on Wilhelm's setting out to travel; and we now find him on horseback, with his saddle-bags behind him, exhilarated by the motion and the free air, approaching the mountains, where he had some affairs to settle.

He winded slowly on his path, through dales and over hills, with a feeling of the greatest satisfaction. Overhanging cliffs, roaring brooks, moss-grown rocky walls, deep precipices, he here saw for the first time; yet his earliest dreams of youth had wandered among such regions. In these scenes, he felt his age renewed; all the sorrows he had undergone were obliterated from his soul; with unbroken cheerfulness he repeated to himself passages of various poems, particularly of the *Pastor Fido*, which, in these solitary places, flocked in crowds into his mind. He also recollected many pieces of his own songs, and recited them with a peculiar contentment. He peopled the world which lay before him with all the forms of the past; and each step into the future was to him full of augury of important operations and remarkable events.

Several men, who came behind him in succession, and saluted him as they passed by to continue their hasty way into the mountains, by steep footpaths, sometimes interrupted his thoughts without attracting his attention to themselves. At last a communicative traveller joined him, and explained the reason of this general pilgrimage.

"At Hochdorf," he said, "there is a play to be acted tonight, and the whole neighbourhood is gathering to see it."

"How!" cried Wilhelm. "In these solitary hills, among these impenetrable forests, has theatric art sought out a place, and built herself a temple? And I am journeying to her festivities!"

"You will wonder more," said the other, "when you learn by whom the piece is to be played. There is in the place a large manufactory which employs many people. The proprietor, who lives, so to speak, remote from all human society, can find no better means of entertaining his workmen during winter, than allowing them to act plays. He suffers no cards among them; and wishes also to withdraw them from all coarse rustic practices. Thus they pass the long evenings; and today, being the old gentleman's birthday, they are giving a particular festival in honour of him."

Wilhelm came to Hochdorf, where he was to pass the night; and alighted at the manufactory, the proprietor of which stood as a debtor in his list.

When he gave his name, the old man cried in a glad surprise: "Ay, sir, are you the son of that worthy man to whom I owe so many thanks; so long have owed money? Your good father has had so much patience with me, I should be a knave if I did not pay you speedily and cheerfully. You come at the proper time to see that I am fully in earnest about it."

He then called out his wife, who seemed no less delighted than himself to see the youth: she declared that he was very like his father; and lamented that, having such a multitude of guests already in the house, she could not lodge him for the night.

The account was clear, and quickly settled; Wilhelm put the roll of gold into his pocket, and wished that all his other business might go on so smoothly. At last the play-hour came: they now waited nothing but the coming of the Head Forester, who at length also arrived; entered with a few hunters, and was received with the greatest reverence.

The company was then led into the playhouse, formed out of a barn that lay close upon the garden. Without any extraordinary taste, both seats and stage were yet decked out in a cheerful and pretty way. One of the painters employed in the manufactory had formerly worked as an understrapper at the Prince's theatre; he had now represented woods, and streets, and chambers, somewhat rudely it is true, yet so as to be recognised for such. The piece itself they had borrowed from a strolling company, and shaped it aright according to their own ideas. As it was, it did not fail to yield some entertainment. The plot of two lovers wishing to carry off a girl from her guardian, and mutually from one another, produced a great variety of interesting situations. Being the first play our friend had witnessed for so long a time, it suggested several reflections to him. It was full of action, but without any true delineation of character. It pleased and delighted. Such are always the beginnings of the scenic art. The rude man is contented if he see but something going on, the man of more refinement must be made to feel, the man entirely refined desires to reflect.

The players he would willingly have helped here and there: for a very little would have made them greatly better.

His silent meditations were somewhat broken in upon by the tobacco-smoke, which now began to rise in great and greater copiousness. Soon after the commencement of the piece, the Head Forester had lit his pipe; by and by, others took the same liberty. The large dogs too, which followed these gentlemen, introduced themselves in no pleasant style. At first they had been bolted out; but soon finding the back-door passage, they entered on the stage; ran against the actors; and at last, jumping over the orchestra, joined their masters, who had taken up the front seats in the pit.

For afterpiece an opera was given. A portrait, representing the old gentleman in his bridegroom dress, stood upon an altar, hung with garlands. All the players paid their reverence to it in the most submissive postures. The youngest child came forward dressed in white, and made a speech in verse; by which the whole family, and even the Head Forester himself, whom it brought in mind of his own children, were melted into tears. So ended the piece; and Wilhelm could not help stepping on the stage, to have a closer view of the actresses, to praise them for their good performance, and give them a little counsel for the future.

The remaining business, which our friend in the following days had to transact in various quarters of the hill-country, was not all so pleasant, or so easy to conclude with satisfaction. Many of his creditors entreated for delay, many were uncourteous, many lied. In conformity with his instructions, he had some of them to sue at law; he was thus obliged to seek out advocates, and give instructions to them, to appear before judges, and to go through many other sorry duties of the same sort.

His case was hardly bettered, when people chanced to incline showing some attentions to him. He found very few that could any way instruct him; few with whom he could hope to establish a useful commercial correspondence. Unhappily, moreover, the weather now grew rainy, and travelling on horseback in this district came to be attended with insufferable difficulties. He therefore thanked his stars on again getting near the level country; and at the foot of the mountains, looking out into a fertile and beautiful plain, intersected by a smooth-flowing river, and seeing a cheerful little town lying on its banks all glittering in the sunshine, he resolved, though without any special business in the place, to pass a day or two there, that he might refresh both himself and his horse, which the bad roads had considerably injured.

CHAPTER IV.

On alighting at an inn, upon the market-place, he found matters going on very joyously, at least very stirringly. A great company of rope-dancers, leapers and jugglers, having a Strong Man along with them, had just arrived with their wives and children; and while preparing for a grand exhibition, they kept up a perpetual racket. They first quarrelled with the landlord; then with one another; and if their contention was intolerable, the expressions of their satisfaction were infinitely more so. Undetermined whether he should go or stay, he was standing in the door, looking at some workmen who had just begun to erect a stage in the middle of the square.

A girl, with roses and other flowers for sale, coming by, held out her basket to him, and he purchased a beautiful nosegay; which, like one that had a taste for these things, he tied up in a different fashion, and was looking at it with a satisfied air, when the window of another inn on the opposite side of the square flew up, and a handsome young lady looked out from it. Notwithstanding the distance, he observed that her face was animated by a pleasant cheerfulness: her fair hair fell carelessly streaming about her neck; she seemed to be looking at the stranger. In a short time afterwards, a boy with a white jacket, and a barber's apron on, came out from the door of her house, towards Wilhelm; saluted him, and said: "The lady at the window bids me ask if you will not favour her with a share of your beautiful flowers."—"They are all at her service," answered Wilhelm, giving the nosegay to this nimble messenger, and making a bow to the fair one, which she returned with a friendly courtesy, and then withdrew from the window.

Amused with this small adventure, he was going up-stairs to his chamber, when a young creature sprang against him, and attracted his attention. A short silk waistcoat with slashed Spanish sleeves, tight trousers with puffs, looked very pretty on the child. Its long black hair was curled, and wound in locks and plaits about the head. He looked at the figure with astonishment, and could not determine whether to take it for a boy or a girl. However, he decided for the latter; and as the child ran by, he took her up in his arms, bade her good-day, and asked her to whom she belonged, though he easily perceived that she must be a member of the vaulting and dancing company lately arrived. She viewed him with a dark sharp side-look, as she pushed herself out of his arms, and ran into the kitchen without making any answer.

On coming up-stairs, he found in the large parlour two men practising the small sword, or seeming rather to make trial which was the better fencer. One of them plainly enough belonged to the vaulting company, the other had a somewhat less savage aspect. Wilhelm looked at them, and had reason to admire them both; and as the black-bearded, sturdy contender soon afterwards forsook the place of action, the other with extreme complaisance offered Wilhelm the rapier.

"If you want to take a scholar under your inspection," said our friend, "I am well content to risk a few passes with you."

Accordingly they fought together; and although the stranger greatly over-matched his new competitor, he politely kept declaring that it all depended upon practice; in fact, Wilhelm, inferior as he was, had made it evident that he had got his first instructions from a good, solid, thoroughpaced German fencing-master.

Their entertainment was disturbed by the uproar with which the parti-coloured brotherhood issued from the inn, to make proclamation of the show, and awaken a desire to see their art, throughout the town. Preceded by a drum, the manager advanced on horseback; he was followed by a female dancer mounted on a corresponding hack, and holding a child before her, all bedizened with ribbons and spangles. Next came the remainder of the troop on foot; some of them carrying children on their shoulders in dangerous postures, yet smoothly and lightly; among these the young, dark, black-haired figure again attracted Wilhelm's notice.

Pickleherring ran gaily up and down the crowding multitude, distributing his hand-bills with much practical fun; here smacking the lips of a girl, there breeching a boy, and awakening generally among the people an invincible desire to know more of him.

On the painted flags, the manifold science of the company was visibly delineated; particularly of a Monsieur Narciss and the Demoiselle Landrinette; both of whom, being main characters, had prudently kept back from the procession, thereby to acquire a more dignified consideration, and excite a greater curiosity.

During the procession, Wilhelm's fair neighbour had again appeared at the window; and he did not fail to inquire about her of his new companion. This person, whom, for the present, we shall call Laertes, offered to take Wilhelm over and introduce him. "I and the lady," said he, laughing, "are two fragments of an acting company that made shipwreck here a short while ago. The pleasantness of the place has induced us to stay in it, and consume our little stock of cash in peace, while one of our friends is out seeking some situation for himself and us."

Laertes immediately accompanied his new acquaintance to Philina's door; where he left him for a moment, and ran to a shop hard by for a few sweetmeats. "I am sure you will thank me," said he on returning, "for procuring you so pleasant an acquaintance."

The lady came out from her room in a pair of tight little slippers with high heels, to give them welcome. She had thrown a black mantle over her, above a white négligé, not indeed superstitiously clean, but which, for that very reason, gave her a more frank and domestic air. Her short dress did not hide a pair of the prettiest feet and ancles in the world.

"You are welcome," she cried to Wilhelm, "and I thank you for your charming flowers." She led him into her chamber with the one hand, pressing the nosegay to her breast with the other.

Being all seated, and got into a pleasant train of general talk, to which she had the art of giving a delightful turn, Laertes threw a handful of gingerbread-nuts into her lap, and she immediately began to eat them.

"Look what a child this young gallant is!" she said: "he wants to persuade you that I am fond of such confectionery; and it is himself that cannot live without licking his lips over something of the kind."

"Let us confess," replied Laertes, "that, in this point, as in others, you and I go hand in hand. For example," he continued, "the weather is delightful today: what if we should take a drive into the country, and eat our dinner at the Mill?"

"With all my heart," said Philina; "we must give our new acquaintance some diversion."

Laertes sprang out, for he never walked; and Wilhelm motioned to return for a minute to his lodgings, to have his hair put in order; for at present it was all dishevelled with riding. "You can do it here!" she said; then called her little servant, and constrained Wilhelm in the politest manner to lay off his coat, to throw her powder-mantle over him, and to have his head dressed in her presence. "We must lose no time," said she: "who knows how short a while we may all be together?"

The boy, out of sulkiness and ill-nature more than want of skill, went on but indifferently with his task; he pulled the hair with his implements, and seemed as if he would not soon be done. Philina more than once reproved him for his blunders, and at last sharply packed him off, and chased him to the door. She then undertook the business herself, and frizzled Wilhelm's locks with great dexterity and grace; though she too appeared to be in no exceeding haste, but found always this and that to improve and put to rights; while at the same time she could not help touching his knees with hers, and holding her nosegay and bosom so near his lips that he was strongly tempted more than once to imprint a kiss on it.

When Wilhelm had cleaned his brow with a little powder-knife, she said to him: "Put it in your pocket, and think of me when you see it." It was a pretty knife; the haft, of inlaid steel, had these friendly words wrought on it, *Think of me*. Wilhelm put it up, and thanked her, begging permission at the same time to make her a little present in return.

At last they were in readiness. Laertes had brought round the coach, and they commenced a very gay excursion. To every beggar, Philina threw out money from the window, giving along with it a merry and friendly word.

Scarcely had they reached the Mill, and ordered dinner, when a strain of music struck up before the house. It was some miners singing various pretty songs, and accompanying their clear and shrill voices with a cithern and triangle. In a short while the gathering crowd had formed a ring about them; and our company nodded approbation to them from the windows. Observing this attention, they expanded their circle, and seemed making preparation for their grandest piece. After some pause, a miner stepped forward with a mattock in his hand; and while the others played a serious tune, he set himself to represent the action of digging.

Ere long a peasant came from among the crowd, and by pantomimic threats let the former know that he must cease and remove. Our company were greatly surprised at this; they did not discover that the peasant was a miner in disguise; till he opened his mouth, and in a sort of recitative, rebuked the other for daring to meddle with his field. The latter did not lose his composure of mind, but began to inform the husbandman about his right to break ground there, giving him withal some primary conceptions of mineralogy. The peasant not being master of his foreign terminology, asked all manner of silly questions; whereat the spectators, as themselves more knowing, set up many a hearty laugh. The miner endeavoured to instruct him; and showed him the advantage which, in the long-run, would reach even him, if the deep-lying treasures of the land were dug out from their secret beds. The peasant, who at first had threatened his instructor with blows, was gradually pacified, and they parted good friends at last; though it was the miner chiefly that got out of this contention with honour.

"In this little dialogue," said Wilhelm, when seated at table, "we have a lively proof how useful the theatre might be to all ranks; what advantage even the State might procure from it, if the occupations, trades and undertakings of men were brought upon the stage; and presented on their praiseworthy side, in that point of view in which the State itself should honour and protect them. As matters stand, we exhibit only the ridiculous side of men; the comic poet is, as it were, but a spiteful tax-gatherer, who keeps a watchful eye over the errors of his fellow-subjects, and seems gratified when he can fix any charge upon them. Might it not be a worthy and pleasing task for a statesman to survey the natural and reciprocal influence of all classes on each other, and to guide some poet, gifted with sufficient humour, in such labours as these? In this way, I am persuaded, many very entertaining, both agreeable and useful pieces, might be executed."

"So far," said Laertes, "as I, in wandering about the world, have been able to observe, statesmen are accustomed merely to forbid, to hinder, to refuse; but very rarely to invite, to further, to reward. They let all things go along, till some mischief happens; then they get into a rage, and lay about them."

"A truce with state and statesmen!" said Philina; "I cannot form a notion of statesmen except in periwigs; and a periwig, wear it who will, always gives my fingers a spasmodic motion; I could like to pluck it off the venerable gentleman, to skip up and down the room with it, and laugh at the bald-head."

So, with a few lively songs, which she could sing very beautifully, Philina cut short their conversation; and urged them to a quick return homewards, that they might arrive in time for seeing the performance of the rope-dancers in the evening. On the road back she continued her lavish generosity, in a style of gaiety reaching to extravagance; for, at last, every coin belonging to herself or her companions being spent, she threw her straw-hat from the window to a girl, and her neckerchief to an old woman, who asked her for alms.

Philina invited both of her attendants to her own apartments; because, she said, the spectacle could be seen more conveniently from her windows than from theirs.

On arriving, they found the stage set up, and the background decked with suspended carpets. The swing-boards were already fastened, the slack-rope fixed to posts, the tight-rope bound over trestles. The square was moderately filled with people, and the windows with spectators of some quality.

Pickleherring, with a few insipidities, at which the lookers-on are generally kind enough to laugh, first prepared the meeting to attention and good humour. Some children, whose bodies were made to exhibit the strangest contortions, awakened astonishment or horror; and Wilhelm could not, without the deepest sympathy, see the child he had at the first glance felt an interest in, go through her fantastic positions with considerable difficulty. But the merry tumblers soon changed the feeling into that of lively satisfaction, when they first singly, then in rows, and at last all together, vaulted up into the air, making somersets backwards and forwards. A loud clapping of hands and a strong huzza echoed from the whole assembly.

The general attention was next directed to quite a different object. The children in succession had to mount the rope; the learners first, that by practising they might prolong the spectacle, and show the difficulties of the art more clearly. Some men and full-grown women likewise exhibited their skill to moderate advantage; but still there was no Monsieur Narciss, no Demoiselle Landrinette.

At last this worthy pair came forth; they issued from a kind of tent with red spread curtains; and, by their agreeable forms and glittering decorations, fulfilled the hitherto increasing hopes of the spectators. He, a hearty knave, of middle stature, with black eyes and a strong head of hair; she, formed with not inferior symmetry, exhibited themselves successively upon the rope, with delicate movements, leaping, and singular postures. Her airy lightness; his audacity; the exactitude with which they both performed their feats of art, raised the universal satisfaction higher at every step and spring. The stateliness with which they bore themselves, the seeming attentions of the rest to them, gave them the appearance of king and queen of the whole troop, and all held them worthy of the rank.

The animation of the people extended itself to the spectators at the windows; the ladies looked incessantly at Narciss, the gentlemen at Landrinette. The populace hurraed, the more cultivated public could not keep from clapping of the hands; Pickleherring now could scarcely raise a laugh. A few, however, slunk away, when some members of the troop began to press through the crowd with their tin plates to collect money.

"They have made their purpose good, I imagine," said Wilhelm to Philina, who was leaning over the window beside him. "I admire the ingenuity with which they have turned to advantage even the meanest parts of their performance: out of the unskilfulness of their children, and exquisiteness of their chief actors, they have made up a whole which at first excited our attention, and then gave us very fine entertainment."

The people by degrees dispersed, and the square was again become empty, while Philina and Laertes were disputing about the forms and the skill of Narciss and Landrinette, and rallying each other on the subject at great length. Wilhelm noticed the wonderful child standing on the street near some other children at play; he showed her to Philina, who, in her lively way, immediately called and beckoned to the little one, and, this not succeeding, tripped singing down stairs, and led her up by the hand.

"Here is the enigma," said she, as she brought her to the door. The child stood upon the threshold, as if she meant again to run off; laid her right hand on her breast, the left on her brow, and bowed deeply. "Fear nothing, my little dear," said Wilhelm, rising and going towards her. She viewed him with a doubting look, and came a few steps nearer.

"What is thy name?" he asked. "They call me Mignon." "How old art thou?" "No one has counted." "Who was thy father?" "The Great Devil is dead."

"Well! this is singular enough," said Philina. They asked her a few more questions; she gave her answers in a kind of broken German, and with a strangely solemn manner, every time laying her hands on her breast and brow, and bowing deeply.

Wilhelm could not satisfy himself with looking at her. His eyes and his heart were irresistibly attracted by the mysterious condition of this being. He reckoned her about twelve or thirteen years of age; her body was well formed, only her limbs gave promise of a stronger growth, or else announced a stunted one. Her countenance was not regular, but striking; her brow full of mystery; her nose extremely beautiful; her mouth, although it seemed too closely shut for one of her age, and though she often threw it to a side, had yet an air of frankness, and was very lovely. Her brownish complexion could scarcely be discerned through the paint. This form stamped itself deeply in Wilhelm's soul; he kept looking at her earnestly, and forgot the present scene in the multitude of his reflections. Philina waked him from his half-dream, by holding out the remainder of her sweetmeats to the child, and giving her a sign to go away. She made her little bow as formerly, and darted like lightning through the door.

As the time drew on when our new friends had to part for the evening, they planned a fresh excursion for the morrow. They purposed now to have their dinner at a neighbouring Jägerhaus. Before taking leave of Laertes, Wilhelm said many things in Philina's praise, to which the other made only brief and careless answers.

Next morning, having once more exercised themselves in fencing for an hour, they went over to Philina's lodging, towards which they had seen their expected coach passing by. But how surprised was Wilhelm, when the coach seemed altogether to have vanished; and how much more so, when Philina was not to be found at home! She had placed herself in the carriage, they were told, with a couple of strangers who had come that morning, and was gone with them. Wilhelm had been promising himself some pleasant entertainment from her company, and could not hide his irritation. Laertes, on the other hand, but laughed at it, and cried: "I love her for this: it looks so like herself! Let us, however, go directly to the Jägerhaus: be Philina where she pleases, we will not lose our promenade on her account."

As Wilhelm, while they walked, continued censuring the inconsistency of such conduct, Laertes said: "I cannot reckon it inconsistent so long as one keeps faithful to his character. If this Philina plans you anything, or promises you anything, she does it under the tacit condition that it shall be quite convenient for her to fulfil her plan, to keep her promise. She gives willingly; but you must ever hold yourself in readiness to return her gifts."

"That seems a singular character," said Wilhelm.

"Anything but singular; only she is not a hypocrite. I like her on that account. Yes, I am her friend, because she represents the sex so truly, which I have so much cause to hate. To me she is another genuine Eve, the great mother of womankind; so are they all, only they will not all confess it."

With abundance of such talk, in which Laertes very vehemently exhibited his spleen against the fair sex, without, however, giving any cause for it, they arrived at the forest; into which Wilhelm entered in no joyful mood, the speeches of Laertes having again revived in him the memory of his relation to Mariana. Not far from a shady well, among some old and noble trees, they found Philina sitting by herself at a stone table. Seeing them, she struck up a merry song; and, when Laertes asked for her companions, she cried out: "I have already cozened them, I have already had my laugh at them, and sent them a-travelling, as they deserved. By the way hither I had put to proof their liberality; and finding that they were a couple of your close-fisted gentry, I immediately determined to have amends of them. On arriving at the inn, they asked the waiter what was to be had. He, with his customary glibness of tongue, reckoned over all that could be found in the house, and more than could be found. I noticed their perplexity; they looked at one another, stammered, and inquired about the cost. 'What is the use of all this studying?' said I; 'the table is the lady's business, allow me to manage it.' I immediately began ordering a most unconscionable dinner; for which many necessary articles would require to be sent for from the neighbourhood. The waiter, of whom, by a wry mouth or two, I had made a confidant, at last helped me out; and so, by the image of a sumptuous feast, we tortured them to such a degree that they fairly determined on having a walk in the forest, from which I imagine we shall look with clear eyes if we see them come again. I have laughed a quarter of an hour for my own behoof; I shall laugh forever when I think of the looks they had." At table, Laertes told of similar adventures: they got into the track of recounting ludicrous stories, mistakes and dextrous cheats.

A young man, of their acquaintance from the town, came gliding through the wood with a book in his hand; he sat down by them, and began praising the beauty of the place. He directed their attention to the murmuring of the brook, to the waving of the boughs, to the checkered lights and shadows, and the music of the birds. Philina commenced a little song of the cuckoo, which did not seem at all to exhilarate the man of taste: he very soon made his compliments and went on.

"O that I might never hear more of nature, and scenes of nature!" cried Philina so soon as he was gone: "there is nothing in the world more intolerable than to hear people reckon up the pleasures you enjoy. When the day is bright you go to walk, as to dance when you hear a tune played. But who would think a moment on the music or the weather? It is the dancer that interests us, not the violin; and to look upon a pair of bright black eyes is the life of a pair of blue ones. But what on earth have we to do with wells, and brooks, and old rotten lindens?" She was sitting opposite to Wilhelm; and while speaking so, she looked into his eyes with a glance which he could not hinder from piercing at least to the very door of his heart.

"You are right," replied he, not without embarrassment; "man is ever the most interesting object to man, and perhaps should be the only one that interests. Whatever else surrounds us is but the element in which we live, or else the instrument which we employ. The more we devote ourselves to such things, the more we attend to and feel concern in them, the weaker will our sense of our own dignity become, the weaker our feelings for society. Men who put a great value on gardens, buildings, clothes, ornaments, or any other sort of property, grow less social and pleasant; they lose sight of their brethren, whom very few can succeed in collecting about them and entertaining. Have you not observed it on the stage? A good actor makes us very soon forget the awkwardness and meanness of paltry decorations; but a splendid theatre is the very thing which first makes us truly feel the want of proper actors."

After dinner Philina sat down among the long over-shaded grass, and commanded both her friends to fetch her flowers in great quantities. She wreathed a complete garland, and put it round her head: it made her look extremely charming. The flowers were still sufficient for another; this too she plaited, while both the young men sat beside her. When at last, amid infinite mirth and sportfulness, it was completed, she pressed it on Wilhelm's head with the greatest dignity, and shifted the posture of it more than once till it seemed to her properly adjusted. "And I, it appears, must go empty," said Laertes.

"Not by any means; you shall not have reason to complain," replied Philina, taking off the garland from her own head, and putting it on his.

"If we were rivals," said Laertes, "we might now dispute very warmly which of us stood higher in thy favour."

"And the more fools you," said she, while she bent herself towards him, and offered him her lips to kiss; and then immediately turned round, threw her arm about Wilhelm, and bestowed a kind salute on him also. "Which of them tastes best?" said she archly.

"Surprisingly!" exclaimed Laertes: "it seems as if nothing else had ever such a tang of wormwood in it."

"As little wormwood," she replied, "as any gift that a man may enjoy without envy and without conceit. But now," cried she, "I should like to have an hour's dancing, and after that we must look to our vaulters."

Accordingly they went into the house, and there found music in readiness. Philina was a beautiful dancer, she animated both her companions. Nor was Wilhelm without skill; but he wanted careful practice, a defect which his two friends voluntarily took charge of remedying.

In these amusements the time passed on insensibly; it was already late when they returned. The rope-dancers had commenced their operations. A multitude of people had again assembled in the square; and our friends, on alighting, were struck by the appearance of a tumult in the crowd, occasioned by a throng of men rushing towards the door of the inn which Wilhelm had now turned his face to. He sprang forward to see what it was; and pressing through the people, he was struck with horror to observe the master of the rope-dancing company dragging poor Mignon by the hair out of the house, and unmercifully beating her little body with the handle of a whip.

Wilhelm darted on the man like lightning, and seized him by the collar. "Quit the child!" he cried in a furious tone, "or one of us shall never leave this spot;" and so speaking, he grasped the fellow by the throat with a force which only rage could have lent him. The showman, on the point of choking, let go the child, and endeavoured to defend himself against his new assailant. But some people, who had felt compassion for Mignon, yet had not dared to begin a quarrel for her, now laid hold of the rope-dancer, wrenched his whip away, and threatened him with great fierceness and abuse. Being now reduced to the weapons of his mouth, he began bullying and cursing horribly: the lazy, worthless urchin, he said, would not do her duty; refused to perform the egg-dance, which he had promised to the public; he would beat her to death, and no one should hinder him. He tried to get loose, and seek the child, who had crept away among the crowd. Wilhelm held him back, and said sternly: "You shall neither see nor touch her, till you have explained before a magistrate where you stole her. I will pursue you to every extremity; you shall not escape me."

These words, which Wilhelm uttered in heat, without thought or purpose, out of some vague feeling, or, if you will, out of inspiration, soon brought the raging showman to composure. "What have I to do with the useless brat?" cried he. "Pay me what her clothes cost, and make of her what you please; we shall settle it tonight." And, being liberated, he made haste to resume his interrupted operations, and to calm the irritation of the public by some striking displays of his craft.

So soon as all was still again, Wilhelm commenced a search for Mignon, whom, however, he could nowhere find. Some said they had seen her on the street, others on the roofs of the adjoining houses; but, after seeking unsuccessfully in all quarters, he was forced to content himself, and wait to see if she would not again turn up of herself.

In the mean time, Narciss had come into the house, and Wilhelm set to question him about the birth-place and history of the child. Monsieur Narciss knew nothing about these things; for he had not long been in the company: but in return he recited, with much volubility and levity, various particulars of his own fortune. Upon Wilhelm's wishing him joy of the great approbation he had gained, Narciss expressed himself as if exceedingly indifferent on that point. "People laugh at us," he said, "and admire our feats of skill; but their admiration does nothing for us. The master has to pay us, and may raise the funds where he pleases." He then took his leave, and was setting off in great haste.

At the question, Whither he was bent so fast? the dog gave a smile, and admitted that his figure and talents had acquired for him a more solid species of favour than the huzzaing of the multitude. He had been invited by some young ladies, who desired much to become acquainted with him, and he was afraid it would be midnight before he could get all his visits over. He proceeded with the greatest candour to detail his adventures; he would have given the names of his patronesses, their streets and houses, had not Wilhelm waved such indiscretion, and politely dismissed him.

Laertes had meanwhile been entertaining Landrinette: he declared that she was fully worthy to be and to remain a woman.

Our friend next proceeded to his bargain with the showman for Mignon. Thirty crowns was the price set upon her; and for this sum the black-bearded hot Italian entirely surrendered all his claims: but of her history, or parentage, he would discover nothing; only that she had fallen into his hands at the death of his brother, who, by reason of his admirable skill, had usually been named the *Great Devil.*

Next morning was chiefly spent in searching for the child. It was in vain that they rummaged every hole and corner of the house and neighbourhood: the child had vanished, and Wilhelm was afraid she might have leapt into some pool of water, or destroyed herself in some other way.

Philina's charms could not dissipate his inquietude; he passed a dreary thoughtful day. Nor at evening could the utmost efforts of the tumblers and dancers, exerting all their powers to gratify the public, divert the current of his thoughts, or clear away the clouds from his mind.

By the concourse of people flocking from all places round, the numbers had greatly increased on this occasion; the general approbation was like a snowball rolling itself into a monstrous size. The feat of leaping over swords, and through the cask with paper ends, made a great sensation. The Strong Man, too, produced a universal feeling of mingled astonishment and horror, when he laid his head and feet on a couple of separate stools, and then allowed some sturdy smiths to place a stithy on the unsupported part of his body, and hammer a horse-shoe till it was completely made by means of it.

The Hercules' Strength, as they called it, was a no less wonderful affair. A row of men stood up; then another row, upon their shoulders; then women and young lads, supported in like manner on the second row; so that finally a living pyramid was formed, the peak being ornamented by a child, placed on its head, and dressed out in the shape of a ball and weather-vane. Such a sight, never witnessed in those parts before, gave a worthy termination to the whole performance. Narciss and Landrinette were then borne in litters, on the shoulders of the rest, along the chief streets of the town, amid the triumphant shouts of the people. Ribbons, nosegays, silks, were thrown upon them; all pressed to get a sight of them. Each thought himself happy if he could behold them, and be honoured with a look of theirs.

"What actor, what author, nay what man of any class, would not regard himself as on the summit of his wishes, could he, by a noble saying or a worthy action, produce so universal an impression? What a precious emotion would it give, if one could disseminate generous, exalted, manly feelings with electric force and speed, and rouse assembled thousands into such rapture, as these people, by their bodily alertness, have done! If one could communicate to thronging multitudes a fellow-feeling in all that belongs to man, by the portraying of happiness and misery, of wisdom and folly, nay of absurdity and silliness; could kindle and thrill their inmost souls, and set their stagnant nature into movement, free, vehement and pure!" So said our friend; and as neither Laertes nor Philina showed any disposition to take part in such a strain, he entertained himself with these darling speculations, walking up and down the streets till late at night, and again pursuing, with all the force and vivacity of a liberated imagination, his old desire to have all that was good and noble and great embodied and shown forth by the theatric art.

CHAPTER V.

NEXT morning, the rope-dancers, not without much parade and bustle, having gone away, Mignon immediately appeared, and came into the parlour as Wilhelm and Laertes were busy fencing. "Where hast thou been hid?" said Wilhelm in a friendly tone. "Thou hast given us a great deal of anxiety." The child looked at him, and answered nothing. "Thou art ours now," cried Laertes, "we have bought thee." "For how much?" inquired the child quite coolly. "For a hundred ducats," said the other; "pay them again, and thou art free." "Is that very much?" she asked. "O yes! thou must now be a good child." "I will try," she said.

From that moment she observed strictly what services the waiter had to do for both her friends: and after next day, she would not any more let him enter the room. She persisted in doing everything herself; and accordingly went through her duties, slowly indeed, and sometimes awkwardly, yet completely and with the greatest care.

She was frequently observed going to a basin of water, and washing her face with such diligence and violence, that she almost wore the skin from her cheeks; till Laertes, by dint of questions and reproofs, learned that she was striving by all means to get the paint from her skin; and that, in her zealous endeavours towards this object, she had mistaken the redness produced by rubbing for the most obdurate dye. They set her right on this point, and she ceased her efforts; after which, having come again to her natural state, she exhibited a fine brown complexion, beautiful, though sparingly intermingled with red.

The siren charms of Philina, the mysterious presence of the child, produced more impression on our friend than he liked to confess; he passed several days in that strange society, endeavouring to elude self-reproaches by a diligent practice of fencing and dancing, accomplishments which he believed might not again be put within his reach so conveniently.

It was with great surprise, and not without a certain satisfaction, that he one day observed Herr Melina and his wife alight at the inn. After the first glad salutation, they inquired about "the lady-manager and the other actors;" and learned, with astonishment and terror, that the lady-manager had long since gone away, and her actors, to a very few, dispersed themselves about the country.

This couple, subsequently to their marriage, in which, as we know, our friend did his best to serve them, had been travelling about in various quarters, seeking an engagement, without finding any; and had at last been directed to this little town by some persons who met them on their journey, and said there was a good theatre in the place.

Melina by no means pleased the lively Laertes, when introduced to him, any more than his wife did Philina. Both heartily wished to be rid of these new-comers; and Wilhelm could inspire them with no favourable feelings on the subject, though he more than once assured them that the Melinas were very worthy people.

Indeed, the previous merry life of our three adventurers was interfered with by this extension of their society, in more ways than one. Melina had taken up his quarters in the inn where Philina stayed, and he very soon began a system of cheapening and higgling. He would have better lodging, more sumptuous diet, and readier attendance, for a smaller charge. In a short while, the landlord and waiter showed very rueful looks; for whereas the others, to get pleasantly along, had expressed no discontent with anything, and paid instantly, that they might avoid thinking longer of payment,. Melina now insisted on regulating every meal, and investigating its contents beforehand; a species of service for which Philina named him, without scruple, a ruminating animal.

Yet more did the merry girl hate Melina's wife. Frau Melina was a young woman not without culture, but wofully defective in soul and spirit. She could declaim not badly, and kept declaiming constantly; but it was easy to observe that her performances were little more than recitations of words. She laboured a few detached passages, but never could express the feeling of the whole. Withal, however, she was seldom disagreeable to any one, especially to men. On the contrary, people who enjoyed her acquaintance commonly ascribed to her a fine understanding; for she was what might be called a kind of *spiritual chameleon,* or *taker-on.*[1] Any friend whose

---

[1] *Anempfinderin* (feeler-by, feeler-according-to) is the new untranslateable word poorly paraphrased so. A new German word, first used here; the like of which might be useful in all languages, for it designates a class of persons extant in all countries.—ED.

favour she had need of, she could flatter with peculiar adroitness: could give in to his ideas so long as she could understand them; and, when they went beyond her own horizon, could hail with ecstasy such new and brilliant visions. She understood well when to speak and when to keep silence; and though her disposition was not spiteful, she could spy out with great expertness where another's weak side lay.

CHAPTER VI.

MELINA, in the mean time, had been making strict inquiry about the wrecks of the late theatrical establishment. The wardrobe, as well as decorations, had been pawned with some traders; and a notary had been empowered, under certain conditions, to dispose of them by sale, should purchasers occur. Melina wished to see this ware; and he took Wilhelm with him. No sooner was the room opened, than our friend felt towards its contents a kind of inclination, which he would not confess to himself. Sad as was the state of the blotched and tarnished decorations; little showy as the Turkish and Pagan garments, the old farce-coats for men and women, the cowls for enchanters, priests and Jews, might be, he was not able to exclude the feeling, that the happiest moments of his life had been spent in a similar magazine of frippery. Could Melina have seen into his heart, he would have urged him more pressingly to lay out a sum of money in liberating these scattered fragments, in furbishing them up, and again combining them into a beautiful whole. "What a happy man could I be," cried Melina, "had I but two hundred crowns, to get into my hands, for a beginning, these fundamental necessaries of a theatre! How soon should I get up a little playhouse, that would draw contributions from the town and neighbourhood, and maintain us all!" Wilhelm was silent. They left these treasures of the stage to be again locked up, and both went away in a reflective mood.

Thenceforth Melina talked of nothing else but projects and plans for setting up a theatre, and gaining profit by it. He tried to interest Philina and Laertes in his schemes; and proposals were made to Wilhelm about advancing money, and taking them as his security. On this occasion, Wilhelm first clearly perceived that he was lingering too long here: he excused himself, and set about making preparations for departure.

In the mean time, Mignon's form and manner of existence was growing more attractive to him every day. In her whole system of proceedings there was something very singular. She never walked up or down the stairs, but jumped. She would spring along by the railing, and before you were aware, would be sitting quietly above upon the landing. Wilhelm had observed, also, that she had a different sort of salutation for each individual. For himself, it had of late been with her arms crossed upon her breast. Often for the whole day she was mute. At times she answered various questions more freely, yet always strangely; so that you could not determine whether it was caused by shrewd sense, or ignorance of the language; for she spoke in broken German, interlaced with French and Italian. In Wilhelm's service she was indefatigable, and up before the sun. On the other hand, she vanished early in the evening, went to sleep in a little room upon the bare floor, and could not by any means be induced to take a bed or even a palliasse. He often found her washing herself. Her clothes, too, were kept scrupulously clean, though nearly all about her was quilted two or three plies thick. Wilhelm was moreover told, that she went every morning early to hear mass. He followed her on one occasion, and saw her kneeling down with a rosary in a corner of the church, and praying devoutly. She did not observe him; and he returned home, forming many a conjecture about this appearance, yet unable to arrive at any probable conclusion.

A new application from Melina for a sum of money to redeem the often-mentioned stage-apparatus, caused Wilhelm to think more seriously than ever about setting off. He proposed writing to his people, who for a long time had heard no tidings of him, by the very earliest post. He accordingly commenced a letter to Werner; and had advanced a considerable way with the history of his adventures, in recounting which he had more than once unintentionally swerved a little from the truth, when, to his vexation and surprise, he observed, upon the back of his sheet, some verses which he had been copying from his album for Madam Melina. Out of humour at this mistake, he tore the paper in pieces, and put off repeating his confession till the next post-day.

CHAPTER VII.

Our party was now again collected; and Philina, who always kept a sharp look-out on every horse or carriage that passed by, exclaimed, with great eagerness: "Our Pedant! Here comes our dearest Pedant! Who the deuce is it he has with him?" Speaking thus, she beckoned at the window, and the vehicle drew up.

A woful-looking genius, whom, by his shabby coat of grayish

brown, and his ill-conditioned lower garments, you must have taken for some unprosperous preceptor, of the sort that moulder in our universities, now descended from the carriage, and, taking off his hat to salute Philina, discovered an ill-powdered but yet very stiff periwig, while Philina threw a hundred kisses of the hand towards him.

As Philina's chief enjoyment lay in loving one class of men, and being loved by them; so there was a second and hardly inferior satisfaction, wherewith she entertained herself as frequently as possible; and this consisted in hoodwinking and passing jokes upon the other class, whom at such moments she happened not to love; all which she could accomplish in a very sprightly style.

Amid the flourish which she made in receiving this old friend, no attention was bestowed upon the rest who followed him. Yet among the party were an oldish man and two young girls, whom Wilhelm thought he knew. Accordingly it turned out, that he had often seen them all, some years ago, in a company then playing in his native town. The daughters had grown since that period; the old man was little altered. He commonly enacted those good-hearted boisterous old gentlemen, whom the German theatre is never without, and whom, in common life, one also frequently enough falls in with. For as it is the character of our countrymen to do good, and cause it, without pomp or circumstance, so they seldom consider that there is likewise a mode of doing what is right with grace and dignity; more frequently, indeed, they yield to the spirit of contradiction, and fall into the error of deforming their dearest virtue by a surly mode of putting it in practice.

Such parts our actor could play very well; and he played them so often and exclusively, that he had himself taken up the same turn of proceeding in his ordinary life.

On recognising him, Wilhelm was seized with a strong commotion: he recollected how often he had seen this man on the stage with his beloved Mariana: he still heard him scolding, still heard the small soothing voice, with which in many characters she had to meet his rugged temper.

The first anxious question put to the strangers, Whether they had heard of any situation in their travels? was answered, alas, with No; and to complete the information, it was farther added, that all the companies they had fallen in with were not only supplied with actors, but many of them were afraid lest, on account of the approaching war, they should be forced to separate. Old Boisterous, with his daughters, moved by spleen and love of change, had given up an advantageous engagement; then meeting with the Pedant by the way, they had hired a carriage to come hither; where, as they found, good counsel was still dear, needful to have, and difficult to get.

The time while the rest were talking very keenly of their circumstances, Wilhelm spent in thought. He longed to speak in private with the old man; he wished and feared to hear of Mariana, and felt himself in the greatest disquietude.

The pretty looks of the stranger damsels could not call him from his dream; but a war of words, which now arose, awakened his attention. It was Friedrich, the fair-haired boy, who used to attend Philina, stubbornly refusing, on this occasion, to cover the table and bring up dinner. "I engaged to serve you," he cried; "but not to wait on everybody." They fell into a hot contest. Philina insisted that he should do his duty; and as he obstinately refused, she told him plainly he might go about his business.

"You think, perhaps, I cannot leave you?" cried he, sturdily; then went to pack up his bundle, and soon hastily quitted the house.

"Go, Mignon," said Philina, "and get us what we want: tell the waiter, and help him to attend us."

Mignon came before Wilhelm, and asked in her laconic way: "Shall I? May I?" To which Wilhelm answered: "Do all that the lady bids thee, child."

She accordingly took charge of everything, and waited on the guests the whole evening, with the utmost carefulness. After dinner, Wilhelm proposed to have a walk with the old man alone. Succeeding in this, after many questions about his late wanderings, the conversation turned upon the former company, and Wilhelm hazarded a question touching Mariana.

"Do not speak to me of that despicable creature," cried the old man; "I have sworn to think of her no more." Terrified at this speech, Wilhelm felt still more embarrassed, as the old man proceeded to vituperate her fickleness and wantonness. Most gladly would our friend have broken off the conversation; but now it was impossible: he was obliged to undergo the whole tumultuous effusions of this strange old gentleman.

"I am ashamed," continued he, "that I felt such a friendship for her. Yet had you known the girl better, you would excuse me. She was so pretty, so natural and good, so pleasing, in every sense so tolerable, I could never have supposed that ingratitude and impudence were to prove the chief features of her character."

Wilhelm had nerved himself to hear the worst of her; when all at once he observed, with astonishment, that the old man's tones grew milder, his voice faltered, and he took out his handkerchief to dry the tears, which at last began to trickle down his cheeks.

"What is the matter with you?" cried Wilhelm. "What is it that suddenly so changes the current of your feelings? Conceal it not from me. I take a deeper interest in the fate of this girl than you suppose. Only tell me all."

"I have not much to say," replied the old man, again taking up his earnest angry tone. "I have suffered more from her than I shall ever forgive. She had always a kind of trust in me. I loved her as my own daughter; indeed, while my wife lived, I had formed a resolution to take the creature to my own house, and save her from the hands of that old crone, from whose guidance I boded no good. But my wife died, and the project went to nothing.

"About the end of our stay in your native town, it is not quite three years ago, I noticed a visible sadness about her. I questioned her, but she evaded me. At last we set out on our journey. She travelled in the same coach with me; and I soon observed, what she herself did not long deny, that she was with child, and suffering the greatest terror, lest our manager might turn her off. In fact, in a short while he did make the discovery; immediately threw up her contract, which at any rate was only for six weeks; paid off her arrears; and in spite of all entreaties, left her behind, in the miserable inn of a little village.

"Devil take all wanton jilts!" cried the old man, with a splenetic tone, "and especially this one, that has spoiled me so many hours of my life! Why should I keep talking how I myself took charge of her, what I did for her, what I spent on her, how in absence I provided for her. I would rather throw my purse into the ditch, and spend my time in nursing mangy whelps, than ever more bestow the smallest care on such a thing. Pshaw! At first I got letters of thanks, notice of places she was staying at; and, finally, no word at all, not even an acknowledgment for the money I had sent to pay the expenses of her lying-in. Oh! the treachery and the fickleness of women are rightly matched, to get a comfortable living for themselves, and to give an honest fellow many heavy hours."

CHAPTER VIII.

WILHELM's feelings, on returning home after this conversation, may be easily conceived. All his old wounds had been torn up afresh; and the sentiment, that Mariana was not wholly unworthy of his love, had again been brought to life. The interest which the old man had shown about her fate, the praises he gave her against his will, displayed her again in all her attractiveness. Nay, even the bitter accusations brought against her contained nothing that could lower her in Wilhelm's estimation; for he, as well as she, was guilty in all her aberrations. Nor did even her final silence seem greatly blamable; it rather inspired him with mournful thoughts. He saw her, as a frail, ill-succoured mother, wandering helplessly about the world; wandering perhaps with his own child. What he knew, and what he knew not, awoke in him the painfullest emotions.

Mignon had been waiting for him; she lighted him up-stairs. On setting down the light, she begged that he would allow her, that evening, to compliment him with a piece of her art. He would rather have declined this, particularly as he knew not what it was; but he had not the heart to refuse anything this kind creature wished. After a little while she again came in. She carried a little carpet below her arm, which she then spread out upon the floor. Wilhelm said she might proceed. She thereupon brought four candles, and placed one upon each corner of the carpet. A little basket of eggs, which she next carried in, made her purpose clearer. Carefully measuring her steps, she then walked to and fro on the carpet, spreading out the eggs in certain figures and positions: which done, she called in a man that was waiting in the house, and could play on the violin. He retired with his instrument into a corner; she tied a band about her eyes, gave a signal, and, like a piece of wheel-work set a-going, she began moving the same instant as the music, accompanying her beats and the notes of the tune with the strokes of a pair of castanets.

Lightly, nimbly, quickly, and with hairsbreadth accuracy, she carried on the dance. She skipped so sharply and surely along between the eggs, and trod so closely down beside them, that you would have thought every instant she must trample one of them in pieces, or kick the rest away in her rapid turns. By no means! She touched no one of them, though winding herself through their mazes with all kinds of steps, wide and narrow, nay even with leaps, and at last half kneeling.

Constant as the movement of a clock, she ran her course; and the strange music, at each repetition of the tune, gave a new impulse to the dance, recommencing and again rushing off as at first. Wilhelm was quite led away by this singular spectacle; he forgot his cares; he followed every movement of the dear little creature, and felt surprised to see how finely her character unfolded itself as she proceeded in the dance.

Rigid, sharp, cold, vehement and in soft postures, stately rather than attractive; such was the light in which it showed her. At this moment, he experienced at once all the emotions he had ever felt for Mignon. He longed to incorporate this forsaken being with his own heart; to take her in his arms, and with a father's love to awaken in her the joy of existence.

The dance being ended, she rolled the eggs together softly with her foot into a little heap, left none behind, harmed none; then placed herself beside it, taking the bandage from her eyes, and concluding her performance with a little bow.

Wilhelm thanked her for having executed, so prettily and unexpectedly, a dance he had long wished to see. He patted her; was sorry she had tired herself so much. He promised her a new suit of clothes; to which she vehemently replied: "Thy colour!" This, too, he promised her, though not well knowing what she meant by it. She then lifted up the eggs, took the carpet under her arm, asked if he wanted anything farther, and skipped out of the door.

The musician, being questioned, said that, for some time, she had taken much trouble in often singing over the tune of this dance, the well-known fandango, to him, and training him till he could play it accurately. For his labour she had likewise offered him some money, which, however, he would not accept.

CHAPTER IX.

AFTER a restless night, which our friend spent sometimes waking, sometimes oppressed with unpleasant dreams, seeing Mariana now in all her beauty, now in woful case, at one time with a child on her arm, then soon bereaved of it, the morning had scarcely dawned, when Mignon entered with a tailor. She brought some gray cloth and blue taffeta, signifying in her own way that she wished to have a new jacket and sailor's trousers, such as she had seen the boys of the town wearing, with blue cuffs and tyers.

Since the loss of Mariana, Wilhelm had laid aside all gay colours. He had used himself to gray, the garment of the shades; and only perhaps a sky-blue lining, or little collar of that dye, in some degree enlivened his sober garb. Mignon, eager to wear his colours, hurried on the tailor, who engaged to have his work soon ready.

The exercise in dancing and fencing, which our friend took this day with Laertes, did not prosper in their hands. Indeed, it was soon interrupted by Melina, who came to show them circumstantially how a little company was now of itself collected, sufficient to exhibit plays in abundance. He renewed the proposal that Wilhelm should advance a little money for setting them in motion; which, however, Wilhelm still declined.

Ere long Philina and the girls came in, racketing and laughing as usual. They had now devised a fresh excursion; for change of place and objects was a pleasure after which they always longed. To eat daily in a different spot was their highest wish. On this occasion they proposed a sail.

The boat, in which they were to fall down the pleasant windings of the river, had already been engaged by the Pedant. Philina urged them on: the party did not linger, and were soon on board.

"What shall we take to now?" said Philina, when all had placed themselves upon the benches.

"The readiest thing," replied Laertes, "were for us to extemporise a play. Let each take a part that suits his character, and we shall see how we get along."

"Excellent!" said Wilhelm. "In a society where there is no dissimulation, but where each without disguise pursues the bent of his own humour, elegance and satisfaction cannot long continue; and where dissimulation always reigns, they do not enter at all. It will not be amiss, then, that we take up dissimulation to begin with; and then, behind our masks, be as candid as we please."

"Yes," said Laertes, "it is on this account that one goes on so pleasantly with women; they never show themselves in their natural form."

"That is to say," replied Madam Melina, "they are not so vain as men, who conceive themselves to be always amiable enough, just as nature has produced them."

In the mean time the river led them between pleasant groves and hills, between gardens and vineyards; and the young women, especially Madam Melina, expressed their rapture at the landscape. The latter even began to recite, in solemn style, a pretty poem of the descriptive sort, upon a similar scene of nature; but Philina interrupted her with the proposal of a law, that no one should presume to speak of any inanimate object. On the other hand, she zealously urged on their project of an extempore play. Old Boisterous was to be a half-pay officer; Laertes a fencing-master taking his vacation; the Pedant a Jew; she herself would act a Tyrolese, leaving to the rest to choose characters according to their several pleasures. They would suppose themselves to be a party of total strangers to each other, who had just met on board a merchant ship.

She immediately began to play her part with the Jew; and a universal cheerfulness diffused itself among them.

They had not sailed far, when the skipper stopped in his course, asking permission of the company to take in a person standing on the shore, who had made a sign to him.

"That is just what we needed," cried Philina; "a chance passenger was wanting to complete the travelling-party."

A handsome man came on board; whom, by his dress and his dignified mien, you might have taken for a clergyman. He saluted the party, who thanked him in their own way, and soon made known to him the nature of their game. The stranger immediately engaged to play the part of a country parson; which, in fact, he accomplished in the adroitest manner, to the admiration of all; now admonishing, now telling stories, showing some weak points, yet never losing their respect.

In the mean time, every one who had made a false step in his part, or swerved from his character, had been obliged to forfeit a pledge; Philina had gathered them with the greatest care; and especially threatened the reverend gentleman with many kisses, though he himself had never been at fault. Melina, on the other hand, was completely fleeced; shirt-buttons, buckles, every moveable about his person was in Philina's hands. He was trying to enact an English traveller, and could not by any means get into the spirit of his part.

Meanwhile the time had passed away very pleasantly. Each had strained his fancy and his wit to the utmost, and each had garnished his part with agreeable and entertaining jests. Thus comfortably occupied, they reached the place where they meant to pass the day; and Wilhelm going out to walk with the clergyman, as both from his appearance and late character he persisted in naming him, soon fell into an interesting conversation.

"I think this practice," said the stranger, "very useful among actors, and even in the company of friends and acquaintances. It is the best mode of drawing men out of themselves, and leading them, by a circuitous path, back into themselves again. It should be a custom with every troop of players to practise in this manner; and the public would assuredly be no loser, if every month an unwritten piece were brought forward; in which, of course, the players had prepared themselves by several rehearsals."

"One should not then," replied our friend, "consider an extempore piece as, strictly speaking, composed on the spur of the moment; but as a piece, of which the plan, action and division of the scenes were given, the filling up of all this being left to the player."

"Quite right," said the stranger; "and, in regard to this very filling up, such a piece, were the players once trained to these performances, would profit greatly. Not in regard to the mere words, it is true; for by a careful selection of these, the studious writer may certainly adorn his work; but in regard to the gestures, looks, exclamations, and everything of that nature; in short, to the mute and half-mute play of the dialogue, which seems by degrees fading away among us altogether. There are indeed some players in Germany, whose bodies figure what they think and feel; who, by their silence, their delays, their looks, their slight graceful movements, can prepare the audience for a speech, and by a pleasant sort of pantomime, combine the pauses of the dialogue with the general whole; but such a practice as this, coöperating with a happy natural turn, and training it to compete with the author, is far from being so habitual as, for the comfort of playgoing people, were to be desired."

"But will not a happy natural turn," said Wilhelm, "as the first and last requisite, of itself conduct the player like every other artist, nay perhaps every other man, to the lofty mark he aims at?"

"The first and the last, the beginning and the end, it may well be; but in the middle, many things will still be wanting to an artist, if instruction, and early instruction too, have not previously made that of him which he was meant to be: and perhaps for the man of genius it is worse in this respect than for the man possessed of only common capabilities; the one may much more easily be misinstructed, and be driven far more violently into false courses, than the other."

"But," said Wilhelm, "will not genius save itself, not heal the wounds which itself has inflicted?"

"Only to a very small extent, and with great difficulty," said the other, "or perhaps not at all. Let no one think that he can conquer the first impressions of his youth. If he has grown up in enviable freedom, surrounded with beautiful and noble objects, in constant intercourse with worthy men; if his masters have taught him what he needed first to know, for comprehending more easily what followed; if he has never learned anything which he requires to unlearn; if his first operations have been so guided, that without altering any of his habits, he can more easily produce what is excellent in future; then such a one will lead a purer, more perfect and happier life, than another man who has wasted the force of his youth in opposition and error. A great deal is said and written about education; yet I meet with very few who can comprehend, and transfer to practice, this simple yet vast idea, which includes within itself all others connected with the subject."

"That may well be true," said Wilhelm, "for the generality of men are limited enough in their conceptions to suppose, that every other should be fashioned by education according to the pattern of themselves. Happy then are those whom fate takes charge of, and educates according to their several natures!"

"Fate," said the other smiling, "is an excellent, but most expensive schoolmaster. In all cases, I would rather trust to the reason of a human tutor. Fate, for whose wisdom I entertain all imaginable reverence, often finds in Chance, by which it works, an instrument not over manageable. At least the latter very seldom seems to execute precisely and accurately what the former had determined."

"You seem to express a very singular opinion," said Wilhelm.

"Not at all!" replied the other. "Most of what happens in the world confirms my opinion. Do not many incidents at their commencement show some mighty purport, and generally terminate in something paltry?"

"You mean to jest."

"And as to what concerns the individual man," pursued the other, "is it not so with this likewise? Suppose Fate had appointed one to be a good player; and why should it not provide us with good players as well as other good things? Chance would perhaps conduct the youth into some puppet-show; where, at such an early age, he could not help taking interest in what was tasteless and despicable, reckoning insipidities endurable or even pleasing, and thus corrupting and misdirecting his primary impressions; impressions which can never be effaced, and whose influence, in spite of all our efforts, cling to us in some degree to the very last."

"What makes you think of puppet-shows?" said Wilhelm, not without some consternation.

"It was an accidental instance; if it does not please you, we shall take another. Suppose Fate had appointed any one to be a great painter, and it pleased Chance that he should pass his youth in sooty huts, in barns and stables; do you think that such a man would ever be enabled to exalt himself to purity, to nobleness, to freedom of soul? The more keenly he may in his youth have seized on the impure, and tried in his own manner to ennoble it, the more powerfully in the remainder of his life will it be revenged on him; because while he was endeavouring to conquer it, his whole being has become inseparably combined with it. Whoever spends his early years in mean and pitiful society, though at an after period he may have the choice of better, will yet constantly look back with longing towards that which he enjoyed of old, and which has left its impression blended with the memory of all his young and unreturning pleasures."

From conversation of this sort, it is easy to imagine, the rest of the company had gradually withdrawn. Philina, in particular, had stept aside at the very outset. Wilhelm and his comrade now rejoined them by a cross-path. Philina brought out her forfeits, and they had to be redeemed in many different ways. During which business, the stranger, by the most ingenious devices, and by his frank participation in their sports, recommended himself much to all the party, and particularly to the ladies; and thus, amid joking, singing, kissing, and railleries of all sorts, the hours passed away in the most pleasant manner.

CHAPTER X.

WHEN our friends began to think of going home, they looked about them for their clergyman; but he had vanished, and was nowhere to be found.

"It is not polite in the man, who otherwise displayed good breeding," said Madam Melina, "to desert a company that welcomed him so kindly, without taking leave."

"I have all the time been thinking," said Laertes, "where I can have seen this singular man before. I fully intended to ask him about it at parting."

"I too had the same feeling," said Wilhelm, "and certainly I should not have let him go, till he had told us something more about his circumstances. I am much mistaken if I have not ere now spoken with him somewhere."

"And you may in truth," said Philina, "be mistaken there. This person seems to have the air of an acquaintance, because he looks like a *man*, and not like Jack or Kit."

"What is this?" said Laertes. "Do not we too look like men?"

"I know what I am saying," cried Philina; "and if you cannot understand me, never mind. In the end my words will be found to require no commentary."

Two coaches now drove up. All praised the attention of Laertes, who had ordered them. Philina, with Madam Melina, took her place opposite to Wilhelm; the rest bestowed themselves as they best could. Laertes rode back on Wilhelm's horse, which had likewise been brought out.

Philina was scarcely seated in the coach, when she began to

sing some pretty songs, and gradually led the conversation to some stories, which she said might be successfully treated in the form of dramas. By this cunning turn she very soon put her young friend into his finest humour: from the wealth of his living imaginative store, he forthwith constructed a complete play, with all its acts, scenes, characters and plots. It was thought proper to insert a few catches and songs; they composed them; and Philina, who entered into every part of it, immediately fitted them with well-known tunes, and sang them on the spot.

It was one of her beautiful, most beautiful days; she had skill to enliven our friend with all manner of diverting wiles; he felt in spirits such as he had not for many a month enjoyed.

Since that shocking discovery had torn him from the side of Mariana, he had continued true to his vow to be on his guard against the encircling arms of woman, to avoid the faithless sex, to lock up his inclinations, his sweet wishes in his own bosom. The conscientiousness, with which he had observed this vow, gave his whole nature a secret nourishment; and as his heart could not remain without affection, some loving sympathy had now become a want with him. He went along once more, as if environed by the first cloudy glories of youth; his eye fixed joyfully on every charming object, and never had his judgment of a lovely form been more favourable. How dangerous, in such a situation, this wild girl must have been to him, is but too easy to conceive.

Arrived at home, they found Wilhelm's chamber all ready to receive them; the chairs set right for a public reading; in midst of them the table, on which the punch-bowl was in due time to take its place.

The German chivalry-plays were new at this period, and had just excited the attention and the inclination of the public. Old Boisterous had brought one of this sort with him; the reading of it had already been determined on. They all sat down: Wilhelm took possession of the pamphlet, and began to read.

The harnessed knights, the ancient keeps, the true-heartedness, honesty and downrightness, but especially the independence of the acting characters, were received with the greatest approbation. The reader did his utmost; and the audience gradually mounted into rapture. Between the third and fourth act, the punch arrived in an ample bowl; and there being much fighting and drinking in the piece itself, nothing was more natural than that, on every such occurrence, the company should transport themselves into the situation of the heroes, should flourish and strike along with them, and drink long life to their favourites among the *dramatis personæ*.

Each individual of the party was inflamed with the noblest fire of national spirit. How it gratified this German company to be poetically entertained, according to their own character, on stuff of their own manufacture! In particular, the vaults and caverns, the ruined castles, the moss and hollow trees, but above all the nocturnal gipsy-scenes, and the Secret Tribunal, produced a quite incredible effect. Every actor now figured to himself how, ere long, in helm and harness; every actress how, with a monstrous spreading ruff, she would present her Germanship before the public. Each would appropriate to himself without delay some name taken from the piece, or from German history; and Madam Melina declared that the son or daughter, she was then expecting, should not be christened otherwise than by the name of Adelbert or of Mathilde.

Towards the fifth act the approbation became more impetuous and louder; and at last, when the hero actually trampled down his oppressor, and the tyrant met his doom, the ecstasy increased to such a height, that all averred they had never passed such happy moments. Melina, whom the liquor had inspired, was the noisiest; and when the second bowl was empty, and midnight near, Laertes swore through thick and thin, that no living mortal was worthy ever more to put these glasses to his lips; and, so swearing, he pitched his own right over his head, through a window-pane, out into the street. The rest followed his example; and notwithstanding the protestations of the landlord, who came running in at the noise, the punch-bowl itself, never after this festivity to be polluted by unholy drink, was dashed into a thousand sherds. Philina, whose exhilaration was the least noticed, the other two girls by that time having laid themselves upon the sofa in no very elegant positions, maliciously encouraged her companions in their tumult. Madam Melina recited some spirit-stirring poems; and her husband, not too amiable in the uproar, began to cavil at the insufficient preparation of the punch, declaring that he could arrange an entertainment altogether in a different style; and at last becoming sulkier and louder as Laertes commanded silence, till the latter, without much consideration, threw the fragments of the punch-bowl about his head, and thereby not a little deepened the confusion.

Meanwhile the town-guard had arrived, and were demanding admission to the house. Wilhelm, much heated by his reading, though he had drunk but little, had enough to do with the landlord's help to content these people by money and good words; and afterwards to get the various members of his party sent home in that unseemly case. On coming back, overpowered with sleep and full of chagrin, he threw himself upon his bed without undressing; and nothing could exceed his disgust, when, opening his eyes next morning, he looked out with dull sight upon the devastations of the bygone day, and saw the uncleanness, and the many bad effects, of which that ingenious, lively and well-intentioned poetical performance had been the cause.

CHAPTER XI.

AFTER a short consideration he called the landlord, and bade him mark to his account both the damage and the regular charge. At the same time he learned, not without vexation, that his horse had been so hard ridden by Laertes last night, that, in all probability, it was foundered, as they term it, the farrier having little hope of its recovering.

A salute from Philina, which she threw him from her window, restored him in some degree to a more cheerful humour; he went forthwith into the nearest shop to buy her a little present, which, in return for the powder-knife, he still owed her; and it must be owned that, in selecting his gift, he did not keep himself within the limits of proportional value. He not only purchased her a pair of earrings; but added likewise a hat and neckerchief, and some other little articles, which he had seen her lavishly throw from her on the first day of their acquaintance.

Madam Melina, happening to observe him as he was delivering his presents, took an opportunity before breakfast to rate him very earnestly about his inclination for this girl; at which he felt the more astonished, the less he thought it merited. He swore solemnly, that he had never once entertained the slightest notion of attaching himself to such a person, whose whole manner of proceeding was well known to him: he excused himself as well as possible for his friendly and polite conduct towards her; yet did not by any means content Madam Melina, whose spite grew ever more determined, as she could not but observe that the flatteries by which she had acquired for herself a sort of partial regard from our friend, were not sufficient to defend this conquest from the attacks of a lively, younger and more gifted rival.

As they sat down to table, her husband joined them, likewise in a very fretful humour; which he was beginning to display on many little things, when the landlord entered to announce a player on the harp. "You will certainly," he said, "find pleasure in the music and the songs of this man: no one who hears him can forbear to admire him, and bestow something on him."

"Let him go about his business," said Melina; "I am anything but in a trim for hearing fiddlers, and we have singers constantly among ourselves disposed to gain a little by their talent." He accompanied these words with a sarcastic side-look at Philina: she understood his meaning; and immediately prepared to punish him, by taking up the cause of the Harper. Turning towards Wilhelm: "Shall we not hear the man?" said she; "shall we do nothing to save ourselves from this miserable *ennui?*"

Melina was going to reply, and the strife would have grown keener, had not the person it related to at that moment entered. Wilhelm saluted him, and beckoned him to come near.

The figure of this singular guest set the whole party in astonishment; he had found a chair before any one took heart to ask him a question, or make any observation. His bald crown was encircled by a few gray hairs; and a pair of large blue eyes looked out softly from beneath his long white eyebrows. To a nose of beautiful proportions, was subjoined a flowing hoary beard, which did not hide the fine shape and position of his lips; and a long dark-brown garment wrapped his thin body from the neck to the feet. He began to prelude on the harp, which he had placed before him.

The sweet tones which he drew from his instrument very soon inspirited the company.

"You can sing too, my good old man," said Philina.

"Give us something that shall entertain the spirit and the heart as well as the senses," said Wilhelm. "The instrument should but accompany the voice; for tunes and melodies without words and meaning seem to me like butterflies or finely-variegated birds, which hover round us in the air, which we could wish to catch and make our own; whereas song is like a blessed genius that exalts us towards heaven, and allures the better self in us to attend him."

The old man looked at Wilhelm; then aloft; then gave some trills upon his harp, and began his song. It contained a eulogy on minstrelsy; described the happiness of minstrels, and reminded men to honour them. He produced his song with so much life and truth, that it seemed as if he had composed it at the moment, for this special occasion. Wilhelm could scarcely refrain from clasping him in his arms; but the fear of awakening a peal of laughter detained him in his chair; for the rest were already in half-whispers making sundry very shallow observations, and debating if the Harper was a Papist or a Jew.

On asking about the author of the song, the man gave no distinct reply; declaring only that he was rich in songs, and anxious that they should please. Most of the party were now merry and joyful; even Melina was grown frank in his way; and whilst they talked and joked together, the old man began to sing the praise of social life, in the most sprightly style. He described the loveliness of unity and courtesy, in soft, soothing tones. Suddenly his music became cold, harsh and jarring, as he turned to deplore repulsive selfishness, short-sighted enmity and baleful division; and every heart willingly threw off those galling fetters, while borne on the wings of a piercing melody, he launched forth in praise of peace-makers, and sang the happiness of souls that, having parted, meet again in love.

Scarcely had he ended, when Wilhelm cried to him: "Whoever thou art, that as a helping spirit comest to us, with a voice which blesses and revives, accept my reverence and my thanks! Feel that we all admire thee, and confide in us if thou wantest anything."

The old man spoke not; he threw his fingers softly across the strings; then struck more sharply, and sang:

> "What notes are those without the wall,
>   Across the portal sounding?
> Let's have the music in our hall,
>   Back from its roof rebounding."
> So spoke the king, the henchman flies;
> His answer heard, the monarch cries:
>   "Bring in that ancient minstrel."
>
> "Hail, gracious king, each noble knight!
>   Each lovely dame, I greet you!
> What glittering stars salute my sight!
>   What heart unmov'd may meet you!
> Such lordly pomp is not for me,
> Far other scenes my eyes must see:
>   Yet deign to list my harping."
>
> The singer turns him to his art,
>   A thrilling strain he raises;
> Each warrior hears with glowing heart,
>   And on his lov'd one gazes.
> The king, who liked his playing well,
> Commands, for such a kindly spell,
>   A golden chain be given him.
>
> "The golden chain give not to me;
>   Thy boldest knight may wear it,
> Who 'cross the battle's purple sea
>   On lion-breast may bear it:

Or let it be thy chancellor's prize,
Amid his heaps to feast his eyes,
   Its yellow glance will please him.

" I sing but as the linnet sings,
   That on the green bough dwelleth;
A rich reward his music brings,
   As from his throat it swelleth:
Yet might I ask, I'd ask of thine
One sparkling draught of purest wine,
   To drink it here before you."

He view'd the wine, he quaff'd it up:
   " O draught of sweetest savour!
O! happy house, where such a cup
   Is thought a little favour!
If well you fare, remember me,
And thank kind Heaven, from envy free,
   As now for this I thank you."

When the Harper, on finishing his song, took up a glass of wine that stood poured out for him, and, turning with a friendly mien to his entertainers, drank it off, a buzz of joyful approbation rose from all the party. They clapped hands, and wished him health from that glass, and strength to his aged limbs. He sang a few other ballads, exciting more and more hilarity among the company.

"Old man," said Philina, "dost thou know the tune, *The shepherd deck'd him for the dance!*"[1]

"Oh yes!" said he; "if you will sing the words, I shall not fail for my part of it."

Philina then stood up, and held herself in readiness. The old man commenced the tune; and she sang a song, which we cannot impart to our readers, lest they might think it insipid, or perhaps undignified.

Meanwhile the company were growing merrier and merrier; they had already emptied several flasks of wine, and were now beginning to get very loud. But our friend, having fresh in his remembrance the bad consequences of their late exhilaration, determined to break up the sitting; he slipped into the old man's hand a liberal remuneration for his trouble, the rest did something likewise; they gave him leave to go and take repose, promising themselves another entertainment from his skill in the evening.

When he had retired, our friend said to Philina: "In this favourite song of yours I certainly find no merit, either moral or poetical; yet, if you were to bring forward any proper composition on the stage, with the same arch simplicity, the same propriety

---

[1] *Der Schäfer putzte sich zum Tanz;* a song of Goethe's.—ED.

and gracefulness, I should engage that strong and universal approbation would be the result."

"Yes," said Philina, "it would be a charming thing indeed to warm one's self at ice."

"After all," said Wilhelm, "this old man might put many a player to the blush. Did you notice how correctly the dramatic part of his ballads was expressed? I maintain, there was more living true representation in his singing, than in many of our starched characters upon the stage. You would take the acting of many plays for a narrative, and you might ascribe to these musical narratives a sensible presence."

"You are hardly just!" replied Laertes. "I pretend to no great skill either as a player or a singer; yet I know well enough, that, when music guides the movements of the body, at once affording to them animation and a scale to measure it; when declamation and expression are furnished me by the composer, I feel quite a different man from what I do when, in prose-dramas, I have all this to create for myself; have both gesture and declamation to invent, and am perhaps disturbed in it too by the awkwardness of some partner in the dialogue."

"Thus much I know," said Melina, "the man certainly may put us to the blush in one point, and that a main one. The strength of his talent is shown by the profit he derives from it. Even us, who perhaps ere long shall be embarrassed where to get a meal, he persuades to share our pittance with him. He has skill enough to wile the money from our pockets with an old song; the money that we should have used to find ourselves employment. So pleasant an affair is it to squander the means which might procure subsistence to oneself and others."

This remark gave the conversation not the most delightful turn. Wilhelm, for whom the reproach was peculiarly intended, replied with some heat; and Melina, at no time over studious of delicacy and politeness, explained his grievances at last in words more plain than courteous. "It is now a fortnight," said he, "since we looked at the theatrical machinery and wardrobe which is lying pawned here; the whole might be redeemed for a very tolerable sum. You then gave me hopes that you would lend me so much; and hitherto I do not see that you have thought more of the matter, or come any nearer a determination. Had you then consented, we should ere now have been under way. Nor has your intention to leave the place been executed; nor has your money in the mean time been spared: at least there are people who have always skill to create opportunities for scattering it faster and faster away."

Such upbraidings, not altogether undeserved, touched Wilhelm to the quick. He replied with keenness, nay with anger; and, as the company arose to part, he took hold of the door, and gave them not obscurely to understand that he would no longer continue with such unfriendly and ungrateful people. He hastened down, in no kindly humour, and seated himself upon the stone-bench without the door of his inn; not observing that, first out of mirth, then out of spleen, he had drunk more wine than usual.

CHAPTER XII.

AFTER a short time, which he passed sitting looking out before him, disquieted by many thoughts, Philina came singing and skipping along through the front door. She sat down by him, nay, we might almost say, on him, so close did she press herself towards him; she leant upon his shoulders, began playing with his hair, patted him, and gave him the best words in the world. She begged of him to stay with them, and not leave her alone in that company, or she must die of tedium: she could not live any longer in the same house with Melina, and had come over to lodge in the other inn for that very reason.

He tried in vain to satisfy her with denials; to make her understand that he neither could nor would remain any longer. She did not cease with her entreaties; nay, suddenly she threw her arm round his neck, and kissed him with the liveliest expression of fondness.

"Are you mad, Philina?" cried Wilhelm, endeavouring to disengage himself; "to make the open street the scene of such caresses, which I nowise merit! Let me go; I cannot and I will not stay."

"And I will hold thee fast," said she, "and kiss thee here on the open street, and kiss thee till thou promise what I want. I shall die of laughing," she continued; "by this familiarity the good people here must take me for thy wife of four weeks' standing; and husbands, who witness this touching scene, will commend me to their wives as a pattern of child-like simple tenderness."

Some persons were just then going by; she caressed him in the most graceful way; and he, to avoid giving scandal, was constrained to play the part of the patient husband. Then she made faces at the people, when their backs were turned; and, in the wildest humour, continued to commit all sorts of improprieties, till at last he was obliged to promise that he would not go that day, or the morrow, or the next day.

"You are a true clod!" said she, quitting him; "and I am but a fool to spend so much kindness on you." She arose with some vexation, and walked a few steps, then turned round laughing, and cried: "I believe it is just that, after all, that makes me so crazy about thee. I will but go and seek my knitting-needles and my stocking, that I may have something to do. Stay there, and let me find the stone man still upon the stone bench when I come back."

She cast a sparkling glance on him, and went into the house. He had no call to follow her; on the contrary, her conduct had excited fresh aversion in him: yet he rose from the bench to go after her, not well knowing why.

He was just entering the door, when Melina passed by, and spoke to him in a respectful tone, asking his pardon for the somewhat too harsh expressions he had used in their late discussion. "You will not take it ill of me," continued he, "if I appear perhaps too fretful in my present circumstances. The charge of providing for a wife, perhaps soon for a child, forbids me from day to day to live at peace, or spend my time, as you may do, in the enjoyment of pleasant feelings. Consider, I pray you; and, if possible, do put me in possession of that stage-machinery that is lying here. I shall not be your debtor long, and I shall be obliged to you while I live."

Our friend, unwilling to be kept upon the threshold, over which an irresistible impulse was drawing him at that moment to Philina, answered, with an absent mind, eager to be gone, and surprised into a transient feeling of good-will: "If I can make you happy and contented by doing this, I will hesitate no longer. Go you and put everything to rights. I shall be prepared this evening, or tomorrow morning, to pay the money." He then gave his hand to Melina in confirmation of his promise, and was very glad to see him hastily proceed along the street; but, alas, his entrance, which he now thought sure, was a second time prohibited, and more disagreeably than at first.

A young man, with a bundle on his back, came walking fast along the street, and advanced to Wilhelm, who at once recognised him for Friedrich. "Here am I again!" cried he, looking with his large blue eyes joyfully up and down, over all the windows of the house. "Where is Mamsell? Devil take me, if I can stroll about the world any longer without seeing her."

The landlord, joining them at this instant, replied that she was above; Friedrich with a few bounds was up-stairs, and Wilhelm continued standing as if rooted to the threshold. At the first instant he was tempted to pluck the younker back, and drag him down by the hair; then all at once the spasm of a sharp jealousy stopped the current of his spirits and ideas; and, as he gradually recovered from this stupefaction, there came over him a splenetic fit of restlessness, a general discomfort, such as he had never felt in his life before.

He went up to his room, and found Mignon busy writing. For some time, the creature had been labouring with great diligence in writing everything she knew by heart, giving always to her master and friend the papers to correct. She was indefatigable, and of good comprehension; but still her letters were irregular, and her lines crooked. Here too the body seemed to contradict the mind. In his usual moods, Wilhelm took no small pleasure in the child's attention; but, at the present moment, he regarded little what she showed him,—a piece of neglect which she felt the more acutely, as on this occasion she conceived her work had been accomplished with peculiar success.

Wilhelm's unrest drove him up and down the passages of the house, and finally again to the street-door. A rider was just prancing towards it, a man of good appearance, of middle age, and a brisk contented look. The landlord ran to meet him, holding out his hand as to an old acquaintance. "Ay, Herr Stallmeister," cried he, "have we the pleasure to see you again?"

"I am just going to bait with you," replied the stranger, "and then along to the Estate, to get matters put in order as soon as possible. The Count is coming over tomorrow with his lady; they mean to stay a while to entertain the Prince von * * * in their best style: he intends to fix his head-quarters in this neighbourhood for some time."

"It is pity," said the landlord, "that you cannot stop with us: we have good company in the house." The ostler came running out, and took the horse from the Stallmeister, who continued talking in the door with the landlord, and now and then giving a look at Wilhelm.

Our friend, observing that he formed the topic of their conversation, went away, and walked up and down the streets.

CHAPTER XIII.

IN the restless vexation of his present humour, it came into his head to go and see the old Harper, hoping by his music to scare away the evil spirits that tormented him. On asking for the man, he was directed to a mean public-house in a remote corner of the little town; and, having mounted up stairs there to the very garret, his ear caught the fine twanging of the harp coming from a little room before him. They were heart-moving, mournful tones, accompanied by a sad and dreary singing. Wilhelm glided to the door; and, as the good old man was performing a sort of voluntary, the few stanzas of which, sometimes chanted, sometimes in recitative, were repeated more than once, our friend succeeded, after listening for a while, in gathering nearly this:

>Who never ate his bread in sorrow,
> Who never spent the darksome hours
>Weeping and watching for the morrow,
> He knows ye not, ye gloomy Powers.
>
>To earth, this weary earth, ye bring us,
> To guilt ye let us heedless go,
>Then leave repentance fierce to wring us:
> A moment's guilt, an age of woe!

The heart-sick plaintive sound of this lament pierced deep into the soul of the hearer. It seemed to him as if the old man were often stopped from proceeding by his tears; his harp would alone be heard for a time, till his voice again joined it in low broken tones. Wilhelm stood by the door; he was much moved; the mourning of this stranger had again opened the avenues of his heart; he could not resist the claim of sympathy, or restrain the tears which this woe-begone complaint at last called forth. All the pains that pressed upon his soul seemed now at once to loosen from their hold; he abandoned himself without reserve to the feelings of the moment. Pushing up the door, he stood before the Harper. The old man was sitting on a mean bed, the only seat, or article of furniture, which his miserable room afforded.

"What feelings hast thou not awakened in me, good old man!" exclaimed he. "All that was lying frozen at my heart thou hast melted, and put in motion. Let me not disturb thee; but continue, in solacing thy own sorrows, to confer happiness upon a friend." The Harper was about to rise, and say something; but Wilhelm hindered him, for he had noticed in the morning that the old man did not like to speak. He sat down by him on the straw bed.

The old man wiped his eyes, and asked, with a friendly smile, "How came you hither? I meant to wait upon you in the evening again."

"We are more quiet here," said Wilhelm. "Sing to me what

thou pleasest, what accords with thy own mood of mind, only proceed as if I were not by. It seems to me, that today thou canst not fail to suit me. I think thee very happy that, in solitude, thou canst employ and entertain thyself so pleasantly; that, being everywhere a stranger, thou findest in thy own heart the most agreeable society."

The old man looked upon his strings, and, after touching them softly by way of prelude, he commenced and sang:

> Who longs in solitude to live,
>   Ah! soon his wish will gain;
> Men hope and love, men get and give,
>   And leave him to his pain.
> Yes, leave me to my moan!
>   When from my bed
>   You all are fled,
> I still am not alone.
>
> The lover glides with footstep light:
>   His love is she not waiting there?
> So glides to meet me, day and night,
>   In solitude my care,
>   In solitude my woe:
> True solitude I then shall know
>   When lying in my grave,
>   When lying in my grave,
> And grief has let me go.

We might describe with great prolixity, and yet fail to express the charms of the singular conversation, which Wilhelm carried on with this wayfaring stranger. To every observation which our friend addressed to him, the old man, with the nicest accordance, answered in some melody, which awakened all the cognate emotions, and opened a wide field to the imagination.

Whoever has happened to assist at a meeting of certain devout people, who conceive that, in a state of separation from the Church, they can edify each other in a purer, more affecting, and more spiritual manner, may form to himself some conception of the present scene. He will recollect how the leader of the meeting would append to his words some verse of a song, that raised the soul till, as he wished, she took wing; how another of the flock would ere long subjoin, in a different tune, some verse of a different song; and to this again a third would link some verse of a third song; by which means the kindred ideas of the songs to which the verses belonged were indeed suggested, yet each passage by its new combination became new and individualised, as if it had been first composed that moment; and thus, from a well-known circle of ideas, from well-known songs and sayings, there was formed, for that particular society in that particular time, an original whole, by means of which their minds were animated, strengthened and refreshed. So likewise did the old man edify his guest: by known and unknown songs and passages, he brought feelings near and distant, emotions sleeping and awake, pleasant and painful, into a circulation, from which, in Wilhelm's actual state, the best effects might be anticipated.

CHAPTER XIV.

ACCORDINGLY, in walking back, he began to think with greater earnestness than ever on his present situation: he had reached home with the firm purpose of altering it, when the landlord disclosed to him, by way of secret, that Mademoiselle Philina had made a conquest of the Count's Stallmeister; who, after executing his commission at his master's Estate, had returned in the greatest haste, and was even now partaking of a good supper with her up in her chamber.

At this very moment Melina came in with a notary: they went into Wilhelm's chamber together, where the latter, though with some hesitation, made his promise good; gave a draught of three hundred crowns to Melina, who, handing it to the lawyer, received in return a note acknowledging the sale of the whole theatrical apparatus, and engaging to deliver it next morning.

Scarcely had they parted, when Wilhelm heard a cry of horror rising from some quarter of the house. He caught the sound of a young voice, uttering menacing and furious tones, which were ever and anon choked by immoderate weeping and howling. He observed this frantic noise move hastily from above; go past his door, and down to the lower part of the house.

Curiosity enticing our friend to follow it, he found Friedrich in a species of delirium. The boy was weeping, grinding his teeth, stamping with his feet, threatening with clenched fists; he appeared beside himself from fury and vexation. Mignon was standing opposite him, looking on with astonishment. The landlord, in some degree, explained this phenomenon.

The boy, he said, being well received at his return by Philina, seemed quite merry and contented; he had kept singing and jumping about, till the time when Philina grew acquainted with the Stallmeister. Then, however, this half-grown younker had begun to show his indignation, to slam the doors, and run up and down in the highest dudgeon. Philina had ordered him to wait at table that evening; upon which he had grown still sulkier and more indignant; till at last, carrying up a plate with a ragout, instead of setting it upon the table, he had thrown the whole between Mademoiselle and her guest, who were sitting moderately close together at the time; and the Stallmeister, after two or three hearty cuffs, had then kicked him out of the room. He, the landlord, had himself helped to clean both of them, and certainly their clothes had suffered much.

On hearing of the good effect of his revenge, the boy began to laugh aloud, whilst the tears were still running down his cheeks. He heartily rejoiced for a time, till the disgrace which he had suffered from the stronger party once more came into his head, and he began afresh to howl and threaten.

Wilhelm stood meditating, and ashamed at this spectacle. It reflected back to him his own feelings, in coarser and exaggerated features: he too was inflamed with a fierce jealousy; and, had not decency restrained him, he would willingly have satisfied his wild humour; with malicious spleen, would have abused the object of his passion, and called out his rival: he could have crushed in pieces all the people round him; they seemed as if standing there but to vex him.

Laertes also had come in, and heard the story; he roguishly spurred on the irritated boy, who was now asserting with oaths that he would make the Stallmeister give him satisfaction; that he had never yet let any injury abide with him; that should the man refuse, there were other ways of taking vengeance.

This was the very business for Laertes. He went up-stairs, with a solemn countenance, to call out the Stallmeister in the boy's name.

"This is a pleasant thing," said the Stallmeister: " such a joke as this I had scarcely promised myself tonight." They went down, and Philina followed them. "My son," said the Stallmeister to Friedrich, " thou art a brave lad, and I do not hesitate to fight thee. Only as our years and strength are unequal, and the attempt a little dangerous on that account, I propose a pair of foils in preference to other weapons. We can rub the buttons of them with a piece of chalk; and whoever marks upon the other's coat the first or the most thrusts, shall be held the victor, and be treated by the other with the best wine that can be had in town."

Laertes decided that the proposition might be listened to: Friedrich obeyed him as his tutor. The foils were produced; Philina took a seat, went on with her knitting, and looked at the contending parties with the greatest peace of mind.

The Stallmeister, who could fence very prettily, was complaisant enough to spare his adversary, and to let a few chalk-scores be marked upon his coat; after which the two embraced, and wine was ordered. The Stallmeister took the liberty of asking Friedrich's parentage and history; and Friedrich told him a long story, which had often been repeated already, and which, at some other opportunity, we purpose communicating to our readers.

To Wilhelm, in the mean time, this contest completed the representation of his own state of mind. He could not but perceive that he would willingly have taken up a foil against the Stallmeister; a sword still more willingly, though evidently much his inferior in the science of defence. Yet he deigned not to cast one look on Philina; he was on his guard against any word or movement that could possibly betray his feelings; and after having once or twice done justice to the health of the duellists, he hastened to his own room, where a thousand painful thoughts came pressing round him.

He called to memory the time when his spirit, rich in hope, and full of boundless aims, was raised aloft, and encircled with the liveliest enjoyments of every kind as with its proper element. He now clearly saw, that of late he had fallen into a broken wandering path, where, if he tasted, it was but in drops what he once quaffed in unrestricted measure. But he could not clearly see what insatiable want it was that nature had made the law of his being; and how this want had been only set on edge, half satisfied, and misdirected by the circumstances of his life.

It will not surprise us, therefore, that, in considering his situation, and labouring to extricate himself, he fell into the greatest perplexity. It was not enough, that, by his friendship for Laertes, his attachment to Philina, his concern for Mignon, he had been detained longer than was proper in a place and a society where he could cherish his darling inclination, content his wishes as it were by stealth, and without proposing any object, again pursue his early dreams. These ties he believed himself possessed of force enough to break asunder: had there been nothing more to hold him, he could have gone at once. But, only a few moments ago, he had entered into money-transactions with Melina; he had seen that mysterious old man, the enigma of whose history he longed with unspeakable desire to clear. Yet of this too, after much balancing of reasons, he at length determined, or thought he had determined, that it should not keep him back. "I must go," he exclaimed; "I will go." He threw himself into a chair; he felt greatly moved. Mignon came in, and asked, Whether she might help to undress him? Her manner was still and shy; it had grieved her to the quick to be so abruptly dismissed by him before.

Nothing is more touching than the first disclosure of a love which has been nursed in silence, of a faith grown strong in secret, and which at last comes forth in the hour of need, and reveals itself to him who formerly has reckoned it of small account. The bud, which had been closed so long and firmly, was now ripe to burst its swathings, and Wilhelm's heart could never have been readier to welcome the impressions of affection.

She stood before him, and noticed his disquietude. "Master!" she cried, "if thou art unhappy, what will become of Mignon?" "Dear little creature," said he, taking her hands, "thou too art part of my anxieties. I must go hence." She looked at his eyes, glistening with restrained tears; and knelt down with vehemence before him. He kept her hands; she laid her head upon his knees, and remained quite still. He played with her hair, patted her, and spoke kindly to her. She continued motionless for a considerable time. At last he felt a sort of palpitating movement in her, which began very softly, and then by degrees with increasing violence diffused itself over all her frame. "What ails thee, Mignon?" cried he; "what ails thee?" She raised her little head, looked at him, and all at once laid her hand upon her heart, with the countenance of one repressing the utterance of pain. He raised her up, and she fell upon his breast; he pressed her towards him, and kissed her. She replied not by any pressure of the hand, by any motion whatever. She held firmly against her heart; and all at once gave a cry, which was accompanied by spasmodic movements of the body. She started up, and immediately fell down before him, as if broken in every joint. It was an excruciating moment! "My child!" cried he, raising her up, and clasping her fast; "my child, what ails thee?" The palpitations continued, spreading from the heart over all the lax and powerless limbs; she was merely hanging in his arms. All at once she again became quite stiff, like one enduring the sharpest corporeal agony; and soon with a new vehemence all her frame once more became alive; and she threw herself about his neck, like a bent spring that is closing; while in her soul, as it were a strong rent took place, and at the same moment a stream of tears flowed from her shut eyes into his bosom. He held her fast. She wept, and no tongue can express the force of these tears. Her long hair had loosened, and was hanging down before her; it seemed as if her whole being was melting incessantly into a brook of tears. Her rigid limbs were again become relaxed; her inmost soul was pouring itself forth; in the wild confusion of the moment, Wilhelm was afraid she would dissolve in his arms, and leave nothing there for him to grasp. He held her faster and faster. "My child!"

cried he, "my child! Thou art indeed mine, if that word can comfort thee. Thou art mine! I will keep thee, I will never forsake thee!" Her tears continued flowing. At last she raised herself; a faint gladness shone upon her face. "My father!" cried she, "thou wilt not forsake me? Wilt be my father? I am thy child!"

Softly, at this moment, the harp began to sound before the door; the old man brought his most affecting songs as an evening offering to our friend, who, holding his child ever faster in his arms, enjoyed the most pure and undescribable felicity.

BOOK III.

CHAPTER I.

> Know'st thou the land where citron-apples bloom,
> And oranges like gold in leafy gloom,
> A gentle wind from deep blue heaven blows,
> The myrtle thick, and high the laurel grows!
> Know'st thou it then!
>   'Tis there! 'tis there,
> O my true lov'd one, thou with me must go!
>
> Know'st thou the house, its porch with pillars tall!
> The rooms do glitter, glitters bright the hall,
> And marble statues stand, and look each one:
> What's this, poor child, to thee they've done!
> Know'st thou it then!
>   'Tis there! 'tis there,
> O my protector, thou with me must go!
>
> Know'st thou the hill, the bridge that hangs on cloud?
> The mules in mist grope o'er the torrent loud,
> In caves lie coil'd the dragon's ancient brood,
> The crag leaps down and over it the flood:
> Know'st thou it then!
>   'Tis there! 'tis there,
> Our way runs; O my father, wilt thou go!

NEXT morning, on looking for Mignon about the house, Wilhelm did not find her; but was informed that she had gone out early with Melina, who had risen betimes to receive the wardrobe and other apparatus of his theatre.

After the space of some hours, Wilhelm heard the sound of music before his door. At first he thought it was the Harper come again to visit him; but he soon distinguished the tones of a cithern, and the voice which began to sing was Mignon's. Wilhelm opened the door; the child came in, and sang him the song we have just given above.

The music and general expression of it pleased our friend extremely, though he could not understand all the words. He made her once more repeat the stanzas, and explain them; he wrote them down, and translated them into his native language. But the originality of its turns he could imitate only from afar; its childlike innocence of expression vanished from it in the process of reducing its broken phraseology to uniformity, and combining its disjointed parts. The charm of the tune, moreover, was entirely incomparable.

She began every verse in a stately and solemn manner, as if she wished to draw attention towards something wonderful, as if she had something weighty to communicate. In the third line, her tones became deeper and gloomier; the *Know'st thou it then?* was uttered with a show of mystery and eager circumspectness; in the *'Tis there! 'tis there!* lay a boundless longing; and her *With me must go!* she modified at each repetition, so that now it appeared to entreat and implore, now to impel and persuade.

On finishing her song for the second time, she stood silent for a moment, looked keenly at Wilhelm, and asked him, "*Know'st* thou the land?" "It must mean Italy," said Wilhelm: "where didst thou get the little song?" "Italy!" said Mignon with an earnest air: "if thou go to Italy, take me along with thee; for I am too cold here." "Hast thou been there already, little dear?" said Wilhelm. But the child was silent, and nothing more could be got out of her.

Melina entered now; he looked at the cithern; was glad that she had rigged it up again so prettily. The instrument had been among Melina's stage-gear; Mignon had begged it of him in the morning; and then gone to the old Harper. On this occasion, she had shown a talent she was not before suspected of possessing.

Melina had already got possession of his wardrobe, with all that pertained to it; some members of the town magistracy had promised him permission to act, for a time, in the place. He was now returning with a merry heart and a cheerful look. His nature seemed altogether changed; he was soft, courteous to every one, nay fond of obliging, and almost attractive. He was happy, he said, at now being able to afford employment to his friends, who had hitherto lain idle and embarrassed; sorry, however, that at first he could not have it in his power to remunerate the excellent actors whom fortune had offered him, in a style corresponding to their talents and capacities; being under the necessity, before all other things, of discharging his debt to so generous a friend as Wilhelm had proved himself to be.

"I cannot describe," said he to Wilhelm, "the friendliness which you have shown, in helping me forward to the management of a theatre. When I found you here, I was in a very curious predicament. You recollect how strongly I displayed to you, on our first acquaintance, my aversion to the stage; and yet on being married, I was forced to look about for a place in some theatre, out of love to my wife, who promised to herself much joy and great applause, if so engaged. I could find none, at least no constant one; but in return I luckily fell in with some commercial men, who, in extraordinary cases, were enabled to employ a person that could handle his pen, that understood French, and was not without a little skill in ciphering. I managed pretty well in this way, for a time; I was tolerably paid; got about me many things which I had need of, and did not feel ashamed of my work. But these commissions of my patrons came to an end; they could afford me no permanent establishment: and ever since, my wife has continued urging me still more to go upon the stage again; though, at present, alas, her own situation is none of the favourablest for exhibiting herself, with honour, in the eyes of the public. But now, I hope, the establishment, which by your kind help I have the means of setting up, will prove a good beginning for me and mine; you I shall thank for all my future happiness, let matters turn out as they will."

Wilhelm listened to him with contentment: the whole fraternity of players were likewise moderately satisfied with the declarations of the new manager; they secretly rejoiced that an offer of employment had occurred so soon; and were disposed to put up, at first, with a smaller salary; the rather, that most of them regarded the present one, so unexpectedly placed within their reach, as a kind of supplement, on which a short while ago they could not count. Melina made haste to profit by this favourable temper; he endeavoured in a sly way to get a little talk with each in private; and ere long had, by various methods, so cockered them all, that they did not hesitate to strike a bargain with him, without loss of time; scarcely thinking of this new engagement, or reckoning themselves secure at worst of getting free again after six weeks' warning.

The terms were now to be reduced to proper form, and Melina was considering with what pieces he would first entice the public, when a courier riding up informed the Stallmeister, that his lord and lady were at hand; on which the latter ordered out his horses.

In a short time after this, the coach with its masses of luggage rolled in; two servants sprang down from the coach-box before the inn; and Philina, according to her custom, foremost in the way of novelties, placed herself within the door.

"Who are you?" said the Countess entering the house.

"An actress, at your Excellency's service," was the answer;

while the cheat, with a most innocent air, and looks of great humility, courtesied, and kissed the lady's gown.

The Count, on seeing some other persons standing round, who also signified that they were players, inquired about the strength of their company, their last place of residence, their manager. "Had they but been Frenchmen," said he to his lady, "we might have treated the Prince with an unexpected enjoyment, and entertained him with his favourite pastime at our house."

"And could we not," said the Countess, "get these people, though unluckily they are but Germans, to exhibit with us at the Castle, while the Prince stays there? Without doubt, they have some degree of skill. A large party can never be so well amused with anything as with a theatre; besides the Baron would assist them."

So speaking they went up-stairs; and Melina presented himself above, as manager. "Call your folk together," said the Count, "and place them before me, that I may see what is in them. I must also have the list of pieces you profess to act."

Melina, with a low bow, hastened from the room, and soon returned with his actors. They advanced in promiscuous succession; some, out of too great anxiety to please, introduced themselves in a rather sorry style; the others, not much better, by assuming an air of unconcern. Philina showed the deepest reverence to the Countess, who behaved with extreme graciousness and condescension; the Count, in the mean time, was mustering the rest. He questioned each about his special province of acting; and signified to Melina, that he must rigorously keep them to their several provinces; a precept which the manager received with the greatest devotion.

The Count then stated to each in particular what he ought especially to study, what about his figure or his postures ought to be amended; showed them luminously in what points the Germans always fail; and displayed such extraordinary knowledge, that all stood in the deepest humility, scarcely daring to draw their breath, before so enlightened a critic and so right honourable a patron.

"What fellow is that in the corner?" said the Count, looking at a subject, who had not yet been presented to him, and who now approached; a lean shambling figure, with a rusty coat patched at the elbows, and a woful periwig covering his submissive head.

This person, whom, from the last Book, we know already as Philina's darling, had been wont to enact pedants, tutors and poets; generally undertaking parts in which any cudgelling or ducking was to be endured. He had trained himself to certain crouching, ludicrous, timid bows; and his faltering, stammering speech befitted the characters he played, and created laughter in the audience; so that he was always looked on as a useful member of the company, being moreover very serviceable and obliging. He approached the Count in his own peculiar way; bent himself before him, and answered every question with the grimaces and gestures he was used to on the stage. The Count looked at him, for some time, with an air of attentive satisfaction and studious observation; then turning to the Countess, " Child," said he, " consider this man well: I will engage for it, he is a great actor, or may become so." The creature here, in the fulness of his heart, made an idiotic bow; the Count burst into laughing, and exclaimed . " He does it excellently well! I bet this fellow can act anything he likes; it is pity that he has not been already used to something better."

So singular a prepossession was extremely galling to the rest; Melina alone felt no vexation, but completely coincided with the Count, and answered with a prostrate look: " Alas! it is too true; both he and others of us have long stood in need of such encouragement, and such a judge, as we now find in your Excellency."

" Is this the whole company?" inquired the Count.

" Some of them are absent," said the crafty Melina; " and at any rate, if we should meet with support, we could soon collect abundant numbers from the neighbourhood."

Philina in the mean while was saying to the Countess: " There is a very pretty young man above, who without doubt would shortly become a first-rate amateur."

" Why does he not appear?" said the Countess.

" I will bring him," cried Philina, hastening to the door.

She found our friend still occupied with Mignon; she persuaded him to come down. He followed her with some reluctance; yet curiosity impelled him: for hearing that the family were people of rank, he longed much to know more of them. On entering the room his eyes met those of the Countess, which were directed towards him. Philina led him to the lady, while the Count was busied with the rest. Wilhelm made his bow; and replied to several questions from the fair dame, not without confusion of mind. Her beauty and youth, her graceful dignity and refined manner, made the most delightful impression on him; and the more so, as her words and looks were accompanied with a certain bashfulness, one might almost say embarrassment. He was likewise introduced to the Count, who however took no special notice of him; but went to the window with his lady, and seemed to ask her about something. It was easy to observe that her opinion accorded strongly with his own; that she even tried to persuade him, and strengthen him in his intentions.

In a short while, he turned round to the company, and said: "I must not stay at present, but I will send a friend to you; and if you make reasonable proposals, and will take very great pains, I am not disinclined to let you play at the Castle."

All testified their joy at this; Philina in particular kissed the hands of the Countess with the greatest vivacity.

"Look you, little thing," said the lady, patting the cheeks of the light-minded girl, "look you, child, you shall come to me again; I will keep my promise; only you must dress better." Philina stated in excuse that she had little to lay out upon her wardrobe; and the Countess immediately ordered her waiting-maids to bring from the carriage a silk neckerchief and an English hat, the articles easiest to come at, and give them to her new favourite. The Countess herself then decked Philina, who continued very neatly to support, by her looks and conduct, that saint-like, guiltless character she had assumed at first.

The Count took his lady's hand and led her down. She bowed to the whole company with a friendly air, in passing by them; she turned round again towards Wilhelm, and said to him, with the most gracious mien: "We shall soon meet again."

These happy prospects enlivened the whole party: every one of them gave free course to his hopes, his wishes, his imaginations; spoke of the parts he would play, and the applause he would acquire. Melina was considering how he might still, by a few speedy exhibitions, gain a little money from the people of the town, before he left it; while others went into the kitchen, to order a better dinner than of late they had been used to.

CHAPTER II.

AFTER a few days, the Baron came; and it was not without fear that Melina received him. The Count had spoken of him as a critic; and it might be dreaded, he would speedily detect the weakness of the little party, and see that it formed no efficient troop, there being scarcely a play which they could act in a suitable manner. But the manager, as well as all the members, were soon delivered from their cares, on finding that the Baron was a man who viewed the German stage with a most patriotic enthusiasm, to whom every player, and every company of players, was welcome and agreeable. He saluted them all with great solemnity; was happy to come upon a German theatre so unexpectedly, to get connected with it, and to introduce their native Muses to the mansion of his relative. He then pulled out from his pocket a bundle of stitched papers, in which Melina hoped to find the terms of their contract specified; but it proved something very different. It was a drama, which the Baron himself had composed, and wished to have played by them: he requested their attention while he read it. Willingly they formed a circle round him; charmed at being able with so little trouble to secure the favour of a man so important; though judging by the thickness of the manuscript, it was clear that a very long rehearsal might be dreaded. Their apprehensions were not groundless; the piece was written in five acts, and that sort of acts which never have an end.

The hero was an excellent, virtuous, magnanimous and at the same time misunderstood and persecuted man; this worthy person, after many trials, gained the victory at last over all his enemies; on whom, in consequence, the most rigorous poetic justice would have been exercised, had he not pardoned them on the spot.

While this piece was rehearsing, each of the auditors had leisure enough to think of himself, and to mount up quite softly from the humble prostration of mind, to which, a little while ago, he had felt disposed, into a comfortable state of contentment with his own gifts and advantages; and from this elevation, to discover the most pleasing prospects in the future. Such of them as found in the play no parts adapted for their own acting, internally pronounced it bad, and viewed the Baron as a miserable author; while the others, every time they noticed any passage which they hoped might procure them a little clapping of the hands, exalted it with the greatest praise, to the immeasurable satisfaction of the author.

The commercial part of their affair was soon completed. Melina made an advantageous bargain with the Baron, and contrived to keep it secret from the rest.

Of our friend, Melina took occasion to declare in passing, that he seemed to be successfully qualifying himself for becoming a dramatic poet, and even to have some capacities for being an actor. The Baron introduced himself to Wilhelm as a colleague; and the latter by and by produced some little pieces, which, with a few other relics, had escaped by chance, on the day when he threw the greater part of his works into the flames. The Baron lauded both his pieces and delivery; he spoke of it as a settled thing, that Wilhelm should come over to the Castle with the rest. For all, at his departure, he engaged to find the best reception, comfortable quarters, a good table, applauses and presents; and Melina further gave the promise of a certain modicum of pocket-money to each.

It is easy to conceive how this visit raised the spirits of the party; instead of a low and harassing situation, they now at once saw honours and enjoyment before them. On the score of these great hopes they already made merry; and each thought it needless and stingy to retain a single groschen of money in his purse.

Meanwhile our friend was taking council with himself, about accompanying the troop to the Castle; and he found it, in more than one sense, advisable to do so. Melina was in hopes of paying off his debt, at least in part, by this engagement; and Wilhelm, who had come from home to study men, was unwilling to let slip this opportunity of examining the great world, where he expected to obtain much insight into life, into himself and the dramatic art. With all this, he durst not confess how greatly he wished again to be near the beautiful Countess. He rather sought to persuade himself in general of the mighty advantages, which a more intimate acquaintance with the world of rank and wealth would procure for him. He pursued his reflections on the Count, the Countess, the Baron; on the security, the grace and propriety of their demeanour; he exclaimed with rapture when alone:

"Thrice happy are they to be esteemed, whom their birth of itself exalts above the lower stages of mankind; who do not need to traverse those perplexities, not even to skirt them, in which many worthy men so painfully consume the whole period of life. Far-extending and unerring must their vision be, on that higher station; easy each step of their progress in the world! From their very birth, they are placed as it were in a ship, which, in this voyage we have all to make, enables them to profit by the favourable winds, and to ride out the cross ones; while others, bare of help, must wear their strength away in swimming, can derive little profit from the favourable breeze, and in the storm must soon become exhausted and sink to the bottom. What convenience, what ease of movement does a fortune we are born to, confer upon us! How securely does a traffic flourish, which is founded on a solid capital, where the failure of one or of many enterprises does not of necessity reduce us to inaction! Who can better know the worth and worthlessness of earthly things, than he that has had within his choice the enjoyment of them from youth upwards; and who can earlier guide his mind to the useful, the necessary, the true, than he that may convince himself of so many errors in an age when his strength is yet fresh to begin a new career!"

Thus did our friend cry joy to all inhabitants of the upper regions; and not to them only, but to all that were permitted to approach their circle, and draw water from their wells. So he thanked his own happy stars, that seemed preparing to grant this mighty blessing to himself.

Melina, in the mean time, was torturing his brains to get the company arranged according to their several provinces, and each of them appointed to produce his own peculiar effect. In compliance with the Count's injunctions and his own persuasions, he made many efforts: but at last, when it came to the point of execution, he was forced to be content, if, in so small a troop, he found his people willing to adjust themselves to this or that part, as they best were able. When matters would admit of it, Laertes played the lover; Philina the lady's-maid; the two young girls took up between them the characters of the artless and tender loved-ones; the boisterous old gentleman of the piece was sure to be the best acted. Melina himself thought he might come forth as chevalier; Madam Melina, to her no small sorrow, was obliged to satisfy herself with personating young wives, or even affectionate mothers; and as in the newer plays a poet or pedant is rarely introduced, and still more rarely for the purpose of being laughed at, the well-known favourite of the Count was now usually transformed into president or minister; these being commonly set forth as knaves, and severely handled in the fifth act. Melina too, in the part of chamberlain or the like, introduced, with great satisfaction, the ineptitudes put into his hands by various honest Germans, according to use and wont, in many well-accepted plays: he delighted in these characters, because he had an opportunity of decking himself out in a fashionable style, and was called upon to assume the airs of a courtier, which he conceived himself to possess in great perfection.

It was not long till they were joined by several actors from different quarters; who being received without very strict examination, were also retained without very burdensome conditions.

Wilhelm had been more than once assailed with persuasions from Melina to undertake an amateur part. This he declined; yet he interested and occupied himself about the general cause with great alacrity, without our new manager's acknowledging his labours in the smallest. On the contrary, it seemed to be Melina's opinion, that with his office he had at the same time picked up all the necessary skill for carrying it on. In particular, the task of curtailment formed one of his most pleasing occupations; he would succeed in reducing any given piece down to the regular measure of time, without the slightest respect to proprieties or proportions, or any thing whatever but his watch. He met with great encouragement; the public was very much delighted; the most knowing inhabitants of the burgh maintained that the Prince's theatre itself was not so well conducted as theirs.

CHAPTER III.

At last the time arrived when the company had to prepare themselves for travelling, and to expect the coaches and other vehicles that were to carry them to the Count's mansion. Much altercation now took place about the mode of travelling, and who should sit with whom. The ordering and distribution of the whole was at length settled and concluded, with great labour, and, alas, without effect. At the appointed hour, fewer coaches came than were expected; they had to accommodate themselves as the case would admit. The Baron, who followed shortly afterwards on horseback, assigned as the reason, that all was in motion at the Castle, not only because the Prince was to arrive a few days earlier than had been looked for, but also because an unexpected party of visitors were already come; the place, he said, was in great confusion; on this account perhaps they would not lodge so comfortably as had been intended; a change which grieved him very much.

Our travellers packed themselves into the carriages the best way they could; and the weather being tolerable, and the Castle but a few leagues distant, the heartiest of the troop preferred setting out on foot to waiting the return of the coaches. The caravan got under way with great jubilee; for the first time, without caring how the landlord's bill was to be paid. The Count's mansion rose like a palace of the fairies on their souls; they were the happiest and merriest mortals in the world. Each throughout the journey, in his own peculiar mode, kept fastening a continued chain of fortune, honour and prosperity to that auspicious day.

A heavy rain, which fell unexpectedly, did not banish these delightful contemplations; though, as it incessantly continued with more and more violence, many of the party began to show traces of uneasiness. The night came on; and no sight could be more welcome than the palace of the Count, which shone upon them from a hill at some distance, glancing with light in all its stories, so that they could reckon every window.

On approaching nearer, they found all the windows in the wings illuminated also. Each of the party thought within himself what chamber would be his; and most of them prudently determined to be satisfied with a room in the attic story, or some of the side buildings.

They were now proceeding through the village, past the inn. Wilhelm stopped the coach, in the mind to alight there; but the landlord protested that it was not in his power to afford the least accommodation: his lordship the Count, he said, being visited by some unexpected guests, had immediately engaged the whole inn; every chamber in the house had been marked with chalk last night, specifying who was to lodge there. Our friend was accordingly obliged, against his will, to travel forward to the Castle, with the rest of the company.

In one of the side buildings, round the kitchen fire, they noticed several cooks running busily about; a sight which refreshed them not a little. Servants came jumping hastily with lights to the staircase of the main-door; and the hearts of the worthy pilgrims overflowed at the aspect of such honours. But how great was their surprise, when this cordial reception changed into a storm of curses. The servants scouted the coachmen for driving in hither; they must wheel out again, it was bawled, and take their loading round to the old Castle; there was no room here for such guests! To this unfriendly and unexpected dismissal, they joined all manner of jeering, and laughed aloud at each other for leaping out in the rain on so false an errand. It was still pouring; no star was visible in the sky; while our company were dragged along a rough jolting road, between two walls, into the old mansion, which stood behind, inhabited by none since the present Count's father had built the new residence in front of it. The carriages drew up, partly in the court-yard, partly in a long arched gateway; and the postillions, people hired from the village, unyoked their horses and rode off.

As nobody came forward to receive the travellers, they alighted from their places, they shouted, and searched. In vain! All continued dark and still. The wind swept through the lofty gate; the court and the old towers were lying gray and dreary, and so dim that their forms could scarcely be distinguished in the gloom. The people were all shuddering and freezing; the women were becoming frightened; the children began to cry; the general impatience was increasing every minute; so quick a revolution of fortune, for which no one of them had been at all prepared, entirely destroyed their equanimity.

Expecting every minute that some person would appear and unbolt the doors; mistaking at one time the pattering of rain, at another the rocking of the wind, for the much-desired footstep of the Castle Bailiff, they continued downcast and inactive; it occurred to none of them to go into the new mansion, and there solicit help from charitable souls. They could not understand where their friend the Baron was lingering; they were in the most disconsolate condition.

At last some people actually arrived: by their voices, they were recognised as the pedestrians who had fallen behind the others on the journey. They intimated that the Baron had tumbled with his horse, and hurt his leg severely; and that on calling at the Castle, they too had been roughly directed hither.

The whole company were in extreme perplexity; they guessed and speculated as to what should now be done; but they could fix on nothing. At length they noticed from afar a lantern advancing, and took fresh breath at sight of it; but their hopes of quick deliverance again evaporated, when the object approached, and came to be distinctly seen. A groom was lighting the well-known Stallmeister of the Castle towards them; this gentleman, on coming nearer, very anxiously inquired for Mademoiselle Philina. No sooner had she stept forth from the crowd, than he very pressingly offered to conduct her to the new mansion, where a little place had been provided for her with the Countess's maids. She did not hesitate long about accepting his proposal; she caught his arm, and recommending her trunk to the care of the rest, was going to hasten off with him directly; but the others intercepted them, asking, entreating, conjuring the Stallmeister; till at last, to get away with his fair one, he promised everything, assuring them that in a little while, the Castle should be opened, and they lodged in the most comfortable manner. In a few moments, they saw the glimmer of his lantern vanish; they long looked in vain for another gleam of light. At last, after much watching, scolding and reviling, it actually appeared, and revived them with a touch of hope and consolation.

An ancient footman opened the door of the old edifice, into which they rushed with violence. Each of them now strove to have his trunk unfastened, and brought in beside him. Most of this luggage, like the persons of its owners, was thoroughly wetted. Having but a single light, the process of unpacking went on very slowly. In the dark passages they pushed against each other, they stumbled, they fell. They begged to have more lights, they begged to have some fuel. The monosyllabic footman, with much ado, consented to put down his own lantern; then went his way, and came not again.

They now began to investigate the edifice. The doors of all the rooms were open; large stoves, tapestry hangings, inlaid floors, yet bore witness to its former pomp: but of other house-gear there was none to be seen; no table, chair, or mirror; nothing but a few monstrous empty bedsteads, stript of every ornament and every necessary. The wet trunks and knapsacks were adopted as seats; a part of the tired wanderers placed themselves upon the floor. Wilhelm had sat down upon some steps; Mignon lay upon his knees. The child was restless; and, when he asked what ailed her, she answered: "I am hungry." He himself had nothing that could still the craving of the child; the rest of the party had consumed their whole provision; so he was obliged to leave the little traveller without refreshment. Through the whole adventure he had been inactive, silently immersed in thought. He was very sullen, and full of indignant regret that he had not kept by his first determination, and remained at the inn, though he should have slept in the garret.

The rest demeaned themselves in various ways. Some of them had got a heap of old wood collected within a vast gaping chimney in the hall; they set fire to the pile with great huzzaing. Unhappily, however, their hopes of warming and drying themselves by means of it, were mocked in the most frightful manner. The chimney, it appeared, was there for ornament alone, and was walled-up above; so the smoke rushed quickly back, and at once filled the whole chamber. The dry wood rose crackling into flames; the flame was also driven back; the draught sweeping through the broken windows gave it a wavering direction. Terrified lest the Castle should catch fire, the unhappy guests had to tear the burning sticks asunder, to smother and trample them under their feet; the smoke increased; their case was rendered more intolerable than before; they were driven to the brink of desperation.

Wilhelm had retreated from the smoke into a distant chamber; to which Mignon soon followed him, leading in a well-dressed servant, with a high clear double-lighted lantern in his hand. He turned to Wilhelm, and holding out to him some fruits and confectionery on a beautiful porcelain plate: "The young lady upstairs," said he, "sends you this, with the request that you would join her party: she bids me tell you," added the lacquey, with a sort of grin, "that she is very well off yonder, and wishes to divide her enjoyments with her friends."

Wilhelm had not at all expected such a message; for, ever since the adventure on the stone bench, he had treated Philina with the most decided contempt: he was still so resolute to have no more concern with her, that he thought of sending back her dainty gifts untasted, when a supplicating look of Mignon's induced him to accept them. He returned his thanks in the name of the child. The invitation he entirely rejected. He desired the servant to exert himself a little for the stranger company, and made inquiry for the Baron. The latter, he was told, had gone to bed; but had already, as the lacquey understood, given orders to some other person to take charge of these unfortunate and ill-lodged gentlemen.

The servant went away, leaving one of his lights, which Wilhelm, in the absence of a candlestick, contrived to fix upon the window casement; and now at least, in his meditations, he could see the four walls of his chamber. Nor was it long till preparations were commenced for conducting our travellers to rest. Candles arrived by degrees, though without snuffers; then a few chairs; an hour afterwards came bed-clothes; then pillows, all well steeped in rain. It was far past midnight when straw-beds and mattresses were produced, which, if sent at first, would have been extremely welcome.

In the interim also, somewhat to eat and drink had been brought in: it was enjoyed without much criticism, though it looked like a most disorderly collection of remains, and offered no very singular proof of the esteem in which our guests were held.

CHAPTER IV.

The disorders and mischievous tricks of some frolicksome companions still farther augmented the disquietudes and distresses of the night; these gay people woke each other, each played a thousand giddy pranks to plague his fellow. The next morning dawned amid loud complaints against their friend the Baron, for having so deceived them, for having given so very false a notion of the order and comfort that awaited their arrival. However, to their great surprise and consolation, at an early hour, the Count himself, attended by a few servants, made his entrance, and inquired about their circumstances. He appeared much vexed on discovering how badly they had fared: and the Baron, who came limping along, supported on the arm of a servant, bitterly accused the Steward for neglecting his commands on this occasion; showing great anxiety to have that person punished for his disobedience.

The Count gave immediate orders that everything should be arranged, in his presence, to the utmost possible convenience of the guests. While this was going on, some officers arrived, who forthwith scraped acquaintance with the actresses. The Count assembled all the company before him, spoke to each by name, introduced a few jokes among his observations; so that every one was charmed at the gracious condescension of his Lordship. At last it came to Wilhelm's turn; he appeared with Mignon holding by his hand. Our friend excused himself, in the best terms he could, for the freedom he had taken; the Count, on the other hand, spoke as if the visit had been looked for.

A gentleman, who stood beside the Count, and who, although he wore no uniform, appeared to be an officer, conversed with Wilhelm; he was evidently not a common man. His large keen blue eyes, looking out from beneath a high brow; his light-coloured hair, thrown carelessly back; his middle stature; everything about him showed an active, firm and decisive mode of being. His questions were lively; he seemed to be at home in all that he inquired about.

Wilhelm asked the Baron what this person was; but found that he had little good to say of him. "He held the rank of Major, was the special favourite of the Prince, managed his most secret affairs, was, in short, regarded as his right arm. Nay, there was reason to believe him the Prince's natural son. He had been on embassies in France, England, Italy; in all those places he had greatly distinguished himself; by which means he was grown conceited, imagining, among other pretensions, that he thoroughly understood the literature of Germany, and allowing himself to vent all kinds of sorry jests upon it. He, the Baron, was in the habit of avoiding all intercourse with him; and Wilhelm would do well to imitate that conduct, for it somehow happened that no one could be near him without being punished for it. He was called Jarno; though nobody knew rightly what to make of such a name."

Wilhelm had nothing to urge against all this: he had felt a sort of inclination for the stranger, though he noticed in him something cold and repulsive.

The company being arranged and distributed throughout the Castle, Melina issued the strictest orders, that they should behave themselves with decency; the women live in a separate quarter; and each direct his whole attention to the study of dramatic art, and of the characters he had to play. He posted up written ordinances, consisting of many articles, upon all the doors. He settled the amount of fine, which should be levied upon each transgressor, and put into a common box.

This edict was but little heeded. Young officers went out and in; they jested not in the most modest fashion with the actresses; made game of the actors; and annihilated the whole system of police, before it had the smallest time to take root in the community. The people ran chasing one another through the rooms, they changed clothes, they disguised themselves. Melina, attempting to be rigorous with a few at first, was exasperated by every sort of insolence; and when the Count soon after sent for him to come and view the place where his theatre was to be erected, matters grew worse and worse. The young gentry devised a thousand broad jokes; by the help of some actors, they became yet coarser; it seemed as if the old Castle had been altogether given up to an infuriate host; and the racket did not end till dinner.

Meanwhile the Count had led Melina over to a large hall, which, though belonging to the old Castle, communicated by a gallery with the new one: it seemed very well adapted for being changed into a little theatre. Here the sagacious lord of the mansion pointed out in person how he wanted everything to be.

The labour now commenced in the greatest haste; the stage-apparatus was erected and furbished up; what decorations they had brought along with them and could employ, were set in order; and what was wanting, was prepared by some skilful workmen of the Count's. Wilhelm likewise put his hand to the business; he assisted in settling the perspective, in laying off the outlines of the scenery; he was very anxious that nothing should be executed clumsily. The Count, who frequently came in to inspect their progress, was highly satisfied; he showed particularly how they should proceed in every case, displaying an uncommon knowledge of all the arts they were concerned with.

Next began the business of rehearsing, in good earnest; and there would have been enough of space and leisure for this undertaking, had the actors not continually been interrupted by the presence of visitors. Some new guests were daily arriving, and each insisted on viewing the operations of the company.

CHAPTER V.

The Baron had, for several days, been cheering Wilhelm with the hope of being formally presented to the Countess. " I have told this excellent lady," said he, " so much about the talent and fine sentiment displayed in your compositions, that she feels quite impatient to see you, and hear one or two of them read. Be prepared, therefore, to come over at a moment's notice; for, the first morning she is at leisure, you will certainly be called on." He then pointed out to him the afterpiece it would be proper to produce on that occasion; adding, that doubtless it would recommend him to no usual degree of favour. The lady, he declared, was extremely sorry that a guest like him had happened to arrive at a time of such confusion, when they could not entertain him in a style more suitable to his merits and their own wishes.

In consequence of this information, Wilhelm, with the most sedulous attention, set about preparing the piece, which was to usher him into the great world. "Hitherto," said he, "thou hast laboured in silence for thyself; applauded only by a small circle of friends. Thou hast for a time despaired of thy abilities, and art yet full of anxious doubts whether even thy present path is the right one, and whether thy talent for the stage at all corresponds with thy inclination for it. In the hearing of such practised judges, in the closet where no illusion can take place, the attempt is far more hazardous than elsewhere; and yet I would not willingly recoil from the experiment; I could wish to add this pleasure to my former enjoyments, and if it might be, to give extension and stability to my hopes from the future."

He accordingly went through some pieces; read them with the keenest critical eye; made corrections here and there; recited them aloud, that he might be perfect in his tones and expression: and finally selected the work, which he was best acquainted with, and hoped to gain most honour by. He put it in his pocket, one morning, on being summoned to attend the Countess.

The Baron had assured him that there would be no one present, but the lady herself and a worthy female friend of hers. On entering the chamber, the Baroness von C * * * advanced with great friendliness to meet him; expressed her happiness at gaining his acquaintance; and introduced him to the Countess, who was then under the hands of her hair-dresser. The Countess received him with kind words and looks; but it vexed him to see Philina kneeling at her chair, and playing a thousand fooleries. "The poor child," said the Baroness, "has just been singing to us. Finish the song you were in the midst of, we should not like to lose it."

Wilhelm listened to her quavering with great patience, being anxious for the friseur's departure before he should begin to read. They offered him a cup of chocolate, the Baroness herself handing him the biscuit. Yet, in spite of these civilities, he relished not his breakfast; he was longing too eagerly to lay before the lovely Countess some performance that might interest and gratify her. Philina too stood somewhat in his way; on former occasions, while listening to him, she had more than once been troublesome. He looked at the friseur with a painful feeling, hoping every moment that the tower of curls would be complete.

Meanwhile the Count came in, and began to talk of the fresh visitors he was expecting, of the day's occupations or amusements, and of various domestic matters that were started. On his retiring, some officers sent to ask permission of the Countess to pay their respects to her, as they had to leave the Castle before dinner. The footman having come to his post at the door, she permitted him to usher in the gentlemen.

The Baroness amid these interruptions gave herself some pains to entertain our friend, and showed him much consideration; all which he accepted with becoming reverence, though not without a little absence of mind. He often felt for the manuscript in his pocket; and hoped for his deliverance every instant. He was almost losing patience, when a man-milliner was introduced, and immediately began without mercy to open his papers, bags and bandboxes; pressing all his various wares upon the ladies, with an importunity peculiar to that species of creature.

The company increased. The Baroness cast a look at Wilhelm, and then whispered with the Countess: he noticed this, but did not understand the purpose of it. The whole, however, became clear enough, when, after an hour of painful and fruitless endurance, he went away. He then found a beautiful pocket-book, of English manufacture, in his pocket. The Baroness had dextrously put it there without his notice; and soon afterwards the Countess' little Black came out, and handed him an elegantly flowered waistcoat, without very clearly saying whence it came.

CHAPTER VI.

This mingled feeling of vexation and gratitude spoiled the remainder of his day; till, towards evening, he once more found employment. Melina informed him that the Count had been speaking of a little prelude, which he wished to have produced, in honour of the Prince, on the day of his Highness' arrival. He meant to have the great qualities of this noble hero and philanthropist personified in the piece. These Virtues were to advance together, to recite his praises, and finally to encircle his bust with garlands of flowers and laurels; behind which a transparency might be inserted, representing the princely Hat, and his name illuminated on it. The Count, Melina said, had ordered him to take charge of getting ready the verses and other arrangements; and Wilhelm, he hoped, to whom it must be an easy matter, would stand by him on this occasion.

"How!" exclaimed our friend in a splenetic tone, "have we nothing but portraits, illuminated names and allegorical figures, to show in honour of a Prince, who, in my opinion, merits quite a different eulogy? How can it flatter any reasonable man to see himself set up in effigy, and his name glimmering on oiled paper! I am very much afraid that your Allegories, particularly in the present state of the wardrobe, will furnish occasion for many ambiguities and jestings. If you mean, however, to compose the piece, or make it be composed, I can have nothing to object against it; only I desire to have no part or lot in the matter."

Melina excused himself; alleging this to be only a casual hint of his Lordship the Count, who for the rest had left the arrangement of the piece entirely in their own hands. "With all my heart," replied our friend, "will I contribute something to the pleasure of this noble family; my Muse has never had so pleasant an employment as to sing, though in broken numbers, the praises of a Prince who merits so much veneration. I will think of the matter; perhaps I may be able to contrive some way of bringing out our little troop, so as at least to produce some effect."

From this moment, Wilhelm eagerly reflected on his undertaking. Before going to sleep, he had got it all reduced to some degree of order; early next morning his plan was ready, the scenes laid out; a few of the most striking passages and songs were even versified and written down.

As soon as he was dressed, our friend made haste to wait upon the Baron, to submit the plan to his inspection, and take his advice upon certain points connected with it. The Baron testified his approbation of it; but not without considerable surprise. For, on the previous evening, he had heard his Lordship talk of having ordered some quite different piece to be prepared and versified.

"To me it seems improbable," replied our friend, "that it could be his Lordship's wish to have the piece got ready, exactly as he gave it to Melina. If I am not mistaken, he intended merely to point out to us from a distance the path we were to follow. The amateur and critic shows the artist what is wanted; and then leaves to him the care of producing it by his own means."

"Not at all," replied the Baron: "his Lordship understands that the piece shall be composed according to that and no other plan, which he has himself prescribed. Yours has indeed a remote similarity with his idea; but, if we mean to accomplish our purpose, and get the Count diverted from his first thought, we shall need to employ the ladies in the matter. The Baroness especially contrives to execute such operations in the most masterly manner: the question is now, whether your plan shall so please her, that she will undertake the business; in that case it will certainly succeed."

"We need the assistance of the ladies," said our friend, "at any rate; for neither our company nor our wardrobe would suffice without them. I have counted on some pretty children, that are running up and down the house, and belong to certain of the servants."

He then desired the Baron to communicate his plan to the ladies. The Baron soon returned with intelligence that they wished to speak with Wilhelm personally. That same evening, when the gentlemen sat down to play, which, owing to the arrival of a certain General, was expected to be deeper and keener than usual, the Countess and her friend, under pretext of some indisposition, would retire to their chamber; where Wilhelm, being introduced by a secret staircase, might submit his project without interruption. This sort of mystery, the Baron said, would give the adventure a peculiar charm; in particular the Baroness was rejoicing like a child, in the prospect of their rendezvous; and the more so, because it was to be accomplished secretly and against the inclination of the Count.

Towards evening, at the appointed time, Wilhelm was sent for, and led in with caution. As the Baroness advanced to meet him in a small cabinet, the manner of their interview brought former happy scenes, for a moment, to his mind. She conducted him along to the Countess' chamber; and they now proceeded earnestly to question and investigate. He exhibited his plan with the utmost warmth and vivacity; so that his fair audience were quite decided in its favour. Our readers also will permit us to present a brief sketch of it here.

The piece was to open with a dance of children in some rural scene; their dance representing that particular game, wherein each has to wheel round and gain the other's place. This was to be followed by several variations of their play; till at last, in performing a dance of the repeating kind, they were all to sing a merry song. Here the old Harper with Mignon should enter, and by the curiosity which they excited, gather several country-people round them; the Harper would sing various songs in praise of peace, repose and joy; and Mignon would then dance the egg-dance.

In these innocent delights, they are disturbed by the sound of martial music; and the party are surprised by a troop of soldiers. The men stand on the defensive, and are overcome; the girls fly, and are taken. In the tumult all seems going to destruction, when a Person (about whose form and qualities the poet was not yet determined) enters, and by signifying that the General is near, restores composure. Whereupon the Hero's character is painted in the finest colours; security is promised in the midst of arms;

violence and lawless disorder are now to be restrained. A universal festival is held in honour of the noble-minded Captain.

The Countess and her friend expressed great satisfaction with the plan; only they maintained that there must of necessity be something of allegory introduced, to make it palatable to his Lordship. The Baron proposed that the leader of the soldiers should be represented as the Genius of Dissension and Violence; that Minerva should then advance to bind fetters on him, to give notice of the hero's approach, and celebrate his praise. The Baroness undertook the task of persuading the Count, that his plan was the one proposed by himself with a few alterations; at the same time expressly stipulating that, without fail, at the conclusion of the piece, the bust, the illuminated name, and the princely Hat, should be exhibited in due order; since otherwise her attempt was vain.

Wilhelm had already figured in his mind how delicately and how nobly he would have the praises of his hero celebrated in the mouth of Minerva; and it was not without a long struggle that he yielded in this point. Yet he felt himself delightfully constrained to yield. The beautiful eyes of the Countess, and her lovely demeanour, would easily have moved him to sin against his conscience as a poet; to abandon the finest and most interesting invention, the keenly wished-for unity of his composition, and all its most suitable details. His conscience as a burgher had a trial no less hard to undergo, when the ladies, in distributing the characters, pointedly insisted that he must undertake one himself.

Laertes had received for his allotment the part of that violent war-god; Wilhelm was to represent the leader of the peasants, who had some very pretty and tender verses to recite. After long resistance he was forced to comply: he could find no excuse, when the Baroness protested that their stage was in all respects to be regarded as a private one, and that she herself would very gladly play on it, if they could find her a fit occasion. On receiving his consent, they parted with our friend on the kindest terms. The Baroness assured him that he was an incomparable man; she accompanied him to the little stairs, and wished him good night with a squeeze of the hand.

CHAPTER VII.

THE interest in his undertakings, which the Countess and her friend expressed and felt so warmly, quickened Wilhelm's faculties and zeal: the plan of his piece, which the process of describing it had rendered more distinct, was now present in the most brilliant vividness before his mind. He spent the greater part of that night, and the whole of next morning, in the sedulous versification of the dialogue and songs.

He had proceeded a considerable way, when a message came requiring his attendance in the Castle; the noble company, who were then at breakfast, wished to speak with him. As he entered the parlour, the Baroness advanced to meet him; and, under pretext of wishing him good morning, whispered cunningly: "Say nothing of your piece, but what you shall be asked."

"I hear," cried the Count to him, "that you are very busy working at my prelude, which I mean to present in honour of the Prince. I consent that you introduce a Minerva into it; and we are just thinking beforehand how the goddess shall be dressed, that we may not blunder in costume. For this purpose I am causing them to fetch from the library all the books that contain any figures of her."

At the same instant, one or two servants entered the parlour, with a huge basket full of books of every shape and appearance.

Montfaucon, the collections of antique statues, gems and coins, all sorts of mythological writings, were turned up, and their plates compared. But even this was not enough. The Count's faithful memory recalled to him all the Minervas to be found in frontispieces, vignettes, or anywhere else; and book after book was, in consequence, carried from the library, till finally the Count was sitting in a chaos of volumes. Unable at last to recollect any other figure of Minerva, he observed with a smile: "I durst bet, that now there is not a single Minerva in all the library; and perhaps it is the first time that a collection of books has been so totally deprived of the presence of its patron goddess."

The whole company were merry at this thought; Jarno particularly, who had all along been spurring on the Count to call for more and more books, laughed quite immoderately.

"Now," said the Count, turning to Wilhelm, "one chief point is: Which goddess do you mean? Minerva or Pallas? The goddess of war or of the arts?"

"Would it not be best, your Excellency," said Wilhelm, "if we were not clearly to express ourselves on this head; if, since the goddess plays a double part in the ancient mythology, we also exhibited her here in a double quality. She announces a warrior, but only to calm the tumults of the people; she celebrates a hero by exalting his humanity; she conquers violence, and restores peace and security."

The Baroness, afraid lest Wilhelm might betray himself, hastily pushed forward the Countess' tailor, to give his opinion how such an antique robe could best be got ready. This man, being frequently employed in making masquerade dresses, very easily contrived the business; and as Madam Melina, notwithstanding her advanced state of pregnancy, had undertaken to enact the celestial virgin, the tailor was directed to take her measure: and the Countess, though with some reluctance, selected from the wardrobe the clothes he was to cut up for that purpose.

The Baroness, in her dextrous way, again contrived to lead Wilhelm aside, and let him know that she had been providing all the other necessaries. Shortly afterwards, she sent him the musician, who had charge of the Count's private band; and this professor set about composing what airs were wanted, or choosing from his actual stock such tunes as appeared suitable. From this time, all went on according to the wishes of our friend: the Count made no more inquiries about the piece; being altogether occupied with the transparent decoration, destined to surprise the spectators at the conclusion of the play. His inventive genius, aided by the skill of his confectioner, produced in fact a very pretty article. In the course of his travels, the Count had witnessed the most splendid exhibitions of this sort; he had also brought home with him a number of copperplates and drawings, and could sketch such things with considerable taste.

Meanwhile Wilhelm finished the play; gave every one his part, and began the study of his own. The musician also, having great skill in dancing, prepared the ballet; so that everything proceeded as it ought.

Yet one unexpected obstacle occurred, which threatened to occasion an unpleasant gap in the performance. He had promised to himself a striking effect from Mignon's egg-dance; and was much surprised when the child, with her customary dryness of manner, refused to dance, saying she was now his, and would no more go upon the stage. He sought to move her by every sort of persuasion, and did not discontinue his attempt till she began weeping bitterly, fell at his feet, and cried out, "Dearest father! stay thou from the boards thyself!" Little heeding this caution, he studied how to give the scene some other turn that might be equally interesting.

Philina, whose appointment was to act one of the peasant girls, and in the concluding dance to give the single-voice part of the song, and lead the chorus, felt exceedingly delighted that it had been so ordered. In other respects too, her present life was altogether to her mind; she had her separate chamber; was constantly beside the Countess, entertaining her with fooleries, and daily receiving some present for her pains. Among other things, a dress had been expressly made for her wearing in this prelude. And being of a light imitative nature, she quickly marked in the procedure of the ladies whatever would befit herself: she had of late grown all politeness and decorum. The attentions of the Stallmeister augmented rather than diminished; and, as the officers also paid zealous court to her, living in so genial an element, it came into her head for once in her life to play the prude, and, in a quiet gradual way, to take upon herself a certain dignity of manner to which she had not before aspired. Cool and sharp-sighted as she was, eight days had not elapsed till she knew the weak side of every person in the house; so that, had she possessed the power of acting from any constant motive, she might very easily have made her fortune. But on this occasion, as on all others, she employed her advantages merely to divert herself, to procure a bright today, and be impertinent, wherever she observed that impertinence was not attended with danger.

The parts were now committed to memory; a rehearsal of the piece was ordered; the Count purposed to be present at it; and his lady began to feel anxious how he might receive it. The Baroness called Wilhelm to her privately: the nearer the hour approached, they all displayed the more perplexity; for the truth was, that of the Count's original idea nothing whatever had been introduced. Jarno, who joined them while consulting together, was admitted to the secret. He felt amused at the contrivance, and was heartily disposed to offer the ladies his good services in carrying it through. "It will go hard," said he, "if you cannot extricate yourselves without help from this affair; but, at all events, I will wait as a body of reserve." The Baroness then told them how she had on various occasions recited the whole piece to the Count, but only in fragments and without order; that consequently he was prepared for each individual passage, yet certainly possessed with the idea that the whole would coincide with his original conception. "I will sit by him," said she, "tonight at the rehearsal, and study to divert his attention. The confectioner I have engaged already to make the decoration as beautiful as possible, but as yet he has not quite completed it."

"I know of a Court," said Jarno, "where I wish we had a few such active and prudent friends as you. If your skill tonight will not suffice, give me a signal; I will take out the Count, and not let him in again till Minerva enter, and you have speedy aid to expect from the illumination. For a day or two, I have had something to report to him about his cousin, which for various reasons

I have hitherto postponed. It will give his thoughts another turn, and that none of the pleasantest."

Business hindered the Count from being present when the play began; the Baroness amused him after his arrival; Jarno's help was not required. For, as the Count had abundance of employment in pointing out improvements, rectifying and arranging the detached parts, he entirely forgot the purport of the whole; and as at last Madam Melina advanced and spoke according to his heart, and the transparency did well, he seemed completely satisfied. It was not till the whole was finished, and his guests were sitting down to cards, that the difference appeared to strike him, and he began to think whether after all this piece was actually of his invention. At a signal from the Baroness, Jarno then came forward into action; the evening passed away; the intelligence of the Prince's approach was confirmed; the people rode out more than once to see his vanguard encamping in the neighbourhood; the house was full of noise and tumult; and our actors, not always served in the handsomest manner by unwilling servants, had to pass their time in practisings and expectations, at their quarters in the old mansion, without any one particularly taking thought about them.

CHAPTER VIII.

At length the Prince arrived, with all his generals, staff-officers and suite accompanying him. These, and the multitude of people coming to visit or do business with him, made the Castle like a bee-hive on the point of swarming. All pressed forward to behold a man no less distinguished by his rank than by his great qualities; and all admired his urbanity and condescension; all were astonished at finding the hero and the leader of armies also the most accomplished and attractive courtier.

By the Count's orders, the inmates of the Castle were required to be all at their posts when the Prince arrived; not a player was allowed to show himself, that his Highness might have no anticipation of the spectacle prepared to welcome him. Accordingly, when at evening he was led into the lofty hall, glowing with light, and adorned with tapestries of the previous century, he seemed not at all prepared to expect a play, and still less a prelude in honour of himself. Everything went off as it should have done: at the conclusion of the show, the whole troop were called and presented individually to the Prince, who contrived with the most pleasing and friendly air to put some question, or make some remark, to every one of them. Wilhelm, as author of the piece, was particularly noticed, and had his tribute of applause liberally paid him.

The prelude being fairly over, no one asked another word about it; in a few days, it was as if it never had existed, except that occasionally Jarno spoke of it to Wilhelm, judiciously praised it, adding however: " It is pity you should play with hollow nuts, for a stake of hollow nuts." This expression stuck in Wilhelm's mind for several days; he knew not how to explain it, or what to infer from it.

Meanwhile the company kept acting every night, as well as their capacities permitted; each doing his utmost to attract the attention of spectators. Undeserved applauses cheered them on: in their old Castle they fully believed, that the great assemblage was crowding thither solely on their account; that the multitude of strangers was allured by their exhibitions; that *they* were the centre round which, and by means of which, the whole was moving and revolving.

Wilhelm alone discovered, to his sorrow, that directly the reverse was true. For although the Prince had waited out the first exhibitions, sitting on his chair, with the greatest conscientiousness, yet by degrees he grew remiss in his attendance, and seized every plausible occasion of withdrawing. And those very people whom Wilhelm, in conversation, had found to be the best informed and most sensible, with Jarno at their head, were wont to spend but a few transitory moments in the hall of the theatre; sitting for the rest of their time in the antechamber, gaming, or seeming to employ themselves in business.

Amid all his persevering efforts, to want the wished and hoped for approbation grieved Wilhelm very deeply. In the choice of plays, in transcribing the parts, in numerous rehearsals, and whatever farther could be done, he zealously coöperated with Melina, who, being in secret conscious of his own insufficiency, at length acknowledged and pursued these counsels. His own parts Wilhelm diligently studied; and executed with vivacity and feeling, and with all the propriety which the little training he had yet received would allow.

At the same time, the unwearied interest which the Baron took in their performances, obliterated every doubt from the minds of the rest of the company: he assured them that their exhibitions were producing the deepest effect, especially while one of his own pieces had been representing; only he was grieved to say, the Prince showed an exclusive inclination for the French theatre; while a part of his people, among whom Jarno was especially distinguished, gave a passionate preference to the monstrous productions of the English stage.

If in this way the art of our players was not adequately noticed and admired, their persons, on the other hand, grew not entirely indifferent to all the gentlemen and all the ladies of the audience. We observed above, that from the very first our actresses had drawn upon them the attention of the young officers; in the sequel they were luckier, and made more important conquests. But omitting these, we shall merely observe, that Wilhelm every day appeared more interesting to the Countess, while in him too a silent inclination towards her was beginning to take root. Whenever he was on the stage, she could not turn her eyes from him; and ere long he seemed to play and to recite with his face towards her alone. To look upon each other was to them the sweetest satisfaction; to which their harmless souls yielded without reserve, without cherishing a bolder wish, or thinking about any consequence.

As two hostile outposts will sometimes peacefully and pleasantly converse together, across the river which divides them, not thinking of the war in which both their countries are engaged, so did the Countess exchange looks full of meaning with our friend, across the vast chasm of birth and rank, both believing for themselves that they might safely cherish their several emotions.

The Baroness, in the mean time, had selected Laertes, who, being a spirited and lively young man, pleased her very much; and who, woman-hater as he was, felt unwilling to refuse a passing adventure. He would actually on this occasion have been fettered, against his will, by the courteous and attractive nature of the Baroness, had not the Baron done him accidentally a piece of good, or if you will, of bad service, by instructing him a little in the habits and temper of this lady.

Laertes happening once to celebrate her praises, and give her the preference to every other of her sex, the Baron with a grin replied: "I see how matters stand; our fair friend has got a fresh inmate for her stalls." This luckless comparison, which pointed too clearly to the dangerous caresses of a Circe, grieved poor Laertes to the heart; he could not listen to the Baron without spite and anger, as the latter continued without mercy:

"Every stranger thinks he is the first, whom this delightful manner of proceeding has concerned: but he is grievously mistaken; for we have all, at one time or another, been trotted round this course. Man, youth, or boy, be who he like, each must devote himself to her service for a season, must hang about her, and toil and long to gain her favour."

To the happy man, just entering the garden of an enchantress, and welcomed by all the pleasures of an artificial spring, nothing can form a more unpleasant surprise, than if, while his ear is watching and drinking-in the music of the nightingales, some transformed predecessor on a sudden grunts at his feet.

After this discovery, Laertes felt heartily ashamed, that vanity should have again misled him to think well, even in the smallest degree, of any woman whatsoever. He now entirely forsook the Baroness; kept by the Stallmeister, with whom he diligently fenced and hunted; conducting himself at rehearsals and representations as if these were but secondary matters.

The Count and his lady would often in the mornings send for some of the company to attend them; and all had continual cause to envy the undeserved good fortune of Philina. The Count kept his favourite, the Pedant, frequently for hours together, at his toilette. This genius had been dressed out by degrees; he was now equipt and furnished even to watch and snuff-box.

Many times, too, particularly after dinner, the whole company were called out before the noble guests; an honour which the artists regarded as the most flattering in the world; not observing, that on these very occasions the servants and huntsmen were ordered to bring in a multitude of hounds, and to lead strings of horses about the court of the Castle.

Wilhelm had been counselled to praise Racine, the Prince's favourite, and thereby to attract some portion of his Highness' favour to himself. On one of these afternoons, being summoned with the rest, he found an opportunity to introduce this topic. The Prince asked him if he diligently read the great French dramatic writers; to which Wilhelm answered with a very eager "Yes." He did not observe that his Highness, without waiting for the answer, was already on the point of turning round to some one else: he fixed upon him, on the contrary, almost stepping in his way; and proceeded to declare, that he valued the French theatre very highly, and read the works of their great masters with delight; particularly he had learned with true joy that his Highness did complete justice to the great talents of Racine. "I can easily conceive," continued he, "how people of high breeding and exalted rank must value a poet, who has painted so excellently and so truly the circumstances of their lofty station. Corneille, if I may say so, has delineated great men; Racine men of eminent rank. In reading his plays, I can always figure to myself the poet as living at a splendid court, with a great king before his eyes, in constant intercourse with the most distinguished persons, and penetrating into the secrets of human nature, as it works concealed behind the gorgeous tapestry of palaces. When I study his Britannicus, his Berenice, it seems as if I were transported in person to the court, were initiated into the great and the little, in the habitations of these earthly gods; through the fine and delicate organs of my author, I see kings whom a nation adores, courtiers whom thousands envy, in their natural forms, with their failings and their pains. The anecdote of Racine's dying of a broken heart, because Louis Fourteenth would no longer attend to him, and had shown him his dissatisfaction, is to me the key to all his works. It was impossible that a poet of his talents, whose life and death depended on the looks of a king, should not write such works as a king and a prince might applaud."

Jarno had stept near, and was listening with astonishment. The Prince, who had made no answer, and had only shown his approbation by an assenting look, now turned aside; though Wilhelm, who did not know that it was contrary to etiquette to continue a discussion under such circumstances and exhaust a subject, would gladly have spoken more, and convinced the Prince that he had not read his favourite poet without sensibility and profit.

"Have you never," said Jarno, taking him aside, "read one of Shakspeare's plays?"

"No," replied Wilhelm: "since the time when they became more known in Germany, I have myself grown unacquainted with the theatre; and I know not whether I should now rejoice that an old taste, and occupation of my youth, has been by chance renewed. In the mean time, all that I have heard of these plays has excited little wish to become acquainted with such extraordinary monsters, which appear to set probability and dignity alike at defiance."

"I would advise you," said the other, "to make a trial, notwithstanding: it can do one no harm to look at what is extraordinary with one's own eyes. I will lend you a volume or two; and you cannot better spend your time, than by casting everything aside, and retiring to the solitude of your old habitation, to look into the magic-lantern of that unknown world. It is sinful of you to waste your hours in dressing out these apes to look more human, and teaching dogs to dance. One thing only I require; you must not cavil at the form; the rest I can leave to your own good sense and feeling."

The horses were standing at the door; and Jarno mounted with some other cavaliers, to go and hunt. Wilhelm looked after him with sadness. He would fain have spoken much with this man, who, though in a harsh unfriendly way, gave him new ideas, ideas that he had need of.

Oftentimes a man when approaching some development of his

powers, capacities and conceptions, gets into a perplexity, from which a prudent friend might easily deliver him. He resembles a traveller, who, at but a short distance from the inn he is to rest at, falls into the water; were any one to catch him then, and pull him to the bank, with one good wetting it were over; whereas though he struggles out himself, it is often at the side where he tumbled in, and he has to make a wide and weary circuit before reaching his appointed object.

Wilhelm now began to have an inkling that things went forward in the world differently from what he had supposed. He now viewed close at hand the solemn and imposing life of the great and distinguished; and wondered at the easy dignity which they contrived to give it. An army on its march, a princely hero at the head of it, such a multitude of coöperating warriors, such a multitude of crowding worshipers, exalted his imagination. In this mood, he received the promised books; and ere long, as may be easily supposed, the stream of that mighty genius laid hold of him, and led him down to a shoreless ocean, where he soon completely forgot and lost himself.

CHAPTER IX.

THE connexion between the Baron and the actors had suffered various changes, since the arrival of the latter. At the commencement, it had been productive of great satisfaction to both parties. As the Baron for the first time in his life now saw one of those pieces, with which he had already graced a private theatre, put into the hands of real actors, and in the fair way for a decent exhibition, he showed the benignest humour in the world. He was liberal in gifts; he bought little presents for the actresses from every millinery-hawker, and contrived to send over many an odd bottle of champaign to the actors. In return for all this, our company took every sort of trouble with his play; and Wilhelm spared no diligence in learning, with extreme correctness, the sublime speeches of that very eminent hero, whose part had fallen to his share.

But, in spite of all these kind reciprocities, some clouds by degrees arose between the players and their patron. The Baron's preference for certain actors became daily more observable; this of necessity chagrined the rest. He exalted his favourites quite exclusively; and thus, of course, he introduced disunion and jealousy among the company. Melina, without skill to help himself in dubious junctures, felt his situation very vexing. The persons eulogised accepted of their praise, without being singularly thankful for it; while the neglected gentlemen showed traces of their spleen by a thousand methods; and constantly found means to make it very disagreeable for their once much-honoured patron to appear among them. Their spite received no little nourishment from a certain poem, by an unknown author, which made a great sensation in the Castle. Previously to this, the Baron's intercourse with the company had given rise to many little strokes of merriment; several stories had been raised about him; certain little incidents, adorned with suitable additions, and presented in the proper light, had been talked of, and made the subject of much bantering and laughter. At last it began to be said, that a certain rivalry of trade was arising between him and some of the actors, who also looked upon themselves as writers. The poem we spoke of was founded upon this report; it ran as follows:

> I poor devil, Lord Baron,
> Must envy you your crest of arms,
> The coach you ride in, coat you've on,
> Your copses, ponds, and rack-rent farms,
> Your father's polish'd ashlar house,
> And all his hounds and hares and grouse.
>
> Me poor devil, Lord Baron,
> You envy my small shred of wit;
> Because it seems, as things have gone,
> Old Nature had a hand in it;
> She made me light of heart and gay,
> With long-necked purse, not brain of clay.
>
> Look you now, dear Lord Baron,
> What if we both should cease to fret,
> You being his Lordship's eldest son,
> And I being mother Nature's brat!
> We live in peace, all envy chase,
> And heed not which o' th' two surpasses;
> I in the Herald's Books no place,
> You having none about Parnassus.

Upon this poem, which various persons were possessed of, in copies scarcely legible, opinions were exceedingly divided. But who the author was, no one could guess; and as some began to draw a spiteful mirth from it, our friend expressed himself against it very keenly.

"We Germans," he exclaimed, "deserve to have our Muses still continue in the low contempt wherein they have languished so long; since we cannot value men of rank who take a share in our literature, no matter how. Birth, rank and fortune are nowise incompatible with genius and taste; as foreign nations, reckoning among their best minds a great number of noblemen, can fully testify. Hitherto indeed it has been rare in Germany for men of high station to devote themselves to science; hitherto few famous names have become more famous by their love of art and learning; while many, on the other hand, have mounted out of darkness to distinction, and risen like unknown stars on the horizon. Yet such will not always be the case; and I greatly err, if the first classes of the nation are not even now in the way of also employing their advantages to earn the fairest laurels of the Muses, at no distant date. Nothing, therefore, grieves me more than to see the burgher jeering at the noble who can value literature; nay even men of rank themselves, with inconsiderate caprice, maliciously scaring off their equal from a path where honour and contentment wait on all."

Apparently this latter observation pointed at the Count, of whom Wilhelm had heard that he liked the poem very much. In truth, this nobleman, accustomed to rally the Baron in his own peculiar way, was extremely glad of such an opportunity to plague his kinsman more effectually. As to who the writer of the squib might be, each formed his own hypothesis; and the Count, never willing that another should surpass him in acuteness, fell upon a thought, which, in a short time, he would have sworn to the truth of. The verses could be written, he believed, by no one but his Pedant, who was a very shrewd knave, and in whom, for a long while, he had noticed some touches of poetic genius. By way of proper treat, he therefore caused the Pedant one morning to be sent for, and made him read the poem, in his own manner, in presence of the Countess, the Baroness, and Jarno; a service he was paid for by applauses, praises and a present: and on the Count's inquiring if he had not still some other poems of an earlier time, he cunningly contrived to evade the question. Thus did the Pedant get invested with the reputation of a poet and a wit; and in the eyes of the Baron's friends, of a pasquinader and a bad-hearted man. From that period, play as he might, the Count applauded him with greater zeal than ever; so that the poor wight grew at last inflated till he nearly lost his senses, and began to meditate having a chamber in the Castle like Philina.

Had this project been fulfilled at once, a great mishap might have been spared him. As he was returning late one evening from the Castle, groping about in the dark narrow way, he was suddenly laid hold of, and kept on the spot by some persons, while some others rained a shower of blows upon him, and battered him so stoutly, that in a few seconds he was lying almost dead upon the place, and could not without difficulty crawl in to his companions. These, indignant as they seemed to be at such an outrage, felt their secret joy in the adventure; they could hardly keep from laughing, at seeing him so thoroughly curried, and his new brown coat bedusted through and through, and bedaubed with white, as if he had had to do with millers.

The Count, who soon got notice of the business, broke into a boundless rage. He treated this act as the most heinous crime; called it an infringement of the Burgfried, or Peace of the Castle, and caused his judge to make the strictest inquisition touching it. The whited coat, it was imagined, would afford a leading proof. Every creature, that possibly could have the smallest trade with flour or powder in the Castle, was submitted to investigation; but in vain.

The Baron solemnly protested on his honour, that although this sort of jesting had considerably displeased him, and the conduct of his Lordship the Count had not been the friendliest, yet he had got over the affair; and with respect to the misfortune which had come upon the poet, or pasquinader, or whatsoever his title might be, he knew absolutely nothing, and had not the most remote concern in it.

The operations of the strangers, and the general commotion of the house, soon effaced all recollection of the matter; and so, without redress, the unlucky favourite had to pay dear for the satisfaction of pluming himself, a short while, in feathers not his own.

Our troop, regularly acting every night, and on the whole very decently treated, now began to make more clamorous demands, the better they were dealt with. Ere long their victuals, drink, attendance, lodging, grew inadequate; and they called upon the Baron, their protector, to provide more liberally for them, and at last make good those promises of comfortable entertainment, which he had been giving them so long. Their complaints grew louder; and the efforts of our friend to still them, more and more abortive.

Meanwhile, excepting in rehearsals and hours of acting, Wilhelm scarcely ever came abroad. Shut up in one of the remotest chambers, to which Mignon and the Harper alone had free access, he lived and moved in the Shaksperean world, feeling or knowing nothing but the movements of his own mind.

We have heard of some Enchanter summoning, by magic formulas, a vast multitude of spiritual shapes into his cell. The conjurations are so powerful that the whole space of the apartment is quickly full; and the spirits crowding on to the verge of the little circle which they must not pass, around this, and above the master's head, keep increasing in number, and ever whirling in perpetual transformation. Every corner is crammed, every crevice is possessed. Embryos expand themselves, and giant forms contract into the size of nuts. Unhappily the Black-artist has forgot the counter-word, with which he might command this flood of sprites again to ebb.

So sat Wilhelm in his privacy; with unknown movements, a thousand feelings and capacities awoke in him, of which he formerly had neither notion nor anticipation. Nothing could allure him from this state; he was vexed and restless if any one presumed to come to him, and talk of news or what was passing in the world.

Accordingly he scarce took notice of the circumstance, when told that a judicial sentence was about being executed in the Castle-yard; the flogging of a boy, who had incurred suspicions of nocturnal housebreaking, and who, as he wore a peruke-maker's coat, had most probably been one of the assaulters of the Pedant. The boy indeed, it seemed, denied most obstinately; so that they could not inflict a formal punishment, but meant to give him a slight memorial as a vagabond, and send him about his business; he having prowled about the neighbourhood for several days, lain at night in the mills, and at last clapped a ladder to the garden-wall, and mounted over by it.

Our friend saw nothing very strange in the transaction, and was dismissing it altogether, when Mignon came running in, and assured him that the criminal was Friedrich, who, since the rencounter with the Stallmeister, had vanished from the company, and not again been heard of.

Feeling an interest in the boy, Wilhelm hastily arose; he found, in the court-yard of the Castle, the preparations almost finished. The Count loved solemnity on these occasions. The boy being now led out, our friend stept forward, and entreated for delay, as he knew the boy, and had various things to say which might perhaps throw light on the affair. He had difficulty in succeeding, notwithstanding all his statements; at length, however, he did get permission to speak with the culprit in private. Friedrich averred, that concerning the assault in which the Pedant had been used so harshly, he knew nothing whatever. He had merely been lurking about; and had come in at night to see Philina, whose room he had discovered, and would certainly have reached, had he not been taken by the way.

For the credit of the company, Wilhelm felt desirous not to have the truth of his adventure published. He hastened to the Stallmeister; he begged him to show favour, and with his intimate knowledge of men and things about the Castle, to find some means of quashing the affair, and dismissing the boy.

This whimsical gentleman, by Wilhelm's help, invented a little story; how the boy had belonged to the troop, had run away from it, but soon wished to get back and be received again into his place; how he had accordingly been trying in the night to come at certain of his well-wishers, and solicit their assistance. It was testified by others that his former behaviour had been good; the ladies put their hands to the work; and Friedrich was let go.

Wilhelm took him in; a third person in that strange family, which for some time he had looked on as his own. The old man and little Mignon received the returning wanderer kindly; and all the three combined to serve their friend and guardian with attention, and procure him all the pleasure in their power.

CHAPTER X.

Philina now succeeded in insinuating farther every day into the favour of the ladies. Whenever they were by themselves, she was wont to lead the conversation on the men whom they saw about the Castle; and our friend was not the last or least important that engaged them. The cunning girl was well aware that he had made a deep impression on the Countess; she therefore talked about him often, telling much that she knew or did not know; only taking care to speak of nothing that might be interpreted against him; eulogising, on the contrary, his nobleness of mind, his generosity, and more than all, his modest and respectful conduct to the fair sex. To all inquiries made about him she replied with equal prudence; and the Baroness, when she observed the growing inclination of her amiable friend, was likewise very glad at the discovery. Her own intrigues with several men, especially of late with Jarno, had not remained hidden from the Countess, whose pure soul could not look upon such levities without disapprobation, and meek though earnest censures.

In this way, both Philina and the Baroness were personally interested in establishing a closer intercourse between the Countess and our friend. Philina hoped, moreover, that there would occur some opportunity, when she might once more labour for herself, and, if possible, get back the favour of the young man she had lost.

One day his Lordship with his guests had ridden out to hunt, and their return was not expected till the morrow. On this, the Baroness devised a frolic, which was altogether in her way: for she loved disguises; and in order to surprise her friends, would suddenly appear among them as a peasant girl at one time, at another as a page, at another as a hunter's boy. By which means she almost gave herself the air of a little fairy, that is present everywhere, and exactly in the place where it is least expected. Nothing could exceed this lady's joy, if, without being recognised, she could contrive to wait upon the company for some time as a servant, or mix among them anyhow, and then at last in some sportful way disclose herself.

Towards night, she sent for Wilhelm to her chamber; and, happening to have something else to do just then, she left Philina to receive him and prepare him.

He arrived, and found to his surprise, not the honourable lady, but the giddy actress in the room. She received him with a certain dignified openness of manner, which she had of late been practising, and so constrained him likewise to be courteous.

At first she rallied him in general on the good fortune which pursued him everywhere, and which, as she could not but see, had led him hither, in the present case. Then she delicately set before him the treatment with which of late he had afflicted her; she blamed and upbraided herself; confessed that she had but too well deserved such punishment; described with the greatest candour what she called her *former* situation; adding, that she would despise herself, if she were not capable of altering, and making herself worthy of his friendship.

Wilhelm was struck with this oration. He had too little knowledge of the world to understand that persons, quite unstable and incapable of all improvement, frequently accuse themselves in the bitterest manner, confessing and deploring their faults with extreme ingenuousness, though they possess not the smallest power within them to retire from that course, along which the irresistible tendency of their nature is dragging them forward. Accordingly, he could not find in his heart to behave inexorably to the graceful sinner; he entered into conversation, and learned from her the project of a singular disguisement, wherewith it was intended to surprise the Countess.

He found some room for hesitation here; nor did he hide his scruples from Philina; but the Baroness, entering at this moment, left him not an instant for reflection; she hurried him away with her, declaring it was just the proper hour.

It was now grown dark. She took him to the Count's wardrobe; made him change his own coat with his Lordship's silk night-gown; and put the cap with red trimmings on his head. She then led him forward to the cabinet; and bidding him sit down upon the large chair, and take a book, she lit the Argand's lamp, which stood before him, and showed him what he was to do, and what kind of part he had to play.

They would inform the Countess, she said, of her husband's unexpected arrival, and that he was in very bad humour. The Countess would come in, walk up and down the room once or twice, then place herself beside the back of his chair, lay her arm upon his shoulder, and speak a few words. He was to play the cross husband as long and as well as possible; and when obliged to disclose himself, he must behave politely, handsomely and gallantly.

Wilhelm was left sitting, restlessly enough, in this singular mask. The proposal had come upon him by surprise; the execution of it got the start of the deliberation. The Baroness had vanished from the room, before he saw how dangerous the post was which he had engaged to fill. He could not deny that the beauty, the youth, the gracefulness of the Countess had made some impression on him; but his nature was entirely averse to all empty gallantry, and his principles forbade any thought of more serious enterprises; so that his perplexity at this moment was in truth extreme. The fear of displeasing the Countess, and that of pleasing her too well, were equally busy in his mind.

Every female charm, that had ever acted on him, now showed itself again to his imagination. Mariana rose before him in her white morning-gown, and entreated his remembrance. Philina's loveliness, her beautiful hair, her insinuating blandishments, had again become attractive by her late presence. Yet all this retired as if behind the veil of distance, when he figured to himself the noble blooming Countess, whose arm in a few minutes he would feel upon his neck, whose innocent caresses he was there to answer.

The strange mode, in which he was to be delivered out of this perplexity, he certainly did not anticipate. We may judge of his astonishment, nay his terror, when the door opened behind him; and at the first stolen look in the mirror, he quite clearly discerned the Count coming in with a light in his hand. His doubt what he should do, whether he should sit still or rise, should fly, confess, deny, or beg forgiveness, lasted but a few instants. The Count, who had remained motionless standing in the door, retired and shut it softly. At the same moment, the Baroness sprang forward by the side-door, extinguished the lamp, tore Wilhelm from his chair, and hurried him with her into the closet. Instantly, he threw off the night-gown, and put it in its former place. The Baroness took his coat under her arm, and hastened with him through several rooms, passages and partitions, into her chamber; where Wilhelm, so soon as she recovered breath, was informed that on her going to the Countess, and delivering the fictitious intelligence about her husband's arrival, the Countess had answered: "I know it already: what can have happened? I saw him riding in, at the postern, even now." On which the Baroness, in an excessive panic, had run to the Count's chamber to give warning.

"Unhappily you came too late!" said Wilhelm. "The Count was in the room before you, and saw me sitting."

"And recognised you?"

"That I know not. He was looking at me in the glass, as I at him; and before I could well determine whether it was he or a spirit, he drew back, and closed the door behind him."

The anxiety of the Baroness increased, when a servant came to call her, signifying that the Count was with his lady. She went with no light heart; and found the Count silent and thoughtful indeed, but milder and kinder in his words than usual. She knew not what to think of it. They spoke about the incidents of the chase, and the causes of his quick return. The conversation soon ran out. The Count became taciturn; and it struck the Baroness particularly, when he asked for Wilhelm, and expressed a wish that he were sent for, to come and read something.

Wilhelm, who had now dressed himself in the Baroness's chamber, and in some degree recovered his composure, obeyed the order, not without anxiety. The Count gave him a book; out of which he read an adventurous tale, very little at his ease. His voice had a certain inconstancy and quivering in it, which fortunately corresponded with the import of the story. The Count more than once gave kindly tokens of approval; and at last dismissed our friend, with praises of his exquisite manner of reading.

CHAPTER XI.

WILHELM had scarcely read one or two of Shakspeare's plays, till their effect on him became so strong that he could go no farther. His whole soul was in commotion. He sought an opportunity to speak with Jarno; to whom, on meeting with him, he expressed his boundless gratitude for such delicious entertainment.

"I clearly enough foresaw," said Jarno, "that you would not remain insensible to the charms of the most extraordinary and most admirable of all writers."

"Yes!" exclaimed our friend; "I cannot recollect that any book, any man, any incident of my life, has produced such important effects on me, as the precious works, to which by your kindness I have been directed. They seem as if they were performances of some celestial genius, descending among men, to make them, by the mildest instructions, acquainted with themselves. They are no fictions! You would think, while reading them, you stood before the unclosed awful Books of Fate, while the whirlwind of most impassioned life was howling through the leaves, and tossing them fiercely to and fro. The strength and tenderness, the power and peacefulness of this man have so astonished and transported me, that I long vehemently for the time when I shall have it in my power to read farther."

"Bravo!" said Jarno, holding out his hand, and squeezing our friend's: "this is as it should be! And the consequences, which I hope for, will likewise surely follow."

"I wish," said Wilhelm, "I could but disclose to you all that is going on within me even now. All the anticipations I have ever had regarding man and his destiny, which have accompanied me from youth upwards, often unobserved by myself, I find developed and fulfilled in Shakspeare's writings. It seems as if he cleared up every one of our enigmas to us, though we cannot say: Here or there is the word of solution. His men appear like natural men, and yet they are not. These, the most mysterious and complex productions of creation, here act before us as if they were watches, whose dial-plates and cases were of crystal; which pointed out, according to their use, the course of the hours and minutes; while, at the same time, you could discern the combination of wheels and springs that turned them. The few glances I have cast over Shakspeare's world incite me, more than anything beside, to quicken my footsteps forward into the actual world, to mingle in the flood of destinies that is suspended over it; and at length, if I shall prosper, to draw a few cups from the great ocean of true nature, and to distribute them from off the stage among the thirsting people of my native land."

"I feel delighted with the temper of mind in which I now behold you," answered Jarno, laying his hand upon the shoulder of the excited youth; "renounce not the purpose of embarking in active life. Make haste to employ with alacrity the years that are granted you. If I can serve you, I will with all my heart. As yet, I have not asked you how you came into this troop, for which you certainly were neither born nor bred. So much I hope and see: you long to be out of it. I know nothing of your parentage, of your domestic circumstances; consider what you shall confide to me. Thus much only I can say: the times of war we live in may produce quick turns of fortune; did you incline devoting your strength and talents to our service, not fearing labour, and if need were, danger, I might even now have an opportunity to put you in a situation, which you would not afterwards be sorry to have filled for a time." Wilhelm could not sufficiently express his gratitude; he was ready to impart to his friend and patron the whole history of his life.

In the course of this conversation, they had wandered far into the park, and at last come upon the highway that crossed it. Jarno stood silent for a moment, and then said: "Deliberate on my proposal, determine, give me your answer in a few days, and then let me have the narrative you mean to trust me with. I assure you, it has all along to me seemed quite incomprehensible, how you ever could have anything to do with such a class of people. I have often thought with vexation and spleen, how, in order to gain a paltry living, you must fix your heart on a wandering balladmonger, and a silly mongrel, neither male nor female."

He had not yet concluded, when an officer on horseback came hastily along; a groom following him with a led horse. Jarno shouted a warm salutation to him. The officer sprang from his horse; Jarno and he embraced, and talked together; while Wilhelm, confounded at the last expressions of his warlike friend, stood thoughtfully at a side. Jarno turned over some papers which the stranger had delivered to him; while the latter came to Wilhelm; held out his hand, and said with emphasis: "I find you in worthy company; follow the counsel of your friend; and by doing so, accomplish likewise the desire of an unknown man, who takes a genuine interest in you." So saying, he embraced Wilhelm and pressed him cordially to his breast. At the same instant, Jarno advanced, and said to the stranger: "It is best that I ride on with you: by this means you may get the necessary orders, and set out again before night." Both then leaped into their saddles, and left our astonished friend to his own reflections.

Jarno's last words were still ringing in his ears. It galled him to see the two human beings, that had most innocently won his affections, so grievously disparaged by a man whom he honoured so much. The strange embracing of the officer, whom he knew not, made but a slight impression on him; it occupied his curiosity and his imagination for a moment: but Jarno's speech had cut him to the heart; he was deeply hurt by it: and now, in his way homewards, he broke out into reproaches against himself, that he should for a single instant have mistaken or forgotten the unfeeling coldness of Jarno, which looked out from his very eyes, and spoke in all his gestures. "No!" exclaimed he, "thou conceivest, dead-hearted worldling, that thou canst be a friend? All that thou hast power to offer me is not worth the sentiment which binds me to these forlorn beings. How fortunate, that I have discovered in time what I had to expect from thee!"

Mignon came to meet him as he entered; he clasped her in his arms, exclaiming: "Nothing, nothing shall part us, thou good little creature! The seeming prudence of the world shall never cause me to forsake thee, or forget what I owe thee."

The child, whose warm caresses he had been accustomed to avoid, rejoiced with all her heart at this unlooked-for show of tenderness, and clung so fast to him, that he had some difficulty to get loose from her.

From this period, he kept a stricter eye on Jarno's conduct: many parts of it he did not think quite praiseworthy; nay several things came out, which totally displeased him. He had strong suspicions, for example, that the verses on the Baron, which the poor Pedant had so dearly paid for, were composed by Jarno. And as the latter, in Wilhelm's presence, had made sport of the adventure, our friend thought here was certainly a symptom of a most corrupted heart; for what could be more depraved than to treat a guiltless person, whose griefs oneself had occasioned, with jeering and mockery, instead of trying to satisfy or to indemnify him? In this matter, Wilhelm would himself willingly have brought about reparation; and ere long a very curious accident led him to obtain some traces of the persons concerned in that nocturnal outrage.

Hitherto his friends had contrived to keep him unacquainted with the fact, that some of the young officers were in the habit of passing whole nights, in merriment and jollity, with certain actors and actresses, in the lower hall of the old Castle. One morning, having risen early according to his custom, he happened to visit this chamber, and found the gallant gentlemen just in the act of performing rather a singular operation. They had mixed a bowl of water with a quantity of chalk, and were plastering this gruel with a brush upon their waistcoats and pantaloons, without stripping; thus very expeditiously restoring the spotlessness of their apparel. On witnessing this piece of ingenuity, our friend was at once struck with the recollection of the poor Pedant's whited and bedusted coat: his suspicions gathered strength, when he learned that some relations of the Baron's were among the party.

To throw some light on his doubts, he engaged the youths to breakfast with him. They were very lively, and told a multitude of pleasant stories. One of them especially, who for a time had been on the recruiting service, was loud in praising the craft and activity of his captain; who, it appeared, understood the art of alluring men of all kinds towards him, and overreaching every one by the deception proper for him. He circumstantially described, how several young people of good families and careful education had been cozened, by playing off to them a thousand promises of honour and preferment; and he heartily laughed at the simpletons, who felt so gratified, when first enlisted, at the thought of being esteemed and introduced to notice by so reputable, prudent, bold and munificent an officer.

Wilhelm blessed his better genius for having drawn him back in time from the abyss, to whose brink he had approached so near. Jarno he now looked upon as nothing better than a crimp; the embrace of the stranger officer was easily explained. He viewed the feelings and opinions of these men with contempt and disgust; from that moment he carefully avoided coming into contact with any one that wore a uniform; and when he heard that the army was about to move its quarters, the news would have been extremely welcome to him, if he had not feared that immediately on its departure, he himself must be banished from the neighbourhood of his lovely friend, perhaps forever.

CHAPTER XII.

MEANWHILE the Baroness had spent several days disquieted by anxious fears and unsatisfied curiosity. Since the late adventure, the Count's demeanour had been altogether an enigma to her. His manner was changed; none of his customary jokes were to be heard. His demands on the company and the servants had very much abated. Little pedantry or imperiousness was now to be discerned in him; he was silent and thoughtful; yet withal he seemed composed and placid; in short, he was quite another man. In choosing the books which now and then he caused to be read to him, those of a serious, often a religious cast were pitched upon; and the Baroness lived in perpetual fright lest, beneath this apparent serenity, a secret rancour might be lurking; a silent purpose to revenge the offence he had so accidentally discovered. She determined, therefore, to make Jarno her confidant; and this the more freely, as that gentleman and she already stood in a relation to each other, where it is not usual to be very cautious in keeping secrets. For some time Jarno had been her dearest friend; yet they had been dextrous enough to conceal their attachment and joys from the noisy world in which they moved. To the Countess alone this new romance had not remained unknown; and very possibly the Baroness might wish to get her fair friend occupied with some similar engagement, and thus to escape the silent reproaches she had often to endure from that noble-minded woman.

Scarcely had the Baroness related the occurrence to her lover, when he cried out, laughing: " To a certainty the old fool believes that he has seen his ghost! He dreads that the vision may betoken some misfortune, perhaps death to him; and so he is become quite tame, as all half-men do, in thinking of that consummation which no one has escaped, or will escape. Softly a little! As I hope he will live long enough, we may now train him at least, so that he shall not again give disturbance to his wife and household."

They accordingly, as soon as any opportunity occurred, began talking, in the presence of the Count, about warnings, visions, apparitions, and the like. Jarno played the sceptic, the Baroness likewise; and they carried it so far, that his Lordship at last took Jarno aside, reproved him for his freethinking, and produced his own experience to prove the possibility, nay actual occurrence, of such preternatural events. Jarno affected to be struck; to be in doubt; and finally to be convinced: but in private with his friend, he made himself so much the merrier at the credulous weakling, who had thus been cured of his evil habits by a bugbear, but who, they admitted, still deserved some praise for expecting dire calamity, or death itself, with such composure.

" The natural result, which the present apparition might have had, would possibly have ruffled him!" exclaimed the Baroness, with her wonted vivacity; to which, when anxiety was taken from her heart, she had instantly returned. Jarno was richly rewarded; and the two contrived fresh projects for frightening the Count still farther; and still farther exciting and confirming the affection of the Countess for Wilhelm.

With this intention, the whole story was related to the Countess. She, indeed, expressed her displeasure at such conduct; but from that time she became more thoughtful, and in peaceful moments seemed to be considering, pursuing and painting out that scene which had been prepared for her.

The preparations, now going forward on every side, left no room for doubt that the armies were soon to move in advance, and the Prince at the same time to change his head-quarters. It was even said that the Count intended leaving his Castle, and returning to the city. Our players could therefore, without difficulty, calculate the aspect of their stars; yet none of them, except Melina, took any measures in consequence: the rest strove only to catch as much enjoyment as they could from the moment that was passing over them.

Wilhelm, in the mean time, was engaged with a peculiar task. The Countess had required from him a copy of his writings; and he looked on this request as the noblest recompense for his labours.

A young author, who has not yet seen himself in print, will, in such a case, apply no ordinary care to provide a clear and beautiful transcript of his works. It is like the golden age of authorship: he feels transported into those centuries, when the press had not inundated the world with so many useless writings, when none but excellent performances were copied, and kept by the noblest men; and he easily admits the illusion, that his own accurately ruled and measured manuscript may itself prove an excellent performance, worthy to be kept and valued by some future critic.

The Prince being shortly to depart, a great entertainment had been appointed in honour of him. Many ladies of the neighbourhood were invited; and the Countess had dressed herself betimes. On this occasion, she had taken a costlier suit than usual. Her head-dress, and the decorations of her hair, were more exquisite and studied: she wore all her jewels. The Baroness, too, had done her utmost to appear with becoming taste and splendour.

Philina, observing that both ladies, in expectation of their guests, felt the time rather tedious, proposed to send for Wilhelm, who was wishing to present his manuscript, now completed, and to read them some other little pieces. He came; and on his entrance was astonished at the form and the graces of the Countess, which her decorations had but made more visible and striking. Being ordered by the ladies, he began to read; but with so much absence of mind, and so badly, that had not his audience been excessively indulgent, they would very soon have dismissed him.

Every time he looked at the Countess, it seemed to him as if a spark of electric fire were glancing before his eyes. In the end, he knew not where to find the breath he wanted for his reading. The Countess had always pleased him; but now it appeared as if he never had beheld a being so perfect and so lovely. A thousand thoughts flitted up and down his soul; what follows might be nearly their substance.

"How foolish is it in so many poets, and men of sentiment as they are called, to make war on pomp and decoration; requiring that women of all ranks should wear no dress but what is simple and conformable to nature! They rail at decoration, without once considering, that when we see a plain or positively ugly person clothed in a costly and gorgeous fashion, it is not the poor decoration that displeases us. I would assemble all the judges in the world, and ask them here if they wished to see one of these folds, of these ribbons and laces, these braids, ringlets and glancing stones removed? Would they not dread disturbing the delightful impression that so naturally and spontaneously meets us here? Yes, naturally I will say! As Minerva sprang in complete armour from the head of Jove, so does this goddess seem to have stept forth with a light foot, in all her ornaments, from the bosom of some flower."

While reading, he turned his eyes upon her frequently, as if he wished to stamp this image on his soul forever; he more than once read wrong, yet without falling into confusion of mind; though, at other times, he used to feel the mistaking of a word or a letter as a painful deformity, which spoiled a whole recitation.

A false alarm of the arrival of the guests put an end to the reading; the Baroness went out; and the Countess, while about to shut her writing-desk, which was standing open, took up her casket, and put some other rings upon her finger. "We are soon to part," said she, keeping her eyes upon the casket: "accept a memorial of a true friend, who wishes nothing more earnestly than that you may always prosper." She then took out a ring, which, underneath a crystal, bore a little plate of woven hair beautifully set with diamonds. She held it out to Wilhelm, who, on taking it, knew neither what to say nor do, but stood as if rooted to the ground. The Countess shut her desk, and sat down upon the sofa.

"And I must go empty?" said Philina, kneeling down at the Countess' right hand. "Do but look at the man; he carries such a store of words in his mouth, when no one wants to hear them; and now he cannot stammer out the poorest syllable of thanks. Quick, sir! Express your services by way of pantomime at least; and if today you can invent nothing, then, for Heaven's sake, be my imitator."

Philina seized the right hand of the Countess, and kissed it warmly. Wilhelm sank upon his knee, laid hold of the left, and pressed it to his lips. The Countess seemed embarrassed, yet without displeasure.

"Ah!" cried Philina, "so much splendour of attire I may have seen before; but never one so fit to wear it. What bracelets, but also what a hand! What a necklace, but also what a bosom!"

"Peace, little cozener!" said the Countess.

"Is this his Lordship then?" said Philina, pointing to a rich medallion, which the Countess wore on her left side, by a particular chain.

"He is painted in his bridegroom dress," replied the Countess.

"Was he then so young?" inquired Philina; "I know it is but a year or two since you were married."

"His youth must be placed to the artist's account," replied the lady.

"He is a handsome man," observed Philina. "But was there never," she continued, placing her hand on the Countess' heart, "never any other image that found its way in secret hither?"

"Thou art very bold, Philina!" cried she; "I have spoiled thee. Let me never hear the like again."

"If you are angry, then am I unhappy," said Philina, springing up, and hastening from the room.

Wilhelm still held that lovely hand in both of his. His eyes were fixed on the bracelet-clasp; he noticed, with extreme surprise that his initials were traced on it, in lines of brilliants.

"Have I then," he modestly inquired, "your own hair in this precious ring?"

"Yes," replied she in a faint voice; then suddenly collecting herself, she said, and pressed his hand: "Arise, and fare you well!"

"Here is my name," cried he, "by the most curious chance!" He pointed to the bracelet-clasp.

"How?" cried the Countess: "it is the cipher of a female friend!"

"They are the initials of my name. Forget me not. Your image is engraven on my heart, and will never be effaced. Farewell! I must be gone."

He kissed her hand, and meant to rise; but as in dreams, some strange thing fades and changes into something stranger, and the succeeding wonder takes us by surprise; so, without knowing how it happened, he found the Countess in his arms; her lips were resting upon his, and their warm mutual kisses were yielding them that blessedness, which mortals sip from the topmost sparkling foam on the freshly poured cup of love.

Her head lay on his shoulder; the disordered ringlets and ruffles were forgotten. She had thrown her arm round him; he clasped her with vivacity; and pressed her again and again to his breast. O that such a moment could but last forever! And woe to envious fate that shortened even this brief moment to our friends!

How terrified was Wilhelm, how astounded did he start from his happy dream, when the Countess, with a shriek, on a sudden tore herself away, and hastily pressed her hand against her heart.

He stood confounded before her; she held the other hand upon her eyes, and, after a moment's pause, exclaimed: "Away! leave me! delay not!"

He continued standing.

"Leave me!" she cried; and taking off her hand from her eyes, she looked at him with an indescribable expression of countenance; and added, in the most tender and affecting voice: "Fly, if you love me."

Wilhelm was out of the chamber, and again in his room, before he knew what he was doing.

Unhappy creatures! What singular warning of chance or of destiny tore them asunder?

BOOK IV.

CHAPTER I.

LAERTES was standing at the window in a thoughtful mood, resting on his arm, and looking out into the fields. Philina came gliding towards him, across the large hall; she leant upon him, and began to mock him for his serious looks.

"Do not laugh," replied he; "it is frightful to think how Time goes on, how all things change and have an end. See here! A little while ago there was a stately camp: how pleasantly the tents looked; what restless life and motion was within them; how carefully they watched the whole enclosure! And behold, it is all vanished in a day! For a short while, that trampled straw, those holes which the cooks have dug, will show a trace of what was here; and soon the whole will be ploughed and reaped as formerly, and the presence of so many thousand gallant fellows in this quarter will but glimmer in the memories of one or two old men."

Philina began to sing, and dragged forth her friend to dance with her in the hall. "Since Time is not a person we can overtake when he is past," cried she, "let us honour him with mirth and cheerfulness of heart while he is passing."

They had scarcely made a step or two, when Frau Melina came walking through the hall. Philina was wicked enough to invite her to join them in the dance, and thus to bring her in mind of the shape to which her pregnancy had reduced her.

"That I might never more see a woman *in an interesting situation!*" said Philina, when her back was turned.

"Yet she feels an *interest* in it," said Laertes.

"But she manages so shockingly. Didst thou notice that wabbling fold of her shortened petticoat, which always travels out before her when she moves? She has not the smallest knack or skill to trim herself a little, and conceal her state."

"Let her be," said Laertes; "time will soon come to her aid."

"It were prettier, however," cried Philina, "if we could shake children from the trees."

The Baron entered, and spoke some kind words to them, adding a few presents, in the name of the Count and the Countess, who had left the place very early in the morning. He then went to Wilhelm, who was busy in the side-chamber with Mignon. She had been extremely affectionate and taking; had asked minutely about Wilhelm's parents, brothers, sisters and relations; and so brought to his mind the duty which he owed his people, to send them some tidings of himself.

With the farewell compliments of the family, the Baron delivered him an assurance from the Count, that his Lordship had been exceedingly obliged by his acting, his poetical labours and his theatrical exertions. For proof of this statement, the Baron then drew forth a purse, through whose beautiful texture the bright glance of new gold coin was sparkling out. Wilhelm drew back, refusing to accept of it.

"Look upon this gift," said the Baron, "as a compensation for your time, as an acknowledgment of your trouble, not as the reward of your talents. If genius procures us a good name and good-will from men, it is fair likewise that, by our diligence and efforts, we should earn the means to satisfy our wants; since, after all, we are not wholly spirit. Had we been in town, where everything is to be got, we should have changed this little sum into a watch, a ring, or something of that sort; but as it is, I must place the magic rod in your own hands; procure a trinket with it, such as may please you best and be of greatest use, and keep it for our sakes. At the same time, you must not forget to hold the purse in honour. It was knit by the fingers of our ladies: they meant that the cover should give to its contents the most pleasing form."

"Forgive my embarrassment," said Wilhelm, "and my doubts about accepting this present. It as it were annihilates the little I have done, and hinders the free play of happy recollection. Money is a fine thing, when any matter is to be completely settled and abolished; I feel unwilling to be so entirely abolished from the recollection of your house."

"That is not the case," replied the Baron; "but feeling so tenderly yourself, you could not wish that the Count should be obliged to consider himself wholly your debtor; especially when I assure you, that his Lordship's highest ambition has always consisted in being punctual and just. He is not uninformed of the labour you have undergone, or of the zeal with which you have devoted all your time to execute his views; nay he is aware that, to quicken certain operations, you have even expended money of your own. With what face shall I appear before him, then, if I cannot say that his acknowledgment has given you satisfaction?"

"If I thought only of myself," said Wilhelm; "if I might follow merely the dictates of my own feelings, I should certainly, in spite of all these reasons, stedfastly refuse this gift, generous and honourable as it is: but I will not deny, that at the very moment when it brings me into one perplexity, it frees me from another, into which I have lately fallen with regard to my relations, and which has in secret caused me much uneasiness. My management, not only of the time, but also of the money, for which I have to give account, has not been the best; and now, by the kindness of his Lordship, I shall be enabled, with confidence, to give my people news of the good fortune to which this curious bypath has led me. I therefore sacrifice those feelings of delicacy, which like a tender conscience admonish us on such occasions, to a higher duty; and, that I may appear courageously before my father, I must consent to stand ashamed before you."

"It is singular," replied the Baron, "to see what a world of hesitation people feel about accepting money from their friends and patrons, though ready to receive any other gift with joy and thankfulness. Human nature manifests some other such peculiarities, by which many scruples of a similar kind are produced and carefully cherished."

"Is it not the same with all points of honour?" said our friend.

"It is so," replied the Baron; "and with several other prejudices. We must not root them out, lest, in doing so, we tear up noble plants along with them. Yet I am always glad when I meet with men, that feel superior to such objections, when the case requires it; and I think with pleasure on the story of that ingenious poet, which I dare say you have heard of. He had written several plays for the court-theatre, which were honoured by the warmest approbation of the monarch. 'I must give him a distinguished recompense,' said the generous prince: 'ask him whether he would choose to have some jewel given him; or if he would disdain to accept a sum of money.' In his humorous way, the poet answered the inquiring courtier: 'I am thankful, with all my heart, for these gracious purposes; and as the Emperor is daily taking money from us, I see not wherefore I should feel ashamed of taking some from him.'"

Scarcely had the Baron left the room, when Wilhelm eagerly began to count the cash, which had come to him so unexpectedly, and, as he thought, so undeservedly. It seemed as if the worth and dignity of gold, not usually felt till later years, had now, by anticipation, twinkled in his eyes for the first time, as the fine glancing coins rolled out from the beautiful purse. He reckoned up, and found that, particularly as Melina had engaged immediately to pay the loan, he had now as much or more on the right-side of his account, as on that day when Philina first asked him for the nosegay. With a little secret satisfaction, he looked upon his talents; with a little pride, upon the fortune which had led him and attended him. He now seized the pen, with an assured mind, to write a letter, which might free his family from their anxieties, and set his late proceedings in the most favourable light. He abstained from any special narrative; and only by significant and mysterious hints, left them room for guessing at what had befallen him. The good condition of his cash-book, the advantage he had earned by his talents, the favour of the great and of the fair, acquaintance with a wider circle, the improvement of his bodily and mental gifts, his hopes from the future, altogether formed such a fair cloud-picture, that Fata Morgagna itself could scarcely have thrown together a stranger or a better.

In this happy exaltation, the letter being folded up, he went on to maintain a conversation with himself, recapitulating what he had been writing, and pointing out for himself an active and glorious future. The example of so many gallant warriors had fired him; the poetry of Shakspeare had opened a new world to him; from the lips of the beautiful Countess he had inhaled an inexpressible inspiration. All this could not and would not be without effect.

The Stallmeister came to inquire whether they were ready with their packing. Alas! with the single exception of Melina, no one of them had thought of it. Now, however, they were speedily to be in motion. The Count had engaged to have the whole party conveyed forward a few days' journey on their way: the horses were now in readiness, and could not long be wanted. Wilhelm asked for his trunk: Frau Melina had taken it to put her own things in. He asked for money; Herr Melina had stowed it all far down at the bottom of his box. Philina said she had still some room in hers; she took Wilhelm's clothes, and bade Mignon bring the rest. Wilhelm, not without reluctance, was obliged to let it be so.

While they were loading, and getting all things ready, Melina said: "I am sorry we should travel like mountebanks and ropedancers; I could wish that Mignon would put on girl's clothes, and that the Harper would let his beard be shorn." Mignon clung firmly to Wilhelm, and cried, with great vivacity: "I am a boy; I will be no girl!" The old man held his peace; and Philina, on this suggestion, made some merry observations on the singularity of their protector the Count. "If the Harper should cut off his beard," said she, "let him sew it carefully upon a ribbon, and keep it by him, that he may put it on again whenever his Lordship the

Count falls in with him in any quarter of the world. It was this beard alone that procured him the favour of his Lordship."

On being pressed to give an explanation of this singular speech, Philina said to them: "The Count thinks it contributes very much to the completeness of theatrical illusion, if the actor continues to play his part, and to sustain his character, even in common life. It was for this reason that he showed such favour to the Pedant; and he judged it, in like manner, very fitting that the Harper not only wore his false beard at nights on the stage, but also constantly by day; and he used to be delighted at the natural appearance of the mask."

While the rest were laughing at this error, and the other strange opinions of the Count, the Harper led our friend aside, took leave of him, and begged with tears that he would even now let him go. Wilhelm spoke to him, declaring that he would protect him against all the world, that no one should touch a hair of his head, much less send him off against his will.

The old man seemed affected deeply; an unwonted fire was glowing in his eyes. "It is not that," cried he, "which drives me away. I have long been reproaching myself in secret for staying with you. I ought to linger nowhere; for misfortune flies to overtake me, and injures all that are connected with me. Dread everything, unless you dismiss me: but ask me no questions; I belong not to myself; I cannot stay."

"To whom dost thou belong? Who can exert such a power on thee?"

"Leave me my horrid secret, and let me go! The vengeance which pursues me is not of the earthly judge. I belong to an inexorable Destiny; I cannot stay, and I dare not."

"In the situation thou art now in, I certainly will not let thee go."

"It were high treason against you, my benefactor, if I should delay. I am secure while with you, but you are in peril. You know not whom you keep beside you. I am guilty, but more wretched than guilty. My presence scares happiness away; and good deeds grow powerless, when I become concerned in them. Fugitive, unresting I should be, that my evil genius might not seize me, which pursues but at a distance, and only appears when I have found a place, and am laying down my head to seek repose. More grateful I cannot show myself, than by forsaking you."

"Strange man! Thou canst neither take away the confidence I place in thee, nor the hope I feel to see thee happy. I wish not to penetrate the secrets of thy superstition; but if thou livest in belief of wonderful forebodings and entanglements of Fate, then, to cheer and hearten thee, I say, unite thyself to my good fortune, and let us see which genius is the stronger, thy dark or my bright one."

Wilhelm seized this opportunity of suggesting to him many other comfortable things; for of late our friend had begun to imagine, that this singular attendant of his must be a man who, by chance or destiny, had been led into some weighty crime, the remembrance of which he was ever bearing on his conscience. A few days ago, Wilhelm, listening to his singing, had observed attentively the following lines:

> For him the light of ruddy morn
> But paints the horizon red with flame;
> And voices, from the depths of nature borne,
> Woe! woe! upon his guilty head proclaim.

But, let the old man urge what arguments he pleased, our friend had constantly a stronger argument at hand. He turned everything on its fairest side; spoke so bravely, heartily and cheerily, that even the old man seemed again to gather spirits, and to throw aside his whims.

CHAPTER II.

MELINA was in hopes to get established with his company, in a small but thriving town at some distance. They had already reached the place where the Count's horses were to turn; and now they looked about for other carriages and cattle to transport them onward. Melina had engaged to provide them a conveyance: he showed himself but niggardly, according to his custom. Wilhelm, on the contrary, had the shining ducats of the Countess in his pocket, and thought he had the fullest right to spend them merrily; forgetting very soon how ostentatiously he had produced them in the stately balance transmitted to his father.

His friend Shakspeare, whom with the greatest joy he acknowledged as his godfather, and rejoiced the more that his name was Wilhelm, had introduced him to a prince, who frolicked for a time among mean, nay vicious companions, and who, notwithstanding his nobleness of nature, found pleasure in the rudeness, indecency and coarse intemperance of these altogether sensual knaves. This ideal likeness, which he figured as the type and the excuse of his own actual condition, was most welcome to our friend; and the process of self-deception, to which already he displayed an almost invincible tendency, was thereby very much facilitated.

He now began to think about his dress. It struck him that a

waistcoat, over which, in case of need, one could throw a little short mantle, was a very fit thing for a traveller. Long knit pantaloons, and a pair of lacing-boots, seemed the true garb of a pedestrian. He next procured a fine silk sash, which he tied about him, under the pretence at first of securing warmth for his person. On the other hand, he freed his neck from the tyranny of stocks; and got a few stripes of muslin sewed upon his shirt; making the pieces of considerable breadth, so that they presented the complete appearance of an ancient ruff. The beautiful silk neckerchief, the memorial of Mariana, which had once been saved from burning, now lay slackly tied beneath this muslin collar. A round hat, with a parti-coloured band, and a large feather, perfected the mask.

The women all asserted that this garb became him very well. Philina in particular appeared enchanted with it. She solicited his hair for herself; beautiful locks, which, the closer to approach the natural ideal, he had unmercifully clipped. By so doing, she recommended herself not amiss to his favour; and our friend, who, by his openhandedness, had acquired the right of treating his companions somewhat in Prince Harry's manner, ere long fell into the humour of himself contriving a few wild tricks, and presiding in the execution of them. The people fenced, they danced, they devised all kinds of sports; and in their gaiety of heart partook of what tolerable wine they could fall in with, in copious proportions; while, amid the disorder of this tumultuous life, Philina lay in wait for the coy hero; over whom let his better Genius keep watch!

One chief diversion, which yielded the company a frequent and very pleasing entertainment, consisted in producing an extempore play, in which their late benefactors and patrons were mimicked and turned into ridicule. Some of our actors had seized very neatly whatever was peculiar in the outward manner of several distinguished people in the Count's establishment; their imitation of these was received by the rest of the party with the greatest approbation; and when Philina produced, from the secret archives of her experience, certain peculiar declarations of love that had been made to her, the audience were like to die with laughing and malicious joy.

Wilhelm censured their ingratitude; but they told him in reply, that these gentry well deserved what they were getting, their general conduct towards such deserving people as our friends believed themselves, not having been by any means the best imaginable. The little consideration, the neglect they had experienced, were now described with many aggravations. The jesting, bantering and mimicry proceeded as before; our party were growing bitterer and more unjust every minute.

"I wish," observed Wilhelm, "there were no envy or selfishness lurking under what you say, but that you would regard those persons and their station in the proper point of view. It is a peculiar thing to be placed, by one's very birth, in an elevated situation in society. The man for whom inherited wealth has secured a perfect freedom of existence; who finds himself from his youth upwards abundantly encompassed with all the secondary essentials, so to speak, of human life,—will generally become accustomed to consider these qualifications as the first and greatest of all; while the worth of that mode of human life, which nature from her own stores equips and furnishes, will strike him much more faintly. The behaviour of noblemen to their inferiors, and likewise to each other, is regulated by external preferences: they give each credit for his title, his rank, his clothes and equipage, but his individual merits come not into play."

This speech was honoured with the company's unbounded applause. They declared it to be shameful, that men of merit should constantly be pushed into the background; and that in the great world, there should not be a trace of natural and hearty intercourse. On this latter point particularly they overshot all bounds.

"Blame them not for it," said Wilhelm, "rather pity them! They have seldom an exalted feeling of that happiness which we admit to be the highest that can flow from the inward abundance of nature. Only to us poor creatures is it granted to enjoy the happiness of friendship, in its richest fulness. Those dear to us we cannot elevate by our countenance, or advance by our favour, or make happy by our presents. We have nothing but ourselves. This whole self we must give away; and if it is to be of any value, we must make our friend secure of it forever. What an enjoyment, what a happiness, for giver and receiver! With what blessedness does truth of affection invest our situation! It gives to the transitory life of man a heavenly certainty; it forms the crown and capital of all that we possess."

While he spoke thus, Mignon had come near him; she threw her little arms round him, and stood with her cheek resting on his breast. He laid his hand on the child's head, and proceeded: "It is easy for a great man to win our minds to him; easy to make our hearts his own. A mild and pleasant manner, a manner only not inhuman, will of itself do wonders: and how many means does he possess of holding fast the affections he has once conquered! To us, all this occurs less frequently, to us it is all more difficult; and we naturally therefore put a greater value on whatever, in the way of mutual kindness, we acquire and accomplish. What touching examples of faithful servants giving themselves up to danger and death for their masters! How finely has Shakspeare painted out such things to us! Fidelity, in this case, is the effort of a noble soul struggling to become equal with one exalted above it. By stedfast attachment and love, the servant is made equal to his lord, who but for this is justified in looking on him as a hired slave. Yes, these virtues belong to the lower class of men alone; that class cannot do without them, and with them it has a beauty of its own. Whoever is enabled to requite all favours easily, will likewise easily be tempted to raise himself above the habit of acknowledgment. Nay, in this sense, I am of opinion, it might almost be maintained, that a great man may possess friends, but cannot be one."

Mignon pressed still closer towards him.

"It may be so," replied one of the party: "we do not need their friendship, and do not ask it. But it were well if they understood a little more about the arts which they affect to patronise. When we played in the best style, there was none to mind us: it was all sheer partiality. Any one they chose to favour pleased; and they did not choose to favour those that merited to please. It was intolerable to observe how often silliness and mere stupidity attracted notice and applause."

"When I abate from this," said Wilhelm, "what seemed to spring from irony and malice, I think we may nearly say, that one fares in art as he does in love. And after all, how shall a fashionable man of the world, with his dissipated habits, attain that intimate presence with a special object, which an artist must long continue in, if he would produce anything approaching to perfection; a state of feeling without which it is impossible for any one to take such an interest, as the artist hopes and wishes, in his work.

"Believe me, my friends, it is with talents as with virtue; one must love them for their own sake, or entirely renounce them. And neither of them is acknowledged and rewarded, except when their possessor can practise them unseen, like a dangerous secret."

"Meanwhile, until some proper judge discovers us, we may all die of hunger," cried a fellow in the corner.

"Not quite inevitably," answered Wilhelm. "I have observed that so long as one stirs and lives, one always finds food and raiment, though they be not of the richest sort. And why should we repine? Were we not, altogether unexpectedly, and when our prospects were the very worst, taken kindly by the hand, and substantially entertained? And now, when we are in want of nothing, does it once occur to us to attempt anything for our improvement; or to strive, though never so faintly, towards advancement in our art? We are busied about indifferent matters; and, like school-boys, we are casting all aside that might bring our lesson to our thoughts."

"In sad truth," said Philina, "it is even so! Let us choose a play; we will go through it on the spot. Each of us must do his best, as if he stood before the largest audience."

They did not long deliberate; a play was fixed on. It was one of those which at that time were meeting great applause in Germany, and have now passed away. Some of the party whistled a symphony; each speedily bethought him of his part; they commenced; and played all the piece with the greatest attention, and really well beyond expectation. Mutual applauses circulated; our friends had seldom been so pleasantly diverted.

On finishing, they all felt exceedingly contented, partly on account of their time being spent so well, partly because each of them experienced some degree of satisfaction with his own performance. Wilhelm expressed himself copiously in their praise; the conversation grew cheerful and merry.

"You would see," cried our friend, "what advances we should make, if we continued this sort of training, and ceased to confine our attention to mere learning by heart, rehearsing, and playing mechanically, as if it were a barren duty, or some handicraft employment. How different a character do our musical professors merit! What interest they take in their art; how correct are they in the practisings they undertake in common! What pains they are at in tuning their instruments; how exactly they observe time; how delicately they express the strength and the weakness of their tones! No one there thinks of gaining credit to himself by a loud accompaniment of the solo of another. Each tries to play in the spirit of the composer, each to express well whatever is committed to him, be it much or little.

"Should not we too go as strictly and as ingeniously to work, seeing we practise an art far more delicate than that of music; seeing we are called on to express the commonest and the strangest emotions of human nature, with elegance and so as to delight? Can anything be more shocking than to slur over our rehearsal, and in our acting to depend on good luck, or the capricious choice of the moment? We ought to place our highest happiness and satisfaction in mutually desiring to gain each other's approbation; we should even value the applauses of the public, only in so far as we have previously sanctioned them among ourselves. Why is the master of the band more secure about his music than the manager about his play? Because, in the orchestra, each individual would feel ashamed of his mistakes, which offend the outward ear: but how seldom have I found an actor disposed to acknowledge or feel ashamed of mistakes, pardonable or the contrary, by which the inward ear is so outrageously offended! I could wish, for my part, that our theatre were as narrow as the wire of a rope-dancer, that so no inept fellow might dare to venture on it; instead of being, as it is, a place where every one discovers in himself capacity enough to flourish and parade."

The company gave this apostrophe a kind reception; each being convinced that the censure conveyed in it could not apply to him, after acting a little while ago so excellently with the rest. On the other hand, it was agreed that during this journey, and for the future, if they remained together, they would regularly proceed with their training in the manner just adopted. Only it was thought, that as this was a thing of good humour and free will, no formal manager must be allowed to have a hand in it. Taking it for an established fact, that among good men, the republican form of government is the best, they declared that the post of manager should go round among them; he must be chosen by universal suffrage, and every time have a sort of little senate joined in authority along with him. So delighted did they feel with this idea, that they longed to put it instantly in practice.

"I have no objection," said Melina, "if you incline making such an experiment while we are travelling; I shall willingly suspend my own directorship until we reach some settled place." He was in hopes of saving cash by this arrangement, and of casting many small expenses on the shoulders of the little senate or of the interim manager. This fixed, they went very earnestly to counsel, how the form of the new commonwealth might best be adjusted.

" 'Tis an itinerating kingdom," said Laertes; " we shall at least have no quarrels about frontiers."

They directly proceeded to the business, and elected Wilhelm as their first manager. The senate also was appointed, the women having seat and vote in it; laws were propounded, were rejected, were agreed to. In such playing, the time passed on unnoticed; and as our friends had spent it pleasantly, they also conceived that they had really been effecting something useful; and by their new constitution had been opening a new prospect for the stage of their native country.

CHAPTER III.

SEEING the company so favourably disposed, Wilhelm now hoped he might farther have it in his power to converse with them on the poetic merit of the pieces which might come before them. "It is not enough," said he next day, when they were all again assembled, "for the actor merely to glance over a dramatic work, to judge of it by his first impression, and thus, without investigation, to declare his satisfaction or dissatisfaction with it. Such things may be allowed in a spectator, whose purpose it is rather to be entertained and moved than formally to criticise. But the actor, on the other hand, should be prepared to give a reason for his praise or censure: and how shall he do this, if he have not taught himself to penetrate the sense, the views and feelings of his author? A common error is, to form a judgment of a drama from a single part in it; and to look upon this part itself in an isolated point of view, not in its connexion with the whole. I have noticed this, within a few days, so clearly in my own conduct, that I will give you the account as an example, if you please to hear me patiently.

"You all know Shakspeare's incomparable Hamlet: our public reading of it at the Castle yielded every one of us the greatest satisfaction. On that occasion, we proposed to act the piece; and I, not knowing what I undertook, engaged to play the Prince's part. This I conceived that I was studying, while I began to get by heart the strongest passages, the soliloquies, and those scenes in which force of soul, vehemence and elevation of feeling have the freest scope; where the agitated heart is allowed to display itself with touching expressiveness.

"I farther conceived that I was penetrating quite into the spirit of the character, while I endeavoured as it were to take upon myself the load of deep melancholy under which my prototype was labouring, and in this humour to pursue him through the strange labyrinths of his caprices and his singularities. Thus learning, thus practising, I doubted not but I should by and by become one person with my hero.

"But the farther I advanced, the more difficult did it become for me to form any image of the whole, in its general bearings; till at last it seemed as if impossible. I next went through the entire piece, without interruption; but here too I found much that I could not away with. At one time the characters, at another time the manner of displaying them, seemed inconsistent;

and I almost despaired of finding any general tint, in which I might present my whole part with all its shadings and variations. In such devious paths I toiled, and wandered long in vain; till at length a hope arose that I might reach my aim in quite a new way.

"I set about investigating every trace of Hamlet's character, as it had shown itself before his father's death: I endeavoured to distinguish what in it was independent of this mournful event; independent of the terrible events that followed; and what most probably the young man would have been, had no such thing occurred.

"Soft, and from a noble stem, this royal flower had sprung up under the immediate influences of majesty: the idea of moral rectitude with that of princely elevation, the feeling of the good and dignified with the consciousness of high birth, had in him been unfolded simultaneously. He was a prince, by birth a prince; and he wished to reign, only that good men might be good without obstruction. Pleasing in form, polished by nature, courteous from the heart, he was meant to be the pattern of youth and the joy of the world.

"Without any prominent passion, his love for Ophelia was a still presentiment of sweet wants. His zeal in knightly accomplishments was not entirely his own; it needed to be quickened and inflamed by praise bestowed on others for excelling in them. Pure in sentiment, he knew the honourable-minded, and could prize the rest which an upright spirit tastes on the bosom of a friend. To a certain degree, he had learned to discern and value the good and the beautiful in arts and sciences; the mean, the vulgar was offensive to him; and if hatred could take root in his tender soul, it was only so far as to make him properly despise the false and changeful insects of a court, and play with them in easy scorn. He was calm in his temper, artless in his conduct; neither pleased with idleness, nor too violently eager for employment. The routine of a university he seemed to continue when at court. He possessed more mirth of humour than of heart; he was a good companion, pliant, courteous, discreet, and able to forget and forgive an injury; yet never able to unite himself with those who overstept the limits of the right, the good, and the becoming.

"When we read the piece again, you shall judge whether I am yet on the proper track. I hope at least to bring forward passages that shall support my opinion in its main points."

This delineation was received with warm approval: the company imagined they foresaw that Hamlet's manner of proceeding might now be very satisfactorily explained; they applauded this method of penetrating into the spirit of a writer. Each of them proposed to himself to take up some piece, and study it on these principles, and so unfold the author's meaning.

CHAPTER IV.

Our friends had to continue in the place for a day or two; and it was not long till sundry of them got engaged in adventures of a rather pleasant kind. Laertes in particular was challenged by a lady of the neighbourhood, a person of some property; but he received her blandishments with extreme, nay unhandsome coldness; and had in consequence to undergo a multitude of jibes from Philina. She took this opportunity of detailing to our friend the hapless love-story which had made the youth so bitter a foe to womankind. "Who can take it ill of him;" she cried, "that he hates a sex which has played him so foul, and given him to swallow, in one stoutly concentrated potion, all the miseries that man can fear from woman? Do but conceive it: within four and twenty hours, he was lover, bridegroom, husband, cuckold, patient and widower! I wot not how you could use a man worse."

Laertes hastened from the room half-vexed, half-laughing; and Philina in her sprightliest style began to relate the story: how Laertes, a young man of eighteen, on joining a company of actors, found in it a girl of fourteen on the point of departing with her father, who had quarrelled with the manager. How, on the instant, he had fallen mortally in love; had conjured the father by all possible considerations to remain, promising at length to marry the young woman. How, after a few pleasing hours of groomship, he had accordingly been wedded, and been happy as he ought; whereupon, next day, while he was occupied at the rehearsal, his wife, according to professional rule, had honoured him with a pair of horns; and how as he, out of excessive tenderness, hastening home far too soon, had, alas, found a former lover in his place, he had struck into the affair with thoughtless indignation, had called out both father and lover, and sustained a grievous wound in the duel. How father and daughter had thereupon set off by night, leaving him behind to labour with a double hurt. How the leech he applied to was unhappily the worst in nature; and the poor fellow had got out of the adventure with blackened teeth and watering eyes. That he was greatly to be pitied, being otherwise the bravest young man on the surface of the earth. "Especially," said she, "it grieves me that the poor soul now hates women; for, hating women, how can one keep living?"

Melina interrupted them with news, that all things being now ready for the journey, they would set out tomorrow morning. He handed them a plan, arranging how they were to travel.

"If any good friend take me on his lap," said Philina, "I shall be content, though we sit crammed together never so close and sorrily: 'tis all one to me."

"It does not signify," observed Laertes, who now entered.

"It is pitiful," said Wilhelm, hastening away. By the aid of money he secured another very comfortable coach, though Melina had pretended that there were no more. A new distribution then took place; and our friends were rejoicing in the thought that they should now travel pleasantly, when intelligence arrived that a party of military volunteers had been seen upon the road, from whom little good could be expected.

In the town, these tidings were received with great attention, though they were but variable and ambiguous. As the contending armies were at that time placed, it seemed impossible that any hostile corps could have advanced, or any friendly one hung arear, so far. Yet every man was eager to exhibit to our travellers the danger that awaited them as truly dangerous; every man was eager to suggest that some other route might be adopted.

By these means, most of our friends had been seized with anxiety and fear; and when, according to the new republican constitution, the whole members of the state had been called together to take counsel on this extraordinary case, they were almost unanimously of opinion that it would be proper either to keep back the mischief by abiding where they were, or to evade it by choosing another road.

Wilhelm alone, not participating in the panic, regarded it as mean to abandon, for the sake of mere rumours, a plan which they had not entered on without much thought. He endeavoured to put heart into them; his reasons were manly and convincing.

"It is but a rumour," he observed; "and how many such arise in time of war! Well-informed people say that the occurrence is exceedingly improbable, nay almost impossible. Shall we, in so important a matter, allow a vague report to determine our proceedings? The route pointed out to us by the Count, and to which our passport was adapted, is the shortest and in the best condition. It leads us to the town, where you see acquaintances, friends before you, and may hope for a good reception. The other way will also bring us thither; but by what a circuit, and along what miserable roads! Have we any right to hope, that, in this late season of the year, we shall get on at all; and what time and money shall we squander in the mean while!" He added many more considerations, presenting the matter on so many advantageous sides, that their fear began to dissipate, and their courage to increase. He talked to them so much about the discipline of regular troops, he painted the marauders and wandering rabble so contemptuously, and represented the danger itself as so pleasant and inspiring, that the spirits of the party were altogether cheered.

Laertes from the first had been of his opinion; he now declared that he would not flinch or fail. Old Boisterous found a consenting phrase or two to utter, in his own vein; Philina laughed at them all; and Madam Melina, who, notwithstanding her advanced state of pregnancy, had lost nothing of her natural stoutheartedness, regarded the proposal as heroic. Herr Melina, moved by this harmonious feeling, hoping also to save somewhat by travelling the short road which had been first contemplated, did not withstand the general consent; and the project was agreed to with universal alacrity.

They next began to make some preparations for defence at all hazards. They bought large hangers, and slung them in well-quilted straps over their shoulders. Wilhelm, farther, stuck a pair of pistols in his girdle. Laertes, independently of this occurrence, had a good gun. They all took the road in the highest glee.

On the second day of their journey, the drivers, who knew the country well, proposed to take their noon's rest in a certain woody spot of the hills; since the town was far off, and in good weather the hill road was generally preferred.

The day being beautiful, all easily agreed to the proposal. Wilhelm on foot went on before them through the hills; making every one that met him stare with astonishment at his singular figure. He hastened with quick and contented steps across the forest; Laertes walked whistling after him; none but the women continued to be dragged along in the carriages. Mignon too ran forward by his side, proud of the hanger, which, when the party were all arming, she would not go without. Around her hat she had bound the pearl necklace, one of Mariana's reliques, which Wilhelm still possessed. Friedrich, the fair-haired boy, carried Laertes' gun. The Harper had the most pacific look; his long cloak was tucked up within his girdle, to let him walk more freely; he leaned upon a knotty staff; his harp had been left behind him in the carriage.

Immediately on reaching the summit of the height, a task not without its difficulties, our party recognised the appointed spot, by the fine beech-trees which encircled and screened it. A spacious green, sloping softly in the middle of the forest, invited one to tarry; a trimly-bordered well offered the most grateful refreshment; and on the farther side, through chasms in the mountains, and over the tops of the woods, appeared a landscape distant, lovely, full of hope. Hamlets and mills were lying in the bottoms, villages upon the plain; and a new chain of mountains, visible in the distance, made the prospect still more significant of hope, for they entered only like a soft limitation.

The first comers took possession of the place; rested a while in the shade, lighted a fire, and so awaited, singing as they worked, the remainder of the party; who by degrees arrived, and with one accord saluted the place, the lovely weather, and the still lovelier scene.

CHAPTER V.

IF our friends had frequently enjoyed a good and merry hour together while within four walls, they were naturally much gayer here, where the freedom of the sky and the beauty of the place seemed as it were to purify the feelings of every one. All felt nearer to each other; all wished that they might pass their whole lives in so pleasant an abode. They envied hunters, charcoal-men and woodcutters; people whom their calling constantly retains in such happy places: but, above all, they prized the delicious economy of a band of gipsies. They envied these wonderful companions, entitled to enjoy in blissful idleness all the adventurous charms of nature; they rejoiced at being in some degree like them.

Meanwhile the women had begun to boil potatoes; and to unwrap and get ready the victuals brought along with them. Some pots were standing by the fire. The party had placed themselves in groups, under the trees and bushes. Their singular apparel, their various weapons, gave them a foreign aspect. The horses were eating their provender at a side. Could one have concealed the coaches, the look of this little horde would have been romantic, even to complete illusion.

Wilhelm enjoyed a pleasure he had never felt before. He could now imagine his present company to be a wandering colony, and himself the leader of it. In this character he talked with those around him, and figured out the fantasy of the moment as poetically as he could. The feelings of the party rose in cheerfulness: they ate and drank and made merry; and repeatedly declared, that they had never passed more pleasant moments.

Their contentment had not long gone on increasing, till activity awoke among the younger part of them. Wilhelm and Laertes seized their rapiers, and began to practise, on this occasion with theatrical intentions. They undertook to represent the duel, in which Hamlet and his adversary find so tragical an end. Both were persuaded that, in this powerful scene, it was not enough merely to keep pushing awkwardly hither and thither, as it is generally exhibited in theatres: they were in hopes to show, by example, how, in presenting it, a worthy spectacle might also be afforded to the critic in the art of fencing. The rest made a circle round them. Both fought with skill and ardour. The interest of the spectators rose higher every pass.

But all at once, in the nearest bush, a shot went off; and immediately another; and the party flew asunder in terror. Next moment, armed men were to be seen pressing forward to the spot where the horses were eating their fodder, not far from the coaches that were packed with luggage.

A universal scream proceeded from the females: our heroes threw away their rapiers, seized their pistols, and ran towards the robbers; demanding, with violent threats, the meaning of such conduct.

This question being answered laconically, with a couple of musket-shots, Wilhelm fired his pistol at a crisp-headed knave, who had got upon the top of the coach, and was cutting the cords of the package. Rightly hit, this artist instantly came tumbling down; Laertes also had not missed. Both of them, encouraged by success, drew their side-arms; when a number of the plundering party rushed out upon them, with curses and loud bellowing; fired a few shots at them, and fronted their impetuosity with glittering sabres. Our young heroes made a bold resistance. They called upon their other comrades, and endeavoured to excite them to a general resistance. But ere long, Wilhelm lost the sight of day, and the consciousness of what was passing. Stupefied by a shot that wounded him between the breast and the left arm, by a stroke that split his hat in two, and almost penetrated to his brain, he sank down, and only by the narratives of others came afterwards to understand the luckless end of this adventure.

On again opening his eyes, he found himself in the strangest posture. The first thing that pierced the dimness, which yet swam before his vision, was Philina's face bent down over his. He felt himself weak; and making a movement to rise, he discovered that he was in Philina's lap; into which, indeed, he again sank down. She was sitting on the sward. She had softly pressed towards her the head of the fallen young man; and made for him an easy couch, as far as in her power. Mignon was kneeling with dishevelled and bloody hair at his feet, which she embraced with many tears.

On noticing his bloody clothes, Wilhelm asked, in a broken

voice, where he was, and what had happened to himself and the rest. Philina begged him to be quiet: the others, she said, were all in safety, and none but he and Laertes wounded. Farther, she would tell him nothing; but earnestly entreated him to keep still, as his wounds had been but slightly and hastily bound. He stretched out his hand to Mignon, and inquired about the bloody locks of the child, who he supposed was also wounded.

For the sake of quietness, Philina let him know that this true-hearted creature, seeing her friend wounded, and in the hurry of the instant being able to think of nothing which would stanch the blood, had taken her own hair that was flowing round her head, and tried to stop the wounds with it; but had soon been obliged to give up the vain attempt: that afterwards they had bound him with moss and dry mushrooms, Philina herself giving up her neckerchief for that purpose.

Wilhelm noticed that Philina was sitting with her back against her own trunk, which still looked firmly locked and quite uninjured. He inquired if the rest also had been so lucky as to save their goods? She answered with a shrug of the shoulders, and a look over the green, where broken chests, and coffers beaten into fragments, and knapsacks ripped up, and a multitude of little wares, lay scattered all round. No person now was to be seen upon the place: this strange group formed the only living object in the solitude.

Inquiring farther, our friend learned more and more particulars. The rest of the men, it appeared, who at all events might still have made resistance, were struck with terror, and soon overpowered. Some fled, some looked with horror at the accident. The drivers, for the sake of their cattle, had held out more obstinately; but they too were at last thrown down and tied; after which, in a few minutes, everything was thoroughly ransacked, and the booty carried off. The hapless travellers, their fear of death being over, had begun to mourn their loss; had hastened with the greatest speed to the neighbouring village, taking with them Laertes, whose wounds were slight, and carrying off but a very few fragments of their property. The Harper having placed his damaged instrument against a tree, had proceeded in their company to the place; to seek a surgeon, and return with his utmost rapidity to help his benefactor, whom he had left apparently upon the brink of death.

CHAPTER VI.

MEANWHILE our three adventurers continued yet a space in their strange position, no one returning to their aid. Evening was advancing; the darkness threatened to come on. Philina's indifference was changing to anxiety; Mignon ran to and fro, her impatience increasing every moment; and at last, when their prayer was granted, and human creatures did approach, a new alarm fell upon them. They distinctly heard a troop of horses coming up the road, which they had lately travelled; they dreaded lest, a second time, some company of unbidden guests might be purposing to visit this scene of battle, and gather up the gleanings.

The more agreeable was their surprise, when, after a few moments, a young lady issued from the thickets, riding on a gray courser, and accompanied by an elderly gentleman and some cavaliers. Grooms, servants and a troop of hussars closed up the rear.

Philina stared at this phenomenon, and was about to call, and entreat the fair Amazon for help; when the latter, turning her astonished eyes on the group, instantly checked her horse, rode up to them, and halted. She inquired eagerly about the wounded man, whose posture in the lap of this light-minded Samaritan seemed to strike her as peculiarly strange.

"Is it your husband?" she inquired of Philina. "Only a good friend," replied the other, with a tone that Wilhelm liked extremely ill. He had fixed his eyes upon the soft, elevated, calm, sympathising features of the stranger: he thought he had never seen aught nobler or more lovely. Her shape he could not see: it was hid by a man's white greatcoat, which she seemed to have borrowed from some of her attendants, to screen her from the chill evening air.

By this, the horsemen also had come near. Some of them dismounted: the lady did so likewise. She asked, with humane sympathy, concerning every circumstance of the mishap which had befallen the travellers; but especially concerning the wounds of the poor youth who lay before her. Thereupon she turned quickly round, and went aside with the old gentleman to some carriages, which were slowly coming up the hill, and which at length stopped upon the scene of action.

The young lady having stood with her conductor a short time at the door of one of the coaches, and talked with the people in it, a man of a squat figure stept out, and came along with them to our wounded hero. By the little box which he held in his hand, and the leathern pouch with instruments in it, you soon recognised him for a surgeon. His manners were rude rather than attractive; but his hand was light, and his help was welcome.

Having examined strictly, he declared that none of the wounds were dangerous. He would dress them, he said, on the spot; after which the patient might be carried to the nearest village.

The anxious attentions of the young lady seemed to augment. "Do but look," she said, after going to and fro once or twice, and again bringing the old gentleman to the place; "look how they have treated him! And is it not on our account that he is suffering?" Wilhelm heard these words, but did not understand them. She went restlessly up and down: it seemed as if she could not tear herself away from the presence of the wounded man, while at the same time she feared to violate decorum by remaining, when they had begun, though not without difficulty, to remove some part of his apparel. The surgeon was just cutting off the left sleeve of his patient's coat, when the old gentleman came near, and represented to the lady, in a serious tone, the necessity of proceeding on their journey. Wilhelm kept his eyes bent on her; and was so enchanted with her looks, that he scarcely felt what he was suffering or doing.

Philina, in the mean time, had risen up to kiss the hand of this kind young lady. While they stood beside each other, Wilhelm thought he had never seen such a contrast. Philina had never till now appeared in so unfavourable a light. She had no right, as it seemed to him, to come near that noble creature, still less to touch her.

The lady asked Philina various things, but in an under tone. At length she turned to the old gentleman, and said, "Dear uncle, may I be generous at your expense?" She took off the greatcoat, with the visible intention to give it to the stript and wounded youth.

Wilhelm, whom the healing look of her eyes had hitherto held fixed, was now, as the surtout fell away, astonished at her lovely figure. She came near, and softly laid the coat above him. At this moment, as he tried to open his mouth, and stammer out some words of gratitude, the lively impression of her presence worked so strongly on his senses, already caught and bewildered, that all at once it appeared to him as if her head were encircled with rays; and a glancing light seemed by degrees to spread itself over all her form. At this moment the surgeon, making preparations to extract the ball from his wound, gave him a sharper twinge: the angel faded away from the eyes of the fainting patient; he lost all consciousness; and on returning to himself, the horsemen and coaches, the fair one with her attendants, had vanished like a dream.

CHAPTER VII.

WILHELM's wounds once dressed, and his clothes put on, the surgeon hastened off; just as the Harper with a number of peasants arrived. Out of some cut boughs, which they speedily wattled with twigs, a kind of litter was constructed; upon which they placed the wounded youth, and under the conduct of a mounted huntsman, whom the noble company had left behind them, carried him softly down the mountain. The Harper, silent and shrouded in his own thoughts, bore with him his broken instrument. Some men brought on Philina's box, herself following with a bundle. Mignon skipped along through copse and thicket, now before the party, now beside them, and looked up with longing eyes at her hurt protector.

He meanwhile, wrapt in his warm surtout, was lying peacefully upon the litter. An electric warmth seemed to flow from the fine wool into his body: in short, he felt himself in the most delightful frame of mind. The lovely being, whom this garment lately covered, had affected him to the very heart. He still saw the coat falling down from her shoulders; saw that noble form, begirt with radiance, stand beside him; and his soul hied over rocks and forests on the footsteps of his vanished benefactress.

It was nightfall when the party reached the village, and halted at the door of the inn where the rest of the company, in the gloom of despondency, were bewailing their irreparable loss. The one little chamber of the house was crammed with people. Some of them were lying upon straw; some were occupying benches; some had squeezed themselves behind the stove. Frau Melina, in a neighbouring room, was painfully expecting her delivery. Fright had accelerated this event. With the sole assistance of the landlady, a young inexperienced woman, nothing good could be expected.

As the party just arrived required admission, there arose a universal murmur. All now maintained, that by Wilhelm's advice alone, and under his especial guidance, they had entered on this dangerous road, and exposed themselves to such misfortunes. They threw the blame of the disaster wholly on him; they stuck themselves in the door to oppose his entrance, declaring that he must go elsewhere and seek quarters. Philina they received with still greater indignation: nor did Mignon and the Harper escape their share.

The huntsman, to whom the care of the forsaken party had been earnestly and strictly recommended by his beautiful mistress, soon grew tired of this discussion: he rushed upon the company with oaths and menaces; commanding them to fall to the right and left, and make way for this new arrival. They now began to pacify themselves. He made a place for Wilhelm on a table, which he shoved into a corner; Philina had her box put there, and then sat down upon it. All packed themselves as they best could; and the huntsman went away to see if he could not find for "the young couple" a more convenient lodging.

Scarcely was he gone, when spite again grew noisy, and one reproach began to follow close upon another. Each described and magnified his loss; censuring the foolhardiness they had so keenly smarted for. They did not even hide the malicious satisfaction they felt at Wilhelm's wounds: they jeered Philina, and imputed to her as a crime the means by which she had saved her trunk. From a multitude of jibes and bitter innuendos you were required to conclude, that during the plundering and discomfiture, she had endeavoured to work herself into favour with the captain of the band, and had persuaded him, Heaven knew by what arts and complaisance, to give her back the chest unhurt. To all this she answered nothing; only clanked with the large padlocks of her box, to impress her censurers completely with its presence, and by her own good fortune to augment their desperation.

CHAPTER VIII.

Though our friend was weak from loss of blood, and though ever since the appearance of that helpful angel his feelings had been soft and mild, yet at last he could not help getting vexed at the harsh and unjust speeches which, as he continued silent, the discontented company went on uttering against him. Feeling himself strong enough to sit up, and expostulate on the annoyance they were causing to their friend and leader, he raised his bandaged head, and propping himself with some difficulty, and leaning against the wall, he began to speak as follows:

"Considering the pain which your losses occasion, I forgive you for assailing me with injuries at a moment when you should condole with me; for opposing me and casting me from you, the first time I have needed to look to you for help. The services I did you, the complaisance I showed you, I regarded as sufficiently repaid by your thanks, by your friendly conduct: do not warp my thoughts, do not force my heart to go back and calculate what I have done for you; the calculation would be painful to me. Chance brought me near you, circumstances and a secret inclination kept me with you. I participated in your labours and your pleasures: my slender abilities were ever at your service. If you now blame me with bitterness for the mishap that has befallen us, you do not recollect that the first project of taking this road came to us from stranger people, was tried by all of you, and sanctioned by every one as well as me.

"Had our journey ended happily, each would have taken credit to himself for the happy thought of suggesting this plan and preferring it to others; each would joyfully have put us in mind of our deliberations and of the vote he gave: but now you make me alone responsible; you force a piece of blame upon me, which I would willingly submit to, if my conscience with a clear voice did not pronounce me innocent, nay if I might not appeal with safety even to yourselves. If you have aught to say against me, bring it forward in order, and I shall defend myself; if you have nothing reasonable to allege, then be silent, and do not torment me now when I have such pressing need of rest."

By way of answer, the girls once more began whimpering and whining, and describing their losses circumstantially. Melina was quite beside himself; for he had suffered more in purse than any of them; more indeed than we can rightly estimate. He stamped like a madman up and down the little room, he knocked his head against the wall, he swore and scolded in the most unseemly manner; and the landlady entering at this very time with news, that his wife had been delivered of a dead child, he yielded to the most furious ebullitions, while in accordance with him all howled and shrieked and bellowed and uproared with double vigour.

Wilhelm, touched to the heart at once with sympathy in their sorrows, and with vexation at their mean way of thinking, felt all the vigour of his soul awakened, notwithstanding the weakness of his body. "Deplorable as your case may be," exclaimed he, "I shall almost be compelled to despise you. No misfortune gives us right to load an innocent man with reproaches. If I had share in this false step, am not I suffering my share? I lie wounded here; and if the company has come to loss, I myself have come to most. The wardrobe of which we have been robbed, the decorations that are gone, were mine; for you, Herr Melina, have not yet paid me, and I here fully acquit you of all obligation in that matter."

"It is well to give what none of us will ever see again," replied Melina. "Your money was lying in my wife's coffer, and it is your own blame that you have lost it. But ah! if that were all!"—And thereupon he began anew to stamp and scold and squeal. Every one recalled to memory the superb clothes from the Count's wardrobe; the buckles, watches, snuff-boxes, hats, for which Melina had so happily transacted with the head valet. Each then thought also of his own, though far inferior treasures. They looked with spleen at Philina's box; and gave Wilhelm to understand, that he had indeed done wisely to connect himself with that fair personage, and to save his own goods also, under the shadow of her fortune.

"Do you think," he exclaimed at last, "that I shall keep anything apart while you are starving? And is this the first time I have honestly shared with you in a season of need? Open the trunk; all that is mine shall go to supply the common wants."

"It is *my* trunk," observed Philina, "and I will not open it till I please. Your rag or two of clothes, which I have saved for you, could amount to little, though they were sold to the most conscientious of Jews. Think of yourself; what your cure will cost, what may befall you in a strange country."

"You, Philina," answered Wilhelm, "will keep back from me nothing that is mine; and that little will help us out of the first perplexity. But a man possesses many things besides coined money to assist his friends with. All that is in me shall be devoted to these hapless persons; who doubtless, on returning to their senses, will repent their present conduct. Yes," continued he, "I feel that you have need of help, and what is mine to do, I will perform. Give me your confidence again; compose yourselves for a moment, and accept of what I promise! Who will receive the engagement of me in the name of all?"

Here he stretched out his hand and cried: "I promise not to flinch from you, never to forsake you till each shall see his losses doubly and trebly repaired; till the situation you are fallen into, by whose blame soever, shall be totally forgotten by all of you, and changed for a better."

He kept his hand still stretched out: but no one would take hold of it. "I promise it again," cried he, sinking back upon his pillow. All continued silent; they felt ashamed, but nothing comforted; and Philina sitting on her chest, kept cracking nuts, a stock of which she had discovered in her pocket.

CHAPTER IX.

THE huntsman now came back with several people, and made preparations for carrying away the wounded youth. He had persuaded the parson of the place to receive the " young couple" into his house; Philina's trunk was taken out; she followed with a natural air of dignity. Mignon ran before; and when the patient reached the parsonage, a wide couch, which had long been standing ready as guest's bed and bed of honour, was assigned him. Here it was first discovered, that his wound had opened and bled profusely. A new bandage was required for it. He fell into a feverish state; Philina waited on him faithfully; and when fatigue overpowered her, she was relieved by the Harper. Mignon, with the firmest purpose to watch, had fallen asleep in a corner.

Next morning, Wilhelm, who felt himself in some degree refreshed, learned by inquiring of the huntsman, that the honourable persons who last night assisted him so nobly, had shortly before left their estates, in order to avoid the movements of the contending armies, and remain till the time of peace in some more quiet district. He named the elderly nobleman as well as his niece; mentioned the place they were first going to; and told how the young lady had charged him to take care of Wilhelm.

The entrance of the surgeon interrupted the warm expressions of gratitude, in which our friend was pouring out his feelings. He made a circumstantial description of the wounds; and certified that they would soon heal, if the patient took care of them, and kept himself at peace.

When the huntsman was gone, Philina signified that he had left with her a purse of twenty louis-d'or; that he had given the parson a remuneration for their lodging, and left with him money to defray the surgeon's bill when the cure should be completed. She added, that she herself passed everywhere for Wilhelm's wife: that she now begged leave to introduce herself once for all to him in this capacity, and would not allow him to look out for any other sick-nurse.

" Philina," said Wilhelm, " in this disaster that has overtaken us, I am already deeply in your debt for kindness shown me; and I should not wish to see my obligations increased. I am restless so long as you are near me: for I know of nothing by which I can repay your labour. Give me my things which you have saved in your trunk; unite yourself to the rest of the company; seek another lodging, take my thanks, and the gold watch as a small acknowledgment: only leave me; your presence disturbs me more than you can fancy."

She laughed in his face when he had ended. "Thou art a fool," she said; "thou wilt not gather wisdom. I know better what is good for thee; I will stay, I will not budge from the spot. I have never counted on the gratitude of men, and therefore not on thine; and if I have a touch of kindness for thee, what hast thou to do with it?"

She stayed accordingly; and soon wormed herself into favour with the parson and his household; being always cheerful, having the knack of giving little presents, and of talking to each in his own vein; at the same time always contriving to do exactly what she pleased. Wilhelm's state was not uncomfortable: the surgeon, an ignorant but no unskilful man, let nature play her part; and the patient was not long till he felt himself recovering. For such a consummation, being eager to pursue his plans and wishes, he vehemently longed.

Incessantly he kept recalling that event, which had made an ineffaceable impression on his heart. He saw the beautiful Amazon again come riding out of the thickets; she approached him, dismounted, went to and fro, and strove to serve him. He saw the garment she was wrapt in fall down from her shoulders; he saw her countenance, her figure vanish in their radiance. All the dreams of his youth now fastened on this image. Here he conceived he had at length beheld the noble, the heroic Clorinda with his own eyes: and again he bethought him of that royal youth, to whose sickbed the lovely sympathising princess came in her modest meekness.

"May it not be," said he often to himself in secret, "that in youth as in sleep, the images of coming things hover round us, and mysteriously become visible to our unobstructed eyes? May not the seeds of what is to betide us be already scattered by the hand of Fate; may not a foretaste of the fruits we yet hope to gather possibly be given us?"

His sickbed gave him leisure to repeat those scenes in every mood. A thousand times he called back the tone of that sweet voice; a thousand times he envied Philina, who had kissed that helpful hand. Often the whole incident appeared before him as a dream; and he would have reckoned it a fiction, if the white surtout had not been left behind to convince him that the vision had a real existence.

With the greatest care for this piece of apparel, he combined the greatest wish to wear it. The first time he arose he put it on;

and was kept in fear all day, lest it might be hurt by some stain or other injury.

CHAPTER X.

LAERTES visited his friend. He had not assisted in that lively scene at the inn, being then confined to bed in an upper chamber. For his loss he was already in a great degree consoled; he helped himself with his customary: "What does it signify?" He detailed various laughable particulars about the company; particularly charging Frau Melina with lamenting the loss of her still-born daughter, solely because she herself could not on that account enjoy the Old-German satisfaction of having a Mechthilde christened. As for her husband, it now appeared that he had been possessed of abundant cash; and even at first had by no means needed the advances which he had cajoled from Wilhelm. Melina's present plan was to set off by the next Postwagen; and he meant to require of Wilhelm an introductory letter to his friend, the Manager Serlo, in whose company, the present undertaking having gone to wreck, he now wished to establish himself.

For some days Mignon had been singularly quiet; when pressed with questions, she at length admitted that her right arm was out of joint. "Thou hast thy own folly to thank for that," observed Philina, and then told how the child had drawn her sword in the battle; and seeing her friend in peril, had struck fiercely at the freebooters; one of whom had at length seized her by the arm, and pitched her to a side. They chid her for not sooner speaking of her ailment; but they easily saw that she was apprehensive of the surgeon, who had hitherto looked on her as a boy. With a view to remove the mischief, she was made to keep her arm in a sling; which arrangement too displeased her; for now she was obliged to surrender most part of her share in the management and nursing of our friend to Philina. That pleasing sinner but showed herself the more active and attentive on this account.

One morning, on awakening, Wilhelm found himself in a strange neighbourhood with her. In the movements of sleep he had hitched himself quite to the back of his spacious bed. Philina was lying across from the front part of it; she seemed to have fallen asleep while sitting on the bed and reading. A book had dropt from her hand; she had sunk back, and her head was lying near his breast, over which her fair and now loosened hair was spread in streams. The disorder of sleep enlivened her charms more than art or purpose could have done; a childlike smiling rest hovered on her countenance. He looked at her for a time; and seemed to blame himself for the pleasure which this gave him. He had viewed her attentively for some moments, when she began to awake. He softly closed his eyes; but could not help glimmering at her through his eyelashes, as she trimmed herself again, and went away to consult about breakfast.

All the actors had at length successively announced themselves to Wilhelm; asking introductory letters, requiring money for their journey with more or less impatience and ill-breeding; and constantly receiving it against Philina's will. It was in vain for her to tell our friend, that the huntsman had already left a handsome sum with these people, and that accordingly they did but cozen him. To these remonstrances he gave no heed; on the contrary, the two had a sharp quarrel on the subject; which ended by Wilhelm signifying once for all, that Philina must now join the rest of the company, and seek her fortune with Serlo.

For an instant or two she lost temper; but speedily recovering her composure, she cried: "If I had but my fair-haired boy again, I should not care a fig for any of you." She meant Friedrich, who had vanished from the scene of battle, and never since appeared.

Next morning Mignon brought news to the bedside, that Philina had gone off by night, leaving all that belonged to Wilhelm very neatly laid out in the next room. He felt her absence; he had lost in her a faithful nurse, a cheerful companion; he was no longer used to be alone. But Mignon soon filled up the blank.

Ever since that light-minded beauty had been near the patient with her friendly cares, the little creature had by degrees drawn back, and remained silent and secluded in herself; but the field being clear once more, she again came forth with her attentions and her love; again was eager in serving, and lively in entertaining him.

CHAPTER XI.

WILHELM was rapidly approaching complete recovery: he now hoped to be upon his journey in a few days. He proposed no more to lead an aimless routine of existence: the steps of his career were henceforth to be calculated for an end. In the first place, he purposed to seek out that beneficent lady, and express the gratitude he felt to her; then to proceed without delay to his friend the Manager, that he might do his utmost to assist the luckless company; intending at the same time to visit the commercial friends whom he had letters for, and to transact the business which had been intrusted to him. He was not without hope that fortune, as formerly, would favour him; and give him opportunity, by some lucky speculation, to repair his losses, and fill up the vacuity of his coffer.

The desire of again beholding his beautiful deliverer augmented every day. To settle his route, he took counsel with the clergyman, a person well skilled in statistics and geography, and possessing a fine collection of charts and books on those subjects. They two searched for the place which this noble family had chosen as their residence while the war continued; they searched for information respecting the family itself. But their place was to be found in no geography or map; and the heraldic manuals made no mention of their name. Wilhelm became restless; and having mentioned the cause of his uneasiness, the Harper told him he had reason to believe that the huntsman, for whatever reason, had concealed the real designations.

Conceiving himself now to be in the immediate neighbourhood of his lovely benefactress, Wilhelm hoped he might obtain some tidings of her, if he sent out the Harper: but in this too he was deceived. Diligently as the old man kept inquiring, he could find no trace of her. Of late days a number of quick movements and unforeseen marches had taken place in that quarter; no one had particularly noticed the travelling party; and the ancient messenger, to avoid being taken for a Jewish spy, was obliged to return, and appear without any olive-leaf before his master and friend. He gave a strict account of his conduct in this commission, striving to keep far from him all suspicions of remissness. He endeavoured by every means to mitigate the trouble of our friend; bethought him of everything that he had learned from the huntsman, and advanced a number of conjectures; out of all which, one circumstance at length came to light, whereby Wilhelm could explain some enigmatic words of his vanished benefactress.

The freebooters, it appeared, had lain in wait, not for the wandering troop, but for that noble company, whom they rightly guessed to be provided with store of gold and valuables, and of whose movements they must have had precise intelligence. Whether the attack should be imputed to some free-corps, to marauders, or to robbers, was uncertain. It was clear, however, that by good fortune for the high and rich company, the poor and low had first arrived upon the place, and undergone the fate which was provided for the others. It was to this that the lady's words referred, which Wilhelm yet well recollected. If he might now be happy and contented, that a prescient Genius had selected him for the sacrifice, which saved a perfect mortal; he was, on the other hand, nigh desperate, when he thought that all hope of finding her and seeing her again was, at least for the present, completely gone.

What increased this singular emotion still farther, was the likeness which he thought he had observed between the Countess and the beautiful unknown. They resembled one another, as two sisters may, of whom neither can be called the younger or the elder, for they seem to be twins.

The recollection of the amiable Countess was to Wilhelm infinitely sweet. He recalled her image but too willingly into his memory. But anon the figure of the noble Amazon would step between; one vision melted and changed into the other, and the form of neither would abide with him.

A new resemblance, the similarity of their handwritings, naturally struck him with still greater wonder. He had a charming song in the Countess' hand laid up in his portfolio; and in the surtout he had found a little note, inquiring with much tender care about the health of an uncle.

Wilhelm was convinced that his benefactress must have penned this billet; that it must have been sent from one chamber to another, at some inn during their journey, and put into the coat-pocket by the uncle. He held both papers together; and if the regular and graceful letters of the Countess had already pleased him much, he found in the similar but freer lines of the stranger a flowing harmony which could not be described. The note contained nothing; yet the strokes of it seemed to affect him, as the presence of their fancied writer once had done.

He fell into a dreamy longing; and well accordant with his feelings was the song which at that instant Mignon and the Harper began to sing, with a touching expression, in the form of an irregular duet:

> You never long'd and lov'd,
> You know not grief like mine:
> Alone and far remov'd
> From joys or hopes, I pine:
> A foreign sky above,
> And a foreign earth below me,
> To the south I look all day;
> For the hearts that love and know me
> Are far, are far away.
> I burn, I faint, I languish,
> My heart is waste, and sick, and sore;
> Who has not long'd in baffled anguish,
> Cannot know what I deplore.

CHAPTER XII.

The soft allurements of his dear presiding angel, far from leading our friend to any one determined path, did but nourish and increase the unrest which he had previously experienced. A secret fire was gliding through his veins; objects distinct and indistinct alternated within his soul, and awoke unspeakable desire. At one time he wished for a horse, at another for wings; and not till it seemed impossible that he could stay, did he look round him to discover whither he was wanting to go.

The threads of his destiny had become so strangely entangled, he wished to see its curious knots unravelled or cut in two. Often, when he heard the tramp of a horse or the rolling of a carriage, he would run to the window and look out, in hopes it might be some one seeking him; some one, even though it were by chance, bringing him intelligence and certainty and joy. He told stories to himself, how his friend Werner might visit these parts and come upon him; how perhaps Mariana might appear. The sound of every post's horn threw him into agitation. It would be Melina sending news to him of his adventures; above all, it would be the huntsman coming back to carry him to the beauty whom he worshiped.

Of all these possibilities, unhappily no one occurred: he was forced at last to return to the company of himself; and in again looking through the past, there was one circumstance, which the more he viewed and weighed it, grew the more offensive and intolerable to him. It was his unprosperous generalship; of which he never thought without vexation. For although, on the evening of that luckless day, he had produced a pretty fair defence of his conduct when accused by the company, yet he could not hide from himself that he was guilty. On the contrary, in hypochondriac moments he took the blame of the whole misfortune.

Self-love exaggerates our faults as well as our virtues. Wilhelm thought he had awakened confidence in him, had guided the will of the rest; that, led by inexperience and rashness, they had ventured on, till a danger seized them, for which they were not match. Loud as well as silent reproaches had then assailed him: and if in their sorrowful condition he had promised to the company, misguided by him, never to forsake them till their loss had been repaid with usury; this was but another folly for which he had to blame himself, the folly of presuming to take upon his single shoulders a misfortune that was spread over many. One instant he accused himself of uttering this promise, under the excitement and the pressure of the moment; the next he again felt that this generous presentation of his hand, which no one deigned to accept, was but a light formality compared with the vow which his heart had taken. He meditated means of being kind and useful to them; he found every cause conspire to quicken his visit to Serlo. Accordingly he packed his things together; and without waiting his complete recovery, without listening to the counsel of the parson or the surgeon, he hastened, in the strange society of Mignon and the Harper, to escape the inactivity, in which his fate had once more too long detained him.

CHAPTER XIII.

SERLO received him with open arms, crying as he met him: "Is it you? Do I see you again? You have scarcely changed at all. Is your love for that noblest of arts still as lively and strong? I myself am so glad at your arrival, I even feel no longer the mistrust which your last letters had excited in me."

Wilhelm asked with surprise for a clearer explanation.

"You have treated me," said Serlo, "not like an old friend, but as if I were a great lord, to whom with a safe conscience you might recommend useless people. Our destiny depends on the opinion of the public; and I fear Herr Melina and his suite can hardly be received among us."

Wilhelm tried to say something in their favour; but Serlo began to draw so merciless a picture of them, that our friend was happy when a lady came into the room, and put a stop to the discussion. She was introduced to him as Aurelia, the sister of his friend: she received him with extreme kindness; and her conversation was so pleasing, that he did not once remark a shade of sorrow visible on her expressive countenance, to which it lent peculiar interest.

For the first time during many months, Wilhelm felt himself in his proper element once more. Of late in talking, he had merely found submissive listeners, and even these not always; but now he had the happiness to speak with critics and artists, who not only fully understood him, but repaid his observations by others equally instructive. With wonderful vivacity they travelled through the latest pieces; with wonderful correctness judged them. The decisions of the public they could try and estimate: they speedily threw light on each other's thoughts.

Loving Shakspeare as our friend did, he failed not to lead round the conversation to the merits of that dramatist. Expressing, as he entertained, the liveliest hopes of the new epoch which these exquisite productions must form in Germany, he ere long introduced his Hamlet, who had busied him so much of late.

Serlo declared that he would long ago have played the piece, had this been possible, and that he himself would willingly engage to act Polonius. He added, with a smile: "An Ophelia, too, will certainly turn up, if we had but a Prince."

Wilhelm did not notice that Aurelia seemed a little hurt at her brother's sarcasm. Our friend was in his proper vein, becoming copious and didactic, expounding how he would have Hamlet played. He circumstantially delivered to his hearers the opinions we before saw him busied with; taking all the trouble possible to make his notion of the matter acceptable, sceptical as Serlo showed himself regarding it. "Well, then," said the latter, finally, "suppose we grant you all this, what will you explain by it?"

"Much, everything," said Wilhelm. "Conceive a prince such as I have painted him, and that his father suddenly dies. Ambition and the love of rule are not the passions that inspire him. As a king's son he would have been contented; but now he is first constrained to consider the difference which separates a sovereign from a subject. The crown was not hereditary; yet a longer possession of it by his father would have strengthened the pretensions of an only son, and secured his hopes of the succession. In place of this, he now beholds himself excluded by his uncle, in spite of specious promises, most probably forever. He is now poor in goods and favour, and a stranger in the scene which from youth he had looked upon as his inheritance. His temper here assumes its first mournful tinge. He feels that now he is not more, that he is less, than a private nobleman; he offers himself as the servant of every one; he is not courteous and condescending, he is needy and degraded.

"His past condition he remembers as a vanished dream. It is in vain that his uncle strives to cheer him, to present his situation in another point of view. The feeling of his nothingness will not leave him.

"The second stroke that came upon him wounded deeper, bowed still more. It was the marriage of his mother. The faithful tender son had yet a mother, when his father passed away. He hoped, in the company of his surviving noble-minded parent, to reverence the heroic form of the departed; but his mother too he loses, and it is something worse than death that robs him of her. The trustful image, which a good child loves to form of its parents, is gone. With the dead there is no help; on the living no hold. She also is a woman, and her name is Frailty, like that of all her sex.

"Now first does he feel himself completely bent and orphaned; and no happiness of life can repay what he has lost. Not reflective or sorrowful by nature, reflection and sorrow have become for him a heavy obligation. It is thus that we see him first enter on the scene. I do not think that I have mixed aught foreign with the piece, or overcharged a single feature of it."

Serlo looked at his sister, and said, "Did I give thee a false picture of our friend? He begins well; he has still many things to tell us, many to persuade us of." Wilhelm asseverated loudly, that he meant not to persuade, but to convince; he begged for another moment's patience.

"Figure to yourselves this youth," cried he, "this son of princes; conceive him vividly, bring his state before your eyes, and then observe him when he learns that his father's spirit walks; stand by him in the terrors of the night, when the venerable ghost itself appears before him. A horrid shudder passes over him; he speaks to the mysterious form; he sees it beckon him; he follows it, and hears. The fearful accusation of his uncle rings in his ears; the summons to revenge, and the piercing oft-repeated prayer, Remember me!

"And when the ghost has vanished, who is it that stands before us? A young hero panting for vengeance? A prince by birth, rejoicing to be called to punish the usurper of his crown? No! trouble and astonishment take hold of the solitary young man: he grows bitter against smiling villains, swears that he will not forget the spirit, and concludes with the significant ejaculation:

> The time is out of joint: O cursed spite,
> That ever I was born to set it right!

"In these words, I imagine, will be found the key to Hamlet's whole procedure. To me it is clear that Shakspeare meant, in the present case, to represent the effects of a great action laid upon a soul unfit for the performance of it. In this view the whole piece seems to me to be composed. There is an oak-tree planted in a costly jar, which should have borne only pleasant flowers in its bosom; the roots expand, the jar is shivered.

"A lovely, pure, noble and most moral nature, without the strength of nerve which forms a hero, sinks beneath a burden which it cannot bear and must not cast away. All duties are holy for him; the present is too hard. Impossibilities have been required of him; not in themselves impossibilities, but such for him. He winds, and turns, and torments himself; he advances and recoils; is ever put in mind, ever puts himself in mind; at last does all but lose his purpose from his thoughts; yet still without recovering his peace of mind."

CHAPTER XIV.

SEVERAL people entering interrupted the discussion. They were musical dilettanti, who commonly assembled at Serlo's once a-week, and formed a little concert. Serlo himself loved music much: he used to maintain, that a player without taste for it never could attain a distinct conception and feeling of the scenic art. "As a man performs," he would observe, "with far more ease and dignity, when his gestures are accompanied and guided by a tune; so the player ought, in idea as it were, to set to music even his prose parts, that he may not monotonously slight them over in his individual style, but treat them in suitable alternation by time and measure."

Aurelia seemed to give but little heed to what was passing; at last, she conducted Wilhelm to another room, and going to the window, and looking out at the starry sky, she said to him: "You have still much to tell us about Hamlet; I will not hurry you; my brother must hear it as well as I: but let me beg to know your thoughts about Ophelia."

"Of her there cannot much be said," he answered; "for a few master-strokes complete her character. The whole being of Ophelia floats in sweet and ripe sensation. Kindness for the Prince, to whose hand she may aspire, flows so spontaneously, her tender heart obeys its impulses so unresistingly, that both father and brother are afraid; both give her warning harshly and directly. Decorum, like the thin lawn upon her bosom, cannot hide the soft, still movements of her heart; it on the contrary betrays them. Her fancy is smit; her silent modesty breathes amiable desire; and if the friendly goddess Opportunity should shake the tree, its fruit would fall."

"And then," said Aurelia, "when she beholds herself forsaken, cast away, despised; when all is inverted in the soul of her crazed lover, and the highest changes to the lowest, and instead of the sweet cup of love he offers her the bitter cup of woe—"

"Her heart breaks," cried Wilhelm; "the whole structure of her being is loosened from its joinings; her father's death strikes fiercely against it; and the fair edifice altogether crumbles into fragments."

Our friend had not observed with what expressiveness Aurelia pronounced those words. Looking only at this work of art, at its connexion and completeness, he dreamed not that his auditress was feeling quite a different influence; that a deep sorrow of her own was vividly awakened in her breast by these dramatic shadows.

Aurelia's head was still resting on her arms; and her eyes, now full of tears, were directed to the sky. At last, no longer able to conceal her secret grief, she seized both hands of her friend, and exclaimed, while he stood surprised before her: "Forgive, forgive a heavy heart! I am girt and pressed together by these people; from my hard-hearted brother I must seek to hide myself: your presence has untied these bonds. My friend!" continued she, "it is but a few minutes since we saw each other first, and already you are going to become my confidant." She could scarcely end the words, and sank upon his shoulder. "Think not worse of me," she said with sobs, "that I disclose myself to you so hastily, that I am so weak before you. Be my friend, remain my friend; I shall deserve it." He spoke to her in his kindest manner: but in vain; her tears still flowed, and choked her words.

At this moment Serlo entered, most unwelcomely; and most unexpectedly, Philina with her hand in his. "Here is your friend," said he to her; "he will be glad to make his compliments to you."

"How!" cried Wilhelm in astonishment: "are you here?" With a modest settled mien, she went up to him; bade him welcome; praised Serlo's goodness, who, she said, without merit on her part, but purely in the hope of her improvement, had agreed to admit her into his accomplished troop. She behaved, all the while, in a friendly manner towards Wilhelm, yet with a dignified distance.

But this dissimulation lasted only till the other two were gone. Aurelia having left them, that she might conceal her trouble, and Serlo being called away, Philina first looked very sharply at the doors, to see that both were really out; then began skipping to and fro about the room, as if she had been mad; at last dropt down upon the floor, like to die of giggling and laughing. She then sprang up, patted and flattered our friend; rejoicing above measure that she had been clever enough to go before, and spy the land and get herself nestled in.

"Pretty things are going on here," she said; "just of the sort I like. Aurelia has had a hapless love-affair with some nobleman, who seems to be a very stately person, one whom I myself could like to see, some day. He has left her a memorial, or I much mistake. There is a boy running about the house, of three years old or so; the papa must be a very pretty fellow. Commonly I cannot suffer children, but this brat quite delights me. I have calculated Aurelia's business. The death of her husband, the new acquaintance, the child's age, all things agree.

"But now her spark has gone his ways; for a year she has not seen a glimpse of him. She is beside herself and inconsolable, on this account. The more fool she! Her brother has a dancing girl in his troop, with whom he stands on pretty terms; an actress to whom he is betrothed; in the town, some other women whom he courts; I too am on his list. The more fool he! Of the rest thou shalt hear tomorrow. And now one word about Philina, whom thou knowest: the arch-fool is fallen in love with thee." She swore that it was true, and a proper joke. She earnestly requested Wilhelm to fall in love with Aurelia; for then the chase would be worth beholding. "She pursues her faithless swain, thou her, I thee, her brother me. If that will not divert us for a quarter of a year, I engage to die at the first episode which occurs in this four-times complicated tale." She begged of him not to spoil her trade, and to show her such respect as her external conduct should deserve.

CHAPTER XV.

Next morning Wilhelm went to visit Frau Melina; but found her not at home. On inquiring here for the other members of the wandering community, he learned that Philina had invited them to breakfast. Out of curiosity, he hastened thither; and found them all cleared up and not a little comforted. The cunning creature had collected them, was treating them with chocolate, and giving them to understand that some prospects still remained for them; that, by her influence, she hoped to convince the manager how advantageous it would be for him to introduce so many clever hands among his company. They listened to her with attention; swallowed cup after cup of her chocolate; thought the girl was not so bad after all; and went away proposing to themselves to speak whatever good of her they could.

"Do you think then," said our friend, who stayed behind, "that Serlo will determine to retain our comrades?" "Not at all," replied Philina; "nor do I care a fig for it. The sooner they are gone the better! Laertes alone I could wish to keep: the rest we shall by and by pack off."

Next she signified to Wilhelm her firm persuasion that he should no longer hide his talent; but, under the direction of a

Serlo, go upon the boards. She was lavish in her praises of the order, the taste, the spirit, which prevailed in this establishment: she spoke so flatteringly to Wilhelm; with such admiration of his gifts, that his heart and his imagination were advancing towards this proposal, as fast as his understanding and his reason were retreating from it. He concealed his inclination from himself and from Philina; and passed a restless day, unable to resolve on visiting his trading correspondents, to receive the letters which might there be lying for him. The anxieties of his people during all this time he easily conceived; yet he shrank from the precise account of them; particularly at the present time, as he promised to himself a great and pure enjoyment from the exhibition of a new piece that evening.

Serlo had refused to let him witness the rehearsal. "You must see us on the best side," he observed, " before we can allow you to look into our cards."

The acting of the piece, however, where our friend did not fail to be present, yielded him a high satisfaction. It was the first time he had ever seen a theatre in such perfection. The actors were evidently all possessed of excellent gifts, of superior capacities, and a high clear notion of their art: they were not equal; but they mutually restrained and supported one another; each breathed ardour into those around him; throughout all their acting, they showed themselves decided and correct. You soon felt that Serlo was the soul of the whole; as an individual he appeared to much advantage. A merry humour, a measured vivacity, a settled feeling of propriety, combined with a great gift of imitation, were to be observed in him the moment he appeared upon the stage. The inward contentment of his being seemed to spread itself over all that looked on him; and the intellectual style, in which he could so easily and gracefully express the finest shadings of his part, excited more delight, as he could conceal the art which, by long-continued practice, he had made his own.

Aurelia, his sister, was not inferior; she obtained still greater approbation, for she touched the souls of the audience, which it was his to exhilarate and amuse.

After a few days had passed pleasantly enough, Aurelia sent to inquire for our friend. He hastened to her: she was lying on a sofa; she seemed to be suffering from headache; her whole frame had visibly a feverish movement. Her eye lighted up as she noticed Wilhelm. "Pardon me!" she cried, as he entered: " the trust you have inspired me with has made me weak. Till now I have contrived to bear up against my woes in secret; nay, they gave me strength and consolation: but now, I know not how it is, you have loosened the bands of silence; you must, against your will, take part in the battle I am fighting with myself."

Wilhelm answered her in friendly and obliging terms. He declared that her image and her sorrows had not ceased to hover in his thoughts; that he longed for her confidence, and devoted himself to be her friend.

While he spoke, his eyes were attracted to the boy, who sat before her on the floor, and was busy rattling a multitude of playthings. This child, as Philina had observed, might be about three years of age; and Wilhelm now conceived how that giddy creature, seldom elevated in her phraseology, had likened it to the sun. For its cheerful eyes and full countenance were shaded by the finest golden locks, which flowed round in copious curls: dark, slender, softly-bending eyebrows showed themselves upon a brow of dazzling whiteness; and the living tinge of health was glancing on its cheeks. " Sit by me," said Aurelia: " you are looking at the happy child with admiration; in truth, I took it into my arms with joy; I keep it carefully: yet by it too I can measure the extent of my sufferings; for they seldom let me feel the worth of such a gift.

"Allow me," she continued, "to speak to you about myself and my destiny; for I have it much at heart that you should not misunderstand me. I thought I should have a few calm instants, and accordingly I sent for you; you are now here, and the thread of my narrative is lost.

"'One more forsaken woman in the world!' you will say. You are a man; you are thinking: 'What a noise she makes, the fool, about a necessary evil; which, certainly as death, awaits a woman, when such is the fidelity of men!' O my friend! if my fate were common, I would gladly undergo a common evil; but it is so singular: why cannot I present it to you in a mirror, why not command some one to tell it you? O, had I, had I been seduced, surprised, and afterwards forsaken, there would then still be comfort in despair: but I am far more miserable; I have been my own deceiver; I have wittingly betrayed myself; and this, this is what shall never be forgiven me."

"With noble feelings, such as yours," said Wilhelm, "you can never be entirely unhappy."

"And do you know to what I am indebted for my feelings?" asked Aurelia. "To the worst education that ever threatened to contaminate a girl; to the vilest examples for misleading the senses and the inclinations.

"My mother dying early, the fairest years of my youth were spent with an aunt, whose principle it was to despise the laws of decency. She resigned herself headlong to every impulse; careless whether the object of it proved her tyrant or her slave, so she might forget herself in wild enjoyment.

"By children, with the pure clear vision of innocence, what ideas of men were necessarily formed in such a scene! How stolid, brutally bold, importunate, unmannerly, was every one whom she allured! How sated, empty, insolent and tasteless, when he left her! I have seen this woman live, for years, humbled under the control of the meanest creatures. What incidents she had to undergo! With what a front she contrived to accommodate herself to her destiny; nay, with how much skill, to wear these shameful fetters!

"It was thus, my friend, that I became acquainted with your sex: and deeply did I hate it, when, as I imagined, I observed that even tolerable men, in their conduct to ours, appeared to renounce every honest feeling, of which Nature might otherwise have made them capable.

"Unhappily, moreover, on such occasions, a multitude of painful discoveries about my own sex were forced upon me: and in truth I was then wiser, as a girl of sixteen, than I now am; now that I scarcely understand myself. Why are we so wise when young; so wise, and ever growing less so?"

The boy began to make a noise; Aurelia became impatient, and rung. An old woman came to take him out. "Hast thou toothache still?" said Aurelia to the crone, whose face was wrapped in cloth. "Unsufferable," said the other, with a muffled voice; then lifted the boy, who seemed to like going with her, and carried him away.

Scarcely was he gone, when Aurelia began bitterly to weep. "I am good for nothing," cried she, "but lamenting and complaining; and I feel ashamed to lie before you like a miserable worm. My recollection is already fled; I can relate no more." She faltered, and was silent. Her friend, unwilling to reply with a commonplace, and unable to reply with anything particularly applicable, pressed her hand, and looked at her for some time without speaking. Thus embarrassed, he at length took up a book, which he noticed lying on the table before him: it was Shakspeare's works, and open at Hamlet.

Serlo at this moment entering, inquired about his sister; and looking in the book which our friend had hold of, cried: "So you are again at Hamlet? Very good! Many doubts have arisen in me, which seem not a little to impair the canonical aspect of the piece as you would have it viewed. The English themselves have admitted that its chief interest concludes with the third act; the last two lagging sorrily on, and scarcely uniting with the rest: and certainly about the end it seems to stand stock-still."

"It is very possible," said Wilhelm, "that some individuals of a nation, which has so many master-pieces to feel proud of, may be led by prejudice and narrowness of mind to form false judgments: but this cannot hinder us from looking with our own eyes, and doing justice where we see it due. I am very far from censuring the plan of Hamlet; on the other hand, I believe there never was a grander one invented; nay, it is not invented, it is real."

"How do you demonstrate that?" inquired Serlo.

"I will not demonstrate anything," said Wilhelm; "I will merely show you what my own conceptions of it are."

Aurelia rose up from her cushion; leaned upon her hand, and looked at Wilhelm; who, with the firmest assurance that he was in the right, went on as follows: "It pleases us, it flatters us to see a hero acting on his own strength; loving and hating as his heart directs him; undertaking and completing; casting every obstacle aside; and at length attaining some great object which he aimed at. Poets and historians would willingly persuade us that so proud a lot may fall to man. In Hamlet we are taught another lesson: the hero is without a plan, but the piece is full of plan. Here we have no villain punished on some self-conceived and rigidly-accomplished scheme of vengeance: a horrid deed occurs; it rolls itself along with all its consequences, dragging guiltless persons also in its course; the perpetrator seems as if he would evade the abyss which is made ready for him; yet he plunges in, at the very point by which he thinks he shall escape and happily complete his course.

"For it is the property of crime to extend its mischief over innocence, as it is of virtue to extend its blessings over many that deserve them not; while frequently the author of the one or of the other is not punished or rewarded at all. Here in this play of ours, how strange! The Pit of darkness sends its spirit and demands revenge; in vain! All circumstances tend one way, and hurry to revenge; in vain! Neither earthly nor infernal thing may bring about what is reserved for Fate alone. The hour of judgment comes: the wicked falls with the good: one race is mowed away, that another may spring up."

After a pause, in which they looked at one another, Serlo said: "You pay no great compliment to Providence, in thus exalting Shakspeare; and besides, it appears to me, that for the honour of your poet, as others for the honour of Providence, you ascribe to him an object and a plan, which he himself had never thought of."

CHAPTER XVI.

"LET me also put a question," said Aurelia. "I have looked at Ophelia's part again; I am contented with it, and conceive that under certain circumstances I could play it. But tell me, should not the poet have furnished the insane maiden with another sort of songs? Could not one select some fragments out of melancholy ballads for this purpose? What have double meanings and lascivious insipidities to do in the mouth of such a noble-minded person?"

"Dear friend," said Wilhelm, "even here I cannot yield you one iota. In these singularities, in this apparent impropriety, a deep sense is hid. Do we not understand from the very first what the mind of the good soft-hearted girl was busied with? Silently she lived within herself, yet she scarce concealed her wishes, her longing; the tones of desire were in secret ringing through her soul; and how often may she have attempted, like an unskilful nurse, to lull her senses to repose with songs which only kept them more awake? But at last, when her self-command is altogether gone, when the secrets of her heart are hovering on her tongue, that tongue betrays her, and in the innocence of insanity she solaces herself, unmindful of king or queen, with the echo of her loose and well-beloved songs: *Tomorrow is Saint Valentine's day*; and *By Gis and by Saint Charity*."

He had not finished speaking, when all at once an extraordinary scene took place before him, which he could not in any way explain.

Serlo had walked once or twice up and down the room, without evincing any special object. On a sudden, he stept forward to Aurelia's dressing-table; caught hastily at something that was lying there, and hastened to the door with his booty. No sooner did Aurelia notice this, than springing up, she threw herself in his way; laid hold of him with boundless vehemence, and had dexterity enough to clutch an end of the article which he was carrying off. They struggled and wrestled with great obstinacy; twisted and threw each other sharply round: he laughed; she exerted all her strength: and as Wilhelm hastened towards them, to separate and soothe them, Aurelia sprang aside with a naked dagger in her hand, while Serlo cast the scabbard, which had stayed with him, angrily upon the floor. Wilhelm started back astonished; and his dumb wonder seemed to ask the cause why so violent a strife, about so strange an implement, had taken place between them.

"You shall judge betwixt us," said the brother. "What has she to do with sharp steel? Do but look at it. That dagger is not fit for any actress: point like a needle's, edge like a razor's! What good is it? Passionate as she is, she will one day chance to do herself a mischief. I have a heart's hatred at such singularities: a serious thought of that sort is insane, and so dangerous a plaything is not in taste."

"I have it back!" exclaimed Aurelia, and held the polished blade aloft; "I will now keep my faithful friend more carefully. Pardon me," she cried, and kissed the steel, "that I have so neglected thee."

Serlo was like to grow seriously angry. "Take it as thou wilt, brother," she continued: "how knowest thou but, under this form, a precious talisman may have been given me; so that, in extreme need, I may find help and counsel in it? Must all be hurtful that looks dangerous?"

"Such talk without a meaning might drive one mad," said Serlo, and left the room with suppressed indignation. Aurelia put the dagger carefully into its sheath, and placed it in her bosom. "Let us now resume the conversation which our foolish brother has disturbed," said she, as Wilhelm was beginning to put questions on the subject of this quarrel.

"I must admit your picture of Ophelia to be just," continued she; "I cannot now misunderstand the object of the poet: I must pity, though as you paint her, I shall rather pity her than sympathise with her. But allow me here to offer a remark, which in these few days you have frequently suggested to me. I observe with admiration the correct, keen, penetrating glance with which you judge of poetry, especially dramatic poetry: the deepest abysses of invention are not hidden from you, the finest touches of representation cannot escape you. Without ever having viewed the objects in nature, you recognise the truth of their images: there seems, as it were, a presentiment of all the universe to lie in you, which by the harmonious touch of poetry is awakened and unfolded. For in truth," continued she, "from without, you receive not much: I have scarcely seen a person that so little knew, so totally misknew the people he lived with, as you do. Allow me to say it: in hearing you expound the mysteries of Shakspeare, one would think you had just descended from a synod of the gods, and had listened there while they were taking counsel how to form men; in seeing you transact with your fellows, I could imagine you to be the first large-born child of the Creation, standing agape, and gazing with strange wonderment and edifying good-nature, at lions and apes and sheep and elephants, and true-heartedly addressing them as your equals, simply because they were there, and in motion like yourself."

"The feeling of my ignorance in this respect," said Wilhelm, "often gives me pain; and I should thank you, worthy friend, if you would help me to get a little better insight into life. From youth, I have been accustomed to direct the eyes of my spirit inwards rather than outwards; and hence it is very natural that to a certain extent I should be acquainted with man, while of men I have not the smallest knowledge."

"In truth," said Aurelia, "I at first suspected that, in giving such accounts of the people whom you sent to my brother, you meant to make sport of us; when I compared your letters with the merits of these persons, it seemed very strange."

Aurelia's remarks, well-founded as they might be, and willing as our friend was to confess himself deficient in this matter, carried with them something painful, nay offensive to him; so that he grew silent, and retired within himself, partly to avoid showing any irritated feeling, partly to search his mind for the truth or error of the charge.

"Let not this alarm you," said Aurelia: "the light of the understanding it is always in our power to reach; but this fulness of the heart no one can give us. If you are destined for an artist, you cannot long enough retain the dim-sightedness and innocence of which I speak; it is the beautiful hull upon the young bud; woe to us if we are forced too soon to burst it! Surely it were well, if we never knew what the people are, for whom we work and study.

"Oh! I too was in that happy case, when I first betrod the stage, with the loftiest opinion of myself and of my nation. What a people, in my fancy, were the Germans; what a people might they yet become! I addressed this people; raised above them by a little joinery, separated from them by a row of lamps, whose glancing and vapour threw an indistinctness over everything before me. How welcome was the tumult of applause, which sounded to me from the crowd; how gratefully did I accept the present, offered me unanimously by so many hands! For a time I rocked myself in these ideas; I affected the multitude, and was again affected by them. With my public I was on the fairest footing; I imagined that I felt a perfect harmony betwixt us, and that on each occasion I beheld before me the best and noblest of the land.

"Unhappily it was not the actress alone that inspired these friends of the stage with interest; they likewise made pretensions to the young and lively girl. They gave me to understand, in terms distinct enough, that my duty was not only to excite emotion in them, but to share it with them personally. This unluckily was not my business: I wished to elevate their minds; but to what they called their hearts I had not the slightest claim. Yet now men of all ranks, ages and characters, by turns afflicted me with their addresses; and it did seem hard that I could not, like an honest young woman, shut my door, and spare myself such a quantity of labour.

"The men appeared, for most part, much the same as I had been accustomed to about my aunt; and here again I should have felt disgusted with them, had not their peculiarities and insipidities amused me. As I was compelled to see them, in the theatre, in open places, in my house, I formed the project of spying out their follies, and my brother helped me with alacrity to execute it. And if you reflect that, up from the whisking shopman and the conceited merchant's son, to the polished calculating man of the world, the bold soldier and the impetuous prince, all in succession passed in review before me, each in his way endeavouring to found his small romance, you will pardon me if I conceived that I had gained some acquaintance with my nation.

"The fantastically dizened student; the awkward, humbly-proud man of letters; the sleek-fed, gouty canon; the solemn, heedful man of office; the heavy country-baron; the smirking, vapid courtier; the young erring parson; the cool, as well as the quick and sharply-speculating merchant; all these I have seen in motion; and I swear to you that there were few among them fitted to inspire me even with a sentiment of toleration: on the contrary, I felt it altogether irksome to collect, with tedium and annoyance, the suffrages of fools; to pocket those applauses in detail, which in their accumulated state had so delighted me, which in the gross I had appropriated with such pleasure.

"If I expected a rational compliment upon my acting; if I hoped that they would praise an author whom I valued, they were sure to make one empty observation on the back of another, and to name some tasteless piece in which they wished to see me play. If I listened in their company, to hear if some noble, brilliant, witty thought had met with a response among them, and would reappear from some of them in proper season, it was rare that I could catch an echo of it. An error that had happened, a mispronunciation, a provincialism of some actor; such were the weighty points by which they held fast, beyond which they could not pass. I knew not, in the end, to what hand I should turn: themselves they thought too clever to be entertained; and me they imagined they were well entertaining, if they romped and made noise enough about me. I began very cordially to despise them all; I felt as if the whole nation had, on purpose, deputed these people to debase it in my eyes. They appeared to me so clownish, so ill-bred, so wretchedly instructed, so void of pleasing qualities, so tasteless; I frequently exclaimed: No German can buckle his shoes, till he has learned to do it of some foreign nation!

"You perceive how blind, how unjust and splenetic I was; and the longer it lasted, my spleen increased. I might have killed myself with these things: but I fell into the contrary extreme; I married, or rather let myself be married. My brother, who had undertaken to conduct the theatre, wished much to have a helper. His choice lighted on a young man, who was not offensive to me; who wanted all that my brother had, genius, vivacity, spirit and impetuosity of mind; but who also in return had all that my brother wanted, love of order, diligence, and precious gifts in housekeeping and the management of money.

"He became my husband, I know not how; we lived together, I do not well know why. Enough, our affairs went prosperously forward. We drew a large income; of this my brother's activity was the cause. We lived with a moderate expenditure; and that was the merit of my husband. I thought no more about world or nation. With the world I had nothing to participate: my idea of the nation had faded away. When I entered on the scene, I did so that I might subsist; I opened my lips because I durst not continue silent, because I had come out to speak.

"Yet let me do the matter justice. I had altogether given myself up to the disposal of my brother. His objects were applause and money; for, between ourselves, he has no dislike to hear his own praises, and his outlay is always great. I no longer played according to my own feeling, to my own conviction; but as he directed me: and if I did it to his satisfaction, I was content. He steered entirely by the caprices of the public. Money flowed upon us; he could live according to his humour, and so we had good times with him.

"Thus had I fallen into a dull, handicraft routine. I spun out my days without joy or sympathy. My marriage was childless, and not of long continuance. My husband grew sick; his strength was visibly decaying; anxiety for him interrupted my general indifference. It was at this time that I formed an acquaintance, which opened a new life for me; a new and quicker one, for it will soon be done."

She kept silence for a time, and then continued: "All at once my prattling humour falters; I have not the courage to go on. Let me rest a little. You shall not go, till you have learned the whole extent of my misfortune. Meanwhile, call in Mignon, and ask her what she wants."

The child had more than once been in the room, while Aurelia and our friend were talking. As they spoke lower on her entrance, she had glided out again, and was now sitting quietly in the hall, and waiting. Being bid return, she brought a book with her, which its form and binding showed to be a small geographical atlas. She had seen some maps, for the first time at the parson's house, with great astonishment; had asked him many questions, and informed herself so far as possible about them. Her desire to learn seemed much excited by this new branch of knowledge. She now earnestly requested Wilhelm to purchase her the book; saying she had pawned her large silver buckle with the printseller for it, and wished to have back the pledge tomorrow morning, as this evening it was late. Her request was granted; and she then began repeating several things she had already learned; at the same time, in her own way, making many very strange inquiries. Here again one might observe, that, with a mighty effort, she could comprehend but little and laboriously. So likewise was it with her writing, at which she still kept busied. She yet spoke very broken German: it was only when she opened her mouth to sing, when she touched her cithern, that she seemed to be employing an organ by which, in some degree, the workings of her mind could be disclosed and communicated.

Since we are at present on the subject, we may also mention the perplexity which Wilhelm had of late experienced from certain parts of her procedure. When she came or went, wished him good-morning or good-night, she clasped him so firmly in her arms, and kissed him with such ardour, that often the violence of this expanding nature gave him serious fears. The spasmodic vivacity of her demeanour seemed daily to increase; her whole being moved in a restless stillness. She would never be without some piece of packthread to twist in her hands; some napkin to tie in knots; some paper or wood to chew. All her sports seemed but the channels which drained off some inward violent commotion. The only thing that seemed to cause her any cheerfulness was being near the boy Felix, with whom she could go on in a very dainty manner.

Aurelia, after a little rest, being now ready to explain to her friend a matter which lay very near her heart, grew impatient at the little girl's delay, and signified that she must go; a hint, however, which the latter did not take; and at last, when nothing else would do, they sent her off expressly and against her will.

"Now or never," said Aurelia, "must I tell you the remainder of my story. Were my tenderly-beloved and unjust friend but a few miles distant, I would say to you: 'Mount on horseback, seek by some means to get acquainted with him; on returning you will certainly forgive me, and pity me with all your heart.' As it is, I can only tell you with words how amiable he was, and how much I loved him.

"It was at the critical season, when care for the illness of my husband had depressed my spirits, that I first became acquainted with this stranger. He had just returned from America, where, in company with some Frenchmen, he had served with much distinction under the colours of the United States.

"He addressed me with an easy dignity, a frank kindliness; he spoke about myself, my state, my acting, like an old acquaintance, so affectionately and distinctly, that now for the first time I enjoyed the pleasure of perceiving my existence reflected in the being of another. His judgments were just, though not severe; penetrating, yet not void of love. He showed no harshness; his pleasantry was courteous, with all his humour. He seemed accustomed to success with women; this excited my attention: he was never in the least importunate or flattering; this put me off my guard.

"In the town he had intercourse with few; he was often on horseback, visiting his many friends in the neighbourhood, and managing the business of his house. On returning, he would frequently alight at my apartments; he treated my ever-ailing husband with warm attention; he procured him mitigation of his sickness by a good physician. And taking part in all that interested me, he allowed me to take part in all that interested him. He told me the history of his campaigns; he spoke of his invincible attachment to military life, of his family relations, of his present business. He kept no secret from me; he displayed to me his inmost thoughts, allowed me to behold the most secret corners of his soul: I became acquainted with his passions and his capabilities. It was the first time in my life that I enjoyed a cordial, intellectual intercourse with any living creature. I was attracted by him, borne along by him, before I thought about inquiring how it stood with me.

"Meanwhile I lost my husband, nearly just as I had taken him. The burden of theatrical affairs now fell entirely on me. My brother, not to be surpassed upon the stage, was never good for anything in economical concerns: I took the charge of all; at the same time, studying my parts with greater diligence than ever. I again played as of old; nay with new life, with quite another force. It was by reason of my friend, it was on his account that I did so; yet my success was not always best when I knew him to be present. Once or twice he listened to me unobserved; and how pleasantly his unexpected applauses surprised me you may conceive.

"Certainly I am a strange creature. In every part I played, it seemed as if I had been speaking it in praise of him; for that was the temper of my heart, the words might be anything they pleased. Did I understand him to be present in the audience, I durst not venture to speak out with all my force; just as I would not press my love or praise on him to his face: was he absent, I had then free scope; I did my best, with a certain peacefulness, with a contentment not to be described. Applause once more delighted me; and when I charmed the people, I longed to call down among them: 'This you owe to him!'

"Yes, my relation to the public, to the nation, had been altered by a wonder. On a sudden they again appeared to me in the most favourable light; I felt astónished at my former blindness.

"How foolish, said I often to myself, was it to revile a nation; foolish, simply since it was a nation. Is it necessary, is it possible, that individual men should generally interest us much? Not at all! The only question is, whether in the great mass there exists a sufficient quantity of talent, force and capability, which lucky circumstances may develop, which men of lofty minds may direct upon a common object. I now rejoiced in discovering so little prominent originality among my countrymen; I rejoiced that they disdained not to accept of guidance from without; I rejoiced that they had found a leader.

"Lothario—allow me to designate my friend by this his first name which I loved—Lothario had always presented the Germans to my mind on the side of valour; and shown me, that when well commanded, there was no braver nation on the face of the earth; and I felt ashamed that I had never thought of this the first quality of a people. History was known to him; he was in connexion and correspondence with the most distinguished persons of the age. Young as he was, his eye was open to the budding youth-hood of his native country; to the silent labours of active and busy men in so many provinces of art. He afforded me a glimpse of Germany; what it was, and what it might be; and I blushed at having formed my judgment of a nation from the motley crowd, that press themselves into the wardrobe of a theatre. He made me look upon it as a duty that I too, in my own department, should be true, spirited, enlivening. I now felt as if inspired, every time I stepped upon the boards. Mediocre passages grew golden in my mouth; had any poet been at hand to support me adequately, I might have produced the most astonishing effects.

"So lived the young widow for a series of months. He could not want me; and I felt exceedingly unhappy when he stayed away He showed me the letters he received from his relations, from his amiable sister. He took an interest in the smallest circumstances that concerned me; more complete, more intimate no union ever was than ours. The name of love was not mentioned. He went and came, came and went—And now, my friend, it is high time that you too should go."

CHAPTER XVII.

WILHELM could put off no longer the visiting of his commercial friends. He proceeded to their place with some anxiety; knowing he should there find letters from his people. He dreaded the reproofs which these would of course contain: it seemed likely also that notice had been given to his trading correspondents, concerning the perplexities and fears which his late silence had occasioned. After such a series of knightly adventures, he recoiled from the school-boy aspect in which he must appear: he proposed within his mind to act with an air of sternness and defiance, and thus hide his embarrassment.

To his great wonder and contentment, however, all went off very easily and well. In the vast, stirring, busy counting-room, the men had scarcely time to seek him out his packet; his delay was but alluded to in passing. And on opening the letters of his father and his friend Werner, he found them all of very innocent contents. His father, in hopes of an extensive journal, the keeping of which he had strongly recommended to his son at parting, giving him also a tabulary scheme for that purpose, seemed pretty well pacified about the silence of the first period; complaining only of a certain enigmatical obscurity in the last and only letter, despatched, as we have seen, from the Castle of the Count. Werner joked in his way; told merry anecdotes, facetious burgh-news; and requested intelligence of friends and acquaintances, whom Wilhelm in the large trading city would now meet with in great numbers. Our friend, extremely pleased at getting off so well, answered without loss of a moment, in some very cheerful letters: promising his father a copious journal of his travels, with all the required geographical, statistical and mercantile remarks. He had seen much on his journey, he said; and hoped to make a tolerably large manuscript out of these materials. He did not observe, that he was almost in the same case as he had once experienced before, when he assembled an audience and lit his lamps to represent a play, which was not written, still less got by heart. Accordingly, so soon as he commenced the actual work of composition, he became aware that he had much to say about emotions and thoughts, and many experiences of the heart and spirit; but not a word concerning outward objects, on which, as he now discovered, he had not bestowed the least attention.

In this embarrassment, the acquisitions of his friend Laertes came very seasonably to his aid. Custom had united these young people, unlike one another as they were; and Laertes, with all his failings and singularities, was actually an interesting man. Endowed with warm and pleasurable senses, he might have reached old age without reflecting for a moment on his situation. But his ill fortune and his sickness had robbed him of the pure feelings of youth; and opened for him instead of it a view into the transitoriness, the discontinuity of man's existence. Hence had arisen a humorous, flighty, rhapsodical way of thinking about all things, or rather of uttering the immediate impressions they produced on him. He did not like to be alone; he strolled about all the coffeehouses and *tables-d'hôte*; and when he did stay at home, books of travels were his favourite, nay his only kind of reading. Having lately found a large circulating library, he had been enabled to content his taste in this respect to the full; and ere long half the world was figuring in his faithful memory.

It was easy for him, therefore, to speak comfort to his friend, when the latter had disclosed his utter lack of matter for the narrative so solemnly promised by him. "Now is the time for a stroke of art," said Laertes, " that shall have no fellow!

"Has not Germany been travelled over, cruised over, walked, crept and flown over, repeatedly from end to end? And has not every German traveller the royal privilege of drawing from the public a repayment of the great or small expenses he may have incurred while travelling? Give me your route previous to our meeting; the rest I know already. I will find you helps and sources of information: of miles that were never measured, populations that were never counted, we shall give them plenty. The revenues of provinces we will take from almanacs and tables, which, as all men know, are the most authentic documents. On these we will ground our political discussions; we shall not fail in sideglances at the ruling powers. One or two princes we will paint as true fathers of their country, that we may gain more ready credence in our allegations against others. If we do not travel through the residence of any noted man, we shall take care to meet such persons at the inn, and make them utter the most foolish stuff to us. Particularly, let us not forget to insert, with all its graces and sentiments, some love-story with a pastoral barmaid. I tell you it shall be a composition, which will not only fill father and mother with delight, but which booksellers themselves shall gladly pay you current money for."

They went accordingly to work; and both of them found pleasure in their labour. Wilhelm, in the mean time, frequenting the play at night, and conversing with Serlo and Aurelia by day, experienced the greatest satisfaction; and was daily more and more expanding his ideas, which had been too long revolving in the same narrow circle.

CHAPTER XVIII.

It was not without deep interest that he became acquainted with the history of Serlo's career. Piecemeal he learned it; for it was not the fashion of that extraordinary man to be confidential, or to speak of anything connectively. He had been, one may say, born and suckled in the theatre. While yet literally an infant, he had been produced upon the stage to move spectators merely by his presence; for authors even then were acquainted with this natural and very guiltless mode of doing so. Thus his first " Father !" or " Mother !" in favourite pieces, procured him approbation, before he understood what was meant by that clapping of the hands. In the character of Cupid, he more than once descended, with terror, in his flying-gear; as harlequin he used to issue from the egg; and as a little chimney-sweep to play the sharpest tricks.

Unhappily, the plaudits of these glancing nights were too bitterly repaid by sufferings in the intervening seasons. His father was persuaded that the minds of children could be kept awake and steadfast by no other means than blows; hence, in the studying of any part, he used to thrash him at stated periods; not because the boy was awkward, but that he might become more certainly and constantly expert. It was thus that in former times, while putting down a landmark, people were accustomed to bestow a hearty drubbing on the children who had followed them; and these, it was supposed, would recollect the place exactly to the latest day of their lives. Serlo waxed in stature, and showed the finest capabilities of spirit and of body; in particular an admirable pliancy at once in his thoughts, looks, movements and gestures. His gift of imitation was beyond belief. When still a boy, he could mimic persons, so that you would think you saw them; though in form, age and disposition, they might be entirely unlike him, and unlike each other. Nor with all this, did he want the knack of suiting himself to his circumstances, and picking out his way in life. Accordingly, so soon as he had grown in some degree acquainted with his strength, he very naturally eloped from his father; who, as the boy's understanding and dexterity increased, still thought it needful to forward their perfection by the harshest treatment.

Happy was the wild boy, now roaming free about the world, where his feats of waggery never failed to secure him a good reception. His lucky star first led him in the Christmas season to a cloister, where the friar, whose business it had been to arrange processions, and to entertain the Christian community by spiritual masquerades, having just died, Serlo was welcomed as a helping angel. On the instant he took up the part of Gabriel in the Annunciation; and did not by any means displease the pretty girl, who, acting the Virgin, very gracefully received his most obliging kiss, with external humility and inward pride. In their Mysteries, he continued to perform the most important parts; and thought himself no slender personage, when at last, in the character of Martyr, he was mocked of the world, and beaten, and fixed upon the cross.

Some Pagan soldiers had, on this occasion, played their parts a little *too* naturally. To be avenged on these heathen in the proper style, he took care at the Day of Judgment to have them decked out in gaudy clothes as emperors and kings; and at the moment when they, exceedingly contented with their situation, were about to take precedence of the rest in heaven as they had done on earth, he on a sudden rushed upon them in the shape of the Devil; and, to the cordial edification of all the beggars and spectators, having thoroughly curried them with his oven-fork, he pushed them without mercy back into the Chasm, where, in the midst of waving flame, they met with the sorriest welcome.

He was acute enough, however, to perceive that these crowned heads might feel offended at such bold procedure; and perhaps forget the reverence due to his privileged office of Accuser and Turnkey. So in all silence, before the Millennium commenced, he withdrew, and betook him to a neighbouring town. Here a society of persons, denominated Children of Joy, received him with open arms. They were a set of clever, strong-headed, lively geniuses, who saw well enough that the sum of our existence, divided by reason, never gives an integer number, but that a surprising fraction is always left behind. At stated times, to get rid of this fraction, which impedes, and if it is diffused over all the mass of our conduct, endangers us, was the object of the Children of Joy. For one day a-week each of them in succession was a fool on purpose; and during this, he in his turn exhibited to ridicule, in allegorical representations, whatever folly he had noticed in himself or the rest, throughout the other six. This practice might be somewhat ruder than that constant training, in the course of which a man of ordinary morals is accustomed to observe, to warn, to punish himself daily; but it was also merrier and surer. For as no Child of Joy concealed his bosom-folly, so he and those about him held it for simply what it was: whereas, on the other plan, by the help of self-deception, this same bosom-folly often gains the head authority within, and binds down reason to a secret servitude, at the very time when reason fondly hopes that she has long since chased it out of doors. The mask of folly circulated round in this society; and each member was allowed, in his particular day, to decorate and characterise it with his own attributes or those of others. At the time of Carnival, they assumed the greatest freedom, vying with the clergy in attempts to instruct and entertain the multitude. Their solemn figurative processions of Virtues and Vices, Arts and Sciences, Quarters of the World, and Seasons of the Year, bodied forth a number of conceptions, and gave images of many distant objects to the people, and hence were not without their use; while, on the other hand, the mummeries of the priesthood tended but to strengthen a tasteless superstition, already strong enough.

Here again young Serlo was altogether in his element. Invention in its strictest sense, it is true, he had not; but, on the other hand, he had the most consummate skill in employing what he found before him; in ordering it; and shadowing it forth. His roguish turns; his gift of mimicry; his biting wit, which at least one day weekly he might use with entire freedom, even against his benefactors, made him precious, or rather indispensable, to the whole society.

Yet his restless mind soon drove him from this favourable scene to other quarters of his country, where other means of instruction awaited him. He came into the polished but also barren part of Germany, where, in worshiping the good and the beautiful, there is indeed no want of truth, but frequently a grievous want of spirit. His masks would here do nothing for him: he had now to aim at working on the heart and mind. For short periods, he attached himself to small or to extensive companies of actors; and marked, on these occasions, what were the distinctive properties both of the pieces and the players. The monotony which then reigned on the German theatre, the mawkish sound and cadence of their Alexandrines, the flat and yet distorted dialogue, the shallowness and commonness of these undisguised preachers of morality, he was not long in comprehending; or in seizing, at the same time, what little there was that moved and pleased.

Not only single parts in the current pieces, but the pieces themselves remained easily and wholly in his memory; and along with them, the special tone of any player who had represented them with approbation. At length, in the course of his rambles, his money being altogether done, the project struck him of acting entire pieces by himself, especially in villages, and noblemen's houses; and thus in all places making sure at least of entertainment and lodging. In any tavern, any room, or any garden, he would accordingly at once set up his theatre: with a roguish seriousness and a show of enthusiasm, he would contrive to gain the imaginations of his audience; to deceive their senses, and before their eyes to make an old press into a tower, or a fan into a dagger. His youthful warmth supplied the place of deep feeling; his vehemence seemed strength, and his flattery tenderness. Such of the spectators as already knew a theatre, he put in mind of all that they had seen and heard; in the rest he awakened a presentiment of something wonderful, and a wish to be more acquainted with it. What produced an effect in one place he did not fail to repeat in others; and his mind overflowed with a wicked pleasure when, by the same means, on the spur of the moment, he could make gulls of all the world.

His spirit was lively, brisk and unimpeded: by frequently repeating parts and pieces, he improved very fast. Ere long he could recite and play with more conformity to the sense, than the models whom he had at first imitated. Proceeding thus, he arrived by degrees at playing naturally, though he did not cease to feign. He seemed transported, yet he lay in wait for the effect; and his greatest pride was in moving, by successive touches, the passions of men. The mad trade he drove did itself soon force him to proceed with a certain moderation; and thus, partly by constraint, partly by instinct, he learned the art of which so few players seem to have a notion, the art of being frugal in the use of voice and gestures.

Thus did he contrive to tame, and to inspire with interest for him, even rude and unfriendly men. Being always contented with food and shelter; thankfully accepting presents of any kind as readily as money; which latter, when he reckoned that he had enough of it, he frequently declined,—he became a general favourite; was sent about from one to another with recommendatory letters; and thus he wandered many a day from castle to castle, exciting much festivity, enjoying much, and meeting in his travels with the most agreeable and curious adventures.

With such inward coldness of temper, he could not properly be said to love any one; with such clearness of vision, he could respect no one. In fact, he never looked beyond the external peculiarities of men; and he merely carried their characters in his mimical collection. Yet withal his selfishness was keenly wounded, if he did not please every one, and call forth universal applause. How this might be attained, he had studied in the course of time so accurately, and so sharpened his sense of the matter, that not only on the stage, but also in common life, he no longer could do otherwise than flatter and deceive. And thus did his disposition, his talent and his way of life, work reciprocally on each other, till by this means he had imperceptibly been formed into a perfect actor. Nay, by a mode of action and reaction, which is quite natural, though it seems paradoxical, his recitation, declamation and gesture, improved, by critical discernment and practice, to a high degree of truth, ease and frankness; while, in his life and intercourse with men, he seemed to grow continually more secret, artful, or even hypocritical and constrained.

Of his fortunes and adventures we perhaps shall speak in another place: it is enough to remark at present, that in later times, when he had become a man of circumstance, in possession of a distinct reputation, and of a very good though not entirely secure employment and rank, he was wont, in conversation, partly in the way of irony, partly of mockery, in a delicate style, to act the sophist, and thus to destroy almost all serious discussion. This kind of speech he seemed peculiarly fond of using towards Wilhelm; particularly when the latter took a fancy, as often happened, for introducing any of his general and theoretical disquisitions. Yet still they liked well to be together; with such different modes of thinking, the conversation could not fail to be lively. Wilhelm always wished to deduce everything from abstract ideas which he had arrived at; he wanted to have art viewed in all its connexions as a whole. He wanted to promulgate and fix down universal laws; to settle what was right, beautiful and good: in short, he treated all things in a serious manner. Serlo, on the other hand, took up the matter very lightly: never answering directly to any question, he would contrive by some anecdote or laughable turn, to give the finest and most satisfactory illustrations; and thus to instruct his audience while he made them merry.

CHAPTER XIX.

While our friend was in this way living very happily, Melina and the rest were in quite a different case. Wilhelm they haunted like evil spirits; and not only by their presence, but frequently by rueful faces and bitter words, they caused him many a sorry moment. Serlo had not admitted them to the most trifling part, far less held out to them any hope of a permanent engagement; and yet he had contrived, by degrees, to get acquainted with the capabilities of every one of them. Whenever any actors were assembled in leisure hours about him, he was wont to make them read, and frequently to read along with them. On such occasions, he took plays which were by and by to be acted, which for a long time had remained unacted; and generally by portions. In like manner, after any first representation, he caused such passages to be repeated as he had anything to say upon; by which means he sharpened the discernment of his actors, and strengthened their certainty of hitting the proper point. And as a person of slender but correct understanding may produce more agreeable effect on others, than a perplexed and unpurified genius, he would frequently exalt men of mediocre talents, by the clear views which he imperceptibly afforded them, to a wonderful extent of power. Nor was it an unimportant item in his scheme, that he likewise had poems read before him in their meetings; for by these he nourished in his people the feeling of that charm, which a well-pronounced rhythm is calculated to awaken in the soul; whereas in other companies, those prose compositions were already getting introduced, for which any tyro was adequate.

On occasions such as these, he had contrived to make himself acquainted with the new-come players: he had decided what they were, and what they might be; and silently made up his mind to take advantage of their talents, in a revolution which was now threatening his own company. For a while he let the matter rest; declined every one of Wilhelm's intercessions for his comrades, with a shrug of the shoulders; till at last he saw his time, and altogether unexpectedly made the proposal to our friend, " that he himself should come upon the stage; that on this condition, the others too might be admitted."

" These people must not be so useless as you formerly described them," answered Wilhelm, " if they can now be all received at once; and I suppose their talents would remain the same without me as with me."

Under seal of secrecy, Serlo hereupon explained his situation: how his first actor was giving hints about a rise of salary at the renewal of their contract; how he himself did not incline conceding this, the rather as the individual in question was no longer in such favour with the public; how, if he dismissed him, a whole train would follow; whereby, it was true, his company would lose some good, but likewise some indifferent actors. He then showed Wilhelm what he hoped to gain in him, in Laertes, Old Boisterous, and even Frau Melina. Nay, he promised to procure for the silly Pedant himself, in the character of Jew, minister, but chiefly of villain, a decided approbation.

Wilhelm faltered; the proposal fluttered him; he knew not what to say. That he might say something, he rejoined, with a deep-drawn breath: "You speak very graciously about the good you find and hope to find in us: but how is it with our weak points, which certainly have not escaped your penetration?"

"These," said Serlo, "by diligence, practice and reflection, we shall soon make strong points. Though you are yet but freshmen and bunglers, there is not one among you that does not warrant expectation more or less: for, so far as I can judge, no stick, properly so called, is to be met with in the company; and your stick is the only person that can never be improved, never bent or guided, whether it be self-conceit, stupidity, or hypochondria, that renders him unpliant."

The Manager next stated, in a few words, the terms he meant to offer; requested Wilhelm to determine soon, and left him in no small perplexity.

In the marvellous composition of those travels, which he had at first engaged with as it were in jest, and was now carrying on in conjunction with Laertes, his mind had by degrees grown more attentive to the circumstances and the every-day life of the actual world, than it was wont. He now first understood the object of his father in so earnestly recommending him to keep a journal. He now, for the first time, felt how pleasant and how useful it might be to become participator in so many trades and requisitions, and to take a hand in diffusing activity and life into the deepest nooks of the mountains and forests of Europe. The busy trading town in which he was; the unrest of Laertes, who dragged him about to examine everything, afforded him the most impressive image of a mighty centre, from which everything was flowing out, to which everything was coming back; and it was the first time that his spirit, in contemplating this species of activity, had really felt delight. At such a juncture Serlo's offer had been made him; had again awakened his desires, his tendencies, his faith in a natural talent, and again brought into mind his solemn obligation to his helpless comrades.

"Here standest thou once more," said he within himself, "at the Parting of the Ways, between the two women who appeared before thee in thy youth. The one no longer looks so pitiful as then; nor does the other look so glorious. To obey the one, or to obey the other, thou art not without a kind of inward calling; outward reasons are on both sides strong enough; and to decide appears to thee impossible. Thou wishest some preponderancy from without would fix thy choice: and yet, if thou consider well, it is external circumstances only that inspire thee with a wish to trade, to gather, to possess; whilst it is thy inmost want that has created, that has nourished the desire still farther to unfold and perfect what endowments soever for the beautiful and good, be they mental or bodily, may lie within thee. And ought I not to honour Fate, which without furtherance of mine has led me hither to the goal of all my wishes? Has not all that I in old times meditated and forecast, now happened accidentally, and without my coöperation? Singular enough! We seem to be so intimate with nothing as we are with our own wishes and hopes, which have long been kept and cherished in our hearts; yet when they meet us, when they as it were press forward to us, then we know them not, then we recoil from them. All that, since the hapless night which severed me from Mariana, I have but allowed myself to dream, now stands before me, entreating my acceptance. Hither I intended to escape by flight; hither I am softly guided: with Serlo I meant to seek a place; he now seeks me, and offers me conditions which, as a beginner, I could not have looked for. Was it then mere love to Mariana that bound me to the stage? Or love to art that bound me to her? Was that prospect, that outlet, which the theatre presented me, nothing but the project of a restless, disorderly and disobedient boy, wishing to lead a life which the customs of the civic world would not admit of? Or, was all this different, worthier, purer? If so, what moved thee to alter the persuasions of that period? Hast thou not hitherto, even without knowing it, pursued thy plan? Is not the concluding step still farther to be justified, now that no side-purposes combine with it; now that in making it thou mayest fulfil a solemn promise, and nobly free thyself from a heavy debt?"

All that could affect his heart and his imagination was now moving, and conflicting in the liveliest strife within him. The thought that he might retain Mignon, that he should not need to put away the Harper, was not an inconsiderable item in the balance; which, however, had not ceased to waver to the one and to the other side, when he went, as he was wont, to see his friend Aurelia.

CHAPTER XX.

She was lying on the sofa; she seemed quiet. "Do you think you will be fit to act tomorrow?" he inquired. "O yes!" cried she with vivacity, "you know there is nothing to prevent me. If I but knew a way," continued she, "to rid myself of those applauses! The people mean it well, but they will kill me. Last night, I thought my very heart would break! Once, when I used to please myself, I could endure this gladly: when I had studied long, and well prepared myself, it gave me joy to hear the sound, 'It has succeeded!' pealing back to me from every corner. But now I speak not what I like, nor as I like; I am swept along, I get confused, I scarce know what I do; and the impression I make is far deeper. The applause grows louder, and I think: Did you but know what charms you! These dark, vague, vehement tones of passion move you, force you to admire; and you feel not that they are the cries of agony, wrung from the miserable being whom you praise.

"I learned my part this morning; just now I have been repeating it and trying it. I am tired, broken down; and tomorrow I must do the same. Tomorrow evening is the play. Thus do I drag myself to and fro: it is wearisome to rise, it is wearisome to go to bed. All moves within me in an everlasting circle. Then come their dreary consolations, and present themselves before me; and I cast them out, and execrate them. I will not surrender, not surrender to necessity: why should that be necessary, which crushes me to the dust? Might it not be otherwise? I am paying the penalty of being born a German; it is the nature of the Germans that they bear heavily on everything, that everything bears heavily on them."

"O my friend!" cried Wilhelm, "could you cease to whet the dagger wherewith you are ever wounding me! Does nothing then remain for you? Are your youth, your form, your health, your talents nothing? Having lost one blessing, without blame of yours, must you throw all the others after it? Is that also necessary?"

She was silent for a few moments, and then burst forth: "I know well it is a waste of time, nothing but a waste of time, this love! What might not, should not I have done! And now it is all vanished into air. I am a poor, wretched, lovelorn creature;

lovelorn, that is all! O, have compassion on me: God knows I am poor and wretched!"

She sank in thought; then, after a brief pause, she exclaimed with violence: "You are accustomed to have all things fly into your arms. No, you cannot feel; no man is qualified to feel the worth of a woman that can reverence herself. By all the holy angels, by all the images of blessedness, which a pure and kindly heart creates, there is not anything more heavenly than the soul of a woman giving herself to the man she loves!

"We are cold, proud, high, clear-sighted, wise, while we deserve the name of women; and all these qualities we lay down at your feet, the instant that we love, that we hope to excite a return of love. O, how have I cast away my whole existence wittingly and willingly! But now will I despair, purposely despair. There is no drop of blood within me but shall suffer, no fibre that I will not punish. Smile, I pray you; laugh at this theatrical display of passion."

Wilhelm was far enough from any tendency to laugh. This horrible, half-natural, half-factitious condition of his friend afflicted him but too deeply. He sympathised in the tortures of that racking misery: his thoughts were wandering in painful perplexities, his blood was in a feverish tumult.

She had risen, and was walking up and down the room. "I see before me," she exclaimed, "all manner of reasons why I should not love him. I know he is not worthy of it: I turn my mind aside, this way and that; I seize upon whatever business I can find. At one time I take up a part, though I have not to play it; at another, I begin to practise old ones, though I know them through and through; I practise them more diligently, more minutely, I toil and toil at them—My friend, my confidant, what a horrid task is it to tear away one's thoughts from oneself! My reason suffers, my brain is racked and strained: to save myself from madness I again admit the feeling that I love him. Yes, I love him, I love him!" cried she with a shower of tears; "I love him, I shall die loving him!"

He took her by the hand, and entreated her in the most earnest manner not to waste herself in such self-torments. "O, it seems hard," said he, "that not only so much that is impossible should be denied us, but so much also that is possible. It was not your lot to meet with a faithful heart that would have formed your perfect happiness. It was mine to fix the welfare of my life upon a hapless creature, whom by the weight of my fidelity I drew to the bottom like a reed, perhaps even broke in pieces!"

He had told Aurelia of his intercourse with Mariana, and could therefore now refer to it. She looked him intently in the face, and asked: " Can you say that you never yet betrayed a woman, that you never tried with thoughtless gallantry, with false asseverations, with cajoling oaths, to wheedle favour from her?"

" I can," said Wilhelm, " and indeed without much vanity; my life has been so simple and sequestered, I have had but few enticements to attempt such things. And what a warning, my beautiful, my noble friend, is this melancholy state in which I see you! Accept of me a vow, which is suited to my heart; which, under the emotion you have caused me, has settled into words and shape, and will be hallowed by the hour in which I utter it: Each transitory inclination I will study to withstand; and even the most earnest I will keep within my bosom; no woman shall receive an acknowledgment of love from my lips, to whom I cannot consecrate my life!"

She looked at him with a wild indifference; and drew back some steps as he offered her his hand. "'Tis of no moment!" cried she: " so many women's tears more or fewer; the ocean will not swell by reason of them. And yet," continued she, " among thousands one woman saved; that still is something: among thousands one honest man discovered; this is not to be refused. Do you know then what you promise?"

" I know it," answered Wilhelm with a smile, and holding out his hand.

" I accept it then," said she, and made a movement with her right hand, as if meaning to take hold of his: but instantly she darted it into her pocket, pulled out her dagger quick as lightning, and scored with the edge and point of it across his hand. He hastily drew it back, but the blood was already running down.

" One must mark you men rather sharply, if one would have you take heed," cried she with a wild mirth, which soon passed into a quick assiduity. She took her handkerchief, and bound his hand with it to stanch the fast-flowing blood. " Forgive a half-crazed being," cried she, " and regret not these few drops of blood. I am appeased, I am again myself. On my knees will I crave your pardon: leave me the comfort of healing you."

She ran to her drawer; brought lint, with other apparatus; stanched the blood, and viewed the wound attentively. It went across the palm, close under the thumb, dividing the life-lines, and running towards the little finger. She bound it up in silence, with a significant, reflective look. He asked once or twice: " Aurelia, how could you hurt your friend?"

" Hush!" replied she, laying her finger on her mouth: " Hush!"

BOOK V.

CHAPTER I.

Thus Wilhelm, to his pair of former wounds, which were yet scarcely healed, had now got the accession of a third, which was fresh and not a little disagreeable. Aurelia would not suffer him to call a surgeon; she dressed the hand with all manner of strange speeches, saws and ceremonies; and so placed him in a very painful situation. Yet not he alone, but all persons who came near her, suffered by her restlessness and singularity: and no one more than little Felix. This stirring child was exceedingly impatient under such oppression, and showed himself still naughtier, the more she censured and instructed him.

He delighted in some practices which commonly are thought bad habits, and in which she would not by any means indulge him. He would drink, for example, rather from the bottle than the glass; and his food seemed visibly to have a better relish when eaten from the bowl than from the plate. Such ill-breeding was not overlooked: if he left the door standing open, or slammed it to; if when bid do anything, he stood stock-still, or ran off violently, he was sure to have a long lecture inflicted on him for the fault. Yet he showed no symptoms of improvement from this training: on the other hand, his affection for Aurelia seemed daily to diminish; there was nothing tender in his tone when he called her Mother; whereas he passionately clung to the old nurse, who let him have his will in everything.

But she likewise had of late become so sick, that they had at last been obliged to take her from the house into a quiet lodging; and Felix would have been entirely alone, if Mignon had not, like a kindly guardian-spirit, come to help him. The two children talked together, and amused each other in the prettiest style. She taught him little songs; and he, having an excellent memory, frequently recited them, to the surprise of those about him. She attempted also to explain her maps to him. With these she was still very busy, though she did not seem to take the fittest method. For, in studying countries, she appeared to care little about any other point than whether they were cold or warm. Of the north and south Poles, of the horrid ice which reigns there, and of the increasing heat the farther one retires from them, she could give a very clear account. When any one was travelling, she merely asked whether he was going northward or southward; and strove to find his route in her little charts. Especially when Wilhelm spoke of travelling, she was all attention, and seemed vexed when anything occurred to change the subject. Though she could not be prevailed upon to undertake a part, or even to enter the theatre when any play was acting, yet she willingly and zealously committed many odes and songs to memory; and by unexpectedly, and as it were on the spur of the moment, reciting some such poem, generally of the earnest and solemn kind, she would often cause astonishment in every one.

Serlo, accustomed to regard with favour every trace of opening talent, encouraged her in such performances: but what pleased him most in Mignon was her sprightly, various and often even mirthful singing. By means of a similar gift, the Harper likewise had acquired his favour.

Without himself possessing genius for music, or playing on any instrument, Serlo could rightly prize the value of the art; he failed not, as often as he could, to enjoy this pleasure, which cannot be compared with any other. He held a concert once a-week; and now, with Mignon, the Harper and Laertes, who was not unskilful on the violin, he had formed a very curious domestic band.

He was wont to say: "Men are so inclined to content themselves with what is commonest; the spirit and the senses so easily grow dead to the impressions of the beautiful and perfect, that every one should study, by all methods, to nourish in his mind the faculty of feeling these things. For no man can bear to be entirely deprived of such enjoyments: it is only because they are not used to taste of what is excellent, that the generality of people take delight in silly and insipid things, provided they be new. For this reason," he would add, " one ought every day at least to hear a little song, read a good poem, see a fine picture, and, if it were possible, to speak a few reasonable words." With such a turn of thought in Serlo, which in some degree was natural to him, the persons who frequented his society could scarcely be in want of pleasant conversation.

It was in the midst of these instructive entertainments, that Wilhelm one day received a letter sealed in black. Werner's hand betokened mournful news; and our friend was not a little shocked when, opening the sheet, he found it to contain the tidings of his father's death, conveyed in a very few words. After a short and sudden illness he had parted from the world, leaving his domestic affairs in the best possible order.

This unlooked-for intelligence struck Wilhelm to the heart. He deeply felt how careless and negligent we often are of friends and relations while they inhabit with us this terrestrial sojourn; and how we first repent of our insensibility when the fair union, at least for this side of time, is finally cut asunder. His grief for the early death of this honest parent was mitigated only by the feeling, that he had loved but little in the world, and the conviction that he had enjoyed but little.

Wilhelm's thoughts soon turned to his own predicament; and he felt himself extremely discomposed. A person can scarcely be put into a more dangerous position, than when external circumstances have produced some striking change in his condition, without his manner of feeling and of thinking having undergone any preparation for it. There is then an epoch without epoch; and the contradiction which arises is the greater, the less the person feels that he is not trained for this new manner of existence.

Wilhelm saw himself in freedom, at a moment when he could not yet be at one with himself. His thoughts were noble, his motives pure, his purposes were not to be despised. All this he could with some degree of confidence acknowledge to himself: but he had of late been frequently enough compelled to notice, that experience was sadly wanting to him; and hence on the experience of others, and on the results which they deduced from it, he put a value far beyond its real one; and thus led himself still deeper into error. What he wanted, he conceived he might most readily acquire if he undertook to collect and retain whatever memorable thought he should meet with, in reading or in conversation. He accordingly recorded his own or other men's opinions, nay wrote whole dialogues, when they chanced to interest him. But unhappily by this means he held fast the false no less firmly than the true; he dwelt far too long on one idea, particularly when it was of an aphoristic shape; and thus he left his natural mode of thought and action, and frequently took foreign lights for his loadstars. Aurelia's bitterness, and Laertes' cold contempt for men, warped his judgment oftener than they should have done: but no one, in his present case, would have been so dangerous as Jarno, a man whose clear intellect could form a just and rigorous decision about present things; but who erred withal in enunciating these particular decisions with a kind of universal application; whereas, in truth, the judgments of the understanding are properly of force but once, and that in the strictest cases, and become inaccurate in some degree when applied to any other.

Thus Wilhelm, striving to become consistent with himself, was deviating farther and farther from wholesome consistency; and this confusion made it easier for his passions to employ their whole artillery against him, and thus still farther to perplex his views of duty.

Serlo did not fail to take advantage of the late tidings: and in truth he daily had more reason to be anxious about some fresh arrangement of his people. Either he must soon renew his old contracts; a measure he was not specially fond of, for several of his actors, who reckoned themselves indispensable, were growing more and more arrogant; or else he must entirely new-model and reform his company; which plan he looked upon as preferable.

Though he did not personally importune our friend, he set Aurelia and Philina on him: and the other wanderers, longing for some kind of settlement, on their side gave Wilhelm not a moment's rest; so that he stood hesitating in his choice, in no slight embarrassment, till he should decide. Who would have thought that a letter of Werner's, written with quite different views, should have forced him on resolving? We shall omit the introduction, and give the rest of it with little alteration.

CHAPTER II.

"—It was, therefore, and it always must be, right for every one, on any opportunity, to follow his vocation and exhibit his activity. Scarcely had the good old man been gone a quarter of an hour, when everything in the house began moving by a different plan than his. Friends, acquaintances, relations, crowded forward; especially all sorts of people who on such occasions use to gain anything. They fetched and carried, they counted, wrote and reckoned; some brought wine and meat, others ate and drank; and none seemed busier than the women getting out the mournings.

" Such being the case, thou wilt not blame me that, in this emergency, I likewise thought of *my* advantage. I made myself as active, and as helpful to thy sister, as I could; and so soon as it was anyway decorous, signified to her that it had now become our business to accelerate a union, which our parents in their too great circumspection had hitherto postponed.

" Do not suppose, however, that it came into our heads to take possession of that monstrous empty house. We are more modest, and more rational. Thou shalt hear our plan: thy sister, so soon as we are married, comes to our house; and thy mother comes along with her. 'How can that be?' thou wilt say; 'you have scarcely room for yourselves in that hampered nest.' There lies the art of it, my friend! Good packing renders all things possible; thou wouldst not believe what space one finds, when one desires to occupy but little. The large house we shall sell; an opportunity occurs for this; and the money we shall draw for it will produce a hundred-fold.

"I hope this meets thy views: I hope also thou hast not inherited the smallest particle of those unprofitable tastes for which thy father and thy grandfather were noted. The latter placed his greatest happiness in having about him a multitude of dull-looking works of art, which no one, I may well say no one, could enjoy with him; the former lived in a stately pomp, which he suffered no one to enjoy with him. We mean to manage otherwise, and we expect thy approbation.

"It is true, I myself in all the house have no place whatever but the stool before my writing-desk; and I see not clearly where they will be able to put a cradle down: but in return, the room we shall have out of doors will be the more abundant. Coffee-houses and clubs for the husband; walks and drives for the wife: and pleasant country jaunts for both. But the chief advantage in our plan is, that the round table being now completely filled, our father cannot ask his friends to dinner, who the more he strove to entertain them, used to laugh at him the more.

"Now no superfluity for us! Not too much furniture and apparatus; no coach, no horses! Nothing but money; and the liberty, day after day, to do what you like in reason. No wardrobe; still the best and newest on your back: the man may wear his coat till it is done; the wife may truck her gown the moment it is going out of fashion. There is nothing so unsufferable to me as an old huckster's shop of property. If you would offer me a jewel, on condition of my wearing it daily on my finger, I would not accept it; for how can one conceive any pleasure in a dead capital? This then is my confession of faith: To transact your business, to make money, to be merry with your household; and about the rest of the earth to trouble yourself no farther than where you can be of service to it.

"But ere now thou art saying: 'And pray what is to be done with me in this sage plan of yours? Where shall I find shelter, when you have sold my own house, and not the smallest room remains in yours?'

"This is in truth the main point, brother; and in this too I shall have it in my power to serve thee. But first I must present the just tribute of my praise for time so spent as thine has been.

"Tell me, how hast thou within a few weeks become so skilled in every useful, interesting object? Highly as I thought of thy powers, I did not reckon such attention and such diligence among the number. Thy journal shows us with what profit thou art travelling. The description of the iron and the copper forges is exquisite; it evinces a complete knowledge of the subject. I myself was once there; but my relation, compared with this, has but a very bungled look. The whole letter on the linen-trade is full of information; the remarks on commercial competition are at once just and striking. In one or two places there are errors in addition, which indeed are very pardonable.

"But what most delights my father and myself is thy thorough knowledge of husbandry, and the improvement of landed property. We have thoughts of purchasing a large estate, at present under sequestration, in a very fruitful district. For paying it, we mean to use the money realised by the sale of the house; another portion we shall borrow; a portion may remain unpaid. And we count on thee for going thither, and superintending the improvement of it; by which means, before many years are passed, the land, to speak in moderation, will have risen above a third in value. We shall then bring it to the market again; seek out a larger piece; improve and trade as formerly. For all this, thou art the man. Our pens, meanwhile, will not lie idle here; and so by and by we shall rise to be enviable people.

"For the present, fare thee well! Enjoy life on thy journey, and turn thy face wherever thou canst find contentment and advantage. For the next half year we shall not need thee; thou canst look about thee in the world as thou pleasest; a judicious person finds his best instruction in his travels. Farewell! I rejoice at being connected with thee so closely by relation, and now united with thee in the spirit of activity."

Well as this letter might be penned, and full of economical truths as it was, Wilhelm felt displeased with it for more than one reason. The praise bestowed on him for his pretended statistical, technological and rural knowledge, was a silent reprimand. The ideal of the happiness of civic life, which his worthy brother sketched, by no means charmed him; on the contrary, a secret spirit of contradiction dragged him forcibly the other way. He convinced himself that, except on the stage, he could nowhere find that mental culture which he longed to give himself: he seemed to grow the more decided in his resolution, the more strongly

Werner, without knowing it, opposed him. Thus assailed, he collected all his arguments together, and buttressed his opinions in his mind the more carefully, the more desirable he reckoned it to show them in a favourable light to Werner; and in this manner he produced an answer, which also we insert.

CHAPTER III.

"Thy letter is so well written, and so prudently and wisely conceived, that no objection can be made to it. Only thou must pardon me, when I declare that one may think, maintain and do directly the reverse, and yet be in the right as well as thou. Thy mode of being and imagining appears to turn on boundless acquisition, and a light mirthful manner of enjoyment: I need scarcely tell thee, that in all this I find little that can charm me.

"First, however, I am sorry to admit, that my journal is none of mine! Under the pressure of necessity, and to satisfy my father, it was patched together by a friend's help, out of many books; and though in words I know the objects it relates to, and more of the like sort, I by no means understand them, or can occupy myself about them. What good were it for me to manufacture perfect iron, while my own breast is full of dross? What would it stead me to put properties of land in order, while I am at variance with myself?

"To speak it in a word; the cultivation of my individual self, here as I am, has from my youth upwards been constantly though dimly my wish and my purpose. The same intention I still cherish, but the means of realising it are now grown somewhat clearer. I have seen more of life than thou believest, and profited more by it also. Give some attention then to what I say, though it should not altogether tally with thy own opinions.

"Had I been a nobleman, our dispute would soon have been decided; but being a simple burgher, I must take a path of my own; and I fear it may be difficult to make thee understand me. I know not how it is in foreign countries; but in Germany, a universal, and if I may say so, personal cultivation is beyond the reach of any one except a nobleman. A burgher may acquire merit; by excessive efforts he may even educate his mind; but his personal qualities are lost, or worse than lost, let him struggle as he will. Since the nobleman, frequenting the society of the most polished, is compelled to give himself a polished manner; since this manner, neither door nor gate being shut against him, grows at last an unconstrained one; since, in court or camp, his figure, his person, are a part of his possessions, and it may be the most necessary part,—he has reason enough to put some value on them, and to show that he puts some. A certain stately grace in common things, a sort of gay elegance in earnest and important ones, becomes him well; for it shows him to be everywhere in equilibrium. He is a public person, and the more cultivated his movements, the more sonorous his voice, the more staid and measured his whole being is, the more perfect is he. If to high and low, to friends and relations, he continues still the same, then nothing can be said against him, none may wish him otherwise. His coldness must be reckoned clearness of head, his dissimulation prudence. If he can rule himself externally at every moment of his life, no man has aught more to demand of him; and whatever else there may be in him or about him, capacities, talents, wealth, all seem gifts of supererogation.

"Now imagine any burgher offering ever to pretend to these advantages, he will utterly fail; and the more completely, the greater inclination and the more endowments nature may have given him for that mode of being.

"Since, in common life, the nobleman is hampered by no limits; since kings, or kinglike figures do not differ from him, he can everywhere advance with a silent consciousness, as if before his equals, everywhere he is entitled to press forward; whereas nothing more beseems the burgher than the quiet feeling of the limits that are drawn round him. The burgher may not ask himself: 'What art thou?' He can only ask: 'What hast thou? What discernment, knowledge, talent, wealth?' If the nobleman, merely by his personal carriage, offers all that can be asked of him, the burgher by his personal carriage offers nothing, and can offer nothing. The former had a right to *seem;* the latter is compelled to *be,* and what he aims at seeming becomes ludicrous and tasteless. The former does and makes, the latter but effects and procures; he must cultivate some single gifts in order to be useful, and it is beforehand settled, that in his manner of existence there is no harmony, and can be none, since he is bound to make himself of use in one department, and so has to relinquish all the others.

"Perhaps the reason of this difference is not the usurpation of the nobles, and the submission of the burghers, but the constitution of society itself. Whether it will ever alter, and how, is to me of small importance: my present business is to meet my own case, as matters actually stand; to consider by what means I may save myself, and reach the object which I cannot live in peace without.

"Now this harmonious cultivation of my nature, which has been denied me by birth, is exactly what I most long for. Since leaving thee, I have gained much by voluntary practice: I have laid aside much of my wonted embarrassment, and can bear myself in very tolerable style. My speech and voice I have likewise been attending to; and I may say, without much vanity, that in society I do not cause displeasure. But I will not conceal from thee, that my inclination to become a public person, and to please and influence in a larger circle, is daily growing more insuperable. With this, there is combined my love for poetry and all that is related to it; and the necessity I feel to cultivate my mental faculties and tastes, that so, in this enjoyment henceforth indispensable, I may esteem as good the good alone, as beautiful the beautiful alone. Thou seest well, that for me all this is nowhere to be met with except upon the stage; that in this element alone can I effect and cultivate myself according to my wishes. On the boards, a polished man appears in his splendour with personal accomplishments, just as he does so in the upper classes of society; body and spirit must advance with equal steps in all his studies; and there I shall have it in my power at once to be and seem, as well as anywhere. If I farther long for solid occupations, we have there mechanical vexations in abundance; I may give my patience daily exercise.

"Dispute not with me on this subject: for ere thou writest, the step is taken. In compliance with the ruling prejudices, I will change my name, as indeed that of Meister or Master does not suit me. Farewell! Our fortune is in good hands: on that subject I shall not disturb myself. What I need I will, as occasion calls, require from thee: it will not be much; for I hope my art will be sufficient to maintain me."

Scarcely was the letter sent away, when our friend made good his words. To the great surprise of Serlo and the rest, he at once declared that he was ready to become an actor, and bind himself by a contract on reasonable terms. With regard to these they were soon agreed: for Serlo had before made offers, with which Wilhelm and his comrades had good reason to be satisfied. The whole of that unlucky company, wherewith we have had so long to occupy ourselves, was now at once received; and except perhaps Laertes, not a member of it showed the smallest thankfulness to Wilhelm. As they had entreated without confidence, so they accepted without gratitude. Most of them preferred ascribing their appointment to the influence of Philina, and directed their thanks to her. Meanwhile the contracts had been written out, and were now a-signing. At the moment when our friend was subscribing his assumed designation, by some inexplicable concatenation of ideas, there arose before his mind's eye the image of that green in the forest, where he lay wounded in Philina's lap. The lovely Amazon came riding on her gray palfrey from the bushes of the wood; she approached him, and dismounted. Her humane anxiety made her come and go; at length she stood before him. The white surtout fell down from her shoulders; her countenance, her form began to glance in radiance, and she vanished from his sight. He wrote his name mechanically only, not knowing what he did; and felt not, till after he had signed, that Mignon was standing at his side, was holding by his arm, and had softly tried to stop him and pull back his hand.

CHAPTER IV.

ONE of the conditions, under which our friend had gone upon the stage, was not acceded to by Serlo without some limitations. Wilhelm had required that Hamlet should be played entire and unmutilated; the other had agreed to this strange stipulation, in so far as it was *possible*. On this point they had many a contest; for as to what was possible or not possible, and what parts of the piece could be omitted without mutilating it, the two were of very different opinions.

Wilhelm was still in that happy season, when one cannot understand how, in the woman one loves, in the writer one honours, there should be anything defective. The feeling they excite in us is so entire, so accordant with itself, that we cannot help attributing the same perfect harmony to the objects themselves. Serlo again was willing to discriminate, perhaps too willing: his acute understanding could usually discern in any work of art nothing but a more or less *im*perfect whole. He thought, that as pieces usually stood, there was little reason to be chary about meddling with them; that of course Shakspeare, and particularly Hamlet, would need to suffer much curtailment.

But when Serlo talked of separating the wheat from the chaff, Wilhelm would not hear of it. "It is not chaff and wheat together," said he: "it is a trunk with boughs, twigs, leaves, buds, blossoms and fruit. Is not the one there with the others, and by means of them?" To which Serlo would reply, that people did not bring a whole tree upon the table; that the artist was required to present his guests with silver apples in platters of silver. They exhausted their invention in similitudes: and their opinions seemed still farther to diverge.

Our friend was on the borders of despair, when, on one occasion, after much debating, Serlo counselled him to take the simple plan; to make a brief resolution, to grasp his pen, to peruse the tragedy; dashing out whatever would not answer, compressing several personages into one: and if he was not skilled in such proceedings, or had not heart enough for going through with them, he might leave the task to him, the Manager, who would engage to make short work with it.

"That is not our bargain," answered Wilhelm. "How can you, with all your taste, show so much levity?"

"My friend," cried Serlo; "you yourself will ere long feel it and show it. I know too well how shocking such a mode of treating works is: perhaps it never was allowed on any theatre till now. But where indeed was ever one so slighted as ours? Authors force us on this wretched clipping system, and the public tolerates it. How many pieces have we, pray, which do not overstep the measure of our numbers, of our decorations and theatrical machinery, of the proper time, of the fit alternation of dialogue, and the physical strength of the actor? And yet we are to play, and play, and constantly give novelties. Ought we not to profit by our privilege, then, since we accomplish just as much by mutilated works as by entire ones? It is the public itself that grants the privilege. Few Germans, perhaps few men of any modern nation, have a proper sense of an æsthetic whole: they praise and blame by passages; they are charmed by passages: and who has greater reason to rejoice at this than actors, since the stage is ever but a patched and piecework matter?"

"Is!" cried Wilhelm; "but *must* it ever be so? Must everything that is continue? Convince me not that you are right: for no power on earth should force me to abide by any contract which I had concluded with the grossest misconceptions."

Serlo gave a merry turn to the business; and persuaded Wilhelm to review once more the many conversations they had had together about Hamlet; and himself to invent some means of properly reforming the piece.

After a few days, which he had spent alone, our friend returned with a cheerful look. "I am much mistaken," cried he, "if I have not now discovered how the whole is to be managed: nay, I am convinced that Shakspeare himself would have arranged it so, had not his mind been too exclusively directed to the ruling interest, and perhaps misled by the novels, which furnished him with his materials."

"Let us hear," said Serlo, placing himself with an air of solemnity upon the sofa; "I will listen calmly; but judge with rigour."

"I am not afraid of you," said Wilhelm; "only hear me. In

the composition of this play, after the most accurate investigation and the most mature reflection, I distinguish two classes of objects. The first are the grand internal relations of the persons and events, the powerful effects which arise from the characters and proceedings of the main figures: these, I hold, are individually excellent; and the order in which they are presented cannot be improved. No kind of interference must be suffered to destroy them, or even essentially to change their form. These are the things which stamp themselves deep into the soul; which all men long to see, which no one dares to meddle with. Accordingly, I understand, they have almost wholly been retained in all our German theatres. But our countrymen have erred, in my opinion, with regard to the second class of objects, which may be observed in this tragedy; I allude to the external relations of the persons, whereby they are brought from place to place, or combined in various ways by certain accidental incidents. These they have looked upon as very unimportant; have spoken of them only in passing, or left them out altogether. Now, indeed, it must be owned, these threads are slack and slender; yet they run through the entire piece, and bind together much that would otherwise fall asunder, and does actually fall asunder, when you cut them off, and imagine you have done enough and more, if you have left the ends hanging.

"Among these external relations I include the disturbances in Norway, the war with young Fortinbras, the embassy to his uncle, the settling of that feud, the march of young Fortinbras to Poland, and his coming back at the end; of the same sort are Horatio's return from Wittenberg, Hamlet's wish to go thither, the journey of Laertes to France, his return, the despatch of Hamlet into England, his capture by pirates, the death of the two courtiers by the letter which they carried. All these circumstances and events would be very fit for expanding and lengthening a novel; but here they injure exceedingly the unity of the piece, particularly as the hero has no plan, and are in consequence entirely out of place."

"For once in the right!" cried Serlo.

"Do not interrupt me," answered Wilhelm; "perhaps you will not always think me right. These errors are like temporary props of an edifice; they must not be removed till we have built a firm wall in their stead. My project therefore is, not at all to change those first-mentioned grand situations, or at least as much as possible to spare them, both collectively and individually; but with respect to these external, single, dissipated and dissipating motives, to cast them all at once away, and substitute a solitary one instead of them."

"And this?" inquired Serlo, springing up from his recumbent posture.

"It lies in the piece itself," answered Wilhelm, "only I employ it rightly. There are disturbances in Norway. You shall hear my plan, and try it.

"After the death of Hamlet the father, the Norwegians, lately conquered, grow unruly. The viceroy of that country sends his son, Horatio, an old school-friend of Hamlet's, and distinguished above every other for his bravery and prudence, to Denmark, to press forward the equipment of the fleet, which, under the new luxurious King, proceeds but slowly. Horatio has known the former king, having fought in his battles, having even stood in favour with him; a circumstance by which the first ghost-scene will be nothing injured. The new sovereign gives Horatio audience, and sends Laertes into Norway with intelligence that the fleet will soon arrive, whilst Horatio is commissioned to accelerate the preparation of it; and the Queen, on the other hand, will not consent that Hamlet, as he wishes, should go to sea along with him."

"Heaven be praised!" cried Serlo; "we shall now get rid of Wittenberg and the university, which was always a sorry piece of business. I think your idea extremely good: for except these two distant objects, Norway and the fleet, the spectator will not be required to *fancy* anything: the rest he will *see;* the rest takes place before him; whereas his imagination, on the other plan, was hunted over all the world."

"You easily perceive," said Wilhelm, "how I shall contrive to keep the other parts together. When Hamlet tells Horatio of his uncle's crime, Horatio counsels him to go to Norway in his company, to secure the affections of the army, and return in warlike force. Hamlet also is becoming dangerous to the King and Queen; they find no readier method of deliverance than to send him in the fleet, with Rosencrantz and Guildenstern to be spies upon him; and as Laertes in the mean time comes from France, they determine that this youth, exasperated even to murder, shall go after him. Unfavourable winds detain the fleet; Hamlet returns: for his wandering through the churchyard perhaps some lucky motive may be thought of; his meeting with Laertes in Ophelia's grave is a grand moment, which we must not part with. After this, the King resolves that it is better to get quit of Hamlet on the spot: the festival of his departure, the pretended reconcilement with Laertes, are now solemnised; on which occasion knightly sports are held, and Laertes fights with Hamlet. Without the four corpses I cannot end the piece; not one of them can possibly be left. The right of popular election now again comes in force, and Hamlet gives his dying voice for Horatio."

"Quick! quick!" said Serlo; "sit down and work the piece: your plan has my entire approbation; only do not let your zeal for it evaporate."

CHAPTER V.

WILHELM had already been for some time busied with translating Hamlet; making use, as he laboured, of Wieland's spirited performance, by means of which he had first become acquainted with Shakspeare. What in Wieland's work had been omitted he replaced; and he had at length procured himself a complete version, at the very time when Serlo and he finally agreed about the way of treating it. He now began, according to his plan, to cut out and insert, to separate and unite, to alter and often to restore; for satisfied as he was with his own conception, it still appeared to him as if in executing it, he were but spoiling the original.

So soon as all was finished, he read his work to Serlo and the rest. They declared themselves exceedingly contented with it; Serlo, in particular, made many flattering observations.

"You have felt very justly," said he, among other things, "that some external circumstances must accompany this piece; but that they must be simpler than those which the great poet has employed. What takes place without the theatre, what the spectator does not see, but must imagine for himself, is like a background, in front of which the acting figures move. Your large and simple prospect of the fleet and Norway will very much improve the piece: if this were altogether taken from it, we should have but a family-scene remaining; and the great idea, that here a kingly house by internal crimes and incongruities goes down to ruin, would not be presented with its proper dignity. But if the former background were left standing, so manifold, so fluctuating and confused, it would hurt the impression of the figures."

Wilhelm again took Shakspeare's part; alleging that he wrote for islanders, for Englishmen, who generally in the distance were accustomed to see little else than ships and voyages, the coasts or France and privateers; and thus what perplexed and distracted others, was to them quite natural.

Serlo assented; and both of them were of opinion, that as the piece was now to be produced upon the German stage, this more serious and simple background was the best adapted for the German mind.

The parts had been distributed before: Serlo undertook Polonius; Aurelia undertook Ophelia; Laertes was already designated by his name; a young, thickset, jolly new-comer was to be Horatio: the King and the Ghost alone occasioned some perplexity. For both of these there was no one but Old Boisterous remaining. Serlo proposed to make the Pedant King; but against this our friend protested in the strongest terms. They could resolve on nothing.

Wilhelm also had allowed both Rosencrantz and Guildenstern to continue in his piece. "Why not compress them into one?" said Serlo. "This abbreviation will not cost you much."

"Heaven keep me from all such curtailments!" answered Wilhelm, "they destroy at once the sense and the effect. What these two persons are and do, it is impossible to represent by one. In such small matters we discover Shakspeare's greatness. These soft approaches, this smirking and bowing, this assenting, wheedling, flattering, this whisking agility, this wagging of the tail, this allness and emptiness, this legal knavery, this ineptitude and insipidity,—how can they be expressed by a single man? There ought to be at least a dozen of these people, if they could be had: for it is only in society that they are anything; they are society itself; and Shakspeare showed no little wisdom and discernment in bringing in a pair of them. Besides, I need them as a couple that may be contrasted with the single, noble, excellent Horatio."

"I understand you," answered Serlo, "and we can arrange it. One of them we shall hand over to Elmira, Old Boisterous' eldest daughter: it will all be right, if they look well enough, and I will deck and trim the puppets so that it shall be a pleasure to behold them."

Philina was rejoicing not a little that she had to act the Duchess in the small subordinate play. "I will show it so natural," cried she, "how you wed a second without loss of time, when you have loved the first immensely. I hope to gain the loudest plaudits, and every man shall wish he were the third."

Aurelia gave a frown· her spleen against Philina was increasing every day.

"'Tis a pity, I declare," said Serlo, "that we have no ballet, else you should dance me a *pas de deux* with your first, and then another with your second husband,—and the first might dance himself to sleep by the measure; and your bits of feet and ancles would look so pretty, tripping to and fro upon the side stage."

"Of my ancles you do not know much," replied she snappishly; "and as to my bits of feet," cried she, hastily reaching below the table, pulling off her slippers, and holding them together out to Serlo; "here are the cases of them, and I give you leave to find me nicer ones."

"It were a serious task," said he, looking at the elegant half-shoes. "In truth, one does not often meet with anything so dainty."

They were of Parisian workmanship: Philina had obtained them as a present from the Countess, a lady whose foot was celebrated for its beauty.

"A charming thing!" cried Serlo; "my heart leaps at the sight of them."

"What gallant throbs!" replied Philina.

"There is nothing in the world beyond a pair of slippers," said he; "of such pretty manufacture, in their proper time and place, when——"

Philina took her slippers from his hands, crying, "You have squeezed them all! They are far too wide for me!" She played with them, and rubbed the soles of them together. "How hot it is!" cried she, clapping the sole upon her cheek, then again rubbing, and holding it to Serlo. He was innocent enough to stretch out his hand to feel the warmth. "Clip! clap!" cried she, giving him a smart rap over the knuckles with the heel, so that he screamed and drew back his hand; "I will teach you to use my slippers better."

"And I will teach you to use old folk like children," cried the other; then sprang up, seized her, and plundered many a kiss, every one of which she artfully contested with a show of serious reluctance. In this romping, her long hair got loose, and floated round the group; the chair overset; and Aurelia, inwardly indignant at such rioting, arose in great vexation.

CHAPTER VI.

Though in this remoulding of Hamlet many characters had been cut off, a sufficient number of them still remained; a number which the company was scarcely adequate to meet.

"If this is the way of it," said Serlo, "our prompter himself must issue from his den, and mount the stage, and become a personage like one of us."

"In his own station," answered Wilhelm, "I have frequently admired him."

"I do not think," said Serlo, "that there is in the world a more perfect artist of his kind. No spectator ever hears him; we upon the stage catch every syllable. He has formed in himself, as it were, a peculiar set of vocal organs for this purpose; he is like a Genius that whispers intelligibly to us in the hour of need. He feels as if by instinct what portion of his task an actor is completely master of; and anticipates from afar where his memory will fail him. I have known cases, in which I myself had scarcely read my part; he said it over to me word for word, and I played happily. Yet he has some peculiarities, which would make another in his place quite useless. For example, he takes such an interest in the pieces, that in giving any moving passage, he does not indeed declaim it, but he reads it with all pomp and pathos. By this ill habit he has nonplussed me on more than one occasion."

"As with another of his singularities," observed Aurelia, "he once left me sticking fast in a very dangerous passage."

"How could this happen, with the man's attentiveness?" said Wilhelm.

"He is so affected," said Aurelia, "by certain passages, that he weeps warm tears, and for a few moments loses all reflection; and it is not properly passages such as we should call affecting that produce this impression on him; but, if I express myself clearly, the *beautiful* passages, those out of which the pure spirit of the poet looks forth, as it were, through open sparkling eyes; passages which others at most rejoice over, and which many thousands altogether overlook."

"And with a soul so tender, why does he never venture on the stage?"

"A hoarse voice," said Serlo, "and a stiff carriage exclude him from it; as his melancholic temper excludes him from society. What trouble have I taken, and in vain, to make myself familiar with him! But he is a charming reader; such another I have never heard; no one can observe like him the narrow limit between declamation and graceful recital."

"The very man!" exclaimed our friend, "the very man! What a fortunate discovery! We have now the proper hand for delivering the passage of *The rugged Pyrrhus*."

"One requires your eagerness," said Serlo, "before one can employ every object, in the use it was meant for."

"In truth," said Wilhelm, "I was very much afraid we should be obliged to leave this passage out; the omission would have lamed the whole play."

"Well! That is what I cannot understand," observed Aurelia.

"I hope you will ere long be of my opinion," answered Wilhelm. "Shakspeare has introduced these travelling players with a double purpose. The person who recites the death of Priam with such feeling, in the *first* place, makes a deep impression on the Prince himself; he sharpens the conscience of the wavering youth: and, accordingly, this scene becomes a prelude to that other, where, in the *second* place, the little play produces such effect upon the King. Hamlet sees himself reproved and put to shame by the player, who feels so deep a sympathy in foreign and fictitious woes: and the thought of making an experiment upon the conscience of his stepfather is in consequence suggested to him. What a royal monologue is that, which ends the second act! How charming it will be to speak it!

> " O what a rogue and peasant slave am I!
> Is it not monstrous that this player here,
> But in a fiction, in a dream of passion,
> Could force his soul so to his own conceit,
> That from her working all his visage wann'd;
> Tears in his eyes, distraction in his aspect,
> A broken voice, and his whole function suiting
> With forms to his conceit? And all for nothing!
> For Hecuba! What's Hecuba to him,
> Or he to Hecuba, that he should weep for her?"

"If we can but persuade our man to come upon the stage," observed Aurelia.

"We must lead him to it by degrees," said Serlo. "At the rehearsal, he may read the passage; we shall tell him that an actor whom we are expecting is to play it; and so, by and by, we shall lead him nearer to the point."

Having agreed on this affair, the conversation next turned upon the Ghost. Wilhelm could not bring himself to give the part of the living King to the Pedant, that so Old Boisterous might play the Ghost: he was of opinion that they ought to wait a while; because some other actors had announced themselves, and among these it was probable they would find a fitter man.

We can easily conceive, then, how astonished Wilhelm must have been, when returning home that evening, he found a billet lying on his table, sealed with singular figures, and containing what follows:

"Strange youth! we know thou art in great perplexity. For thy Hamlet thou canst hardly find men enough, not to speak of Ghosts. Thy zeal deserves a miracle: miracles we cannot work; but somewhat marvellous shall happen. If thou have faith, the Ghost shall arise at the proper hour! Be of courage and keep firm! This needs no answer: thy determination will be known to us."

With this curious sheet he hastened back to Serlo, who read

it and re-read it, and at last declared with a thoughtful look, that it seemed a matter of some moment; that they must consider well and seriously whether they could risk it. They talked the subject over at some length; Aurelia was silent, only smiling now and then; and a few days after, when speaking of the incident again, she gave our friend, not obscurely, to understand, that she held it all for a joke of Serlo's. She desired him to cast away anxiety, and to expect the Ghost with patience.

Serlo, for most part, was in excellent humour: the actors that were going to leave him took all possible pains to play well, that their absence might be properly regretted; and this, combined with the newfangled zeal of the others, gave promise of the best results.

His intercourse with Wilhelm had not failed to exert some influence on him. He began to speak more about art: for, after all, he was a German; and Germans like to give themselves account of what they do. Wilhelm wrote down many of their conversations; which, as our narrative must not be so often interrupted here, we shall communicate to such of our readers as feel an interest in dramaturgic matters, by some other opportunity.

In particular, one evening, the Manager was very merry in speaking of the part of Polonius, and how he meant to take it up. "I engage," said he, "on this occasion, to present a very meritorious person in his best aspect. The repose and security of this old gentleman, his emptiness and his significance, his exterior gracefulness and interior meanness, his frankness and sycophancy, his sincere roguery and deceitful truth, I will introduce with all due elegance in their fit proportions. This respectable, gray-haired, enduring, time-serving half-knave I will represent in the most courtly style: the occasional roughness and coarseness of our author's strokes will further me here. I will speak like a book, when I am prepared beforehand; and like an ass, when I utter the overflowings of my heart. I will be insipid and absurd enough to chime-in with every one; and acute enough never to observe when people make a mock of me. I have seldom taken up a part with so much zeal and roguishness."

"Could I but hope as much from mine!" exclaimed Aurelia. "I have neither youth nor softness enough to be at home in this character. One thing alone I am too sure of; the feeling that turns Ophelia's brain, I shall not want."

"We must not take the matter up so strictly," said our friend. "For my share, I am certain, that the wish to act the character of Hamlet has led me exceedingly astray, throughout my study of the piece. And now the more I look into the part, the more clearly do

I see, that in my whole form and physiognomy, there is not one feature such as Shakspeare meant for Hamlet. When I consider with what nicety the various circumstances are adapted to each other, I can scarcely hope to produce even a tolerable effect."

"You are entering on your new career with becoming conscientiousness," said Serlo. "The actor fits himself to his part as he can, and the part to him as it must. But how has Shakspeare drawn his Hamlet? Is he then so utterly unlike you?"

"In the first place," answered Wilhelm, "he is fair-haired."

"That I call farfetched," observed Aurelia. "How do you infer that?"

"As a Dane, as a Northman, he is fair-haired and blue-eyed by descent."

"And you think Shakspeare had this in view?"

"I do not find it specially expressed; but, by comparison of passages, I think it incontestable. The fencing tires him; the sweat is running from his brow; and the Queen remarks: *He's fat and scant of breath*. Can you conceive him to be otherwise than plump and fair-haired? Brown-complexioned people, in their youth, are seldom plump. And does not his wavering melancholy, his soft lamenting, his irresolute activity, accord with such a figure? From a dark-haired young man you would look for more decision and impetuosity."

"You are spoiling my imagination," cried Aurelia: "away with your fat Hamlets! Do not set your well-fed Prince before us! Give us rather any succedaneum that will move us, will delight us. The intention of the author is of less importance to us than our own enjoyment, and we need a charm that is adapted for us."

CHAPTER VII.

One evening a dispute arose among our friends about the novel and the drama, and which of them deserved the preference. Serlo said it was a fruitless and misunderstood debate; both might be superior in their kinds, only each must keep within the limits proper to it.

"About their limits and their kinds," said Wilhelm, "I confess myself not altogether clear."

"Who *is* so?" said the other; "and yet perhaps it were worth while to come a little closer to the business."

They conversed together long upon the matter; and in fine, the following was nearly the result of their discussion:

"In the novel as well as in the drama, it is human nature and human action that we see. The difference between these sorts of fiction lies not merely in their outward form; not merely in the circumstance that the personages of the one are made to speak, while those of the other have commonly their history narrated. Unfortunately many dramas are but novels, which proceed by dialogue; and it would not be impossible to write a drama in the shape of letters.

"But in the novel, it is chiefly *sentiments* and *events* that are exhibited; in the drama, it is *characters* and *deeds*. The novel must go slowly forward; and the sentiments of the hero, by some means or another, must restrain the tendency of the whole to unfold itself and to conclude. The drama, on the other hand, must hasten, and the character of the hero must press forward to the end; it does not restrain, but is restrained. The novel-hero must be suffering, at least he must not in a high degree be active; in the dramatic one, we look for activity and deeds. Grandison, Clarissa, Pamela, the Vicar of Wakefield, Tom Jones himself, are, if not suffering, at least retarding personages; and the incidents are all in some sort modelled by their sentiments. In the drama the hero models nothing by himself; all things withstand him, and he clears and casts away the hinderances from off his path, or else sinks under them."

Our friends were also of opinion, that in the novel some degree of scope may be allowed to Chance; but that it must always be led and guided by the sentiments of the personages; on the other hand, that Fate, which, by means of outward unconnected circumstances, carries forward men, without their own concurrence, to an unforeseen catastrophe, can have place only in the drama; that Chance may produce pathetic situations, but never tragic ones; Fate, on the other hand, ought always to be terrible; and is in the highest sense tragic, when it brings into a ruinous concatenation the guilty man, and the guiltless that was unconcerned with him.

These considerations led them back to the play of Hamlet, and the peculiarities of its composition. The hero in this case, it was observed, is endowed more properly with sentiments than with a character; it is events alone that push him on; and accordingly the piece has in some measure the expansion of a novel. But as it is Fate that draws the plan; as the story issues from a deed of terror, and the hero is continually driven forward to a deed of terror, the work is tragic in the highest sense, and admits of no other than a tragic end.

They were now to study and peruse the piece in common; to commence what are called the book-rehearsals. These Wilhelm had looked forward to as to a festival. Having formerly collated all the parts, no obstacle on this side could oppose him. The whole of the actors were acquainted with the piece; he endeavoured to impress their minds with the importance of these book-rehearsals. "As you require," said he, "of every musical performer, that he shall, in some degree, be able to play from the book; so every actor, every educated man, should train himself to recite from the book, to catch immediately the character of any drama, any poem, any tale he may be reading, and exhibit it with grace and readiness. No committing of the piece to memory will be of service, if the actor have not in the first place penetrated into the sense and spirit of his author; the mere letter will avail him nothing."

Serlo declared, that he would overlook all subsequent rehearsals, the last rehearsal itself, if justice were but done to these rehearsals from the book. "For commonly," said he, "there is nothing more amusing than to hear an actor speak of study; it is as if freemasons were to talk of building."

The rehearsal passed according to their wishes; and we may assert, that the fame and favour which our company acquired afterwards, had their foundation in these few but well-spent hours.

"You did right, my friend," said Serlo, when they were alone, "in speaking to our fellow-labourers so earnestly; and yet I am afraid they will scarcely fulfil your wishes."

"How so?" asked Wilhelm.

"I have noticed," answered Serlo, "that as easily as you may set in motion the imaginations of men, gladly as they listen to your tales and fictions, it is yet very seldom that you find among them any touch of an imagination you can call productive. In actors this remark is strikingly exemplified. Any one of them is well content to undertake a beautiful, praiseworthy, brilliant part; and seldom will any one of them do more than self-complacently transport himself into his hero's place, without in the smallest troubling his head whether other people view him so or not. But to seize with vivacity what the author's feeling was in writing; what portion of your individual qualities you must cast off, in order to do justice to a part; how by your own conviction that you are become another man, you may carry with you the convictions of the audience; how by the inward truth of your conceptive power, you can change these boards into a temple, this pasteboard into woods; to seize and execute all this is given to very few. That internal strength of soul, by which alone deception can be brought about; that lying truth, without which nothing will affect us rightly, have by most men never even been imagined.

"Let us not then press too hard for spirit and feeling in our friends! The surest way is first coolly to instruct them in the sense and letter of the piece; if possible, to open their understandings. Whoever has the talent will then, of his own accord, eagerly adopt the spirited feeling and manner of expression; and those who have it not, will at least be prevented from acting or reciting altogether falsely. And among actors, as indeed in all cases, there is no worse arrangement than for any one to make pretensions to the spirit of a thing, while the sense and letter of it are not ready and clear to him."

CHAPTER VIII.

COMING to the first stage-rehearsal very early, Wilhelm found himself alone upon the boards. The appearance of the place surprised him, and awoke the strangest recollections. A forest and village-scene stood exactly represented as he once had seen it in the theatre of his native town. On that occasion also, a rehearsal was proceeding; and it was the morning when Mariana first confessed her love to him, and promised him a happy interview. The peasants' cottages resembled one another on the two stages, as they did in nature; the true morning sun, beaming through a half-closed window-shutter, fell upon a part of a bench ill-joined to a cottage-door; but unhappily it did not now enlighten Mariana's waist and bosom. He sat down, reflecting on this strange coincidence: he almost thought that perhaps on this very spot he would soon see her again. And alas! the truth was nothing more, than that an afterpiece to which this scene belonged was at that time very often played upon the German stage.

Out of these meditations he was roused by the other actors; along with whom two amateurs, frequenters of the wardrobe and the stage, came in, and saluted Wilhelm with a show of great enthusiasm. One of these was in some degree attached to Frau Melina: but the other was entirely a pure friend of art; and both were of the kind which a good company should always wish to have about it. It was difficult to say whether their love for the stage or their knowledge of it was the greater. They loved it too much to know it perfectly; they knew it well enough to prize the good, and to discard the bad. But their inclination being so powerful, they could tolerate the mediocre; and the glorious joy, which they experienced from the foretaste and the aftertaste of excellence, surpassed expression. The mechanical department gave them pleasure, the intellectual charmed them; and so strong was their susceptibility, that even a discontinuous rehearsal afforded them a species of illusion. Deficiencies appeared in their eyes to fade away in distance; the successful touched them like an object near at hand. In a word, they were judges such as every artist wishes in his own department. Their favourite movement was from the side-scenes to the pit, and from the pit to the side-scenes; their happiest place was in the wardrobe; their busiest employment was in trying to improve the dress, position, recitation, gesture of the actor; their liveliest conversation was on the effect produced by him; their most constant effort was to keep him accurate, active and attentive, to do him service or kindness, and, without squandering, to procure for the company a series of enjoyments. The two had obtained the exclusive privilege of being present on the stage at rehearsals as well as exhibitions. In regard to Hamlet, they had not in all points agreed with Wilhelm; here and there he had yielded; but for most part he had stood by his opinion; and, upon the whole, these discussions had been very useful in the forming of his taste. He showed both gentlemen how much he valued them; and they again predicted nothing less, from these combined endeavours, than a new epoch for the German theatre.

The presence of these persons was of great service during the rehearsals. In particular, they laboured to convince our players that, throughout the whole of their preparations, the posture and action, as they were intended ultimately to appear, should always be combined with the words, and thus the whole be mechanically united by habit. In rehearsing a tragedy especially, they said, no common movement with the hands should be allowed: a tragic actor that took snuff in the rehearsal always frightened them; for, in all probability, on coming to the same passage in the exhibition he would miss his pinch. Nay, on the same principles, they maintained that no one should rehearse in boots, if his part were to be played in shoes. But nothing, they declared, afflicted them so much as when the women, in rehearsing, stuck their hands into the folds of their gowns.

By the persuasion of our friends, another very good effect was brought about; the actors all began to learn the use of arms. Since military parts occur so frequently, said they, can anything look more absurd than men without the smallest particle of discipline, trolling about the stage in captains' and majors' uniforms.

Wilhelm and Laertes were the first that took lessons of a subaltern: they continued their practising of fence with the greatest zeal.

Such pains did our two amateurs give themselves for perfecting a company, which had so fortunately come together. They were thus providing for the future satisfaction of the public, while the public was usually laughing at their taste. People did not know what gratitude they owed our friends; particularly for performing one service, the service of frequently impressing on the actor the fundamental point, that it was his duty to speak so loud as to be heard. In this simple matter, they experienced more opposition and repugnance than could have been expected. Most part maintained that they were heard well enough already; some laid the blame upon the building; others said, one could not yell and bellow, when one had to speak naturally, secretly, or tenderly.

Our two friends having an immeasurable stock of patience, tried every means of undoing this delusion, of getting round this obstinate self-will. They spared neither arguments nor flatteries; and at last they reached their object, being aided not a little by the good example of Wilhelm. By him they were requested to sit down in the remotest corners of the house; and every time they did not hear him perfectly, to rap on the bench with a key. He articulated well, spoke out in a measured manner, raised his tones gradually, and did not overcry himself in the most vehement passages. The rapping of the key was heard less and less every new rehearsal: by and by the rest submitted to the same operation; and at last it seemed rational to hope, that the piece would be heard by every one in all the nooks of the house.

From this example, we may see how desirous people are to reach their object in their own way; what need there often is of enforcing on them truths which are self-evident; and how difficult it may be to reduce the man, who aims at effecting something, to admit the primary conditions under which alone his enterprise is possible.

CHAPTER IX.

THE necessary preparations for scenery and dresses, and whatever else was requisite, were now proceeding. In regard to certain scenes and passages, our friend had whims of his own, which Serlo humoured, partly in consideration of their bargain, partly from conviction, and because he hoped by these civilities to gain Wilhelm, and to lead him according to his own purposes the more implicitly in time to come.

Thus, for example, the King and Queen were, at the first audience, to appear sitting on the throne, with the courtiers at the sides, and Hamlet standing undistinguished in the crowd. "Hamlet," said he, "must keep himself quiet; his sable dress will sufficiently point him out. He should rather shun remark than seek it. Not till the audience is ended, and the King speaks with him as with a son, should he advance, and allow the scene to take its course."

A formidable obstacle still remained, in regard to the two pictures, which Hamlet so passionately refers to in the scene with his mother. "We ought," said Wilhelm, "to have both of them visible, at full length, in the bottom of the chamber, near the main door; and the former King must be clad in armour, like the Ghost, and hang at the side where it enters. I could wish that the figure held its right hand in a commanding attitude; were somewhat turned away; and as it were looked over its shoulder, that so it might perfectly resemble the Ghost at the moment when he issues from the door. It will produce a great effect, when at this instant Hamlet looks upon the Ghost, and the Queen upon the picture. The stepfather may be painted in royal ornaments, but not so striking."

There were several other points of this sort, about which we shall perhaps elsewhere have opportunity to speak.

"Are you then inexorably bent on Hamlet's dying at the end?" inquired Serlo.

"How can I keep him alive," said Wilhelm, "when the whole piece is pressing him to death? We have already talked at large on that matter."

"But the public wishes him to live."

"I will show the public any other complaisance; but as to this, I cannot. We often wish that some gallant useful man, who is dying of a chronic disease, might yet live longer. The family weep, and conjure the physician, but he cannot stay him; and no more than this physician can withstand the necessity of nature, can we give law to an acknowledged necessity of art. It is a false compliance with the multitude, to raise in them emotions which they *wish*, when these are not emotions which they *ought*, to feel."

"Whoever pays the cash," said Serlo, "may require the ware according to his liking."

"Doubtless, in some degree," replied our friend; "but a great public should be reverenced, not used as children are, when pedlars wish to hook the money from them. By presenting excellence to the people, you should gradually excite in them a taste and feeling for the excellent; and they will pay their money with double satisfaction, when reason itself has nothing to object against this outlay. The public you may flatter, as you do a well-beloved child, to better, to enlighten it; not as you do a pampered child of quality, to perpetuate the error you profit from."

In this manner, various other topics were discussed relating to the question: What might still be changed in the piece, and what must of necessity remain untouched? We shall not enter farther on those points at present; but perhaps at some future time we may submit this altered Hamlet itself to such of our readers as feel any interest in the subject.

CHAPTER X.

THE main rehearsal was at length concluded; it had lasted very long. Serlo and Wilhelm still found much to care for: notwithstanding all the time which had already been consumed in preparation, some highly necessary matters had been left to the very last moment.

Thus, the pictures of the kings, for instance, were not ready; and the scene between Hamlet and his Mother, from which so powerful an effect was looked for, had a very helpless aspect, as the business stood; for neither Ghost nor painted image of him was at present forthcoming. Serlo made a jest of this perplexity: "We should be in a pretty scrape," said he, "if the Ghost were to decline appearing, and the guard had nothing to fight with but the air, and our prompter were obliged to speak the spirit's part from the side-scenes."

"We will not scare away our strange friend by unbelief," said Wilhelm: "doubtless at the proper season he will come, and astonish us as much as the spectators."

"Well, certainly," said Serlo, "I shall be a happy man tomorrow night, when once this piece is fairly acted. It costs us more arrangement than I dreamed of."

"But none of you," exclaimed Philina, "will be happier than I, little as my part disturbs me. Really, to hear a single subject talked of forever and forever, when after all there is nothing to come of it, beyond an exhibition which will be forgotten like so many hundred others, this is what I have not patience for. In Heaven's name, not so many *pros* and *cons!* The guests you entertain have always something to object against the dinner; nay, if you could hear them talk of it at home, they cannot understand how it was possible to undergo so sad a business."

"Let me turn your illustration, pretty one, to my own advantage," answered Wilhelm. "Consider how much must be done by art and nature, by traffickers and tradesmen, before an entertainment can be given. How many years the stag must wander in the forest, the fish in the river or the sea, before they can deserve to grace our table! And what cares and consultations with her cooks and servants has the lady of the house submitted to! Observe with what indifference the people swallow the production of the distant vintager, the seaman and the vintner, as if it were a thing of course. And ought these men to cease from labouring, providing and preparing; ought the master of the house to cease from purchasing and laying up the fruit of their exertions, because at last the enjoyment it affords is transitory? But no enjoyment can be transitory; the impression which it leaves is permanent; and what is done with diligence and effort communicates to the spectator a hidden force, of which we cannot say how far its influence may reach."

" 'Tis all one to me," replied Philina; " only here again I must observe that you men are constantly at variance with yourselves. With all this conscientious horror at curtailing Shakspeare, you have missed the finest thought there was in Hamlet!"

" The finest?" cried our friend.

" Certainly the finest," said Philina; " the Prince himself takes pleasure in it."

" And it is?" inquired Serlo.

" If you wore a wig," replied Philina, " I would pluck it very coolly off you; for I think you need to have your understanding opened."

The rest began to think what she could mean; the conversation paused. The party arose; it was now grown late; they seemed about to separate. While they were standing in this undetermined mood, Philina all at once struck up a song, with a very graceful, pleasing tune:

> Sing me not with such emotion
>   How the night so lonesome is;
> Pretty maids, I've got a notion
>   It is the reverse of this.
>
> For as wife and man are plighted,
>   And the better half the wife;
> So is night to day united,
>   Night's the better half of life.
>
> Can you joy in bustling daytime,
>   Day when none can get his will?
> It is good for work, for haytime,
>   For much other it is ill.
>
> But when, in the nightly glooming,
>   Social lamp on table glows,
> Face for faces dear illuming,
>   And such jest and joyance goes;

When the fiery pert young fellow,
  Wont by day to run or ride,
Whispering now some tale would tell O,—
  All so gentle by your side;

When the nightingale to lovers
  Lovingly her songlet sings,
Which for exiles and sad rovers
  Like mere woe and wailing rings:

With a heart how lightsome feeling
  Do ye count the kindly clock,
Which, twelve times deliberate pealing,
  Tells you none tonight shall knock!

Therefore, on all fit occasions,
  Mark it, maidens, what I sing:
Every day its own vexations,
  And the night its joys will bring.

She made a little courtesy on concluding, and Serlo gave a loud "Bravo!" She scuttled off, and left the room with a tee-hee of laughter. They heard her singing and skipping as she went down-stairs.

Serlo passed into another room; Wilhelm bade Aurelia good night; but she continued looking at him for a few moments, and said:

"How I dislike that woman! Dislike her from my heart, and to her very slightest qualities! Those brown eyelashes, with her fair hair, which our brother thinks so charming, I cannot bear to look at; and that scar upon her brow has something in it so repulsive, so low and base, that I could recoil ten paces every time I meet her. She was lately telling as a joke, that her father, when she was a child, threw a plate at her head, of which this is the mark. It is well that she is marked in the eyes and brow, that those about her may be on their guard."

Wilhelm made no answer, and Aurelia went on, apparently with greater spleen:

"It is next to impossible to speak a friendly or civil word to her, so deeply do I hate her, with all her wheedling. Would that we were rid of her! And you too, my friend, have a certain complaisance for the creature, a way of acting towards her, that grieves me to the soul; an attention which borders on respect; which, by Heaven! she does not merit."

"Whatever she may be," replied our friend, "I owe her thanks. Her upbringing is to blame: to her natural character I would do justice."

"Character!" exclaimed Aurelia; "and do you think such a creature has a character? O you men! It is so like you! These are the women you deserve!"

"My friend, can you suspect me?" answered Wilhelm. "I will give account of every minute I have spent beside her."

"Come, come," replied Aurelia; "it is late, we will not quarrel. All like each, and each like all! Good night, my friend! Good night, my sparkling bird of Paradise!"

Wilhelm asked how he had earned this title.

"Another time," cried she; "another time. They say it has no feet, but hovers in the air, and lives on æther. That, however, is a story, a poetic fiction. Good night! Dream sweetly, if you are in luck!"

She proceeded to her room; and he, being left alone, made haste to his.

Half angrily he walked along his chamber to and fro. The jesting but decided tone of Aurelia had hurt him: he felt deeply how unjust she was. Could he treat Philina with unkindness or ill-nature? She had done no evil to him: but for any love to her, he could proudly and confidently take his conscience to witness that it was not so.

On the point of beginning to undress, he was going forward to his bed to draw aside the curtains, when, not without extreme astonishment, he saw a pair of women's slippers lying on the floor before it. One of them was resting on its sole, the other on its edge. They were Philina's slippers; he recognised them but too well. He thought he noticed some disorder in the curtains; nay it seemed as if they moved. He stood, and looked with unaverted eyes.

A new impulse, which he took for anger, cut his breath: after a short pause, he recovered, and cried in a firm tone:

"Come out, Philina! What do you mean by this? Where is your sense, your modesty? Are we to be the speech of the house tomorrow?"

Nothing stirred.

"I do not jest," continued he; "these pranks are little to my taste."

No sound! No motion!

Irritated and determined, he at last went forward to the bed, and tore the curtains asunder. "Arise," said he, "if I am not to give you up my room tonight."

With great surprise, he found his bed unoccupied; the sheets and pillows in the sleekest rest. He looked around; he searched, and searched, but found no traces of the rogue. Behind the bed, the stove, the drawers, there was nothing to be seen: he sought with great and greater diligence; a spiteful looker-on might have believed that he was seeking in the hope of finding.

All thought of sleep was gone. He put the slippers on his table; went past it up and down; often paused before it; and a wicked sprite that watched him has asserted, that our friend employed himself for several hours about these dainty little shoes; that he viewed them with a certain interest; that he handled them and played with them: and it was not till towards morning that he threw himself on the bed, without undressing, where he fell asleep amidst a world of curious fantasies.

He was still slumbering, when Serlo entered hastily: "Where are you?" cried he: "Still in bed? Impossible! I want you in the theatre; we have a thousand things to do."

CHAPTER XI.

THE forenoon and the afternoon fled rapidly away. The playhouse was already full; our friend hastened to dress. It was not with the joy which it had given him when he first essayed it, that he now put on the garb of Hamlet: he only dressed himself that he might be in readiness. On joining the women in the stage-room, they unanimously cried that nothing sat upon him right; the fine feather stood awry; the buckle of his belt did not fit: they began to slit, to sew, and piece together. The music started: Philina still objected somewhat to his ruff; Aurelia had much to say against his mantle. "Leave me alone, good people," cried he, "this negligence will make me liker Hamlet." The women would not let him go, but continued trimming him. The music ceased; the acting was begun. He looked at himself in the glass; pressed his hat closer down upon his face, and retouched the painting of his cheeks.

At this instant, somebody came rushing in and cried: "The Ghost! The Ghost!"

Wilhelm had not once had time all day to think of the Ghost, and whether it would come or not. His anxiety on that head was at length removed, and now some strange assistant was to be expected. The stage-manager came in, inquiring after various matters: Wilhelm had not time to ask about the Ghost; he hastened to present himself before the throne, where King and Queen, surrounded with their court, were already glancing in all the splendours of royalty, and waiting till the scene in front of them should be concluded. He caught the last words of Horatio, who was speaking of the Ghost in extreme confusion, and seemed to have almost forgotten his part.

The intermediate curtain went aloft, and Hamlet saw the crowded house before him. Horatio having spoken his address, and been dismissed by the King, pressed through to Hamlet; and, as if presenting himself to the Prince, he said; "The Devil is in harness; he has put us all in fright."

In the mean while two men of large stature, in white cloaks and capuches, were observed standing in the side-scenes. Our friend, in the distraction, embarrassment and hurry of the moment, had failed in the first soliloquy; at least such was his own opinion, though loud plaudits had attended his exit. Accordingly he made his next entrance in no pleasant mood, with the dreary wintry feeling of dramatic condemnation. Yet he girded up his mind; and spoke that appropriate passage on the "rouse and wassel," the "heavy-headed revel" of the Danes, with suitable indifference; he had, like the audience, in thinking of it, quite forgotten the Ghost; and he started in real terror, when Horatio cried out, "Look, my lord, it comes!" He whirled violently round; and the tall noble figure, the low inaudible tread, the light movement in the heavy-looking armour, made such an impression on him, that he stood as if transformed to stone, and could utter only in a half-voice his: "Angels and ministers of grace defend us!" He glared at the form; drew a deep breathing once or twice, and pronounced his address to the Ghost in a manner so confused, so broken, so constrained, that the highest art could not have hit the mark so well.

His translation of this passage now stood him in good stead. He had kept very close to the original; in which the arrangement of the words appeared to him expressive of a mind confounded, terrified and seized with horror:

> "Be thou a spirit of health, or goblin damn'd,
> Bring with thee airs from Heaven or blasts from Hell,
> Be thy intents wicked or charitable,
> Thou com'st in such a questionable shape,
> That I will speak to thee; I'll call thee Hamlet,
> King, father, royal Dane: O answer me!"

A deep effect was visible in the audience. The Ghost beckoned, the Prince followed him amid the loudest plaudits.

The scene changed; and when the two had re-appeared, the Ghost on a sudden stopped, and turned round; by which means Hamlet came to be a little too close upon it. With a longing curiosity, he looked in at the lowered vizor, but except two deep-lying eyes, and a well-formed nose, he could discern nothing. Gazing timidly, he stood before the Ghost; but when the first tones issued from the helmet, and a somewhat hoarse yet deep and penetrating voice pronounced the words: "I am thy father's spirit," Wilhelm, shuddering, started back some paces, and the audience shuddered with him. Each imagined that he knew the voice; Wilhelm thought he noticed in it some resemblance with his father's. These strange emotions and remembrances; the curiosity he felt about discovering his secret friend, the anxiety about offending him, even the theatric impropriety of coming too near him in the present situation, all this affected Wilhelm with powerful and conflicting impulses. During the long speech of the Ghost, he changed his place so frequently; he seemed so unsettled and perplexed, so attentive and so absent-minded, that his acting caused a universal admiration, as the Spirit caused a universal horror. The latter spoke with a feeling of melancholy anger rather than of sorrow; but of an anger spiritual, slow and inexhaustible. It was the mistemper of a noble soul, that is severed from all earthly things, and yet devoted to unbounded woe. At last he vanished; but in a curious manner; for a thin, gray, transparent gauze arose from the place of descent like a vapour, spread itself over him, and sank along with him.

Hamlet's friends now entered, and swore upon the sword. Old Truepenny, in the mean time, was so busy under ground, that wherever they might take their station, he was sure to call out right beneath them: "Swear!" and they started, as if the soil had taken fire below them, and hastened to another spot. On each of these occasions, too, a little flame pierced through at the place where they were standing. The whole produced on the spectators a profound impression.

After this, the piece proceeded calmly on its course: nothing failed, all prospered; the audience manifested their contentment, and the actors seemed to rise in heart and spirits every scene.

CHAPTER XII.

THE curtain fell; and rapturous applauses sounded out of every corner of the house. The four princely corpses sprang aloft, and embraced each other. Polonius and Ophelia likewise issued from their graves, and listened with extreme satisfaction, as Horatio, who had stept before the curtain to announce the following piece, was welcomed with the most thundering plaudits. The people would not hear of any other play, but violently required the repetition of the present.

"We have won," cried Serlo: "and so not another reasonable word this night! Every thing depends on the first impression: we should never take it ill of any actor that, on occasion of his first appearance, he is provident and even self-willed."

The box-keeper came and delivered him a heavy sum. "We have made a good beginning," cried the Manager, "and prejudice itself will now be on our side. But where is the supper that you promised us? Tonight we may be allowed to relish it a little."

It had been agreed that all the party were to stay together in their stage-dresses, and enjoy a little feast among themselves. Wilhelm had engaged to have the place in readiness, and Frau Melina to provide the victuals.

A room, which commonly was occupied by scene-painters, had accordingly been polished up as well as possible; our friends had hung it round with little decorations; and so decked and trimmed it, that it looked half like a garden, half like a colonnade. On entering it, the company were dazzled with the glitter of a multitude of lights, which, across the vapours of the sweetest and most copious perfumes, spread a stately splendour over a well-decorated and well-furnished table. These preparations were hailed with joyful interjections by the party: all took their places with a certain genuine dignity; it seemed as if some royal family had met together in the Kingdom of the Shades. Wilhelm sat between Aurelia and the Frau Melina; Serlo between Philina and Elmira; nobody was discontented with himself or with his place.

Our two theatric amateurs, who had from the first been present, now increased the pleasure of the meeting. While the exhibition was proceeding, they had several times stept round, and come upon the stage, expressing, in the warmest terms, the delight which they and the audience felt. They now descended to particulars; and each was richly rewarded for his efforts.

With boundless animation, the company extolled man after man and passage after passage. To the prompter, who had modestly sat down at the bottom of the table, they gave a liberal commendation for his *rugged Pyrrhus;* the fencing of Hamlet and Laertes was beyond all praise; Ophelia's mourning had been inexpressibly exalted and affecting; of Polonius they would not trust themselves to speak.

Every individual present heard himself commended through the rest and by them; nor was the absent Ghost defrauded of his share of praise and admiration. He had played the part, it was asserted, with a very happy voice, and in a lofty style; but what surprised them most was the information which he seemed to have about their own affairs. He entirely resembled the painted figure, as if he had sat to the painter of it; and the two amateurs described, in glowing language, how awful it had looked when the spirit entered near the picture, and stept across before his own image. Truth and error, they declared, had been commingled in the strangest manner; they had felt as if the Queen really did not see the Ghost. And Frau Melina was especially commended, because on this occasion she had gazed upwards at the picture, while Hamlet was pointing downwards at the Spectre.

Inquiry was now made how the apparition could have entered. The stage-manager reported that a back-door, usually blocked up by decorations, had that evening, as the Gothic hall was occupied, been opened; that two large figures in white cloaks and hoods, one of whom was not to be distinguished from the other, had entered by this passage; and by the same, it was likely, they had issued when the third act was over.

Serlo praised the Ghost for one merit; that he had not whined and lamented like a tailor; nay, to animate his son, had even introduced a passage at the end, which more beseemed such a hero. Wilhelm had kept it in memory; he promised to insert it in his manuscript.

Amid the pleasures of the entertainment, it had not been noticed that the children and the Harper were absent. Ere long they made their entrance, and were blithely welcomed by the company. They came in together, very strangely decked: Felix was beating a triangle, Mignon a tambourine; the old man had his large harp hung round his neck, and was playing on it whilst he carried it before him. They marched round and round the table, and sang a multitude of songs. Eatables were handed them; and the guests seemed to think they could not do a greater kindness to the children, than by giving them as much sweet wine as they chose to have. For the company themselves had not by any means neglected a stock of savoury flasks, presented by the two amateurs, which had arrived that evening in baskets. The children tripped about, and sang; Mignon, in particular, was frolicsome beyond all wont. She beat the tambourine with the greatest liveliness and grace: now, with her finger pressed against the parchment, she hummed across it swiftly to and fro; now rattled on it with her knuckles, now with the back of her hand; nay sometimes, with alternating rhythm, she struck it first against her knee and then against her head; and anon twirling it in her hand, she made the shells jingle by themselves; and thus, from the simplest instrument, elicited a great variety of tones. After she and Felix had long rioted about, they sat down upon an elbow-chair which was standing empty at the table, exactly opposite to Wilhelm.

"Keep out of the chair!" cried Serlo: "it is waiting for the Ghost, I think; and when he comes, it will be worse for you."

"I do not fear him," answered Mignon: "if he come, we can rise. He is my uncle, and will not harm me." To those who did not know that her reputed father had been named the Great Devil, this speech was unintelligible.

The party looked at one another; they were more and more confirmed in their suspicion that the Manager was in the secret of the Ghost. They talked and tippled, and the girls from time to time cast timid glances towards the door.

The children, who, sitting in the great chair, looked from over the table but like puppets in their box, did actually at length start a little drama in the style of Punch. The screeching tone of these people Mignon imitated very well; and Felix and she began to knock their heads together, and against the edges of the table, in such a way as only wooden puppets could endure. Mignon, in particular, grew frantic with gaiety; the company, much as they had laughed at her at first, were in fine obliged to curb her. But persuasion was of small avail; for she now sprang up, and raved and shook her tambourine, and capered round the table. With her hair flying out behind her, with her head thrown back, and her limbs as it were cast into the air, she seemed like one of those antique Menads, whose wild and all but impossible positions still, on classic monuments, often strike us with amazement.

Incited by the talents and the uproar of the children, each endeavoured to contribute something to the entertainment of the night. The girls sung several *canons*; Laertes whistled in the manner of a nightingale; and the Pedant gave a symphony *pianissimo* upon the Jew's-harp. Meanwhile the youths and damsels, who sat near each other, had begun a great variety of games; in which, as the hands often crossed and met, some pairs were favoured with a transient squeeze, the emblem of a hopeful kindness. Madam Melina in particular seemed scarcely to conceal a decided tenderness for Wilhelm. It was late; and Aurelia, perhaps the only one retaining self-possession in the party, now stood up, and signified that it was time to go.

By way of termination, Serlo gave a firework, or what resembled one; for he could imitate the sound of crackers, rockets and firewheels with his mouth, in a style of nearly inconceivable correctness. You had only to shut your eyes, and the deception was complete. In the mean time, they had all risen; the men gave their arms to the women to escort them home. Wilhelm was walking last with Aurelia. The stage-manager met him on the stairs, and said to him: "Here is the veil our Ghost vanished in: it was hanging fixed to the place where he sank; we found it this moment."

"A curious relique!" said our friend, and took it with him.

At this instant his left arm was laid hold of, and he felt a smart twinge of pain in it. Mignon had hid herself in the place; she had seized him, and bit his arm. She rushed past him, down-stairs, and disappeared.

On reaching the open air, almost all of them discovered that they had drunk too liberally. They glided asunder without taking leave.

The instant Wilhelm gained his room, he stripped, and extinguishing his candle, hastened into bed. Sleep was overpowering him without delay, when a noise, that seemed to issue from behind the stove, aroused him. In the eye of his heated fancy, the image of the harnessed King was hovering there: he sat up that he might address the Spectre; but he felt himself encircled with soft arms, and his mouth was shut with kisses, which he had not force to push away.

CHAPTER XIII.

NEXT morning, Wilhelm started up with an unpleasant feeling, and found himself alone. His head was still dim with the tumult, which he had not yet entirely slept off; and the recollection of his nightly visitant disquieted his mind. His first suspicion lighted on Philina; but, on second thoughts, he conceived that it could not have been she. He sprang out of bed, and, while putting on his clothes, he noticed that the door, which commonly he used to bolt, was now ajar; though whether he had shut it on the previous night or not, he could not recollect.

But what surprised him most was the Spirit's veil, which he found lying on his bed. Having brought it up with him, he had most probably thrown it there himself. It was a gray gauze; on the hem of it he noticed an inscription broidered in dark letters. He unfolded it, and read the words: "FOR THE FIRST AND THE LAST TIME! FLY, YOUTH! FLY!" He was struck with it, and knew not what to think or say.

At this moment Mignon entered with his breakfast. The aspect of the child astonished Wilhelm, we may almost say frightened him. She appeared to have grown taller overnight: she entered with a stately, noble air; and looked him in the face so earnestly, that he could not endure her glances. She did not touch him, as at other times, when, for morning salutation, she would press his hand, or kiss his cheek, his lips, his arm, or shoulder; but having put his things in order, she retired in silence.

The appointed time of a first-rehearsal now arrived: our friends assembled, all of them entirely out of tune from yesternight's debauch. Wilhelm roused himself as much as possible, that he might not at the very outset violate the principles of diligence, which he had preached so lately with such emphasis. His practice in the matter helped him through: for practice and habit must, in every art, fill up the voids, which genius and temper in their fluctuations will so often leave.

But in the present case, our friends had especial reason to admit the truth of the remark, that no one should begin with a festivity any situation that is meant to last, particularly that is meant to be a trade, a mode of living. Festivities are fit for what is happily concluded: at the commencement, they but waste the force and zeal which should inspire us in the struggle, and support us through a long-continued labour. Of all festivities, the marriage-festival appears the most unsuitable: calmness, humility and silent hope befit no ceremony more than this.

So passed the day, which to Wilhelm seemed the most insipid he had ever spent. Instead of their accustomed conversation in the evening, the company began to yawn: the interest of Hamlet was exhausted; they rather felt it disagreeable than otherwise that the piece was to be given again next night. Wilhelm showed the veil which the Royal Dane had left; it was to be inferred from this, that he would not come again. Serlo was of that opinion; he appeared to be deep in the secrets of the Ghost; but, on the other hand, the inscription, "Fly, youth! Fly!" seemed inconsistent with the rest. How could Serlo be in league with any one whose aim it was to take away the finest actor of his troop?

It had now become a matter of necessity to confer on Boisterous the Ghost's part, and on the Pedant that of the King. Both declared that they had studied these sufficiently: nor was it wonderful; for, in such a number of rehearsals, and so copious a treatment of the subject, all of them had grown familiar with it; each could have exchanged his part with any other. Yet they rehearsed a little here and there, and prepared the new adventurers as fully as the hurry would admit. When the company was breaking up at a pretty late hour, Philina softly whispered Wilhelm as she passed: "I must have my slippers back: thou wilt not bolt the door?" These words excited some perplexity in Wilhelm, when he reached his chamber: they strengthened the suspicion that Philina was the secret visitant: and we ourselves are forced to coincide with this idea; particularly as the causes, which awakened in our friend another and a stranger supposition, cannot be disclosed. He kept walking up and down his chamber, in no quiet frame: his door was actually not yet bolted.

On a sudden, Mignon rushed into the room; laid hold of him, and cried: "Master! save the house! It is on fire!" Wilhelm sprang through the door; and a strong smoke came rushing down upon him from the upper story. On the street he heard the cry of fire; and the Harper, with his instrument in his hand, came down-stairs breathless through the smoke. Aurelia hurried out of her chamber, and threw little Felix into Wilhelm's arms.

"Save the child!" cried she; "and we will mind the rest."

Wilhelm did not look upon the danger as so great; his first thought was to penetrate to the source of the fire, and try to stifle it before it reached a head. He gave Felix to the Harper; commanding him to hasten down the stone stairs, which led across a little garden-vault out into the garden, and to wait with the children in the open air. Mignon took a light to show the way. He begged Aurelia to secure her things there also. He himself pierced upwards through the smoke; but it was in vain that he exposed himself to such danger. The flame appeared to issue from a neighbouring house; it had already caught the wooden floor and staircase: some others, who had hastened to his help, were suffering like himself from fire and vapour. Yet he kept inciting them; he called for water; he conjured them to dispute every inch with the flame; and promised to abide by them to the last. At this instant, Mignon came springing up, and cried: "Master! save thy Felix! The old man is mad! He is killing him." Scarcely knowing what he did, Wilhelm darted down-stairs, and Mignon followed close behind him.

On the last steps, which led into the garden-vault, he paused with horror. Some heaps of fire-wood branches, and large masses of straw, which had been stowed in the place, were burning with a clear flame; Felix was lying on the ground and screaming; the Harper stood aside holding down his head, and leaned against the wall. "Unhappy creature! what is this?" said Wilhelm. The old man spoke not; Mignon lifted Felix, and carried him with difficulty to the garden; while Wilhelm strove to pull the fire asunder and extinguish it; but only by his efforts made the flame more violent. At last he too was forced to fly into the garden, with his hair and his eyelashes burnt; tearing the Harper with him through the conflagration, who, with singed beard, unwillingly accompanied him.

Wilhelm hastened instantly to seek the children. He found them on the threshold of a summer-house at some distance: Mignon was trying every effort to pacify her comrade. Wilhelm took him on his knee; he questioned him, felt him; but could obtain no satisfactory account from either him or Mignon.

Meanwhile the fire had fiercely seized on several houses; it was now enlightening all the neighbourhood. Wilhelm looked at the child in the red glare of the flames; he could find no wound, no blood, no hurt of any kind. He groped over all the little creature's body; but it gave no sign of pain; on the contrary, it by degrees grew calm, and began to wonder at the blazing houses, and express its pleasure at the spectacle of beams and rafters burning all in order, like a grand illumination, so beautifully there.

Wilhelm thought not of the clothes or goods he might have lost; he felt deeply how inestimable to him was this pair of human beings, who had just escaped so great a danger. He pressed little Felix to his heart with a new emotion; Mignon too he was about to clasp with joyful tenderness, but she softly avoided this; she took him by the hand and held it fast.

"Master," said she,—(till the present evening she had hardly ever named him master; at first she used to name him sir, and afterwards to call him father)—"Master! we have escaped an awful danger; thy Felix was on the point of death."

By many inquiries, Wilhelm learned from her at last, that when they came into the vault, the Harper tore the light from her hand, and set on fire the straw. That he then put Felix down; laid his hands with strange gestures on the head of the child, and drew a knife as if he meant to sacrifice him. That she sprang forward, and snatched it from him; that she screamed, and some one from the house, who was carrying something down into the garden, came to her help, but must have gone away again in the confusion, and left the old man and the child alone.

Two or even three houses were now flaming in a general blaze. Owing to the conflagration in the vault, no person had been able to take shelter in the garden. Wilhelm was distressed about his friends, and in a less degree about his property. Not venturing to quit the children, he was forced to sit, and see the mischief spreading more and more.

In this anxious state, he passed some hours. Felix had fallen asleep on his bosom; Mignon was lying at his side, and holding fast his hand. The efforts of the people finally subdued the fire. The burnt houses sank, with successive crashes, into heaps; the morning was advancing; the children awoke, and complained of bitter cold; even Wilhelm in his light dress could scarcely brook the chillness of the falling dew. He took the young ones to the rubbish of the prostrate building; where, among the ashes and the embers, they found a very grateful warmth.

The opening day collected, by degrees, the various individuals of the party. All of them had got away unhurt, no one had lost much. Wilhelm's trunk was saved among the rest.

Towards ten o'clock, Serlo called them to rehearse their Hamlet, at least some scenes of the piece, in which fresh players were to act. He had some debates to manage, on this point, with the municipal authorities. The clergy required, that after such a visitation of Providence, the playhouse should be shut for some time; and Serlo on the other hand maintained that, both for the purpose of repairing the damage he had suffered, and of exhilarating the depressed and terrified spirits of the people, nothing could be more in place than the exhibition of some interesting piece. His opinion in the end prevailed; and the house was full. The actors played with singular fire, with more of a passionate freedom than at first. The feelings of the audience had been heightened by the horrors of the previous night, and their appetite for entertainment had been sharpened by the tedium of a wasted and dissipated day; every one had more than usual susceptibility for what was strange and moving. Most of them were new spectators, invited by the fame of the piece; they could not compare the present with the preceding evening. Boisterous played altogether in the style of the unknown Ghost; the Pedant too had accurately seized the manner of his predecessor; nor was his own woful aspect without its use to him; for it seemed as if, in spite of his purple cloak and his ermine collar, Hamlet were fully justified in calling him a "king of shreds and patches."

Few have ever reached the throne by a path more singular than his had been. But although the rest, and especially Philina, made sport of his preferment, he himself signified that the Count, a consummate judge, had at the first glance predicted this and much more of him. Philina, on the other hand, recommended lowliness of mind to him; saying, she would now and then powder the sleeves of his coat, that he might remember that unhappy night in the Castle, and wear his crown with meekness.

CHAPTER XIV.

Our friends had sought out other lodgings, on the spur of the moment, and were by this means much dispersed. Wilhelm had conceived a liking for the garden-house, where he had spent the night of the conflagration: he easily obtained the key, and settled himself there. But Aurelia being greatly hampered in her new abode, he was obliged to retain little Felix with him. Mignon, indeed, would not part with the boy.

He had placed the children in a neat chamber on the upper floor: he himself was in the lower parlour. The young ones were asleep at this time: Wilhelm could not sleep.

Adjoining the lovely garden, which the full moon had just risen to illuminate, the black ruins of the fire were visible, and here and there a streak of vapour was still mounting from them. The air was soft, the night extremely beautiful. Philina in issuing from the theatre had jogged him with her elbow, and whispered something to him, which he did not understand. He felt perplexed and out of humour: he knew not what he should expect or do. For a day or two Philina had avoided him: it was not till tonight that she had given him any second signal. Unhappily the doors, that he was not to bolt, were now consumed; the slippers had evaporated into smoke. How the girl would gain admission to the garden, if her aim was such, he knew not. He wished she might not come; and yet he longed to have some explanation with her.

But what lay heavier at his heart than this, was the fate of the Harper, whom, since the fire, no one had seen. Wilhelm was afraid that, in clearing off the rubbish, they would find him buried under it. Our friend had carefully concealed the suspicion which he entertained, that it was the Harper who had fired the house. The old man had been first seen, as he rushed from the burning and smoking floor; and his desperation in the vault appeared a natural consequence of such a deed. Yet, from the inquiry which the magistrates had instituted touching the affair, it seemed likely that the fire had not originated in the house where Wilhelm lived, but had accidentally been kindled in the third from that, and had crept along, beneath the roofs, before it burst into activity.

Seated in a grove, our friend was meditating all these things, when he heard a low footfall in a neighbouring walk. By the melancholy song which arose along with it, he recognised the Harper. He caught the words of the song without difficulty: it turned on the consolations of a miserable man, conscious of being on the borders of insanity. Unhappily our friend forgot the whole of it except the last verse:

> Wheresoe'er my steps may lead me,
> Meekly at the door I'll stay;
> Pious hands will come to feed me,
> And I'll wander on my way.

> Each will feel a touch of gladness,
> When my aged form appears;
> Each will shed a tear of sadness,
> Though I reck not of his tears.

So singing, he had reached the garden-door, which led into an unfrequented street. Finding it bolted, he was making an attempt to climb the railing, when Wilhelm held him back, and addressed some kindly words to him. The old man begged to have the door unlocked, declaring that he would and must escape. Wilhelm represented to him, that he might indeed escape from the garden, but could not from the town; showing, at the same time, what suspicions he must needs incur by such a step. But it was in vain: the old man held by his opinion. Our friend, however, would not yield; and at last he brought him, half by force, into the garden-house, in which he locked himself along with him. The two carried on a strange conversation; which, however, not to afflict our readers with repeating unconnected thoughts and dolorous emotions, we had rather pass in silence than detail at large.

CHAPTER XV.

UNDETERMINED what to do with this unhappy man, who displayed such indubitable symptoms of madness, Wilhelm would have been in great perplexity, had not Laertes come that very morning, and delivered him from his uncertainty. Laertes, as usual, rambling everywhere about the town, had happened, in some coffee-house, to meet with a man who, a short time ago, had suffered under violent attacks of melancholy. This person, it appeared, had been intrusted to the care of some country clergyman, who made it his peculiar business to attend to people in such situations. In the present instance, as in many others, his treatment had succeeded: he was still in town; and the friends of the patient were showing him the greatest honour.

Wilhelm hastened to find out this person: he disclosed the case to him, and agreed with him about the terms. The Harper was to be brought over to him, under certain pretexts. The separation deeply pained our friend; so used was he to see the man beside him, and to hear his spirited and touching strains. The hope of soon beholding him recovered, served in some degree to moderate this feeling. The old man's harp had been destroyed in the burning of the house: they purchased him another, and gave it him when he departed.

Mignon's little wardrobe had in like manner been consumed. As Wilhelm was about providing her with new apparel, Aurelia proposed that now at last they should dress her as a girl.

"No! no! not at all!" cried Mignon; and insisted on it with such earnestness, that they let her have her way.

The company had not much leisure for reflection: the exhibitions followed close on one another.

Wilhelm often mingled with the audience, to ascertain their feelings; but he seldom heard a criticism of the kind he wished: more frequently the observations which he listened to distressed or angered him. Thus, for instance, shortly after Hamlet had been acted for the first time, a youth was telling, with considerable animation, how happy he had been that evening in the playhouse. Wilhelm hearkened; and was scandalised to learn that his neighbour had, on that occasion, in contempt of those behind him, kept his hat on, stubbornly refusing to remove it till the piece was done; to which heroical transaction he still looked back with great contentment.

Another gentleman declared that Wilhelm played Laertes very well; but that the actor who had undertaken Hamlet did not seem too happy in *his* part. This permutation was not quite unnnatural; for Wilhelm and Laertes did resemble one another, though in a very distant manner.

A third critic warmly praised his acting, particularly in the scene with his mother; only he regretted much, that in this fiery moment a white strap had peered out from below the Prince's waistcoat, whereby the illusion had been greatly marred.

Meanwhile, in the interior of the company, a multitude of alterations were occurring. Philina, since the evening subsequent to that of the fire, had never given our friend the smallest sign of closer intimacy. She had, as it seemed on purpose, hired a remote lodging; she associated with Elmira, and came seldomer to Serlo, an arrangement very gratifying to Aurelia. Serlo continued still to like her; and often visited her quarters, particularly when he hoped to find Elmira there. One evening he took Wilhelm with him. At their entrance, both of them were much surprised to see Philina, in the inner room, sitting in close contact with a young officer. He wore a red uniform with white pantaloons; but his face being turned away, they could not see it. Philina came into the outer room to meet her visitors, and shut the door behind her. "You surprise me in the middle of a very strange adventure," cried she.

"It does not appear so strange," said Serlo: "but let us see this handsome, young, enviable gallant. You have us in such training, that we dare not show any jealousy, however it may be."

"I must leave you to suspicion for a time," replied Philina, in a jesting tone; "yet I can assure you, the gallant is a lady of my friends, who wishes to remain a few days undiscovered. You shall know her history in due season; nay, perhaps you shall even behold the beautiful spinster in person; and then most probably I shall have need of all my prudence and discretion, for it seems too likely that your new acquaintance will drive your old friend out of favour."

Wilhelm stood as if transformed to stone. At the first glance, the red uniform had reminded him of Mariana; the figure too was hers, the fair hair was hers; only the present individual seemed to be a little taller.

"For Heaven's sake," cried he, "let us know something more about your friend; let us see this lady in disguise! We are now partakers of your secret: we will promise, we will swear; only let us see the lady!"

"What a fire he is in!" cried Philina: "but be cool, be calm; for today there will nothing come of it."

"Let us only know her name!" cried Wilhelm.

"It were a fine secret then," replied Philina.

"At least her first name!"

"If you can guess it, be it so. Three guesses I will give you; not a fourth. You might lead me through the whole calendar."

"Well!" said Wilhelm, "Cecilia, then?"

"None of your Cecilias!"

"Henrietta?"

"Not at all! Have a care, I pray you; guess better, or your curiosity will have to sleep unsatisfied."

Wilhelm paused and shivered: he tried to speak, but the sound died away within him. "Mariana?" stammered he at last, "Mariana!"

"Bravo!" cried Philina. "Hit to a hair's-breadth!" said she, whirling round upon her heel, as she was wont on such occasions.

Wilhelm could not utter a word; and Serlo, not observing his emotion, urged Philina more and more to let them in.

Conceive the astonishment of both, when Wilhelm, suddenly and vehemently interrupting their raillery, threw himself at Philina's feet, and with an air and tone of the deepest passion begged and conjured her: "Let me see the stranger," cried he; "she is mine; she is my Mariana! She, for whom I have longed all the days of my life; she, who is still more to me than all the women in this world! Go in to her at least, and tell her that I am here; that the man is here who linked to her his earliest love, and all the happiness of his youth. Say that he will justify himself, though he left her so unkindly; he will pray for pardon of her; and will grant her pardon, whatsoever she may have done to him; he will even make no pretensions further, if he may but see her, if he may but see that she is living, and in happiness."

Philina shook her head, and said: "Speak low! Do not betray us! If the lady is indeed your friend, her feelings must be spared; for she does not in the least suspect that you are here. Quite a different sort of business brings her hither: and you know well enough, one had rather see a spectre than a former lover, at an inconvenient time. I will ask her, and prepare her; we will then consider what is farther to be done. Tomorrow I shall write you a note, saying when you are to come, or whether you may come at all. Obey me punctually; for I protest that, without her own and my consent, no eye shall see this lovely creature. I shall keep my doors better bolted; and with axe and crow you surely will not visit me."

Our friend conjured her, Serlo begged of her; but all in vain: they were obliged to yield, and leave the chamber and the house.

With what feelings Wilhelm passed the night is easy to conceive. How slowly the hours of the day flowed on, while he sat expecting a message from Philina, may also be imagined. Unhappily he had to play that evening: such mental pain he had never endured. The moment his part was done, he hastened to Philina's house, without inquiring whether he had got her leave or not. He found her doors bolted: and the people of the house informed him, that Mademoiselle had set out early in the morning, in company with a young officer; that she had talked about returning shortly; but they had not believed her, she having paid her debts, and taken everything along with her.

This intelligence drove Wilhelm almost frantic. He hastened to Laertes, that he might take measures for pursuing her, and, cost what it would, for attaining certainty regarding her attendant. Laertes, however, represented to him the imprudence of such passion and credulity. "I dare wager, after all," said he, "that it is no one else but Friedrich. The boy is of a high family, I know; he is madly in love with Philina; it is likely he has cozened from his friends a fresh supply of money, so that he can once more live with her in peace for a while."

These considerations, though they did not quite convince our friend, sufficed to make him waver. Laertes showed him how improbable the story was, with which Philina had amused them;

reminded him how well the stranger's hair and figure answered Friedrich; that with the start of him by twelve hours, they could not easily be overtaken; and what was more than all, that Serlo could not do without him at the theatre.

By so many reasons, Wilhelm was at last persuaded to postpone the execution of his project. That night Laertes got an active man, to whom they gave the charge of following the runaways. It was a steady person, who had often officiated as courier and guide to travelling parties, and was at present without employment. They gave him money, they informed him of the whole affair; instructing him to seek and overtake the fugitives, to keep them in his eye, and instantly to send intelligence to Wilhelm, where and how he found them. That very hour he mounted horse, pursuing this ambiguous pair; by which exertions Wilhelm was, in some degree at least, composed.

CHAPTER XVI.

The departure of Philina did not make a deep sensation, either in the theatre or in the public. She never was in earnest with anything: the women universally detested her; the men rather wished to see her selves-two than on the boards. Thus her fine, and for the stage even happy talents were of no avail to her. The other members of the company took greater labour on them to supply her place: the Frau Melina, in particular, was much distinguished by her diligence and zeal. She noted down, as formerly, the principles of Wilhelm; she guided herself according to his theory and his example; there was of late a something in her nature that rendered her more interesting. She soon acquired an accurate mode of playing; she attained the natural tone of conversation altogether, that of keen emotion she attained in some degree. She contrived, moreover, to adapt herself to Serlo's humours; she took pains in singing for his pleasure, and succeeded in that matter moderately well.

By the accession of some other players, the company was rendered more complete: and while Wilhelm and Serlo were busied each in his degree, the former insisting on the general tone and spirit of the whole, the latter faithfully elaborating the separate passages, a laudable ardour likewise inspired the actors, and the public took a lively interest in their concerns.

"We are on the right path," said Serlo once; "if we can continue thus, the public too will soon be on it. Men are easily astonished and misled by wild and barbarous exhibitions; yet lay before them anything rational and polished, in an interesting manner, and doubt not they will catch at it.

"What forms the chief defect of our German theatre, what prevents both actor and spectator from obtaining proper views, is the vague and variegated nature of the objects it contains. You nowhere find a barrier, on which to prop your judgment. In my opinion, it is far from an advantage to us, that we have expanded our stage into as it were a boundless arena for the whole of nature: yet neither manager nor actor need attempt contracting it, until the taste of the nation shall itself mark out the proper circle. Every good society submits to certain conditions and restrictions; so also must every good theatre. Certain manners, certain modes of speech, certain objects and fashions of proceeding, must altogether be excluded. You do not grow poorer by limiting your household expenditure."

On these points our friends were more or less accordant or at variance. The majority, with Wilhelm at their head, were for the English theatre; Serlo and a few others for the French.

It was also settled, that in vacant hours, of which unhappily an actor has too many, they should in company peruse the finest plays in both these languages; examining what parts of them seemed best and worthiest of imitation. They accordingly commenced with some French pieces. On these occasions, it was soon observed, Aurelia went away whenever they began to read. At first they supposed she had been sick: Wilhelm once questioned her about it.

"I would not assist at such a reading," said she: "for how could I hear and judge, when my heart was torn in pieces? I hate the French language from the bottom of my soul."

"How can you be hostile to a language," cried our friend, "to which we Germans are indebted for the greater part of our accomplishments; to which we must become indebted still more, if our natural qualities are ever to assume their proper form?"

"It is no prejudice!" replied Aurelia: "a painful impression, a hated recollection of my faithless friend, has robbed me of all enjoyment in that beautiful and cultivated tongue. How I hate it now, with my whole strength and heart! During the period of our kindliest connexion, he wrote in German, and what genuine, powerful, cordial German! It was not till he wanted to get quit of me, that he began seriously to write in French. I marked, I felt what he meant. What he would have blushed to utter in his mother-tongue, he could by this means write with a quiet conscience. It is the language of reservations, equivocations and lies: it is a *perfidious* language. Heaven be praised! I cannot find another word to express this *perfide* of theirs in all its compass. Our poor *treulos*, the *faithless* of the English, are innocent as babes beside it. *Perfide* means faithless with pleasure, with insolence and malice. How enviable is the culture of a nation that can figure out so many shades of meaning by a single word! French is exactly the language of the world; worthy to become the universal language, that all may have it in their power to cheat, and cozen, and betray each other! His French letters were always smooth and pleasant, while you read them. If you chose to believe it, they sounded warmly, even passionately: but if you examined narrowly, they were but phrases, accursed phrases! He has spoiled my feeling to the whole language, to French literature, even to the beautiful delicious expressions of noble souls which may be found in it. I shudder when a French word is spoken in my hearing."

In such terms, she could for hours continue to give utterance to her chagrin, interrupting or disturbing every other kind of conversation. Sooner or later, Serlo used to put an end to such peevish lamentations by some bitter sally; but, by this means, commonly the talk for the evening was destroyed.

In all provinces of life, it is unhappily the case, that whatever is to be accomplished by a number of coöperating men and circumstances, cannot long continue perfect. Of an acting company as well as of a kingdom, of a circle of friends as well as of an army, you may commonly select the moment when it may be said that all was standing on the highest pinnacle of harmony, perfection, contentment and activity. But alterations will ere long occur: the individuals that compose the body often change; new members are added; the persons are no longer suited to the circumstances, or the circumstances to the persons; what was formerly united, quickly falls asunder. Thus it was with Serlo's company. For a time, you might have called it as complete as any German company could ever boast of being. Most of the actors were occupying their proper places; all had enough to do, and all did it willingly. Their private personal condition was not bad; and each appeared to promise great things in his art, for each commenced with animation and alacrity. But it soon became apparent that a part of them were mere automatons, who could not reach beyond what was attainable without the aid of feeling. Nor was it long till grudgings and envyings arose among them, such as commonly obstruct every good arrangement, and easily distort and tear in pieces everything that reasonable and thinking men would wish to keep united.

The departure of Philina was not quite so insignificant as it had at first appeared. She had always skilfully contrived to entertain the Manager, and keep the others in good humour. She had endured Aurelia's violence with amazing patience; and her dearest task had been to flatter Wilhelm. Thus she was, in some respects, a bond of union for the whole: the loss of her was quickly felt.

Serlo could not live without some little passion of the love sort. Elmira was of late grown up, we might almost say grown beautiful: for some time she had been attracting his attention, and Philina, with her usual dexterity, had favoured this attachment so soon as she observed it. "We should train ourselves in time," she would say, "to the business of procuress; nothing else remains for us when we are old." Serlo and Elmira had by this means so approximated to each other, that, shortly after the departure of Philina, both were of a mind; and their small romance was rendered doubly interesting, as they had to hide it sedulously from the father; Old Boisterous not understanding jokes of that description. Elmira's sister had been admitted to the secret: and Serlo was in consequence obliged to overlook a multitude of things in both of them. One of their worst habits was an excessive love of junketing, nay, if you will, an intolerable gluttony. In this respect they altogether differed from Philina, to whom it gave a new tint of loveliness, that she seemed as it were to live on air; eating very little; and for drink, merely skimming off, with all imaginable grace, the foam from a glass of champagne.

Now, however, Serlo, if he meant to please his doxies, was obliged to join breakfast with dinner; and with this, by a substantial bever, to connect the supper. But amid gormandising, Serlo entertained another plan, which he longed to have fulfilled. He imagined that he saw a kind of inclination beween Wilhelm and Aurelia; and he anxiously wished that it might assume a serious shape. He hoped to cast the whole mechanical department of his theatrical economy on Wilhelm's shoulders; to find in him, as in the former brother, a faithful and industrious tool. Already he had, by degrees, shifted over to him most of the cares of management: Aurelia kept the strong-box; and Serlo once more lived as he had done of old, entirely according to his humour. Yet there was a circumstance which vexed him in secret, as it did his sister likewise.

The world has a particular way of acting towards public persons of acknowledged merit: it gradually begins to be indifferent to them; and to favour talents which are new, though far inferior; it makes excessive requisitions of the former, and accepts of anything with approbation from the latter.

Serlo and Aurelia had opportunity enough to meditate on this peculiarity. The strangers, especially the young and handsome ones, had drawn the whole attention and applause upon themselves; and Serlo and his sister, in spite of the most zealous efforts, had in general to make their exits without the welcome sound of clapping hands. It is true, some special causes were at work on this occasion. Aurelia's pride was palpable, and her contempt for the public was known to many. Serlo indeed flattered every individual; but his cutting jibes against the whole were often circulated and repeated. The new members again were not only strangers, unknown and wanting help, but some of them were likewise young and amiable; thus all of them found patrons.

Ere long, too, there arose internal discontents, and many bickerings among the actors. Scarcely had they noticed that our friend was acting as director, when most of them began to grow the more remiss, the more he strove to introduce a better order, greater accuracy, and chiefly to insist that everything mechanical should be performed in the most strict and regular manner.

Thus, by and by, the whole concern, which actually for a time had nearly looked ideal, grew as vulgar in its attributes as any mere itinerating theatre. And unhappily, just as Wilhelm, by his labour, diligence and vigorous efforts, had made himself acquainted with the requisitions of the art, and trained completely both his person and his habits to comply with them, he began to feel, in melancholy hours, that this craft deserved the necessary outlay of time and talents less than any other. The task was burdensome, the recompense was small. He would rather have engaged with any occupation in which, when the period of exertion is past, one can enjoy repose of mind, than with this, wherein, after undergoing much mechanical drudgery, the aim of one's activity cannot still be attained but by the strongest effort of thought and emotion. Besides, he had to listen to Aurelia's complaints about her brother's wastefulness; he had to misconceive the winks and nods of Serlo, trying from afar to lead him to a marriage with Aurelia. He had withal to hide his own secret sorrow, which pressed heavy on his heart, because of that ambiguous officer, whom he had sent in quest of. The messenger returned not, sent no tidings; and Wilhelm feared that his Mariana was lost to him a second time.

About this period, there occurred a public mourning, which obliged our friends to shut their theatre for several weeks. Wilhelm seized this opportunity to pay a visit to the Clergyman, with whom the Harper had been placed to board. He found him in a pleasant district; and the first thing that he noticed in the parsonage, was the old man teaching a boy to play upon his instrument. The Harper showed no little joy at sight of Wilhelm; he rose, held out his hand, and said: "You see, I am still good for something in the world; permit me to continue; for my hours are all distributed, and full of business."

The Clergyman saluted Wilhelm very kindly; and told him that the Harper promised well, already giving hopes of a complete recovery.

Their conversation naturally turned upon the various modes of treating the insane.

"Except physical derangements," observed the Clergyman, "which often place insuperable difficulties in the way, and in regard to which I follow the prescriptions of a wise physician, the means of curing madness seem to me extremely simple. They are the very means by which you hinder sane persons from becoming mad. Awaken their activity; accustom them to order; bring them to perceive that they hold their being and their fate in common with many millions; that extraordinary talents, the highest happiness, the deepest misery, are but slight variations from the general lot: in this way, no insanity will enter; or, if it has entered, will gradually disappear. I have portioned out the old man's hours; he gives lessons to some children on the harp; he works in the garden; he is already much more cheerful. He wishes to enjoy the cabbages he plants; my son, to whom in case of death he has bequeathed his harp, he is ardent to instruct, that the boy may be able to make use of his inheritance. I have said but little to him, as a clergyman, about his wild mysterious scruples; but a busy life brings on so many incidents, that ere long he must feel how true it is, that doubt of any kind can be removed by nothing but activity. I go softly to work; yet if I could get his beard and hood removed, I should reckon it a weighty point; for nothing more exposes us to madness, than distinguishing ourselves from others, and nothing more contributes to maintain our common sense, than living in the universal way with multitudes of men. Alas! how much there is in education, in our social institutions, to prepare us and our children for insanity!"

Wilhelm stayed some days with this intelligent divine; heard from him many curious narratives, not of the insane alone, but of persons such as commonly are reckoned wise and rational, though they may have peculiarities which border on insanity.

The conversation became doubly animated on the entrance of the Doctor, with whom it was a custom to pay frequent visits to his friend the Clergyman, and to assist him in his labours of humanity. The physician was an oldish man, who, though in weak health, had spent many years in the practice of the noblest virtues.

He was a strong advocate for country life, being himself scarcely able to exist except in the open air. Withal he was extremely active and companionable. For several years, he had shown a special inclination to make friends with all the country clergymen within his reach. Such of these as were employed in any useful occupation, he strove by every means to help; into others, who were still unsettled in their aims, he endeavoured to infuse a taste for some profitable species of exertion. Being at the same time in connexion with a multitude of noblemen, magistrates, judges, he had in the space of twenty years, in secret, accomplished much towards the advancement of many branches of husbandry; he had done his best to put in motion every project that seemed capable of benefiting agriculture, animals, or men; and had thus forwarded improvement in its truest sense. "For man," he used to say, "there is but one misfortune; when some idea lays hold of him, which exerts no influence upon active life, or still more, which withdraws him from it. At the present time," continued he on this occasion, "I have such a case before me; it concerns a rich and noble couple; and hitherto has baffled all my skill. The affair belongs in part to your department, worthy Pastor, and your friend here will forbear to mention it again.

"In the absence of a certain nobleman, some persons of the house, in a frolic not entirely commendable, disguised a young man in the master's clothes. The lady was to be imposed upon by this deception; and although it was described to me as nothing but a joke, I am much afraid the purpose of it was to lead this noble and most amiable lady from the path of honour. Her husband, however, unexpectedly returns; enters his chamber; thinks he sees his spirit; and from that time falls into a melancholy temper, firmly believing that his death is near.

"He has now abandoned himself to men who pamper him with religious ideas; and I see not how he is to be prevented from going among the Herrnhuthers with his lady; and as he has no children, from depriving his relations of the chief part of his fortune."

"With his lady?" cried our friend, in great agitation; for this story had affrighted him extremely.

"And alas!" replied the Doctor, who regarded Wilhelm's exclamation only as the voice of common sympathy; "this lady is herself possessed with a deeper sorrow, which renders a removal from the world desirable to her also. The same young man was taking leave of her: she was not circumspect enough to hide a nascent inclination towards him; the youth grew bolder, clasped her in his arms, and pressed a large portrait of her husband, which was set with diamonds, forcibly against her breast. She felt a sharp pain, which gradually went off, leaving first a little redness, then no trace at all. As a man, I am convinced that she has nothing farther to reproach herself with, in this affair; as a physician, I am certain that this pressure could not have the smallest ill effect. Yet she will not be persuaded that an induration is not taking place in the part; and if you try to overcome her notion by the evidence of feeling, she maintains, that though the evil is away this moment, it will return the next. She conceives that the disease will end in cancer; and thus her youth and loveliness be altogether lost to others and herself."

"Wretch that I am!" cried Wilhelm, striking his brow, and rushing from the company into the fields. He had never felt himself in such a miserable case.

The clergyman and the physician were of course exceedingly astonished at this singular discovery. In the evening, all their skill was called for, when our friend returned, and, with a circumstantial disclosure of the whole occurrence, uttered the most violent accusations of himself. Both took interest in him; both felt a real concern about his general condition, particularly as he painted it in the gloomy colours which arose from the humour of the moment.

Next day the physician, without much entreaty, was prevailed upon to accompany him in his return; both that he might bear him company, and that he might, if possible, do something for Aurelia, whom our friend had left in rather dangerous circumstances.

In fact, they found her worse than they expected. She was afflicted with a sort of intermittent fever, which could the less be mastered, as she purposely maintained and aggravated the attacks of it. The stranger was not introduced as a physician: he behaved with great courteousness and prudence. They conversed about her situation bodily and mental: her new friend related many anecdotes of persons who, in spite of lingering disorders, had attained a good old age; adding, that in such cases, nothing could be more injurious than the intentional recalling of passionate and disagreeable emotions. In particular he stated, that for persons labouring under chronic and partly incurable distempers, he had always found it a very happy circumstance when they chanced to entertain, and cherish in their minds, true feelings of religion. This he signified in the most unobtrusive manner; as it were historically; promising Aurelia at the same time the reading of a very interesting manuscript, which he said he had received from the hands of an excellent lady of his friends, who was now deceased. "To me," he said, "it is of uncommon value; and I shall trust you even with the original. Nothing but the title is in my handwriting: I have called it, *Confessions of a Fair Saint.*"

Touching the medical and dietetic treatment of the racked and hapless patient, he also left his best advice with Wilhelm. He then departed; promising to write; and, if possible, to come again in person.

Meanwhile, in Wilhelm's absence, there had changes been preparing such as he was not aware of. During his directorship, our friend had managed all things with a certain liberality and freedom; looking chiefly at the main result. Whatever was required for dresses, decorations and the like, he had usually provided in a plentiful and handsome style; and for securing the coöperation of his people, he had flattered their self-interest, since he could not reach them by nobler motives. In this he felt his conduct justified the more, as Serlo for his own part never aimed at being a strict economist; but liked to hear the beauty of his theatre commended; and was contented, if Aurelia, who conducted the domestic matters, on defraying all expenses, signified that she was free from debt, and could besides afford the necessary sums for clearing off such scores as Serlo in the interim, by lavish kindness to his mistresses or otherwise, might have incurred.

Melina, who was charged with managing the wardrobe, had all the while been silently considering these things, with the cold spiteful temper peculiar to him. On occasion of our friend's departure, and Aurelia's increasing sickness, he contrived to signify to Serlo, that more money might be raised and less expended; and consequently something be laid up, or at least a merrier life be led. Serlo hearkened gladly to such allegations, and Melina risked the exhibition of his plan.

"I will not say," continued he, "that any of your actors has at present too much salary; they are meritorious people, they would find a welcome anywhere; but for the income which they bring us in, they have too much. My project would be, to set up an opera: and as to what concerns the playhouse, I may be allowed to say it, you are the person for maintaining that establishment upon your single strength. Observe how at present your merits are neglected; and justice is refused you, not because your fellow-actors are excellent, but merely good.

"Come out alone, as used to be the case; endeavour to attract around you middling, I will even say inferior people, for a slender salary; regale the public with mechanical displays, as you can so cleverly do; apply your remaining means to the opera, which I am talking of; and you will quickly see, that with the same labour and expense, you will give greater satisfaction, while you draw incomparably more money than at present."

These observations were so flattering to Serlo, that they could not fail of making some impression on him. He readily admitted, that, loving music as he did, he had long wished for some arrangement such as this: though he could not but perceive that the public taste would thus be still more widely led astray; and that with such a mongrel theatre, not properly an opera, not properly a playhouse, any residue of true feeling for regular and perfect works of art must shortly disappear.

Melina ridiculed, in terms more plain than delicate, our friend's pedantic notions in this matter, and his vain attempts to form the public mind, instead of being formed by it. Serlo and he at last agreed, with full conviction, that the sole concern was, how to gather money, and grow rich, or live a joyous life; and they scarcely concealed their wish to be delivered from those persons who at present hindered them. Melina took occasion to lament Aurelia's weak health, and the speedy end which it threatened; thinking all the while directly the reverse. Serlo affected to regret that Wilhelm could not sing; thus signifying that his presence was by no means indispensable. Melina then came forward with a whole catalogue of savings, which, he said, might be effected; and Serlo saw in him his brother-in-law replaced threefold. Both of them felt well that secrecy was necessary in the matter; but this mutual obligation only joined them closer in their interests. They failed not to converse together privately, on everything that happened; to blame whatever Wilhelm or Aurelia undertook; and to elaborate their own project, and prepare it more and more for execution.

Silent as they both might be about their plan, little as their words betrayed them, in their conduct they were not so politic as constantly to hide their purposes. Melina now opposed our friend in many points that lay within the province of the latter; and Serlo, who had never acted smoothly to his sister, seemed to grow more bitter, the more her sickness deepened, the more her passionate and variable humours would have needed toleration.

About this period, they took up the *Emilie Galotti* of Lessing. The parts were very happily distributed and filled; within the narrow circle of this tragedy, the company found room for showing all the complex riches of their acting. Serlo in the character of Marinelli was altogether in his place; Odoardo was very well exhibited; Madam Melina played the Mother with considerable skill; Elmira gained distinction as Emilie; Laertes made a stately Appiani; and Wilhelm had bestowed the study of some months upon the Prince's part. On this occasion, both internally and with Aurelia and Serlo, he had often come upon this question: What is the distinction between a noble and a well-bred manner; and how far must the former be included in the latter, though the latter is not in the former?

Serlo, who himself in Marinelli had to act the courtier accurately, without caricature, afforded him some valuable thoughts on this. "A well-bred carriage," he would say, "is difficult to imitate; for in strictness it is negative; and it implies a long-continued previous training. You are not required to exhibit in your manner anything that specially betokens dignity; for, by this means, you are like to run into formality and haughtiness; you are rather to avoid whatever is undignified and vulgar. You are never to forget yourself; are to keep a constant watch upon yourself and others; to forgive nothing that is faulty in your own conduct, in that of others neither to forgive too little nor too much. Nothing must appear to touch you, nothing to agitate: you must never overhaste yourself, must ever keep yourself composed, retaining still an outward calmness, whatever storms may rage within. The noble character at certain moments may resign himself to his emotions; the well-bred never. The latter is like a man dressed out in fair and spotless clothes: he will not lean on anything; every person will beware of rubbing on him. He distinguishes himself from others, yet he may not stand apart; for as in all arts, so in this, the hardest must at length be done with ease: the well-bred man of rank, in spite of every separation, always seems united with the people round him; he is never to be stiff or uncomplying; he is always to appear the first, and never to insist on so appearing.

"It is clear, then, that to seem well-bred, a man must actually be so. It is also clear why women generally are more expert at taking up the air of breeding than the other sex; why courtiers and soldiers catch it more easily than other men."

Wilhelm now despaired of doing justice to his part; but Serlo aided and encouraged him; communicated the acutest observations on detached points; and furnished him so well, that on the exhibition of the piece, the public reckoned him a very proper Prince.

Serlo had engaged to give him, when the play was over, such remarks as might occur upon his acting; a disagreeable contention with Aurelia prevented any conversation of that kind. Aurelia had acted the character of Orsina, in such a style as few have ever done. She was well acquainted with the part; and during the rehearsals she had treated it indifferently: but in the exhibition of the piece, she had opened as it were all the sluices of her personal sorrow; and the character was represented, so as never poet in the first glow of invention could have figured it. A boundless applause rewarded her painful efforts; but her friends, on visiting her when the play was finished, found her half fainting in her chair.

Serlo had already signified his anger at her over-charged acting, as he called it; at this disclosure of her inmost heart before the public, to many individuals of which the history of her fatal passion was more or less completely known. He had spoken bitterly and fiercely; grinding with his teeth, and stamping with his feet, as was his custom when enraged. "Never mind her," cried he, when he saw her in the chair, surrounded by the rest; "she will go upon the stage stark-naked one of these days; and then the approbation will be perfect."

"Ungrateful, inhuman man!" exclaimed she; "soon shall I be carried naked to the place where approbation or disapprobation can no longer reach our ears!" With these words she started up, and hastened to the door. The maid had not yet brought her mantle; the sedan was not in waiting; it had been raining lately; a cold, raw wind was blowing through the streets. They endeavoured to persuade her to remain, for she was very warm. But in vain: she purposely walked slow; she praised the coolness, seemed to inhale it with peculiar eagerness. No sooner was she home, than she became so hoarse that she could hardly speak a word: she did not mention that there was a total stiffness in her neck and along her back. Shortly afterwards, a sort of palsy in the tongue came on, so that she pronounced one word instead of another. They put her to bed; by numerous and copious remedies, the evil changed its form, but was not mastered. The fever gathered strength; her case was dangerous.

Next morning she enjoyed a quiet hour. She sent for Wilhelm, and delivered him a letter. "This sheet," said she, "has long been waiting for the present moment. I feel that my end is drawing nigh: promise me that you yourself will take this paper; that by a word or two, you will avenge my sorrows on the faithless man. He is not void of feeling; my death will pain him for a moment."

Wilhelm took the letter; still endeavouring to console her, and to drive away the thought of death.

"No," said she, "do not deprive me of my nearest hope. I have waited for him long; I will joyfully clasp him when he comes."

Shortly after this, the manuscript arrived, which the physician had engaged to send her. She called for Wilhelm; made him read it to her. The effect, which it produced upon her, the reader will be better able to appreciate after looking at the following Book. The violent and stubborn temper of our poor Aurelia was mollified by hearing it. She took back the letter, and wrote another as it seemed in a meeker tone; charging Wilhelm at the same time to console her friend, if he should be distressed about her death; to assure him that she had forgiven him, and wished him every kind of happiness.

From this time, she was very quiet; and appeared to occupy herself with but a few ideas, which she endeavoured to extract and appropriate from the manuscript, out of which she frequently made Wilhelm read to her. The decay of her strength was not perceptible: nor had Wilhelm been anticipating the event, when one morning as he went to visit her, he found that she was dead.

Entertaining such respect for her as he had done, and accustomed as he was to live in her society, the loss of her affected him with no common sorrow. She was the only person that had truly wished him well; the coldness of Serlo he had felt of late but too keenly. He hastened therefore to perform the service she had entrusted to him; he wished to be absent for a time.

On the other hand, this journey was exceedingly convenient for Melina; in the course of his extensive correspondence, he had lately entered upon terms with a male and a female singer, who, it was intended, should, by their performances in interludes, prepare the public for his future opera. The loss of Aurelia, and Wilhelm's absence, were to be supplied in this manner; and our friend was satisfied with anything that could facilitate his setting out.

He had formed, within himself, a singular idea of the importance of his errand. The death of his unhappy friend had moved him deeply; and having seen her pass so early from the scene, he could not but be hostilely inclined against the man, who had abridged her life, and made that shortened term so full of woe.

Notwithstanding the last mild words of the dying woman, he resolved that, on delivering his letter, he would pass a strict sentence on her faithless friend: and not wishing to depend upon the temper of the moment, he studied an address, which in the course of preparation became more pathetic than just. Having fully convinced himself of the good composition of his essay, he began committing it to memory, and at the same time making ready for departure. Mignon was present as he packed his articles; she asked him whether he intended travelling south or north; and learning that it was the latter, she replied: "Then I will wait here for thee." She begged of him the pearl necklace which had once been Mariana's. He could not refuse to gratify the dear little creature, and he gave it her: the neckerchief she had already.

On the other hand, she put the veil of Hamlet's Ghost into his travelling bag, though he told her it could not be of any service to him.

Melina took upon him the directorship; his wife engaged to keep a mother's eye upon the children, whom Wilhelm parted with unwillingly. Felix was very merry at the setting out, and when asked what pretty thing he wished to have brought back for him, he said: "Hark you! bring me a papa!" Mignon seized the traveller's hand; then, standing on her tiptoes, she pressed a warm and cordial, though not a tender kiss, upon his lips, and cried: "Master! forget us not, and come soon back."

And so we leave our friend, entering on his journey, amid a thousand different thoughts and feelings; and here subjoin, by way of close, a little poem, which Mignon had recited once or twice with great expressiveness, and which the hurry of so many singular occurrences prevented us from inserting sooner:

> O, ask me not to speak, I pray thee!
>   It must not be reveal'd but hid;
> How gladly would my tongue obey thee,
>   Did not the voice of Fate forbid!
>
> At his appointed time revolving,
>   The sun these shades of night dispels;
> The rock, its rugged breast dissolving,
>   Gives up to Earth its hidden wells.
>
> In Friendship's arms each heart reposes;
>   There soul to soul pours out its woe:
> My lips an oath forever closes,
>   My sorrows God alone can know.

BOOK VI.

CONFESSIONS OF A FAIR SAINT.

TILL my eighth year, I was always a healthy child; but of that period I can recollect no more than of the day when I was born. About the beginning of my eighth year, I was seized with a hemorrhage; and from that moment my soul became all feeling, all memory. The smallest circumstances of that accident are yet before my eyes, as if they had occurred but yesterday.

During the nine months, which I then spent patiently upon a sick-bed, it appears to me, the ground-work of my whole turn of thought was laid; as the first means were then afforded my mind of developing itself in its own manner.

I suffered and I loved; this was the peculiar form of my heart. In the most violent fits of coughing, in the depressing pains of fever, I lay quiet, like a snail drawn back within its house: the moment I obtained a respite, I wanted to enjoy something pleasant; and as every other pleasure was denied me, I endeavoured to amuse myself with the innocent delights of eye and ear. The people brought me dolls and picture-books; and whoever would sit by my bed, was obliged to tell me something.

From my mother I rejoiced to hear the Bible histories: and my father entertained me with natural curiosities. He had a very pretty cabinet; from which he brought me first one drawer and then another, as occasion served; showing me the articles, and pointing out their properties. Dried plants and insects, with many kinds of anatomical preparations, such as human skin, bones, mummies and the like, were in succession laid upon the sick-bed of the little one; the birds and animals he killed in hunting were shown to me, before they passed into the kitchen: and that the Prince of the World might also have a voice in this assembly, my aunt related to me love-adventures out of fairy tales. All was accepted, all took root. There were hours in which I vividly conversed with the Invisible Power. I can still repeat some verses, which I then dictated, and my mother wrote down.

Often I would tell my father back again what I had learned from him. Rarely did I take any physic without asking where the simples it was made of grew, what look they had, what names they bore. Nor had the stories of my aunt lighted on stony ground. I figured myself out in pretty clothes; and met the most delightful princes, who could find no peace or rest, till they discovered who the unknown beauty was. One adventure of this kind, with a charming little angel, dressed in white, with golden wings, who warmly courted me, I dwelt upon so long, that my imagination painted out his form almost to visibility.

After a year, I was pretty well restored to health; but nothing of the giddiness of childhood remained with me. I could not play with dolls; I longed for beings able to return my love. Dogs, cats and birds, of which my father kept a great variety, afforded me delight: but what would I have given for such a creature as my aunt once told me of! It was a lamb, which a peasant girl took up and nourished in a wood; but in the guise of this pretty beast an enchanted prince was hid; who at length appeared in his native shape, a lovely youth, and rewarded his benefactress by his hand. Such a lamb I would have given the world for.

But there was none to be had; and as everything about me went on in such a quite natural manner, I by degrees all but abandoned nearly all hopes of such a treasure. Meanwhile I comforted myself by reading books, in which the strangest incidents were set forth. Among them all, my favourite was the *Christian German Hercules*: that devout love-history was altogether in my way. Whenever anything befell his dear Valiska, and cruel things befell her, he always prayed before hastening to her aid, and the prayers stood there *verbatim*. My longing after the Invisible, which I had always dimly felt, was strengthened by such means: for, in short, it was ordained that God should also be my confidant.

As I grew older, I continued reading, Heaven knows what, in chaotic order. The *Roman Octavia* was the book I liked beyond all others. The persecutions of the first Christians, decorated with the charms of a romance, awoke the deepest interest in me.

But my mother now began to murmur at my constant reading; and to humour her, my father took away my books today, but gave them back tomorrow. She was wise enough to see that nothing could be done in this way; she next insisted merely that my Bible should be read with equal diligence. To this I was not disinclined: and I accordingly perused the sacred volume with a lively interest. Withal my mother was extremely careful that no books of a corruptive tendency should come into my hands: immodest writings I would, of my own accord, have cast away; for my princes and my princesses were all extremely virtuous.

To my mother, and my zeal for knowledge, it was owing that with all my love of books I also learned to cook; for much was to be seen in cookery. To cut up a hen, a pig, was quite a feast for me. I used to bring the entrails to my father, and he talked with me about them, as if I had been a student of anatomy. With suppressed joy, he would often call me his misfashioned son.

My twelfth year was now behind me. I learned French, dancing and drawing; I received the usual instructions in religion. In the latter, many thoughts and feelings were awakened; but nothing properly relating to my own condition. I liked to hear the people speak of God; I was proud that I could speak on these points better than my equals. I zealously read many books which put me in a condition to talk about religion; but it never once struck me to think how matters stood with *me*, whether *my* soul was formed according to these holy precepts, whether it was like a glass from which the everlasting sun could be reflected in its glancing. From the first, I had presupposed all this.

My French I learned with eagerness. My teacher was a clever man. He was not a vain empiric, not a dry grammarian: he had learning, he had seen the world. Instructing me in language, he satisfied my zeal for knowledge in a thousand ways. I loved him so much, that I used to wait his coming with a palpitating heart. Drawing was not hard for me: I should have made greater progress had my teacher possessed head and science; he had only hands and practice.

Dancing was, at first, one of my smallest amusements: my body was too sensitive for it; I learned it only in the company of my sisters. But our dancing-master took a thought of gathering all his scholars, male and female, and giving them a ball. This event gave dancing quite another charm for me.

Amid a throng of boys and girls, the most remarkable were two sons of the Marshal of the Court. The youngest was of my age, the other two years older; they were children of such beauty that, according to the universal voice, no one had seen their like. For my part, scarcely had I noticed them, when I lost sight of all the other crowd. From that moment I began to dance with care, and to wish that I could dance with grace. How came it, on the other hand, that these two boys distinguished me from all the rest? No matter; before an hour had passed, we had become the warmest friends; and our little entertainment did not end, till we had fixed upon the time and place where we were next to meet. What a joy for me! And how charmed was I next morning when both of them inquired for my health, each in a gallant note, accompanied with a nosegay! I have never since felt as I then did! Compliment was met by compliment; letter answered letter. The church and the public walks were grown a rendezvous; our young acquaintances, in all their little parties, now invited us together; while, at the same time, we were sly enough to veil the business from our parents, so that they saw no more of it than we thought good.

Thus had I at once got a pair of lovers. I had yet decided upon neither; they both pleased me, and we did extremely well together. All at once, the eldest of the two fell very sick. I myself had often been sick; and thus I was enabled, by rendering him many little dainties and delicacies suited for a sick person, to afford some solace to the sufferer. His parents thankfully acknowledged my attention: in compliance with the prayer of their beloved son, they invited me, with all my sisters, to their house, so soon as he had risen from his sick-bed. The tenderness, which he displayed on meeting me, was not the feeling of a child; from that day I gave the preference to him. He warned me to keep our secret from his brother; but the flame could no longer be concealed; and the jealousy of the younger completed our romance. He played us a thousand tricks; eager to annihilate our joys, he but increased the passion he was seeking to destroy.

At last, then, I had actually found the wished-for lamb; and this attachment acted on me like my sickness; it made me calm, and drew me back from noisy pleasures. I was solitary, I was moved; and thoughts of God again occurred to me. He was again my confidant, and I well remember with what tears I often prayed for this poor boy, who still continued sickly.

The more childishness there was in this adventure, the more did it contribute to the forming of my heart. Our French teacher had now turned us from translating, into daily writing him some letter of our own invention. I brought my little history to market, shrouded in the names of Phyllis and Damon. The old man soon saw through it; and to render me communicative, praised my labour very much. I still waxed bolder; came openly out with the affair, adhering even in the minute details to truth. I do not now remember what the passage was at which he took occasion to remark: "How pretty, how natural it is! But the good Phyllis had better have a care; the thing may soon grow serious."

It vexed me that he did not look upon the matter as already serious; and I asked him, with an air of pique, what he meant by serious. I had not to repeat the question; he explained himself so clearly, that I could scarcely hide my terror. Yet, as anger came along with it, as I took it ill that he should entertain such thoughts, I kept myself composed; I tried to justify my nymph; and said with glowing cheeks: "But, sir, Phyllis is an honourable girl."

He was rogue enough to banter me about my honourable heroine. While we were speaking French, he played upon the word *honnête*, and hunted the honourableness of Phyllis over all its meanings. I felt the ridicule of this, and was extremely puzzled. He, not to frighten me, broke off; but afterwards often led the conversation to such topics. Plays and little histories, such as I was reading and translating with him, gave him frequent opportunity to show how feeble a security against the calls of inclination our boasted virtue was. I no longer contradicted him; but I was in secret scandalised; and his remarks became a burden to me.

With my worthy Damon, too, I by degrees fell out of all connexion. The chicanery of the younger boy destroyed our intercourse. Soon after, both these blooming creatures died. I lamented sore; however, in a short time I forgot.

But Phyllis rapidly increased in stature; was altogether healthy, and began to see the world. The hereditary Prince now married; and a short time after, on his father's death, began his rule. Court and town were in the liveliest motion: my curiosity had copious nourishment. There were plays and balls, with all their usual accompaniments; and though my parents kept retired as much as possible, they were obliged to show themselves at court, where I was of course introduced. Strangers were pouring in from every side; high company was in every house; even to us some cavaliers were recommended, others introduced; and at my uncle's, men of every nation might be met with.

My honest Mentor still continued, in a modest and yet striking way, to warn me; and I in secret to take it ill of him. With regard to his assertion, that women under every circumstance were weak, I did not feel at all convinced; and here perhaps I was in the right, and my Mentor in the wrong; but he spoke so earnestly, that once I grew afraid he might be right, and said to him, with much vivacity: "Since the danger is so great, and the human heart so weak, I will pray to God that He may keep me."

This simple answer seemed to please him, for he praised my purpose; but on my side, it was anything but seriously meant. It was, in truth, but an empty word; for my feelings towards the Invisible were almost totally extinguished. The hurry and the crowd I lived in, dissipated my attention, and carried me along as in a rapid stream. These were the emptiest years of my life. All day long, to speak of nothing, to have no solid thought; never to do anything but revel: such was my employment. On my beloved books I never once bestowed a thought. The people I lived among had not the slightest tinge of literature or science: they were German courtiers; a class of men at that time altogether destitute of culture.

Such society, it may be thought, must naturally have led me to the brink of ruin. I lived away in mere corporeal cheerfulness; I never took myself to task, I never prayed, I never thought about myself or God. Yet I look upon it as a providential guidance, that none of these many handsome, rich and well-dressed men could take my fancy. They were rakes, and did not conceal it; this scared me back: they adorned their speech with double meanings; this offended me, made me act with coldness towards them. Many times their improprieties exceeded belief; and I did not restrain myself from being rude.

Besides, my ancient counsellor had once in confidence contrived to tell me, that, with the greater part of these lewd fellows, health as well as virtue was in danger. I now shuddered at the sight of them; I was afraid, if one of them in any way approached too near me. I would not touch their cups or glasses, even the chairs they had been sitting on. Thus morally and physically I remained apart from them; all the compliments they paid me I haughtily accepted, as incense that was due.

Among the strangers then resident among us, was one young man peculiarly distinguished, whom we used in sport to call Narciss. He had gained a reputation in the diplomatic line; and among the various changes now occurring at court, he was in hopes of meeting with some advantageous place. He soon became acquainted with my father: his acquirements and manners opened for him the way to a select society of most accomplished men. My father often spoke in praise of him: his figure, which was very handsome, would have made a still better impression, had it not been for something of self-complacency, which breathed from the whole carriage of the man. I had seen him; I thought well of him; but we had never spoken.

At a great ball, where we chanced to be in company, I danced a minuet with him; but this too passed without results. The more violent dances, in compliance with my father, who felt anxious about my health, I was accustomed to avoid: in the present case, when these came on, I retired to an adjoining room, and began to talk with certain of my friends, elderly ladies, who had set themselves to cards.

Narciss, who had jigged it for a while, at last came into the room where I was; and having got the better of a bleeding at the nose, which had overtaken him in dancing, he began speaking with me about a multitude of things. In half an hour, the talk had grown so interesting, that neither of us could think of dancing any more. We were rallied by our friends; but we did not let their bantering disturb us. Next evening, we recommenced our conversation, and were very careful not to hurt our health.

The acquaintance, then, was made. Narciss was often with my sisters and myself; and I now once more began to reckon over and consider what I knew, what I thought of, what I had felt, and what I could express myself about in conversation. My new friend had mingled in the best society; besides the department of history and politics, with every part of which he was familiar, he had gained extensive literary knowledge; there was nothing new that issued from the press, especially in France, that he was unacquainted with. He brought or sent me many a pleasant book; but this we had to keep as secret as forbidden love. Learned women had been made ridiculous, nor were well-informed women tolerated,—apparently, because it would have been uncivil to put so many ill-informed men to shame. Even my father, much as he delighted in this new opportunity of cultivating my mind, expressly stipulated that our literary commerce should remain secret.

Thus our intercourse continued for almost year and day; and still I could not say that, in any wise, Narciss had ever shown me aught of love or tenderness. He was always complaisant and kind; but manifested nothing like attachment: on the contrary, he even seemed to be in some degree affected by the charms of my youngest sister, who was then extremely beautiful. In sport, he gave her many little friendly names, out of foreign tongues; for he could speak two or three of these extremely well, and loved to mix their idiomatic phrases with his German. Such compliments she did not answer very liberally; she was entangled in a different noose; and being very sharp, while he was very sensitive, the two were often quarrelling about trifles. With my mother and my aunt he kept on very pleasant terms; and thus by gradual advances, he was grown to be a member of the family.

Who knows how long we might have lived in this way, had not a curious accident altered our relations all at once. My sisters and I were invited to a certain house, to which we did not like to go. The company was too mixed; and persons of the stupidest, if not the rudest stamp were often to be met there. Narciss, on this occasion, was invited also; and on his account I felt inclined to go, for I was sure of finding one, at least, whom I could converse with as I desired. Even at table, we had many things to suffer; for several of the gentlemen had drunk too much: then, in the drawing-room, they insisted on a game at forfeits. It went on, with great vivacity and tumult. Narciss had lost a forfeit: they ordered him, by way of penalty, to whisper something pleasant in the ear of every member of the company. It seems, he stayed too long beside my next neighbour, the lady of a captain. The latter on a sudden struck him such a box with his fist, that the powder flew about me, into my eyes. When I had got my eyes cleared, and in some degree recovered from my terror, I saw that both gentlemen had drawn their swords. Narciss was bleeding; and the other, mad with wine and rage and jealousy, could scarcely be held back by all the company. I seized Narciss, led him by the arm up-stairs; and as I did not think my friend safe even here from his frantic enemy, I shut the door and bolted it.

Neither of us considered the wound serious; for a slight cut across the hand was all we saw. Soon, however, I discovered that there was a stream of blood running down his back, that there was a deep wound on the head. I now began to be afraid. I hastened to the lobby, to get help; but I could see no person; every one had stayed below to calm the raving captain. At last a daughter of the family came skipping up; her mirth annoyed me; she was like to die with laughing at the bedlam spectacle. I conjured her, for the sake of Heaven, to get a surgeon; and she, in her wild way, sprang down-stairs to fetch me one herself.

Returning to my wounded friend, I bound my handkerchief about his hand; and a neckerchief, that was hanging on the door, about his head. He was still bleeding copiously: he now grew pale, and seemed as if he were about to faint. There was none at hand to aid me: I very freely put my arm round him; patted his cheek, and tried to cheer him by little flatteries. It seemed to act on him like a spiritual remedy; he kept his senses, but sat as pale as death.

At last the active housewife arrived: it is easy to conceive her terror when she saw my friend in this predicament, lying in my arms, and both of us bestreamed with blood. No one had supposed he was wounded; all imagined I had carried him away in safety.

Now smelling-bottles, wine and everything that could support and stimulate were copiously produced. The surgeon also came; and I might easily have been dispensed with. Narciss, however, held me firmly by the hand; I would have stayed without holding. During the dressing of his wounds, I continued wetting his lips with wine; I minded not though all the company were now about us. The surgeon having finished, his patient took a mute but tender leave of me, and was conducted home.

The mistress of the house now led me to her bedroom: she had to strip me altogether; and I must confess, while they washed the blood from me, I saw with pleasure, for the first time, in a mirror, that I might be reckoned beautiful without help of dress. No portion of my clothes could be put on again; and as the people of the house were all either less or larger than myself, I was taken home in a strange disguise. My parents were, of course, astonished. They felt exceedingly indignant at my fright, at the wounds of their friend, at the captain's madness, at the whole occurrence. A very little would have made my father send the captain a challenge, that he might avenge his friend without delay. He blamed the gentlemen that had been there, because they had not punished on the spot such a murderous attempt; for it was but too clear, that the captain, instantly on striking, had drawn his sword, and wounded the other from behind. The cut across the hand had been given, just when Narciss himself was grasping at his sword. I felt unspeakably affected, altered; or, how shall I express it? The passion which was sleeping at the deepest bottom of my heart, had at once broken loose, like a flame getting air. And if joy and pleasure are well suited for the first producing and the silent nourishing of love, yet this passion, bold by nature, is most easily impelled by terror to decide and to declare itself. My mother gave her little flurried daughter some medicine, and made her go to bed. With the earliest morrow, my father hastened to Narciss, whom he found lying very sick of a wound-fever.

He told me little of what passed between them; but tried to quiet me about the probable results of this event. They were now considering whether an apology should be accepted, whether the affair should go before a court of justice, and many other points of that description. I knew my father too well to doubt that he would be averse to see the matter end without a duel: but I held my peace; for I had learned from him before, that women should not meddle in such things. For the rest, it did not strike me as if anything had passed between the friends, in which my interests were specially concerned: but my father soon communicated to my mother the purport of their farther conversation. Narciss, he said, appeared to be exceedingly affected at the help afforded by me; had embraced him, declared himself my debtor forever; signified that he desired no happiness except what he could share with me, and concluded by entreating that he might presume to ask my hand. All this mamma repeated to me, but subjoined the safe reflection, that "as for what was said in the first agitation of mind in such a case, there was little trust to be placed in it." "Of course, none," I answered, with affected coldness; though all the while I was feeling Heaven knows what.

Narciss continued sick for two months; owing to the wound in his right hand, he could not even write. Yet, in the mean time, he showed me his regard by the most obliging courtesies. All these unusual attentions I combined with what my mother had disclosed to me; and constantly my head was full of fancies. The whole city talked of the occurrence. With me they spoke of it in a peculiar tone; they drew inferences which, greatly as I struggled to avoid them, touched me very close. What had formerly been habitude and trifling, was now grown seriousness and inclination. The anxiety in which I lived was the more violent, the more carefully I studied to conceal it from every one. The idea of losing him frightened me; the possibility of any closer union made me tremble. For a half-prudent girl, there is really something awful in the thought of marriage.

By such incessant agitations, I was once more led to recollect myself. The gaudy imagery of a thoughtless life, which used to hover day and night before my eyes, was at once blown away. My soul again began to awaken: but the greatly interrupted intimacy with my Invisible Friend was not so easy to renew. We still continued at a frigid distance: it was again something; but little to the times of old.

A duel had been fought, and the captain severely wounded, before I ever heard of it. The public feeling was, in all senses, strong on the side of my lover, who at length again appeared upon the scene. But first of all, he came, with his head tied up and his arm in a sling, to visit us. How my heart beat while he was there! The whole family was present; general thanks and compliments were all that passed on either side; Narciss, however, found an opportunity to show some secret tokens of his love to me, by which means my inquietude was but increased. After his recovery, he visited us throughout the winter on the former footing; and in spite of all the soft private marks of tenderness which he contrived to give me, the whole affair remained unsettled, undiscussed.

In this manner was I kept in constant practice. I could trust my thoughts to no mortal; and from God I was too far removed. Him I had quite forgotten, those four wild years: I now again began to think of him occasionally; but our acquaintance had grown cool; they were visits of mere ceremony these; and as, moreover, in waiting on him, I used to dress in fine apparel, to set before him self-complacently my virtue, honour and superiorities to others, he did not seem to notice me, or know me in that finery.

A courtier would have been exceedingly distressed, if the prince who held his fortune in his hands had treated him in this way: but for me, I did not sorrow at it. I had what I required, health and conveniences: if God should please to think of me, well; if not, I reckoned I had done my duty.

This, in truth, I did not think at that period; yet it was the true figure of my soul. But, to change and purify my feelings, preparations were already made.

The spring came on: Narciss once visited me, unannounced, and at a time when I happened to be quite alone. He now appeared in the character of lover; and asked me if I could bestow on him my heart, and so soon as he should obtain some lucrative and honourable place, my hand along with it.

He had been received into our service: but at first they kept him back, and would not rapidly promote him, because they dreaded his ambition. Having some little fortune of his own, he was left with a slender salary.

Notwithstanding my regard for him, I knew that he was not a man to treat with altogether frankly. I drew up, therefore, and referred him to my father. About my father he did not seem to doubt; but wished first to be at one with me, now and here. I at last said, Yes; but stipulated as an indispensable condition that my parents should concur. He then spoke formally with both of them; they signified their satisfaction; mutual promises were given, on the faith of his advancement, which it was expected would be speedy. Sisters and aunts were informed of this arrangement, and the strictest secrecy enjoined on them.

Thus from a lover I had got a bridegroom. The difference between the two soon showed itself to be considerable. If one could change the lovers of all honourable maidens into bridegrooms, it would be a kindness to our sex, even though marriage should not follow the connexion. The love between two persons does not lessen by the change, but it becomes more reasonable. Innumerable little follies, all coquetries and caprices, disappear. If the bridegroom tells us, that we please him better in a morning-cap than in the finest head-dress, no discreet young woman will disturb herself about her hair-dressing; and nothing is more natural than that he too should think solidly, and rather wish to form a housewife for himself, than a gaudy doll for others. And thus it is in every province of the business.

Should a young woman, of this kind, be fortunate enough to have a bridegroom who possesses understanding and acquirements, she learns from him more than universities and foreign lands can teach. She not only willingly receives instruction when he offers it, but she endeavours to elicit more and more from him. Love makes much that was impossible possible. By degrees too, that subjection, so necessary and so graceful for the female sex, begins: the bridegroom does not govern like the husband; he only asks: but his mistress seeks to discover what he wants, and to offer it before he asks it.

So did experience teach me what I would not for much have missed. I was happy; truly happy, as woman could be in the world; that is to say, for a while.

Amid these quiet joys, a summer passed away. Narciss gave not the slightest reason to complain of him; he daily became more dear to me; my whole soul was his; this he well knew, and knew also how to prize it. Meanwhile, from seeming trifles, something rose, which by and by grew hurtful to our union.

Narciss behaved to me as to a bride, and never dared to ask of me such favours as were yet forbidden us. But, about the boundaries of virtue and decorum, we were of very different opinions. I meant to walk securely; and so never granted him the smallest freedom which the whole world might not have witnessed. He, used to dainties, thought this diet very strict. On this point there was continual variance: he praised my modesty, and sought to undermine my resolution.

The *serious* of my old French teacher now occurred to me, as well as the defence which I had once suggested in regard to it.

With God I had again become a little more acquainted. He had given me a bridegroom whom I loved; and for this I felt some thankfulness. Earthly love itself concentrated my soul, and put its powers in motion; nor did it contradict my intercourse with God. I naturally complained to him of what alarmed me: but I did not perceive that I myself was wishing and desiring it. In my own eyes I was strong; I did not pray: 'Lead us not into temptation!' My thoughts were far beyond temptation. In this flimsy tinsel-work of virtue I came to God; he did not drive me back. On the smallest movement towards him, he left a soft impression in my soul; and this impression caused me always to return.

Except Narciss, the world was altogether dead to me; excepting him, there was nothing in it that had any charm. Even my love for dress was but the wish to please him; if I knew that he was not to see me, I could spend no care upon it. I liked to dance; but if he was not beside me, it seemed as if I could not bear the motion. At a brilliant festival, if he was not invited, I could neither take the trouble of providing new things, nor of putting on the old according to the mode. To me they were alike agreeable, or rather, I might say, alike burdensome. I used to reckon such an evening very fairly spent, when I could join myself to any ancient card-party, though formerly I had not the smallest taste for such things; and if some old acquaintance came and rallied me about it, I would smile, perhaps for the first time all that night. So likewise it was with promenades, and every social entertainment that can be imagined:

> Him had I chosen from all others,
> His would I be, and not another's;
> To me his love was all in all.

Thus was I often solitary in the midst of company; and real solitude was generally acceptable to me. But my busy soul could neither sleep nor dream; I felt and thought; and acquired, by degrees, some faculty to speak about my feelings and my thoughts with God. Then were feelings of another sort unfolded; but these did not contradict the former feelings: my affection to Narciss accorded with the universal scheme of nature: it nowhere hindered the performance of a duty. They did not contradict each other, yet they were immensely different. Narciss was the only living form which hovered in my mind, and to which my love was all directed; but the other feeling was not directed towards any form, and yet it was unspeakably agreeable. I no longer have it, I no longer can impart it.

My lover, whom I used to trust with all my secrets, did not know of this. I soon discovered that he thought far otherwise: he often gave me writings which opposed, with light and heavy weapons, all that can be called connexion with the Invisible. I used to read the books, because they came from him; but at the end, I knew no word of all that had been argued in them.

Nor, in regard to sciences and knowledge, was there want of contradiction in our conduct. He did as all men do, he mocked at learned women; and yet he kept continually instructing me. He used to speak with me on all subjects, law excepted; and while constantly procuring books of every kind for me, he frequently repeated the uncertain precept, "That a lady ought to keep the knowledge she might have more secret than the Calvinist his creed in Catholic countries." And while I, by natural consequence, endeavoured not to show myself more wise or learned than formerly before the world, Narciss himself was commonly the first who yielded to the vanity of speaking about me and my superiorities.

A nobleman of high repute, and at that time valued for his influence, his talents and accomplishments, was living at our Court with great applause. He bestowed especial notice on Narciss, whom he kept continually about him. They once had an argument about the virtue of women. Narciss repeated to me what had passed between them; I was not wanting with my observations; and my friend required of me a written essay on the subject. I could write French fluently enough; I had laid a good foundation with my teacher. My correspondence with Narciss was likewise carried on in French: except in French books, there was then no elegant instruction to be had. My essay pleased the Count; I was obliged to let him have some little songs, which I had lately been composing. In short, Narciss appeared to revel without stint in the renown of his beloved: and the story, to his great contentment, ended with a French epistle in heroic verse, which the Count transmitted to him on departing; in which their argument was mentioned, and my friend reminded of his happiness in being destined, after all his doubts and errors, to learn most certainly what virtue was, in the arms of a virtuous and charming wife.

He showed this poem first of all to me, and then to almost every one; each thinking of the matter what he pleased. Thus did he act in several cases; every stranger, whom he valued, must be made acquainted in our house.

A noble family was staying for a season in the place, to profit by the skill of our physician. In this house too Narciss was looked on as a son: he introduced me there; we found among these worthy persons the most pleasant entertainment for mind and heart. Even the common pastimes of society appeared less empty here than elsewhere. All knew how matters stood with us: they treated us as circumstances would allow, and left the main relation unalluded to. I mention this one family, because in the after-period of my life it had a powerful influence upon me.

Almost a year of our connexion had elapsed; and along with it, our spring was over. The summer came, and all grew drier and more earnest.

By several unexpected deaths, some offices fell vacant which Narciss might make pretensions to. The instant was at hand, when my whole destiny must be decided; and while Narciss, and all our friends, were making every effort to efface some impressions which obstructed him at Court, and to obtain for him the wished-for situation, I turned with my request to my Invisible Friend. I was received so kindly, that I gladly came again. I confessed, without disguise, my wish that Narciss might obtain the place: but my prayer was not importunate; and I did not require that it should happen for the sake of my petition.

The place was obtained by a far inferior competitor. I was

dreadfully troubled at this news; I hastened to my room, the door of which I locked behind me. The first fit of grief went off in a shower of tears; the next thought was, "Yet it was not by chance that it happened;" and instantly I formed the resolution to be well content with it, seeing even this apparent evil would be for my true advantage. The softest emotions then pressed in upon me, and divided all the clouds of sorrow. I felt that, with help like this, there was nothing one might not endure. At dinner I appeared quite cheerful, to the great astonishment of all the house.

Narciss had less internal force than I, and I was called upon to comfort him. In his family, too, he had many crosses to encounter, some of which afflicted him considerably; and, such true confidence subsisting between us, he intrusted me with all. His negotiations for entering on foreign service were not more fortunate; all this I felt deeply on his account and mine; all this too I ultimately carried to the place where my petitions had already been so well received.

The softer these experiences were, the oftener did I endeavour to renew them; I hoped continually to meet with comfort where I had so often met with it. Yet I did not always meet with it: I was as one that goes to warm him in the sunshine, while there is something standing in the way that makes a shadow. "What is this?" I asked myself. I traced the matter zealously, and soon perceived that it all depended on the situation of my soul: if this was not turned in the straightest direction towards God, I still continued cold; I did not feel his counter-influence; I could obtain no answer. The second question was: "What hinders this direction?" Here I was in a wide field; I perplexed myself in an inquiry, which lasted nearly all the second year of my attachment to Narciss. I might have ended the investigation sooner; for it was not long till I had got upon the proper trace; but I would not confess it, and I sought a thousand outlets.

I very soon discovered that the straight direction of my soul was marred by foolish dissipations, and employment with unworthy things. The How and the Where were clear enough to me. Yet by what means could I help myself, or extricate my mind from the calls of a world where everything was either cold indifference or hot insanity? Gladly would I have left things standing as they were, and lived from day to day, floating down with the stream, like other people whom I saw quite happy; but I durst not; my inmost feelings contradicted me too often. Yet if I determined to renounce society, and alter my relations to others, it was not in my power. I was hemmed in as by a ring drawn round me; certain connexions I could not dissolve; and, in the matter which lay nearest to my heart, fatalities accumulated and oppressed me more and more. I often went to bed with tears; and, after a sleepless night, arose again with tears: I required some strong support; and God would not vouchsafe it me, while I was running with the cap and bells.

I proceeded now to estimate my doings, all and each; dancing and play were first put upon their trial. Never was there anything spoken, thought or written for or against these practices, which I did not examine, talk of, read, weigh, reject, aggravate, and plague myself about. If I gave up these habits, I was certain that Narciss would be offended; for he dreaded exceedingly the ridicule which any look of straightlaced conscientiousness gives one in the eyes of the world. And doing what I now looked upon as folly, noxious folly, out of no taste of my own, but merely to gratify him, it all grew wofully irksome to me.

Without disagreeable prolixities and repetitions, it is not in my power to represent what pains I took, in trying so to counteract those occupations which distracted my attention and disturbed my peace of mind, that my heart, in spite of them, might still be open to the influences of the Invisible Being. But at last, with pain, I was compelled to admit, that in this way the quarrel could not be composed. For no sooner had I clothed myself in the garment of folly, than it came to be something more than a mask, than the foolishness pierced and penetrated me through and through.

May I here overstep the province of a mere historical detail, and offer one or two remarks on what was then taking place within me? What could it be which so changed my tastes and feelings, that, in my twenty-second year, nay earlier, I lost all relish for the recreations with which people of that age are harmlessly delighted? Why were they not harmless for me? I may answer, Just because they were not harmless; because I was not, like others of my years, unacquainted with my soul. No! I knew, from experiences which had reached me unsought, that there are loftier emotions, which afford us a contentment such as it is vain to seek in the amusements of the world; and that, in these higher joys, there is also kept a secret treasure for strengthening the spirit in misfortune.

But the pleasures of society, the dissipations of youth, must needs have had a powerful charm for me, since it was not in my power to engage in them without participation, to act among them as if they were not there. How many things could I now do, if I liked, with entire coldness, which then dazzled and confounded me, nay threatened to obtain the mastery over me! Here there could no medium be observed: either those delicious amusements, or my nourishing and quickening internal emotions, must be given up.

But in my soul, the strife had, without my own consciousness, already been decided. Even if there still was anything within me that longed for earthly pleasures, I had now become unfitted for enjoying them. Much as a man might hanker after wine, all desire of drinking would forsake him, if he should be placed among full barrels in a cellar, where the foul air was like to suffocate him. Free air is more than wine: this I felt but too keenly; and from the first, it would have cost me little studying to prefer the good to the delightful, if the fear of losing the affection of Narciss had not restrained me. But at last, when after many thousand struggles, and thoughts continually renewed, I began to cast a steady eye upon the bond which held me to him, I discovered that it was but weak, that it might be torn asunder. I at once perceived it to be only as a glass bell, which shut me up in the exhausted airless space: One bold stroke to break the bell in pieces, and thou art delivered!

No sooner thought than tried. I drew off the mask, and on all occasions acted as my heart directed. Narciss I still cordially loved: but the thermometer, which formerly had stood in hot water, was now hanging in the natural air; it could rise no higher than the warmth of the atmosphere directed.

Unhappily it cooled very much. Narciss drew back, and began to assume a distant air: this was at his option; but my thermometer descended as he drew back. Our family observed this; questioned me, and seemed to be surprised. I explained to them with stout defiance, that heretofore I had made abundant sacrifices; that I was ready, still farther and to the end of my life, to share all crosses that befell him; but that I required full freedom in my conduct, that my doings and avoidings must depend upon my own conviction; that indeed I would never bigotedly cleave to my own opinion, but on the other hand would willingly be reasoned with; yet, as it concerned my own happiness, the decision must proceed from myself, and be liable to no manner of constraint. The greatest physician could not move me by his reasonings to take an article of food, which perhaps was altogether wholesome and agreeable to many, so soon as my experience had shown that on all occasions it was noxious to me; as I might produce coffee for an instance: and just as little, nay still less, would I have any sort of conduct which misled me, preached up and demonstrated upon me as morally profitable.

Having so long prepared myself in silence, these debates were rather pleasant than vexatious to me. I gave vent to my soul; I felt the whole worth of my determination. I yielded not a hairsbreadth; and those to whom I owed no filial respect were sharply handled and despatched. In the family I soon prevailed. My mother from her youth had entertained these sentiments, though in her they had never reached maturity; for no necessity had pressed upon her, and exalted her courage to achieve her purpose. She rejoiced in beholding her silent wishes fulfilled through me. My younger sisters seemed to join themselves with me; the second was attentive and quiet. Our aunt had the most to object. The arguments which she employed appeared to her irrefragable; and they were irrefragable, being altogether commonplace. At last I was obliged to show her, that she had no voice in the affair in any sense; and after this, she seldom signified that she persisted in her views. She was indeed the only person that observed this transaction close at hand, without in some degree experiencing its influence. I do not calumniate her, when I say that she had no character, and the most limited ideas.

My father had acted altogether in his own way. He spoke not much, but often, with me on the matter: his arguments were rational; and being *his* arguments, they could not be impugned. It was only the deep feeling of my right that gave me strength to dispute against him. But the scenes soon changed; I was forced to make appeal to his heart. Straitened by his understanding, I came out with the most pathetic pleadings. I gave free course to my tongue and to my tears. I showed him how much I loved Narciss; how much constraint I had for two years been enduring; how certain I was of being in the right; that I was ready to testify that certainty, by the loss of my beloved bridegroom and prospective happiness; nay, if it were necessary, by the loss of all that I possessed on earth; that I would rather leave my native country, my parents and my friends, and beg my bread in foreign lands, than act against these dictates of my conscience. He concealed his emotion; he said nothing on the subject for a while, and at last he openly declared in my favour.

During all this time Narciss forbore to visit us; and my father now gave up the weekly club, where he was used to meet him. The business made a noise at court, and in the town. People talked about it, as is common in such cases, which the public takes a vehement interest in, because its sentence has usurped an influence on the resolutions of weak minds. I knew enough about the world to understand that one's conduct is often censured by the very persons who would have advised it, had one consulted them: and independently of this, with my internal composure, I should have looked on all such transitory speculations just as if they had not been.

On the other hand, I hindered not myself from yielding to my inclination for Narciss. To me he had become invisible, and to him my feelings had not altered. I loved him tenderly; as it were anew, and much more steadfastly than before. If he chose to leave my conscience undisturbed, then I was his: wanting this condition, I would have refused a kingdom with him. For several months, I bore these feelings and these thoughts about with me; and finding, at last, that I was calm and strong enough to go peacefully and firmly to work, I wrote him a polite but not a tender note, inquiring why he never came to see me.

As I knew his manner of avoiding to explain himself in little matters, but of silently doing what seemed good to him, I purposely urged him in the present instance. I got a long and, as it seemed to me, pitiful reply, in vague style and unmeaning phrases, stating, that without a better place, he could not fix himself, and offer me his hand; that I best knew how hard it had fared with him hitherto; that as he was afraid lest a fruitless intercourse, so long continued, might prove hurtful to my reputation, I would give him leave to continue at his present distance; so soon as it was in his power to make me happy, he would look upon the word which he had given me as sacred.

I answered him on the spot, that as our intercourse was known to all the world, it might perhaps be rather late to spare my reputation; for which, at any rate, my conscience and my innocence were the surest pledges: however, that I hereby freely gave him back his word, and hoped the change would prove a happy one for him. The same hour I received a short reply, which was, in all essential particulars, entirely synonymous with the first. He adhered to his former statement, that so soon as he obtained a situation, he would ask me, if I pleased to share his fortune with him.

This I interpreted as meaning simply nothing. I signified to my relations and acquaintances, that the affair was altogether settled; and it was so in fact. Having, nine months afterwards, obtained the much-desired preferment, he offered me his hand; but under the condition, that as the wife of a man who must keep house like other people, I should alter my opinions. I returned him many thanks: and hastened with my heart and mind away from this transaction; as one hastens from the playhouse when the curtain falls. And as he, a short time afterwards, had found a rich and advantageous match, a thing now easy for him;

and as I now knew him to be happy in the way he liked, my own tranquillity was quite complete.

I must not pass in silence the fact, that several times before he got a place, and after it, there were respectable proposals made to me; which, however, I declined without the smallest hesitation, much as my father and my mother could have wished for more compliance on my part.

At length, after a stormy March and April, the loveliest May weather seemed to be allotted me. With good health, I enjoyed an indescribable composure of mind: look around me as I pleased, my loss appeared a gain to me. Young and full of sensibility, I thought the universe a thousand times more beautiful than formerly, when I required to have society and play, that in the fair garden tedium might not overtake me. And now, as I did not conceal my piety, I likewise took heart to own my love for the sciences and arts. I drew, painted, read; and found enow of people to support me: instead of the great world, which I had left, or rather which had left me, a smaller one formed itself about me, which was infinitely richer and more entertaining. I had a turn for social life; and I do not deny that, on giving up my old acquaintances, I trembled at the thought of solitude. I now found myself abundantly, perhaps excessively, indemnified. My acquaintances ere long were very numerous; not at home only, but likewise among people at a distance. My story had been noised abroad; and many persons felt a curiosity to see the woman who had valued God above her bridegroom. There was a certain pious tone to be observed, at that time, generally over Germany. In the families of several counts and princes, a care for the welfare of the soul had been awakened. Nor were there wanting noblemen who showed a like attention; while in the inferior classes, sentiments of this kind were diffused on every side.

The noble family, whom I mentioned above, now drew me nearer to them. They had, in the mean while, gathered strength; several of their relations having settled in the town. These estimable persons courted my familiarity, as I did theirs. They had high connexions; I became acquainted, in their house, with a great part of the princes, counts and lords of the Empire. My sentiments were not concealed from any one; they might be honoured or be tolerated; I obtained my object, none attacked me.

There was yet another way, by which I was again led back into the world. About this period, a step-brother of my father, who till now had never visited the house except in passing, stayed with us for a considerable time. He had left the service of his court, where he enjoyed great influence and honour, simply because all matters were not managed quite according to his mind. His intellect was just, his character was rigid. In these points he was very like my father; only the latter had withal a certain touch of softness, which enabled him with greater ease to yield a little in affairs, and though not to do, yet to permit, some things against his own conviction; and then to evaporate his anger at them, either in silence by himself, or in confidence amid his family. My uncle was a great deal younger; and his independence of spirit had been favoured by his outward circumstances. His mother had been very rich; and he still had large possessions to expect from her near and distant relatives; so he needed no foreign increase; whereas my father, with his moderate fortune, was bound to his place by the consideration of his salary.

My uncle had become still more unbending from domestic sufferings. He had early lost an amiable wife and a hopeful son; and from that time he appeared to wish to push away from him everything that did not hang upon his individual will.

In our family it was whispered now and then with some complacency, that probably he would not wed again, and so we children might anticipate inheriting his fortune. I paid small regard to this: but the demeanour of the rest was not a little modified by their hopes. In his own imperturbable firmness of character, my uncle had grown into the habit of never contradicting any one in conversation. On the other hand, he listened with a friendly air to every one's opinion; and would himself elucidate and strengthen it by instances and reasons of his own. All who did not know him fancied that he thought as they did: for he was possessed of a preponderating intellect, and could transport himself into the mental state of any man, and imitate his manner of conceiving. With me he did not prosper quite so well: for here the question was about emotions, of which he had not any glimpse; and with whatever tolerance, and sympathy, and rationality, he spoke about my sentiments, it was palpable to me that he had not the slightest notion of what formed the ground of all my conduct.

With all his secrecy, we by and by found out the aim of his unusual stay with us. He had, as we at length discovered, cast his eyes upon our youngest sister, with the view of giving her in marriage, and rendering her happy as he pleased: and certainly, considering her personal and mental attractions, particularly when a handsome fortune was laid into the scale along with them, she might pretend to the first matches. His feelings towards me he likewise showed us pantomimically, by procuring me a post of Canoness, the income of which I very soon began to draw.

My sister was not so contented with his care as I. She now

disclosed to me a tender secret, which hitherto she had very wisely kept back; fearing, as in truth it happened, that I would by all means counsel her against connexion with a man who was not suited to her. I did my utmost, and succeeded. The purpose of my uncle was too serious and too distinct; the prospect for my sister, with her worldly views, was too delightful, to be thwarted by a passion which her own understanding disapproved: she mustered force to give it up.

On her ceasing to resist the gentle guidance of my uncle, the foundation of his plan was quickly laid. She was appointed Maid of Honour at a neighbouring court, where he could commit her to the oversight and the instructions of a lady, his friend, who presided there as Governess, with great applause. I accompanied her to the place of her new abode. Both of us had reason to be satisfied with the reception we met with: and frequently I could not help, in secret, smiling at the character, which now as Canoness, as young and pious Canoness, I was enacting in the world.

In earlier times, a situation such as this would have confused me dreadfully; perhaps have turned my head: but now, in midst of all the splendours that surrounded me, I felt extremely cool. With great quietness, I let them frizzle me, and deck me out for hours; and thought no more of it than that my place required me to wear that gala livery. In the thronged saloons, I spoke with all and each, though no shape or character among them made any impression on me. On returning to my house, nearly all the feeling I brought back with me was that of tired limbs. Yet my understanding drew advantage from the multitude of persons whom I saw; and I became acquainted with some ladies, patterns of every virtue, of a noble and good demeanour; particularly with the Governess, under whom my sister was to have the happiness of being formed.

At my return, however, the consequences of this journey, in regard to health, were found to be less favourable. With the greatest temperance, the strictest diet, I had not been, as I used to be, completely mistress of my time and strength. Food, motion, rising and going to sleep, dressing and visiting, had not depended, as at home, on my own conveniency and will. In the circle of social life, you cannot stop without a breach of courtesy: all that was needful I had willingly performed; because I looked upon it as my duty, because I knew that it would soon be over, and because I felt myself completely healthy. Yet this unusual restless life must have had more effect upon me than I was aware of. Scarcely had I reached home, and cheered my parents with a comfortable narrative, when I was attacked by a hemorrhage, which, although it did not prove dangerous or lasting, yet left a weakness after it, perceptible for many a day.

Here, then, I had another lesson to repeat. I did it joyfully. Nothing bound me to the world; and I was convinced that here the true good was never to be found: so I waited in the cheerfullest and meekest state; and after having abdicated life, I was retained in it.

A new trial was awaiting me: my mother took a painful and oppressive ailment, which she had to bear five years, before she paid the debt of nature. All this time we were sharply proved. Often, when her terror grew too strong, she would have us all summoned, in the night, to her bed, that so at least she might be busied, if not bettered, by our presence. The load grew heavier, nay scarcely to be borne, when my father too became unwell. From his youth, he had frequently had violent headaches; which, however, at longest never used to last beyond six-and-thirty hours. But now they were continual; and when they mounted to a high degree of pain, his moanings tore my very heart. It was in these tempestuous seasons that I chiefly felt my bodily weakness; because it kept me from my holiest and dearest duties, or rendered the performance of them hard to an extreme degree.

It was now that I could try whether the path, which I had chosen, was the path of phantasy or truth; whether I had merely thought as others showed me, or the object of my trust had a reality. To my unspeakable support, I always found the latter. The straight direction of my heart to God, the fellowship of the "Beloved Ones"[1] I had sought and found; and this was what made all things light to me. As a traveller in the dark, my soul, when all was pressing on me from without, hastened to the place of refuge, and never did it return empty.

In later times, some champions of religion, who seem to be animated more by zeal than feeling for it, have required of their brethren to produce examples of prayers actually heard; apparently as wishing to have seal and signature, that so they might proceed juridically in the matter. How unknown must the true feeling be to these persons; how few real experiences can they themselves have made!

I can say that I never returned empty, when in straits and oppression I called on God. This is saying infinitely much; more I must not and cannot say. Important as each experience was at the critical moment for myself, the recital of them would be flat, improbable and insignificant, were I to specify the separate cases. Happy was I, that a thousand little incidents in combination

[1] So in the original.—ED.

proved, as clearly as the drawing of my breath proved me to be living, that I was not without God in the world. He was near to me, I was before him. This is what, with a diligent avoidance of all theological systematic terms, I can with the greatest truth declare.

Much do I wish that, in those times too, I had been entirely without system. But which of us arrives early at the happiness of being conscious of his individual self, in its own pure combination, without extraneous forms? I was in earnest with religion. I timidly trusted in the judgments of others; I entirely gave in to the Hallean system of conversion; but my nature would by no means tally with it.

According to this scheme of doctrine, the alteration of the heart must begin with a deep terror on account of sin; the heart in this agony must recognise, in a less or greater degree, the punishment which it has merited, must get a foretaste of Hell, and so embitter the delight of sin. At last it feels a very palpable assurance of grace; which, however, in its progress often fades away, and must again be sought with earnest prayer.

Of all this no jot or tittle happened with me. When I sought God sincerely, he let himself be found of me, and did not reproach me about bygone things. On looking back, I saw well enough where I had been unworthy, where I still was so; but the confession of my faults was altogether without terror. Not for a moment did the fear of Hell occur to me: nay the very notion of a wicked Spirit, and a place of punishment and torment after death, could nowise gain admission into the circle of my thoughts. I considered the men who lived without God, whose hearts were shut against the trust in and the love of the Invisible, as already so unhappy that a Hell and external pains appeared to promise rather an alleviation than an increase of their misery. I had but to look upon the persons, in this world, who in their breasts gave scope to hateful feelings; who hardened their hearts against the Good of whatever kind, and strove to force the Evil on themselves and others; who shut their eyes by day, that so they might deny the shining of the sun: How unutterably wretched did these persons seem to me! Who could have formed a Hell to make their situation worse?

This mood of mind continued in me, without change, for half a score of years. It maintained itself through many trials; even at the moving death-bed of my beloved mother. I was frank enough, on this occasion, not to hide my comfortable frame of mind from certain pious but rigorously orthodox people; and I had to suffer many a friendly admonition on that score. They reckoned they were just in season, for explaining with what earnestness one should be diligent to lay a right foundation in the days of health and youth.

In earnestness I too determined not to fail. For the moment, I allowed myself to be convinced; and fain would I have grown, for life, distressed and full of fears. But what was my surprise on finding that I absolutely could not. When I thought of God, I was cheerful and contented: even at the painful end of my dear mother, I did not shudder at the thought of death. Yet I learned many and far other things than my uncalled teachers thought of, in these solemn hours.

By degrees, I grew to doubt the dictates of so many famous people, and retained my own sentiments in silence. A certain lady of my friends, to whom I had at first disclosed too much, insisted always on interfering with my business. Of her too I was obliged to rid myself; I at last firmly told her, that she might spare herself this labour, as I did not need her counsel; that I knew my God, and would have no guide but him. She was greatly offended; I believe she never quite forgave me.

Such determination, to withdraw from the advices and the influence of my friends, in spiritual matters, produced the consequence, that also in my temporal affairs I gained sufficient courage to obey my own persuasions. But for the assistance of my faithful invisible Leader, I could not have prospered here. I am still gratefully astonished at his wise and happy guidance. No one knew how matters stood with me; even I myself did not know.

The thing, the wicked and inexplicable thing, which separates us from the Being to whom we owe our life, and in whom all that deserves the name of life must find its nourishment; the thing which we call Sin, I yet knew nothing of.

In my intercourse with my invisible Friend, I felt the sweetest enjoyment of all my powers. My desire of constantly enjoying this felicity was so predominant, that I abandoned without hesitation whatever marred our intercourse; and here experience was my best teacher. But it was with me as with sick persons, who have no medicine, and try to help themselves by diet. Something is accomplished, but far from enough.

I could not always live in solitude; though in it I found the best preservative against the dissipation of my thoughts. On returning to the tumult, the impression it produced upon me was the deeper for my previous loneliness. My most peculiar advantage lay in this, that love for quiet was my ruling passion, and that in the end I still drew back to it. I perceived, as in a kind of twilight, my weakness and my misery; and tried to save myself by avoiding danger and exposure.

For seven years, I had used my dietetic scheme. I held myself not wicked, and I thought my state desirable. But for some peculiar circumstances and occurrences, I had remained in this position: it was by a curious path that I got farther. Contrary to the advice of all my friends, I entered on a new connexion. Their objections, at first, made me pause. I turned to my invisible Leader, and, as he permitted me, I went forward without fear.

A man of spirit, heart and talents had bought a property beside us. Among the strangers whom I grew acquainted with, were this person and his family. In our manners, domestic economy and habits we accorded well; and thus we soon approximated to each other.

Philo, as I propose to call him, was already middle-aged: in certain matters he was highly serviceable to my father, whose strength was now decaying. He soon became the friend of the family; and finding in me, as he was pleased to say, a person free alike from the extravagance and emptiness of the great world, and from the narrowness and aridness of the still world in the country, he courted intimacy with me, and ere long we were in one another's confidence. To me he was very pleasing and useful.

Though I did not feel the smallest inclination or capacity for mingling in public business, or seeking any influence on it, yet I liked to hear about such matters, liked to know whatever happened far and near. Of worldly things, I loved to get a clear though unconcerned perception: feeling, sympathy, affection, I reserved for God, for my people and my friends.

The latter were, if I may say so, jealous of Philo, in my new connexion with him. In more than one sense, they were right in warning me about it. I suffered much in secret; for even I could not consider their remonstrances as altogether empty or selfish. I had been accustomed, from of old, to give a reason for my views and conduct; but in this case my conviction would not follow. I prayed to God, that here as elsewhere he would warn, restrain and guide me; and as my heart on this did not dissuade me, I went forward on my way with comfort.

Philo, on the whole, had a remote resemblance to Narciss; only a pious education had more enlivened and concentrated his feelings. He had less vanity, more character; and, in business, if Narciss was delicate, exact, persevering, indefatigable, the other was clear, sharp, quick and capable of working with incredible ease. By means of him, I learned the secret history of almost every noble personage with whose exterior I had got acquainted in society. It was pleasant for me to behold the tumult, off my watch-tower, from afar. Philo could now hide nothing from me:

he confided to me, by degrees, his own concerns both inward and outward. I was in fear because of him; for I foresaw certain circumstances and entanglements; and the mischief came more speedily than I had looked for. There were some confessions he had still kept back; and even at last he told me only what enabled me to guess the worst.

What an effect had this upon my heart! I attained experiences which to me were altogether new. With infinite sorrow, I beheld an Agathon, who, educated in the groves of Delphi, still owed his school-fees, which he was now obliged to pay with their accumulated interest; and this Agathon was my especial friend. My sympathy was lively and complete; I suffered with him; both of us were in the strangest state.

After having long occupied myself with the temper of his mind, I at last turned round to contemplate my own. The thought, ' Thou art no better than he,' rose like a little cloud before me, and gradually expanded till it darkened all my soul.

I now not only thought myself no better than he; I felt this, and felt it as I should not wish to do again. Nor was it any transitory mood. For more than a year, I was compelled to feel that, had not an unseen hand restrained me, I might have become a Girard, a Cartouche, a Damiens, or any wretch you can imagine. The tendencies to this I traced too clearly in my heart. Heavens, what a discovery!

If hitherto I had never been able, in the faintest degree, to recognise in myself the reality of sin by experience, its possibility was now become apparent to me by anticipation, in the frightfullest manner. And yet I knew not evil; I but feared it: I felt that I might be guilty, and could not accuse myself of being so.

Deeply as I was convinced that such a temperament of soul, as I now saw mine to be, could never be adapted for that union with the invisible Being, which I hoped for after death; I did not, in the smallest, fear that I should finally be separated from him. With all the wickedness which I discovered in my heart, I still loved *Him*; I hated what I felt, nay wished to hate it still more earnestly; my whole desire was to be delivered from this sickness, and this tendency to sickness; and I was persuaded that the great Physician would at length vouchsafe his help.

The sole question was: What medicine will cure this malady? The practice of virtue? This I could not for a moment think. For ten years, I had already practised more than mere virtue; and the horrors now first-discovered had, all the while, lain hidden at the bottom of my soul. Might they not have broken out with me, as they did with David when he looked on Bathsheba? Yet was not he a friend of God; and was not I assured in my inmost heart that God was my friend?

Was it then an unavoidable infirmity of human nature? Must we just content ourselves in feeling and acknowledging the sovereignty of inclination? And, with the best will, is there nothing left for us but to abhor the fault we have committed, and on the like occasion to commit it again?

From systems of morality I could obtain no comfort. Neither their severity, by which they try to bend our inclinations, nor their attractiveness, by which they try to place our inclinations on the side of virtue, gave me any satisfaction. The fundamental notions, which I had imbibed from intercourse with my invisible Friend, were of far higher value to me.

Once, while I was studying the songs composed by David after that tremendous fall, it struck me very much that he traced his indwelling corruption even in the substance out of which he had been shaped; yet that he wished to be freed from sin, and that he earnestly entreated for a pure heart.

But how was this to be attained? The answer from Scripture I was well aware of; 'that the blood of Jesus cleanseth us from all sin,' was a Bible truth which I had long known. But now for the first time, I observed that as yet I had never understood this oft-repeated saying. The questions: What does it mean? How is it to be? were day and night working out their answers in me. At last I thought I saw, as by a gleam of light, that what I sought was to be found in the incarnation of the everlasting Word, by whom all things, even we ourselves, were made. That the Eternal descended as an inhabitant to the depths in which we dwell, which he surveys and comprehends; that he passed through our lot from stage to stage, from conception and birth to the grave; that by this marvellous circuit he again mounted to those shining Heights, whither we too must rise in order to be happy: all this was revealed to me, as in a dawning remoteness.

Oh! why must we, in speaking of such things, make use of figures, which can only indicate external situations! Where is there in his eyes aught high or deep, aught dark or clear? It is we only that have an Under and Upper, a night and day. And even for this did he become like us, since otherwise we could have had no part in him.

But how shall we obtain a share in this priceless benefit? 'By faith,' the Scripture says. And what is faith? To consider the account of an event as true, what help can this afford me? I must be enabled to appropriate its effects, its consequences. This appropriating faith must be a state of mind peculiar, and to the natural man unknown.

'Now, gracious Father, grant me faith!' so prayed I once, in the deepest heaviness of heart. I was leaning on a little table, where I sat; my tear-stained countenance was hidden in my hands. I was now in the condition in which we seldom are, but in which we are required to be, if God is to regard our prayers.

O, that I could but paint what I felt then! A sudden force drew my soul to the cross where Jesus once expired: it was a sudden force, a pull, I cannot name it otherwise, such as leads our soul to an absent loved one; an approximation, which perhaps is far more real and true than we imagine. So did my soul approach the Son of Man, who died upon the cross; and that instant did I know what faith was.

'This is faith!' said I; and started up as if half frightened. I now endeavoured to get certain of my feeling, of my view; and shortly I became convinced that my soul had acquired a power of soaring upwards, which was altogether new to it.

Words fail us in describing such emotions. I could most distinctly separate them from all phantasy: they were entirely without phantasy, without image; yet they gave us just such certainty of their referring to some object, as our imagination gives us when it paints the features of an absent lover.

When the first rapture was over, I observed that my present condition of mind had formerly been known to me; only I had never felt it in such strength; I had never held it fast, never made it mine. I believe, indeed, every human soul at intervals feels something of it. Doubtless it is this which teaches every mortal that there is a God.

With such faculty, wont from of old to visit me now and then, I had hitherto been well content; and had not, by a singular arrangement of events, that unexpected sorrow weighed upon me for a twelvemonth; had not my own ability and strength, on that occasion, altogether lost credit with me; I perhaps might have remained content with such a state of matters all my days.

But now, since that great moment, I had as it were got wings. I could mount aloft above what used to threaten me; as the bird can fly singing and with ease across the fiercest stream, while the little dog stands anxiously baying on the bank.

My joy was indescribable; and though I did not mention it to any one, my people soon observed an unaccustomed cheerfulness in me, and could not understand the reason of my joy. Had I but forever held my peace, and tried to nourish this serene temper in my soul! Had I not allowed myself to be misled by circumstances, so as to reveal my secret! I might then have been saved, once more, a long and tedious circuit.

As in the previous ten years of my Christian course, this necessary force had not existed in my soul, I had just been in the case of other worthy people; had helped myself by keeping my fancy always full of images, which had some reference to God: a practice so far truly useful; for noxious images and their baneful consequences are by that means kept away. Often too our spirit seizes one or other of these spiritual images, and mounts with it a little way upwards; like a young bird fluttering from twig to twig.

Images and impressions pointing towards God are presented to us by the institutions of the Church, by organs, bells, singing, and particularly by the preaching of our pastors. Of these I used to be unspeakably desirous: no weather, no bodily weakness could keep me from church; the sound of the Sunday bells was the only thing that rendered me impatient on a sick-bed. Our head Court-chaplain, a gifted man, I heard with great pleasure; his colleagues too I liked; and I could pick the golden apple of the word from the common fruit, with which on earthen platters it was mingled. With public ordinances, all sorts of private exercises were combined; and these too only nourished fancy and a finer kind of sense. I was so accustomed to this track, I reverenced it so much, that even now no higher one occurred to me. For my soul has only feelers, and not eyes; it gropes, but does not see: Ah! that it could get eyes and look!

Now again, therefore, I went with a longing mind to sermon: but alas, what happened! I no longer found what I was wont to find. These preachers were blunting their teeth on the shell, while I enjoyed the kernel. I soon grew weary of them; and I had already been so spoiled, that I could not be content with the little they afforded me. I required images, I wanted impressions from without; and reckoned it a pure spiritual desire that I felt.

Philo's parents had been in connexion with the Herrnhuther Community: in his library were many writings of Count Zinzendorf's. He had spoken with me, more than once, very candidly and clearly on the subject; inviting me to turn over one or two of these treatises, if it were but for the sake of studying a psychological phenomenon. I looked upon the Count, and those that followed him, as very heterodox: and so the Ebersdorf Hymn-book, which my friend had pressed upon me, lay unread.

However, in this total destitution of external excitements for my soul, I opened the Hymn-book, as it were by chance; and found in it, to my astonishment, some songs which actually, though under a fantastic form, appeared to shadow what I felt. The originality and simplicity of their expression drew me on. It seemed to be peculiar emotions expressed in a peculiar way; no school technology suggested any notion of formality or commonplace. I was persuaded that these people felt as I did: I was very happy to lay hold of here and there a stanza in their songs, to fix it in my memory, and carry it about with me for days.

Since the moment when the truth had been revealed to me, some three months had in this way passed on. At last I came to the resolution of disclosing everything to Philo, and asking him to let me have those writings, about which I had now become immoderately curious. Accordingly I did so, notwithstanding there was something in my heart which earnestly dissuaded me

I circumstantially related to him all the story; and, as he was himself a leading person in it, and my narrative conveyed the sharpest reprimand on him, he felt surprised and moved to an extreme degree. He melted into tears. I rejoiced; believing that, in his mind also, a full and fundamental change had taken place.

He provided me with all the writings I could require; and now I had excess of nourishment for my imagination. I made rapid progress in the Zinzendorfic mode of thought and speech. And be it not supposed that I am yet incapable of prizing the peculiar turn and manner of the Count. I willingly do him justice; he is no empty phantast; he speaks of mighty truths, and mostly in a bold figurative style; the people who despise him know not either how to value or discriminate his qualities.

At that time, I became exceedingly attached to him. Had I been mistress of myself, I would certainly have left my friends and country, and gone to join him. We should infallibly have understood each other, and should hardly have agreed together long.

Thanks to my better genius that now kept me so confined by my domestic duties. I reckoned it a distant journey if I visited the garden. The charge of my aged weakly father afforded me employment enough, and in hours of recreation, I had Fancy to procure me pastime. The only mortal whom I saw was Philo; he was highly valued by my father; but with me, his intimacy had been cooled a little by the late explanation. Its influence on him had not penetrated deep; and as some attempts to talk in my dialect had not succeeded with him, he avoided touching on this subject; and the rather, as his extensive knowledge put it always in his power to introduce new topics in his conversation.

I was thus a Herrnhuth sister on my own footing. I had especially to hide this new turn of my temper and my inclinations from the head Court-chaplain; whom, as my father confessor, I had much cause to honour; and whose high merits his extreme aversion to the Herrnhuth Community did not diminish, in my eyes, even then. Unhappily this worthy person had to suffer many troubles on account of me and others.

Several years ago, he had become acquainted with an upright pious gentleman, residing in a distant quarter; and had long continued in unbroken correspondence with him, as with one who truly sought God. How painful was it with the spiritual leader, when this gentleman subsequently joined himself to the Community of Herrnhuth, where he lived for a long while! How delightful, on the other hand, when at length he quarrelled with the Brethren; determined to settle in our neighbourhood; and seemed once more to yield himself completely to the guidance of his ancient friend!

The stranger was presented, as in triumph, by the upper Pastor to all the chosen lambs of his fold. To our house alone he was not introduced, because my father did not now see company. The gentleman obtained no little approbation: he combined the polish of the court with the winning manner of the Brethren; and having also many fine qualities by nature, he soon became the favourite saint with all who knew him; a result at which the chaplain was exceedingly contented. But, alas! it was merely in externals that the gentleman had split with the Community; in his heart he was yet entirely a Herrnhuther. He was, in truth, concerned for the reality of the matter: but yet the gimcracks which the Counnt had stuck round it were, at the same time, quite adapted to his taste. Besides, he had now become accustomed to this mode of speaking and conceiving; and if he had to hide it carefully from his old friend, the gladder was he, in any knot of trusty persons, to come forth with his couplets, litanies and little figures; in which, as might have been supposed, he met with great applause.

I knew nothing of the whole affair, and wandered quietly along in my separate path. For a good while we continued mutally unknown.

Once, in a leisure hour, I happened to visit a lady who was sick. I found several acquaintances with her; and soon perceived that my appearance had cut short their conversation. I affected not to notice anything; but saw ere long, with great surprise, some Herrnhuth figures stuck upon the wall in elegant frames. Quickly comprehending what had passed before my entrance, I expressed my pleasure at the sight, in a few suitable verses.

Conceive the wonder of my friends! We explained ourselves; instantly we were agreed, and in each other's confidence.

I often henceforth sought opportunities of going out. Unhappily I found such only once in the three or four weeks; yet I grew acquainted with our gentleman apostle, and by degrees with all the body. I visited their meetings, when I could: with my social disposition, it was quite delightful for me to communicate to others, and to hear from them the feelings which, till now, I had conceived and harboured by myself.

But I was not so completely taken with my friends, as not to see that few of them could really feel the sense of those affecting words and emblems; and that from these they drew as little benefit, as formerly they did from the symbolic language of the Church. Yet, notwithstanding, I went on with them, not letting this disturb me. I thought, I was not called to search and try the hearts of others. Had not I too, by long-continued innocent exercisings of that sort, been prepared for something better? I had my share of profit from our meetings: in speaking, I insisted on attending to the sense and spirit, which, in things so delicate, is rather apt to be disguised by words than indicated by them; and for the rest, I left, with silent tolerance, each to act according to his own conviction.

These quiet times of secret social joy were shortly followed by storms of open bickering and contradiction; contentions which excited great commotion, I might almost say occasioned not a little scandal, in court and town. The period was now arrived when our Chaplain, that stout gainsayer of the Herrnhuth Brethren, must discover, to his deep, but I trust, sanctified humiliation, that his best and once most zealous hearers were now all leaning to the side of that Community. He was excessively provoked: in the first moments, he forgot all moderation; and could not, even if he had inclined it, retract afterwards. Violent debates took place; in which happily I was not mentioned; both as being but an accidental member of those hated meetings; and then because, in respect of certain civic matters, our zealous preacher could not safely disoblige either my father or my friend. With silent satisfaction, I continued neutral. It was irksome to me to converse about such feelings and objects, even with well-affected people, when they could not penetrate the deepest sense, and lingered merely on the surface. But to strive with adversaries, about things on which even friends could scarcely understand each other, seemed to me unprofitable, nay pernicious. For I soon perceived that many amiable noblemen, who on this occurrence could not shut their hearts to enmity and hatred, had rapidly passed over to injustice; and in order to defend an outward form, had almost sacrificed their most substantial duties.

Far as the worthy clergyman might, in the present case, be wrong; much as others tried to irritate me at him, I could never hesitate to give him my sincere respect. I knew him well: I could candidly transport myself into his way of looking at these matters. I have never seen a man without his weaknesses; only, in distinguished men they strike us more. We wish, and will at all rates have it, that persons privileged as they are should at the same time pay no tribute, no tax whatever. I honoured him as a superior man; and hoped to use the influence of my calm neutrality to bring about, if not a peace, at least a truce. I know not what my efforts might have done: but God concluded the affair more briefly, and took the Chaplain to himself. On his coffin all wept, who had lately been striving with him about words. His uprightness, his fear of God, no one had ever doubted.

I too was, ere long, forced to lay aside this Herrnhuth dollwork, which, by means of these contentions, now appeared before me in a rather different light. Our uncle had, in silence, executed his intentions with my sister. He offered her a young man of rank and fortune as a bridegroom; and showed, by a rich dowry, what might be expected of himself. My father joyfully consented; my sister was free and forewarned, she did not hesitate to change her state. The bridal was appointed at my uncle's castle: family and friends were all invited; and we came together in the cheerfullest mood.

For the first time in my life, the aspect of a house excited admiration in me. I had often heard of my uncle's taste, of his Italian architect, of his collections and his library; but, comparing this with what I had already seen, I had formed a very vague and fluctuating picture of it in my thoughts. Great, accordingly, was my surprise at the earnest and harmonious impression which I felt on entering the house, and which every hall and chamber deepened. If elsewhere pomp and decoration had but dissipated my attention, I felt here concentrated and drawn back upon myself. In like manner, the preparatives for these solemnities and festivals produced a silent pleasure, by their air of dignity and splendour; and to me it seemed as inconceivable that one man could have invented and arranged all this, as that more than one could have worked together in so high a spirit. Yet withal, the landlord and his people were entirely natural; not a trace of stiffness or of empty form was to be seen.

The wedding itself was managed in a striking way: an exquisite strain of vocal music came upon us by surprise; and the clergyman went through the ceremony with a singular solemnity. I was standing by Philo at the time; and instead of a congratulation, he whispered in my ear: "When I saw your sister give away her hand, I felt as if a stream of boiling water had been poured over me." "Why so?" I inquired. "It is always the way with me," said he, "when I see two people joined." I laughed at him; but I have often since had cause to recollect his words

The revel of the party, among whom were many young people, looked particularly glittering and airy, as everything around us was dignified and serious. The furniture, plate, table-ware and table-ornaments, accorded with the general whole; and if in other houses you would say the architect was of the school of the confectioner, it here appeared as if even our confectioner and butler had taken lessons from the architect.

We stayed together several days; and our intelligent and gifted landlord had variedly provided for the entertainment of his guests. I did not in the present case repeat the melancholy proof, which has so often in my life been forced upon me, how unhappily a large mixed company are situated, when, altogether left to themselves, they have to select the most general and vapid pastimes, that the fools of the party may not want amusement, however it may fare with those that are not such.

My uncle had arranged it altogether differently. Two or three marshals, if I may call them so, had been appointed by him: one of them had charge of providing entertainment for the young. Dances, excursions, little games, were of his invention, and under his direction: and as young people take delight in being out of doors, and do not fear the influences of the air, the garden and garden-hall had been assigned to them; while some additional pavilions and galleries had been erected and appended to the latter, formed of boards and canvas merely, but in such proportions, so elegant and noble, they reminded one of nothing but stone and marble. How rare is a festivity, in which the person who invites the guests feels also that it is his duty to provide for their conveniences and wants of every kind! Hunting and card parties, short promenades, opportunities for trustful private conversations, were afforded the elder persons: and whoever wished to go earliest to bed was sure to be lodged the farthest from noise.

By this happy order, the space we lived in appeared to be a little world; and yet, considered narrowly, the castle was not large; without an accurate knowledge of it, and without the spirit of its owner, it would have been impossible to entertain so many people here, and quarter each according to his humour.

As the aspect of a well-formed person pleases us, so also does a fair establishment, by means of which the presence of a rational intelligent mind is manifested. We feel a joy in entering even a cleanly house, though it may be tasteless in its structure and its decorations; because it shows us the presence of a person cultivated in at least one sense. Doubly pleasing is it therefore, when, from a human dwelling, the spirit of a higher though merely sensual culture speaks to us.

All this was vividly impressed on my observation at my uncle's castle. I had heard and read much of art; Philo too was a lover of pictures, and had a fine collection; I myself had often practised drawing: but I had been too deeply occupied with my emotions striving exclusively after the one thing needful, which alone I was bent on carrying to perfection; and then such objects of art as I had hitherto seen, appeared, like all other worldly objects, to distract my thoughts. But now, for the first time, outward things had led me back upon myself: I now first perceived the difference between the natural charm of the nightingale's song, and that of a four-voice anthem pealed from the expressive organs of men.

My joy over this discovery I did not hide from my uncle; who, when all the rest were settled at their posts, was wont to come and talk with me in private. He spoke with great modesty of what he possessed and had produced here; with great decision, of the views in which it had been gathered and arranged: and I could easily observe that he spoke with a forbearance towards me; seeming, in his usual way, to rate the excellence which he himself possessed, below that other excellence, which, in my way of thinking, was the best and properest.

"If we can conceive it possible," he once observed, "that the Creator of the world himself assumed the form of his creature, and lived in that manner for a time upon earth, this creature must appear to us of infinite perfection, because susceptible of such a combination with its Maker. Hence, in our idea of man there can be no inconsistency with our idea of God: and if we often feel a certain disagreement with Him and remoteness from Him, it is but the more on that account our duty, not like advocates of the wicked Spirit, to keep our eyes continually upon the nakedness and weakness of our nature; but rather to seek out every property and beauty, by which our pretension to a similarity with the Divinity may be made good."

I smiled and answered: "Do not make me blush, dear uncle, by your complaisance in talking in my language! What you have to say is of such importance to me, that I wish to hear it in your own most peculiar style; and then what parts of it I cannot quite appropriate, I will endeavour to translate."

"I may continue," he replied, "in my own most peculiar way, without any alteration of my tone. Man's highest merit always is, as much as possible to rule external circumstances, and as little as possible to let himself be ruled by them. Life lies before us, as a huge quarry lies before the architect: he deserves not the name of architect, except when, out of this fortuitous mass, he can combine, with the greatest economy, and fitness, and durability, some form, the pattern of which originated in his spirit. All things without us, nay I may add, all things on us, are mere elements: but deep within us lies the creative force, which out of these can produce what they were meant to be; and which leaves us neither sleep nor rest, till in one way or another, without us or on us, that same have been produced. You, my dear niece, have, it may be, chosen the better part: you have striven to bring your moral being, your earnest lovely nature into accordance with itself and with the Highest: but neither ought we to be blamed, when we strive to get acquainted with the sentient man in all his comprehensiveness, and to bring about an active harmony among his powers."

By such discoursing, we in time grew more familiar; and I begged of him to speak with me as with himself, omitting every sort of condescension. "Do not think," replied my uncle, "that I flatter you, when I commend your mode of thinking and acting. I reverence the individual who understands distinctly what it is he wishes; who unweariedly advances, who knows the means conducive to his object, and can seize and use them. How far his object may be great or little, may merit praise or censure, is the next consideration with me. Believe me, love, most part of all the misery and mischief, of all that is denominated evil, in the world, arises from the fact that men are too remiss to get a proper knowledge of their aims, and when they do know them, to work intensely in attaining them. They seem to me like people who have taken up a notion, that they must and will erect a tower, and who yet expend on the foundation not more stones and labour than would be sufficient for a hut. If you, my friend, whose highest want it was to perfect and unfold your moral nature, had, instead of those bold and noble sacrifices, merely trimmed between your duties to yourself and to your family, your bridegroom, or perhaps your husband, you must have lived in constant contradiction with your feelings, and never could have had a peaceful moment."

"You employ the word sacrifice," I answered here; "and I have often thought that to a higher purpose, as to a divinity, we offer up, by way of sacrifice, a thing of smaller value; feeling like persons who should willingly and gladly bring a favourite lamb to the altar for the health of a beloved father."

"Whatever it may be," said he, "reason or feeling, that commands us to give up the one thing for the other, to choose the one before the other, decision and perseverance are, in my opinion, the noblest qualities of man. You cannot have the ware and the money both at once: and he who always hankers for the ware without having heart to give the money for it, is no better off than he who repents him of the purchase when the ware is in his hands. But I am far from blaming men on this account: it is not they that are to blame; it is the difficult entangled situation they are in; they know not how to guide themselves in its perplexities. Thus, for instance, you will on the average find fewer bad economists in the country than in towns, and fewer again in small towns than in great; and why? Man is intended for a limited condition; objects that are simple, near, determinate, he comprehends, and he becomes accustomed to employ such means as are at hand: but on entering a wider field, he now knows neither what he would nor what he should; and it amounts to quite the same, whether his attention is distracted by the multitude of objects, or is overpowered by their magnitude and dignity. It is always a misfortune for him, when he is induced to struggle after anything, with which he cannot connect himself by some regular exertion of his powers.

"Certainly," pursued he, "without earnestness there is nothing to be done in life: yet among the people whom we name cultivated men, little earnestness is to be found: in labours and employments, in arts, nay even in recreations, they proceed, if I may say so, with a sort of self-defence; they live, as they read a heap of newspapers, only to have done with it; they remind one of that young Englishman at Rome, who said, with a contented air, one evening in some company, that today he had despatched six churches and two galleries. They wish to know and learn a multitude of things, and precisely those they have the least concern with; and they never see that hunger is not stilled by snapping at the air. When I become acquainted with a man, my first inquiry is: With what does he employ himself, and how, and with what degree of perseverance? The answer regulates the interest I shall take in him, for life."

"My dear uncle," I replied, "you are perhaps too rigorous; you perhaps withdraw your helping hand from here and there a worthy man to whom you might be useful."

"Can it be imputed as a fault," said he, "to one who has so long and vainly laboured on them and about them? How much we have to suffer, in our youth, from men who think they are inviting us to a delightful pleasure-party, when they undertake to introduce us to the Danaides or Sisyphus! Heaven be praised! I have rid myself of these people: if one of them unfortunately comes within my sphere, I forthwith, in the politest manner, compliment him out again. It is from such persons that you hear the bitterest complaints about the miserable course of things, the aridity of science, the levity of artists, the emptiness of poets, and much more of that sort. They do not recollect that they, and the many like them, are the very persons who would never read a book which had been written just as they require it; that true poetry is alien to them; that even an excellent work of art can never gain their approbation, except by means of prejudice. But let us now break off; for this is not the time to rail or to complain."

He directed my attention to the different pictures hanging on the wall: my eye dwelt on those whose look was beautiful or subject striking. This he permitted for a while; at last he said: "Bestow a little notice on the spirit manifested in these other works. Good minds delight to trace the finger of the Deity in nature: why not likewise pay some small regard to the hand of his imitator?" He then led my observation to some unobtrusive figures; endeavouring to make me understand, that it was the history of art alone which could give us an idea of the worth and dignity of any work of art; that we should know the weary steps of mere handicraft and mechanism, over which the man of talents has struggled in the course of centuries, before we can conceive how it is possible for the man of genius to move with airy freedom, on the pinnacle whose very aspect makes us giddy.

With this view he had formed a beautiful series of works; and whilst he explained it, I could not help conceiving that I saw before me a similitude of moral culture. When I expressed my thought to him, he answered: "You are altogether right; and we see from this, that those do not act well, who, in a solitary exclusive manner, follow moral cultivation by itself. On the contrary, it will be found that he whose spirit strives for a development of that kind, has likewise every reason, at the same time, to improve his finer sentient powers; that so he may not run the risk of sinking from his moral height, by giving way to the enticements of a lawless fancy, and degrading his moral nature by allowing it to take delight in tasteless baubles, if not in something worse."

I did not suspect him of levelling at me; but I felt myself struck, when I reflected how many insipidities there might be in the songs that used to edify me; and how little favour the figures, which had joined themselves to my religious ideas, would have found in the eyes of my uncle.

Philo, in the mean time, had frequently been busied in the

library: he now took me along with him. We admired the selection, as well as the multitude of books. They had been collected on my uncle's general principle; there were none to be found among them but such as either lead to correct knowledge, or teach right arrangement; such as either give us fit materials, or further the concordance of our spirit.

In the course of my life I had read very largely; in certain branches, there was almost no work unknown to me: the more pleasant was it here, to speak about the general survey of the whole; to mark deficiencies, and not, as elsewhere, see nothing but a hampered confusion or a boundless expansion.

Here too we became acquainted with a very interesting, quiet man. He was a physician and a naturalist; he seemed rather one of the Penates than of the inmates. He showed us the museum, which like the library was fixed in glass-cases to the walls of the chambers; adorning and ennobling the space, which it did not crowd. On this occasion, I recalled with joy the days of my youth; and showed my father many of the things he had been wont to lay upon the sick-bed of his little child, just opening its little eyes to look into the world then. At the same time, the Physician, in our present and following conversations, did not scruple to avow how near he approximated to me in respect of my religious sentiments: he warmly praised my uncle for his tolerance, and his esteem of all that testified or forwarded the worth and unity of human nature; admitting also, that he called for a similar return from others, and would shun and condemn nothing else so heartily as individual pretension, and narrow exclusiveness.

Since the nuptials of my sister, joy had sparkled in the eyes of our uncle: he often spoke with me of what he meant to do for her and for her children. He had several fine estates; he managed them himself, and hoped to leave them in the best condition to his nephews. Regarding the small estate, where we at present were, he appeared to entertain peculiar thoughts. "I will leave it to none," said he, "but to a person who can understand and value and enjoy what it contains, and who feels how loudly every man of wealth and rank, especially in Germany, is called on to exhibit something like a model to others."

Most of his guests were now gone; we too were making ready for departure, thinking we had seen the final scene of this solemnity; when his attention in affording us some dignified enjoyment produced a new surprise. We had mentioned to him the delight which the chorus of voices, suddenly commencing without accompaniment of any instrument, had given us, at my sister's marriage.

We hinted, at the same time, how pleasant it would be were such a thing repeated; but he seemed to pay no heed to us. The livelier was our surprise, when he said one evening: "The music of the dance has died away; our transitory, youthful friends have left us; the happy pair themselves have a more serious look than they had some days ago: to part at such a time, when perhaps we shall never meet again, certainly never without changes, exalts us to a solemn mood, which I know not how to entertain more nobly than by the music you were lately signifying a desire to have repeated."

The chorus, which had in the mean while gathered strength, and by secret practice more expertness, was accordingly made sing to us a series of four and of eight-voiced melodies, which, if I may say so, gave a real foretaste of bliss. Till then, I had only known the pious mode of singing, as good souls practise it, frequently with hoarse pipes, imagining, like wild birds, that they are praising God, while they procure a pleasant feeling to themselves. Or perhaps I had listened to the vain music of concerts, in which you are at best invited to admire the talent of the singer, and very seldom have even a transient enjoyment. Now, however, I was listening to music, which, as it originated in the deepest feeling of the most accomplished human beings, was, by suitable and practised organs in harmonious unity, made again to address the deepest and best feelings of man, and to impress him at that moment with a lively sense of his likeness to the Deity. They were all devotional songs, in the Latin language: they sat like jewels in the golden ring of a polished intellectual conversation; and without pretending to edify, they elevated me and made me happy in the most spiritual manner

At our departure, he presented all of us with handsome gifts. To me he gave the cross of my order, more beautifully and artfully worked and enamelled than I had ever seen it before. It was hung upon a large brilliant, by which also it was fastened to the chain: this he gave me, he said, "as the noblest stone in the cabinet of a collector."

My sister with her husband went to their estates: the rest of us to our abodes; appearing to ourselves, so far as outward circumstances were concerned, to have returned to quite an every-day existence. We had been, as it were, dropped from a palace of the fairies down upon the common earth; and were again obliged to help ourselves as we best could.

The singular experiences, which this new circle had afforded, left a fine impression on my mind. This, however, did not long continue in its first vivacity; though my uncle tried to nourish and renew it, by sending me certain of his best and most pleasing works of art; changing them, from time to time, with others which I had not seen.

I had been so much accustomed to be busied with myself, in regulating the concerns of my heart and temper, and conversing on these matters with persons of a like mind, that I could not long study any work of art attentively without being turned by it back upon myself. I was used to look at a picture or copperplate merely as at the letters of a book. Fine printing pleases well: but who would read a book for the beauty of the printing? In like manner, I required of each pictorial form that it should tell me something, should instruct, affect, improve me: and after all my uncle's letters to expound his works of art, say what he would, I continued in my former humour.

Yet not only my peculiar disposition, but external incidents and changes in our family still farther drew me back from contemplations of that nature, nay for some time even from myself. I had to suffer and to do, more than my slender strength seemed fit for.

My maiden sister had till now been as a right arm to me. Healthy, strong, unspeakably good-natured, she had managed all the housekeeping, I myself being busied with the personal nursing of our aged father. She was seized with a catarrh, which changed to a disorder of the lungs; in three weeks she was lying in her coffin. Her death inflicted wounds on me, the scars of which I am not yet willing to examine.

I was lying sick before they buried her: the old ailment in my breast appeared to be awakening; I coughed with violence, and was so hoarse, I could not speak beyond a whisper

My married sister, out of fright and grief, was brought to bed before her time. Our old father thought he was about to lose at once his children and the hope of their posterity: his natural tears increased my sorrow; I prayed to God that he would give me back a sufferable state of health. I asked him but to spare my life till my father should die. I recovered; I was what I reckoned well; being able to discharge my duties, though with pain.

My sister was again with child. Many cares, which in such cases are committed to the mother, in the present instance fell to me. She was not altogether happy with her husband; this was to be hidden from our father: I was often made judge of their disputes; in which I could decide with the greater safety, as my brother trusted in me, and the two were really worthy persons, only each of them, instead of humouring, endeavoured to convince the other; and out of eagerness to live in constant harmony, never could agree. I now learned to mingle seriously in worldly matters, and to practise what of old I had but sung.

My sister bore a son: the frailty of my father did not hinder him from travelling to her. The sight of the child exceedingly enlivened and cheered him; at the christening, contrary to his custom, he seemed as if inspired; nay I might say, like a Genius with two faces. With the one, he looked joyfully forward to those regions which he soon hoped to enter; with the other, to the new, hopeful, earthly life which had arisen in the boy descended from him. On our journey home, he never wearied talking to me of the child, its form, its health, and his wish that the gifts of this new denizen of earth might be rightly cultivated. His reflections on the subject lasted when we had arrived at home: it was not till some days afterwards, that I observed a kind of fever in him; which displayed itself, without shivering, in a sort of languid heat commencing after dinner. He did not yield, however; he went out as usual in the mornings, faithfully attending to the duties of his office, till at last continuous serious symptoms kept him within doors.

I never shall forget with what distinctness, clearness and repose of mind, he settled in the greatest order the concerns of his house, nay the arrangements of his funeral, as he would have done a business of some other person.

With a cheerfulness, which he never used to show, and which now mounted to a lively joy, he said to me: "Where is the fear of death which I once felt? Shall I shrink at departing? I have a gracious God; the grave awakens no terror in me; I have an eternal life."

To recall the circumstances of his death, which shortly followed, forms one of the most pleasing entertainments of my solitude: the visible workings of a higher Power in that solemn time, no one shall ever argue from me.

The death of my beloved father altogether changed my mode of life. From the strictest obedience, the narrowest confinement, I passed at once into the greatest freedom; I enjoyed it like a sort of food from which one has long abstained. Formerly I very seldom spent two hours from home; now I very seldom lived a day there. My friends, whom I had been allowed to visit only by hurried snatches, wished now to have my company without interruption, as I did to have theirs. I was often asked to dinner; at walks and pleasure-jaunts I never failed. But when once the circle had been fairly run, I saw that the invaluable happiness of liberty consisted, not in doing what one pleases and what circumstances may invite to, but in being able, without hinderance or restraint, to do in the direct way what one regards as right and proper; and, in this instance, I was old enough to reach a valuable truth, without smarting for my ignorance.

One pleasure I could not deny myself: it was, as soon as might be, to renew and strengthen my connexion with the Herrnhuth Brethren. I hastened, accordingly, to visit one of their establishments at no great distance: but here I by no means found what I had been anticipating. I was frank enough to signify my disappointment, which they tried to soften by alleging that the present settlement was nothing to a full and fitly organised Community. This I did not take upon me to deny; yet in my thought, the genuine spirit of the matter might have displayed itself in a small body as well as in a great one.

One of their Bishops who was present, a personal disciple of the Count, took considerable pains with me. He spoke English perfectly, and as I too understood a little of it, he reckoned this a token that we both belonged to one class. I, however, reckoned nothing of the kind; his conversation did not in the least satisfy me. He had been a cutler; was a native of Moravia: his mode of thought still savoured of the artisan. With Herr Von L*, who had been a Major in the French service, I got upon a better footing: yet I could never bring myself to the submissiveness he showed to his superiors; nay I felt as if you had given me a box on the ear, when I saw the Major's wife, and other women more or less like ladies, take the Bishop's hand and kiss it. Meanwhile a journey into Holland was proposed; which, however, doubtless for my good, did not take place.

About this time, my sister was delivered of a daughter; and now it was the turn of us women to exult, and consider how the little creature should be bred like one of us. The husband, on the other hand, was not so satisfied, when in the following year another daughter saw the light: with his large estates, he wanted to have boys about him, who in future might assist him in his management.

My health was feeble: I kept myself in peace, and, by a quiet mode of life, in tolerable equilibrium. I was not afraid of death; nay I wished to die; yet I secretly perceived that God was granting time for me to prove my soul, and to advance still nearer to himself. In my many sleepless nights, especially, I have at times felt something which I cannot undertake to describe.

It was as if my soul were thinking separately from the body: she looked upon the body as a foreign substance, as we look upon a garment. She pictured with extreme vivacity events and times long past, and felt by means of this, events that were to follow.

Those times are all gone by; what follows likewise will go by; the body too will fall to pieces like a vesture; but I, the well-known I, I am.

The thought is great, exalted and consoling; yet an excellent friend, with whom I every day became more intimate, instructed me to dwell on it as little as I could. This was the Physician whom I met in my uncle's house, and who had since accurately informed himself about the temper of my body and my spirit. He showed me how much these feelings, when we cherish them within us independently of outward objects, tend as it were to excavate us, and to undermine the whole foundation of our being. "To be active," he would say, "is the primary vocation of man; all the intervals in which he is obliged to rest, he should employ in gaining clearer knowledge of external things, for this will in its turn facilitate activity."

This friend was acquainted with my custom of looking on my body as an outward object; he knew also that I pretty well understood my constitution, my disorder, and the medicines of use for it; nay that by continual sufferings of my own or other people's, I had really grown a kind of half doctor: he now carried forward my attention from the human body, and the drugs which act upon it, to the kindred objects of creation: he led me up and down as in the Paradise of the First Man; only, if I may continue my comparison, allowing me to trace, in dim remoteness, the Creator walking in the Garden in the cool of the evening.

How gladly did I now see God in nature, when I bore him with such certainty within my heart! How interesting to me was his handiwork; how thankful did I feel that he had pleased to quicken me with the breath of his mouth!

We again had hopes that my sister would present us with a boy; her husband waited anxiously for that event, but did not live to see it. He died in consequence of an unlucky fall from horseback; and my sister followed him, soon after she had brought into the world a lovely boy. The four orphans they had left I could not look at but with sadness. So many healthy people had been called away before poor sickly me; might I not also have blights to witness among these fair and hopeful blossoms? I knew the world sufficiently to understand what dangers threaten the precarious breeding of a child, especially a child of quality; and it seemed as if, since the period of my youth, these dangers had increased. I felt that weakly as I was, I could not be of much, perhaps of any service to the little ones; and I rejoiced the more on finding that my uncle, as indeed might have been looked for, had determined to devote his whole attention to the education of these amiable creatures. And this they doubtless merited in every sense; they were handsome, and with great diversities, all promised to be well-conditioned, reasonable persons.

Since my worthy Doctor had suggested it, I loved to trace out family likenesses among our relatives and children. My father had carefully preserved the portraits of his ancestors, and got his own and those of his descendants drawn by tolerable masters; nor had my mother and her people been forgotten. We accurately knew the characters of all the family; and as we had frequently compared them with each other, we now endeavoured to discover in the children the same peculiarities outward or inward. My sister's eldest son, we thought, resembled his paternal grandfather, of whom there was a fine youthful picture in my uncle's collection: he had been a brave soldier; and in this point too the boy took after him, liking arms above all things, and busying himself with them whenever he paid me a visit. For my father had left a very pretty armory; and the boy got no rest till I had given him a pair of pistols and a fowling-piece, and he had learned the proper way of using them. At the same time, in his conduct or bearing there was nothing like rudeness: far from that, he was always meek and sensible.

The eldest daughter had attracted my especial love; of which perhaps the reason was that she resembled me, and of all the four seemed to like me best. But I may well admit that the more closely I observed her as she grew, the more she shamed me: I could not look on her without a sentiment of admiration, nay I may almost say, of reverence. You would scarcely have seen a nobler form, a more peaceful spirit, an activity so equable and universal. No moment of her life was she unoccupied; and every occupation in her hands became dignified. All seemed indifferent to her, so that she could but accomplish what was proper in the place and time; and in the same manner, she could patiently continue unemployed, when there was nothing to be done. This activity without need of occupation, I have never elsewhere met with. In particular, her conduct to the suffering and destitute was, from her earliest youth, inimitable. For my part, I freely confess I never had the gift to make a business of beneficence: I was not niggardly to the poor; nay I often gave too largely for my means; yet this was little more than buying myself off; and a person needed to be made for me, if I was to bestow attention on him. Directly the reverse was the conduct of my niece. I never saw her give a poor man money; whatever she obtained from me for this purpose, she failed not in the first place to change for some necessary article. Never did she seem more lovely in my eyes, than when rummaging my clothes-presses: she was always sure to light on something which I did not wear and did not need: to sew these old cast articles together, and put them on some ragged child, she thought her highest happiness.

Her sister's turn of mind appeared already different: she had much of her mother; she promised to become very elegant and beautiful, and she now bids fair to keep her promise. She is greatly taken up with her exterior; from her earliest years she could decorate and carry herself in a way that struck you. I still remember with what ecstasy, when quite a little creature, she saw herself in a mirror, decked in certain precious pearls, once my mother's, which she had by chance discovered, and made me try upon her.

Reflecting on these diverse inclinations, it was pleasant for me to consider how my property would, after my decease, be shared among them, and again called into use. I saw the fowling-pieces of my father once more travelling round the fields on my nephew's shoulder, and birds once more falling from his hunting-pouch: I saw my whole wardrobe issuing from the church, at Easter Confirmation, on the persons of tidy little girls; while the best pieces of it were employed to decorate some virtuous burgher maiden on her marriage-day. In furnishing such children and poor little girls, Natalia had a singular delight; though, as I must here remark, she showed not the smallest love, or if I may say it, smallest need, of a dependence upon any visible or invisible Being, such as I had in my youth so strongly manifested.

When I also thought that the younger sister, on that same day, would wear my jewels and pearls at court, I could see with peace my possessions, like my body, given back to the elements.

The children waxed apace: to my comfort, they are healthy, handsome, clever creatures. That my uncle keeps them from me, I endure without repining: when staying in the neighbourhood, or even in town, they seldom see me.

A singular personage, regarded as a French Clergyman, though no one rightly knows his history, has been intrusted with the oversight of all these children. He has them taught in various places; they are put to board now here, now there.

At first I could perceive no plan whatever in this mode of education; till at last our Doctor told me the Abbé had convinced my uncle, that in order to accomplish anything by education, we must first become acquainted with the pupil's tendencies and wishes; that these once ascertained, he ought to be transported to a situation where he may, as speedily as possible, content the former and attain the latter; and so if he have been mistaken, may still in time perceive his error; and at last having found what suits him, may hold the faster by it, may the more diligently fashion himself according to it. I wish this strange experiment may prosper: with such excellent natures it is perhaps possible.

But there is one peculiarity in these instructors, which I never shall approve of: they study to seclude the children from whatever might awaken them to an acquaintance with themselves and with the invisible, sole, faithful Friend. I often take it ill of my uncle that, on this account, he considers me dangerous for the little ones. Thus in practice there is no man tolerant! Many assure us that they willingly leave each to take his own way; yet all endeavour to exclude from action every one that does not think as they do.

This removal of the children troubles me the more, the more I am convinced of the reality of my belief. How can it fail to have a heavenly origin, an actual object, when in practice it is so effectual? Is it not by practice alone that we prove our own existence? Why then may we not, by a like mode, prove to ourselves the influence of that Power who gives us all good things?

That I am still advancing, never retrograding; that my conduct is approximating more and more to the image I have formed of perfection; that I every day feel more facility in doing what I reckon proper, even while the weakness of my body so obstructs me: can all this be accounted for upon the principles of human nature, whose corruption I have so clearly seen into? For me, at least, it cannot.

I scarcely remember a commandment; to me there is nothing that assumes the aspect of law; it is an impulse that leads me, and guides me always aright. I freely follow my emotions, and know as little of constraint as of repentance. God be praised that I know to whom I am indebted for such happiness, and that I cannot think of it without humility! There is no danger I should ever become proud of what I myself can do or can forbear to do; I have seen too well what a monster might be formed and nursed in every human bosom, did not higher Influence restrain us.

END OF VOL. I.

LONDON:
PRINTED BY LEVEY, ROBSON, AND FRANKLYN;
Great New Street and Fetter Lane.